Building A Houseful of Furniture

Building A Houseful of Furniture

43 Plans with comments on design and construction

Simon Watts

The Taunton Press

First printing: October 1983
Second printing: September 1984
International Standard Book Number: 0-918804-16-7
Library of Congress Catalog Card Number: 82-060352
Printed in the United States of America

A FINE WOODWORKING Book

FINE WOODWORKING® is a trademark of The Taunton Press, Inc.,
registered in the U.S. Patent and Trademark Office.

The Taunton Press, Inc.
52 Church Hill Road
Newtown, Connecticut 06470

Contents

Acknowledgments

Thanking all the people involved in the making of this book by
name would be an impossible task. Much of the furniture was made
years ago and is now scattered across the country. The owners,
without exception, were most cooperative in loaning pieces to be
measured and photographed. I especially want to thank Peter and
Phyllis Rees, Steve and Ursula McAllister, Dick and Harriet Virkstis,
Robin and Todd Bayer, Patricia Jatczak, and my mother, Marjorie
Watts, for her valuable help with the historical photographs. Also
Lilian Farber and Bern Fridelson, who allowed their home to be
invaded several times by the blazing quartz lights and other
paraphernalia of modern photography. I also want to thank my
former partner, David Powell, and the two or three dozen apprentices
who have passed through the shop in the past twenty years.
Their energy and enthusiasm helped keep the game alive for me.
Finally, I want to thank my friend and neighbor Fred Picker for
his unfailing support and his practical help.

For Richard, Alison and Rebecca

Introduction

The furniture in this book is the fruit of twenty years of professional woodworking. Of the hundreds of pieces that I have designed and made during that time, I have selected these because they cover the whole range of furniture needed in an average home. They are all mature designs, designs that have evolved over the years to a point where I don't want to make any further changes.

The roles of designer and maker are frequently combined by today's craftspeople, many of whom feel compelled to make each of their designs original. I think that it is given to very few of us to be truly original, and then only when aided by the arrival of a new material, such as steel tubing or fiberglass, or a technical innovation. As a designer, I borrow freely from the past, and enjoy making contemporary versions of classic pieces. From time to time I even make exact copies of pieces that I particularly admire. I see nothing wrong with borrowing or copying, as long as it is done honestly, the materials and construction of the copy are comparable to the original, and no attempt is made to deceive a buyer by antiquing.

I have often been asked to define the style in which I have chosen to work—Danish Modern, Arts and Crafts, or whatever. After several futile attempts to sum up what I was doing and why, I began calling the style "transitional," which seemed to satisfy those people who wanted the assurance of legitimacy that a label gives.

The architect Ludwig Mies van der Rohe, designer of the superb Barcelona chair, expressed his design philosophy in two phrases: "Less is more," and "God is in the details." I have great respect for this approach, and hope that it is evident in my designs.

I became a furniture maker by a circuitous route. I never had any formal training as a woodworker, and have learned by making many humiliating mistakes—some of which I have had to live with for years. Learning by trial and error takes a long time and many things get made that should never be allowed off the drawing board, but I found it had one advantage: Not knowing the proper way to do something, I was willing to use any method that worked. Had I served a formal apprenticeship, I might have lost this flexibility.

The closest I came to being taught woodworking was spending one evening a week with the local carpenter when I was six or seven years old. He would ask me what I wanted to make, I would tell him, and then he would make it for me. Not being allowed to make anything myself simply whetted my appetite, so I collected a few simple tools and pursued my interest.

It was soon noticed that I was a handy little boy, but in the 1930s, handy little middle-class boys in England did not become craftsmen. My family and teachers, as well as myself, assumed I would become an engineer, and ten years later I did. I took my engineering degree at Cambridge and then, rather ungratefully, emigrated from England to Canada with the ink on my diploma scarcely dry.

In Canada, I specialized in soil mechanics and the design of prefabricated timber bridges, work that took me into some of the remote areas of British Columbia. Designing, but never being involved in the construction of the designs—often not seeing the final results—became increasingly frustrating to me. Also, with a twenty-three-year-old's arrogance, I was appalled by the aesthetic myopia of my fellow engineers, most of whom had no interest in how things looked and were quite content to leave that to the architects. Architecture and civil engineering, I realized, were actually two parts of a whole. If I wanted to function as a designer, I had to understand the aesthetics as well as the mechanics of a structure. After four more years in engineering, saving money and gaining experience, I applied to the School of Architecture at the Massachusetts Institute of Technology in Boston, and was accepted as an undergraduate.

The school was very exciting for me. I felt that after years of nothing but apple cores, I was finally getting my teeth into a whole apple. The first projects were fairly simple: a Coast Guard station, a vacation house, a small airport. Early in my third year, however, the class was asked to plan buildings, roads, services and car parks for sixty acres of Philadelphia waterfront, and here I got lost. I was forced to realize I was more suited to design on a smaller scale— houses, furniture and other things I could make myself. A regular user of the Institute's well-equipped woodworking shop, I now turned to it full-time, making furniture for friends, relatives and my new family.

The shop was only open office hours, so I had to learn to organize my work and to do it fast. I think this was of crucial importance later on when I was earning my living as a furniture maker. As far as I am concerned, the only real difference between an amateur and professional is that the professional has to keep one eye on the clock.

Living with my own furniture has been an important part of my education as a craftsman and also of my development as a designer. Even minor flaws in workmanship or design become painfully obvious when encountered every day, and really gross errors are not tolerated for long. One of the first projects I made, a set of stools for my house in Boston, is a good example of this.

The stools were much admired when I brought them home, but their shortcomings soon became evident. Because the seats were only 10 in. in diameter and nearly 2 in. thick and the legs did not splay out much, the stools were rather unstable and were constantly being knocked over. I also dished the seats, believing that this would make the stools more comfortable, but the raised ridge cut into people's thighs. The legs, which I had tapered down to a fine point, made dents in the floor, like those made by stiletto heels. Finally, I through-tenoned-and-wedged the legs into the seat, aligning each wedge along a radius of the seat because I liked the pattern the wedges made. This inevitably led to split seats.

These stools had four major design flaws: They were unstable, uncomfortable, impractical for softwood floors, and structurally unsound. All these faults could have been avoided by making a full-size mock-up and living with it for a week. We lived with the stools for years, until the edges were battered and the children stool-shy.

I tell this story to help dispel the widespread notion that if you wade into a pile of lumber with a love for wood and a bright idea, a good piece of furniture is bound to be the result. If you have thirty or forty years of experience this is likely, but if you are a beginner, it is an invitation to disaster. Furniture making is a deliberate craft, not a spontaneous art form. If you don't start with a clear idea of what you want and how to achieve it, the result is most likely to be a muddle.

Every piece in this book has been well tested by several people in the best laboratory of all—their homes. Some pieces have been made a dozen times, each time with slight modifications and improvements. If you make them as drawn and described, they'll give years of service. You can also use the drawings as a starting point for developing your own ideas. There's nothing sacred about the dimensions in the plan drawings. It's the proportions that matter— the relationship of the parts to each other, the parts to the whole, and the whole to the users. The pieces can be altered to suit your needs, but by changing them too much, you may dissipate the force of the original idea and end up with a cloud of uneasy compromise.

As important as proportion to a successful piece of furniture is the design and execution of the details. Here, careful workmanship and sensitive design must go hand in hand. Pleasing transitions from one part to another—the chair leg to the rail, headboard to bed post— and from one surface to another can make a simple piece elegant, or if done badly, can make an elegant piece crude. Rounding, for example, is an effective way of making a transition at the juncture of two surfaces (called the arris). Rounded arrises are simple to make using a router and a rounding-over bit with a ball-bearing pilot, but the crispness is easily lost by careless sanding. I prefer rounds that don't fade completely into the adjacent surfaces, but leave two arrises to mark the transition of each surface into the round.

I have always given a lifetime (my lifetime) guarantee on any furniture I sold. At one point it looked as if I might spend the second half of my career repairing the errors made during the first half. I am glad I followed that policy, though, because it has been a valuable experience to see what limps, or has to be carried, back through the shop door. I have also repaired a lot of furniture built by others, some old pieces, some not so old, which is another excellent way to find out what doesn't hold up and why. Unless the furniture has been abused, failure can always be traced to one of three causes: faulty design, wrong choice of wood or poor workmanship. Occasionally all three faults are combined, and then the only solution is a bonfire.

Old furniture has always interested me. I like to know how things were done one hundred, five hundred or five thousand years ago. I enjoy the feeling of continuity, of working with an ancient material, using tools and techniques most of which were invented long before the birth of Christ. I hope the brief historical background included in several of the chapters will help put modern work, mine as well as that of others, in some context, while giving a glimpse of a few of the marvelous things that have been made in the past.

I don't think that the survival of a particular piece of antique furniture, when hundreds have perished over the years, is entirely a matter of accident. Time has an inexorable way of sorting the excellent from the mediocre and the mediocre from the bad. The worst soon falls apart and the mediocre will be tolerated for a while, but the truly excellent may survive long after its maker has been forgotten. Wood is a very durable material and furniture makers should be taking a long view of their work. Will it still be around to be enjoyed in a hundred years' time? Two hundred? If not, why not?

While still at school, I lost the use of my left hand and arm in the polio epidemic of 1947. Although some strength returned, I am still essentially one-armed and have had to develop methods of work suited to my limitations—for example, I use hold-downs more than most people. Other handicapped people should not think that the furniture in this book is beyond their capabilities—there are always more ways than one to achieve a result. It may take longer, but all that really matters is the quality of the finished furniture.

Using This Book
Most of the pieces were made originally for a particular client, then repeated with slight variations to suit the needs of others. Each time the piece was made, it was refined; the lessons I learned from making it and seeing it in use were incorporated into the next version. Eventually there were no more significant changes to be made. These final versions are shown in the plan drawings.

The text and photographs that accompany each plan drawing are not intended as a step-by-step guide to making the piece; neither do they provide comprehensive instruction in woodworking techniques. I assume that you have some woodworking experience and are looking for ways to develop your skills while making furniture with which you will be happy to live.

Where a construction technique is difficult or interesting, I have described how I would do the job. Discussions of technique, though specific to the piece being described, apply to other pieces in the book, and are cross-referenced rather than repeated each time. The information in the appendices on joining boards, selection and movement of wood, glues, finishing and several other topics is more general, and you may want to read it before starting any project.

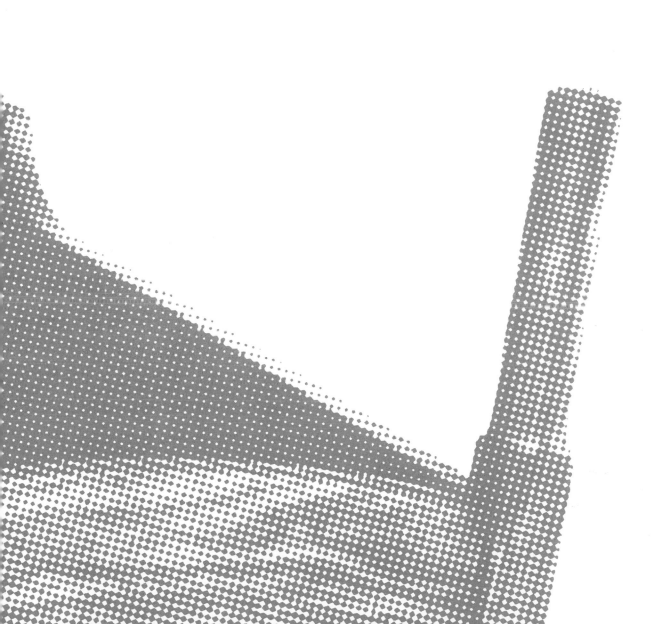

The Bedroom

Beds

Introduction to Beds

I have chosen to begin with beds because they have a symbolic importance in our lives that is shared by no other piece of furniture. One only has to think of the words *marriage bed, childbed* and *deathbed* to realize the truth of this. From the cradle on, we spend a third of our lives in bed, so all the attention lavished on beds isn't surprising.

The physical requirements for a bed are simple: It must be dry, warm, somewhat soft and reasonably level. The first beds were probably leaves, grass or animal skins, spread on the floor of a cave. Other requirements are less easy to define, but just as real. Most of us like to sleep feeling enclosed, secure and free from sudden intrusion, loud noise or harsh light. A swaying bed, like a hammock or a ship's bunk, can be conducive to sleep, but its movement must be gentle and without vibration.

When the need for sleep becomes overwhelming, people will sleep anywhere. During World War II, many London subway stations were turned into dormitories for families who had lost their homes in the bombing. The Hampstead station near my home was particularly favored because it was the deepest. I remember waiting for trains while people were methodically undressing and climbing into their bunks. I wondered how they could sleep in such a noisy and public place, but when our turn came to sleep in a bomb shelter, I found I actually enjoyed the security of being underground.

Our custom in North America is to sleep either alone or in pairs. In other ages, people slept in groups for companionship, security and also for warmth. In the sixteenth and seventeenth centuries, English inns typically accommodated all their guests in one large bed, latecomers climbing in at one side. An old nursery rhyme that undoubtedly refers to this practice begins, "There were ten in the bed and the little one said 'roll over' and they all rolled over and one fell out...." The Greate Bed of Ware, shown in the top photo on the opposite page, probably the best-known piece of furniture in England, carries the idea of a community bed to the point of freakishness.

Four-poster beds, such as The Greate Bed of Ware, were really rooms within rooms. Hung with heavy curtains, they gave the occupants some privacy and protected them from drafts. The style persisted until quite recently when heated bedrooms became the rule rather than the exception.

An aumbrey, or snack cupboard, stocked with bread, beer and spiced wine, was usually placed next to the bed so sleepers could defeat night starvation and brace themselves for the rigors of the morning without getting out of bed. This arrangement prompted a sixteenth-century poet to exclaim: "Some slovens from sleeping no sooner be up / but hand is in aumbrie and nose in the cup."

Elaborate bedsteads were only for the wealthy; the lowly made do with straw mattresses or rush mats on the floor. It was common for masters and servants to sleep in the same room, the servants on a trundle or truckle bed, which could be rolled out of sight when not in use. This idea persisted, and some early American beds included a child's bed that could fit underneath the larger one.

Unlike the portable sleeping accessories of the ancient Egyptians, many early European beds were a structural part of the building and could not be moved. Others could be dismantled, and it was quite usual for royal visitors to bring their beds, costly hangings and bed linen with them.

Although we seldom travel with our beds today, they do have to be moved sometimes, so all the beds in this book are made so they can be taken apart. (The only exception is the dovetailed platform bed on p. 19, which can't be disassembled.) Various concealed, patented bed fasteners are available, but I use 5/16-in. carriage bolts with captive nuts in the rails, so the bed can be tightened easily if it should loosen up. I find the practice of putting lag screws into the end grain of the rails deplorable. After the bed is taken apart once or twice, lag screws lose their grip and cannot be tightened.

I like headboards. They not only keep pillows from falling off, but they allow you to sit up in bed to read, breakfast or write letters. Footboards (also called blanket rails) are less obviously functional, but they do add a sense of coziness and provide a place to hang clothes and extra covers. Modern materials provide adequate and inexpensive alternatives to box springs and innerspring mattresses; all the beds I make have a solid-wood mattress support, which can be used with a foam-plastic or foam-rubber mattress. Beds have lengthened by nearly one foot over the last three generations, and mattress sizes have become standardized: A twin mattress is 39 in. by 75 in., a double is 54 in. by 75 in., a queen is 60 in. by 80 in., and a king is 76 in. by 80 in. (There are nonstandard sizes, too, so check your mattress to make sure.) You can adapt the length and width of the beds to suit your mattress preference.

The Greate Bed of Ware, 8 ft. 9 in. long and 10 ft. 8 in. wide, could comfortably accommodate eight people. Made in England around 1590, the carved, oak bed frame has inlaid and painted decoration. It was an oddity even in its own day and soon became notorious—Shakespeare mentions it in his play Twelfth Night.

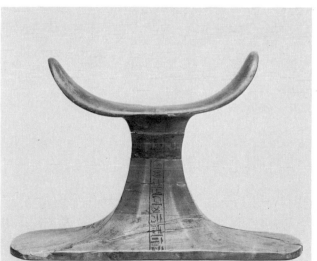

Not all furniture for sleeping needs to be elaborate. Wooden headrests, similar to this ancient Egyptian example, are used in many cultures.

During the Middle Ages, an aumbrey would have been placed next to a bed to help stave off late-night hunger pangs. This frame-and-panel aumbrey dates from about 1500. Its front panels are pierced with Gothic tracery in the English Perpendicular style.

Four-Poster Bed

The four-poster bed has lingered on long after the need for a private sleeping space in a communal room has vanished. People still like the air of formal elegance these beds possess and, perhaps less consciously, they enjoy sleeping in a bed whose pedigree stretches back to the Middle Ages.

The first four-poster I made was for a wealthy young man whose dog liked to sleep lengthwise across the foot of the bed. The dog measured just over 4 ft., so I made the bed 54 in. wide and 76 in. long, which takes a standard double mattress. The proportions looked right, and the same bed is shown at left, with a few minor changes. I recently made one in cherry for my daughter, who has managed to give it a carnival air by stringing colored lights between the posts. A blanket rail could fit this style of bed, so that option is included in the drawings.

Construction

I feel this design looks best in a dark wood, such as walnut, cherry or mahogany, because it is a rather traditional piece. Also, the bedposts are so slender that if made of a blond wood, such as ash or oak, they might get lost altogether. The posts, rails, headboard and blanket rail will all be visible and should be made of the same wood, but the mattress support can be a cheaper wood, such as ¾-in. pine.

The headboard should be one piece of wood, or at least have that appearance. If you can't get a board 16 in. wide, get one a bit over 8 in. wide, and long enough to be cut in half and joined edge to edge. This method can create a nicely balanced pattern. It may be difficult to find straight, clear boards the length of the rails. I buy rough lumber at least ¼ in. thicker than the final dimension, to allow for waste when flattening it on the jointer. For these ⅞-in.-thick rails, I would buy 1¼-in.-thick rough stock.

The posts must be of straight-grained stock, as posts with any short grain would be too fragile, and it would be difficult to hand-plane the tapers into rising grain. At their largest final dimension, the posts are 1⅞ in. square. Cut the rough stock 2¼ in. square (or as much oversized as you can) and 1 in. or so over the final length. Set the posts aside for several weeks so that any movement can be corrected as you plane them to final dimension. Kiln-dried (and some air-dried) boards frequently contain mechanical stresses that are released when the boards are ripsawn or surface-planed. Also, as the newly exposed surface fibers adjust to the humidity prevailing in the workshop, the wood will move. An unbraced part of the structure, such as a bedpost or a table leaf, is particularly vulnerable to this kind of distortion. Any warping or twisting of the posts will be conspicuous and impossible to remedy once they've been cut and finished.

When the posts have settled down, joint or hand-plane two adjacent surfaces straight and at right angles to each other. Saw the other two faces slightly oversized and plane them so that each post is exactly 1⅞ in. square, then cut them to final length. It's best to mark out and cut the mortises before tapering the posts. The short rails are through-tenoned and wedged; the long ones stub-tenoned and held with ⁵⁄₁₆-in. bronze carriage bolts and captive nuts. (I prefer the quiet tone of bronze to the brightness of brass, which can distract the eye from the bed's overall design.) The headboard has a double tenon (one tenon, divided lengthwise) because a single, long mortise would weaken the post. A single tenon is sufficient for the narrower blanket rail. Lay all four posts next to each other and measure from their bottom ends to mark out the mortises. All the mortises are centered on the faces of the posts.

Cut the blind mortises for the long rails first. This mortise should not intersect the through mortise for the short rail; even a thin bridge of wood between the two will help keep the post strong. If you are using a hollow-chisel mortising machine or drill-press attachment, use a ⅜-in. hollow chisel to clear the waste for the ½-in. through mortises. Even a new hollow chisel makes a slightly ragged cut, which can be ignored if it's concealed by the shoulder of a tenon. But a through mortise shows, so I center the chisel between the gauge lines and enter from both sides, then chisel to the gauge marks by hand. If you cut the mortises completely by hand, the same care is necessary. All the mortises finish the same width, so you only have to cut ½-in. tenons.

Next, machine the rails, headboard and footboard to their final dimensions. The curve on the headboard is best marked using a long, thin wooden batten about ⅛ in. thick. (The radius of the arc is so long that marking it with a beam compass would require a very long beam and a very large room.) Clamp the middle of the batten lightly at the curve's highest point on the headboard—I clamp with large spring clips. Spring both ends down to establish a curve that pleases you, then clip them. (A few brads in the waste side of the wood will hold the strip in place, too.)

I cut all the tenons using the tablesaw. To cut the cheeks, I hold the piece vertically against the fence. For long, heavy pieces like these rails, I screw an 8-in.-wide piece of hardwood to the fence to help steady the work. My workshop has a high ceiling; if yours doesn't, or if the piece is too unwieldy, lay it flat and remove the waste with a dado head, or else saw the cheeks by hand. In any case, the two cuts that form the narrow cheeks (the tenon's two edges) are best made as rip cuts with the stock held flat on the tablesaw, one edge against the fence. A stop clamped to the fence prevents cutting into the shoulder. (You can cut the kerfs for the wedges in the same way, stopping them just short of the shoulders.)

The shoulders can also be cut on the tablesaw, but you'll need a helper to support the long rails, and if your sawblade is not sharp enough, the fibers will tear out. Instead, I cut the shoulders with a backsaw, cutting clear of the knifed shoulder line, then I chisel to it by hand. Shoulders should not be undercut, but left square so as to give enough bearing surface. I fit the joints individually by trimming where needed with a shoulder plane, and then marking each joint with a letter or number in pencil.

The shallow round on the top edges of the rails is easy on the hands when tucking in the sheets. Routed rounds can too easily become a woodworking cliché, so I often work them with a hand plane, taking care to keep the arrises crisp. Round the top edges of the headboard and blanket rail as well.

Next, assemble the whole bed dry and accurately mark with a pencil the points at which the tapers and the chamfers begin. The bottom part of each post is tapered, and the top part is both tapered and chamfered to form an octagon. I put the bed together to do the marking because it's difficult to keep separate pieces straight. Remember that the faces of the posts must not be tapered where the headboard and blanket rail join. Also mark the positions of the holes for the carriage bolts.

To lay out the tapers, set a marking gauge and scribe a ¹³⁄₁₆-in. square at the top of each post and a 1⅛-in. square at the bottom. Plane each post down to these lines, keeping the faces at right angles to one another in section at every point along the length of the taper. These sections will not be perfect squares

The tapers and chamfers on the inside face of each post begin above and below the headboard and footboard.

The rails at the head and foot of the bed are through-tenoned and wedged in the bedposts. The long rails are bolted in place so that the bed can be knocked down. Chisel the cheeks of the through mortise carefully so the joint finishes crisp and clean.

because the taper of one face of each post begins above the headboard or blanket rail.

Lay out the chamfers by penciling an octagon on the top end of each post. The width of each chamfer is constant along its length, so the post is a true octagon only at the top. To prevent mistakes, I mark the wood that is to be removed with a colored crayon—chamfers are impossible to fix if cut incorrectly. With a sharp chisel, cut the tight curve that starts the chamfer, spokeshave a flat beyond the curve, then plane along the length with a bench plane. You may want to make a cardboard template to help you keep the width of the chamfer constant.

For planing long chamfers and tapers, I use an old, iron, 18-in. Bailey fore plane. I like its weight, the ease with which the cutting iron can be adjusted up, down and sideways, and the comfortable grip. I have little use for wooden planes except when planing green oak, which stains easily, or when doing overhead work on boats, where an iron plane is too heavy. You are better off buying an old iron plane, because most of today's large manufacturers machine their castings too soon after pouring them, and this often produces distortion. A plane whose sole is out of true is fit only for scrap.

I chisel a slight crown on the tops of the posts and chamfer the bottoms to keep them from splitting when the bed is slid around. I like to leave the posts as they come from the plane—sanding blunts the arrises, which look best when they're crisp.

The bed is ready for final assembly when the rails, headboard and blanket rail have been finish-sanded. Glue up the ends, wedge the through tenons and flush them off with a plane. A wedge should be as long as the kerf and should taper gently, its midpoint being as thick as the kerf. Alternate hammer blows between the two wedges so they spread the tenon evenly.

Bore the holes for the bolts next. Clamp one or both long rails squarely in place (I use long pipe clamps). The holes must be exactly centered in the rails so that the recesses for the captive nuts come no closer than ⅛ in. to the rail's outside face. I use a self-centering doweling jig and a ⁵⁄₁₆-in. twist bit to bore the holes through the post and about 1 in. into the long rail. I then take the bed apart again and, using the same self-centering jig as a guide, bore about 3 in. into the end of the rail. Make the recesses for the nuts by boring a 1½-in. hole from the inside of the rail. Place these recesses so that the bolt will project the thickness of a nut into the hole. If you don't have a flat-bottomed Forstner or a centerless bit, you can grind down the spur of a flat spade bit so it won't come through. The hole should be trimmed with a chisel on the side nearest the bolt so that the nut has a flat surface to bear against. It's awkward to move a wrench in such a spot, so I file or saw a slot in the head of the bolt and grind the square shank round; this way, the bolt can be tightened easily with a large screwdriver while the wrench just holds the nut.

The hangers for the mattress-support crosspieces should be screwed to the long rails and a ledge screwed to each of the short rails. The crosspieces should fit snugly in notches cut in the hangers. The mattress rests on ½-in. plywood or ¾-in. solid-wood slats screwed to the crosspieces and ledges. I often use cedar slats because of their pleasant smell. The grain of the plywood or slats should run along the length of the bed.

The final step before applying a finish is to label the ends of the rails and posts with dimples made with a center punch. The dimples won't fade, like pencil marks will, so the bed can be taken apart and reassembled correctly—unless you have been clever enough to make the rails interchangeable.

The four-poster style also looks well with short posts, which are suitable for beds with narrow mattresses or for beds in an attic or a room with a low ceiling. I have made several such beds with head-

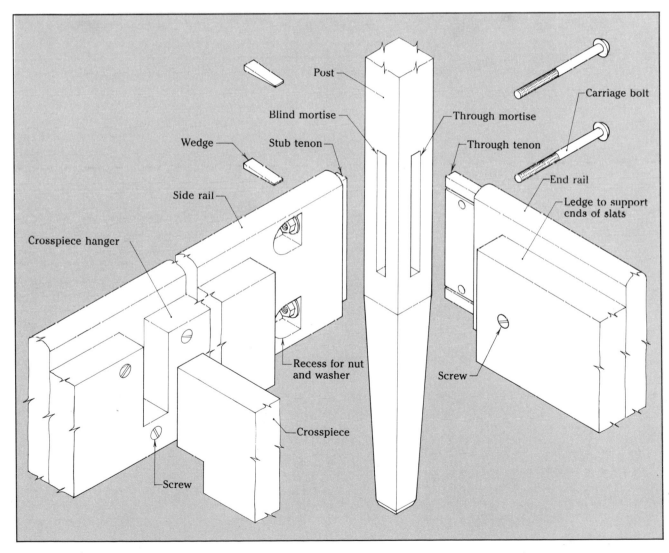

The rails and headboard are mortised to the posts. The long rails are positioned by stub tenons and bolted to the posts. Access to the nuts is from the inside face of the rails. Crosspieces and hangers support slats or plywood on which the mattress rests.

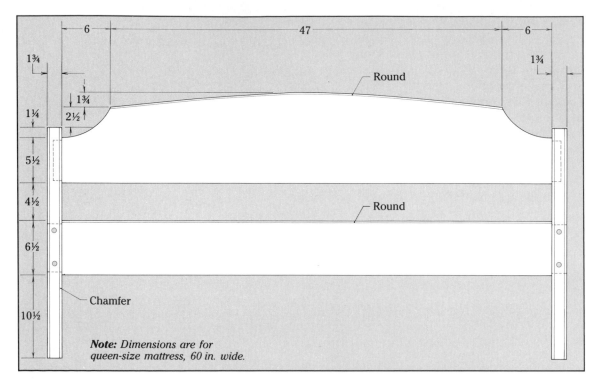

Note: Dimensions are for queen-size mattress, 60 in. wide.

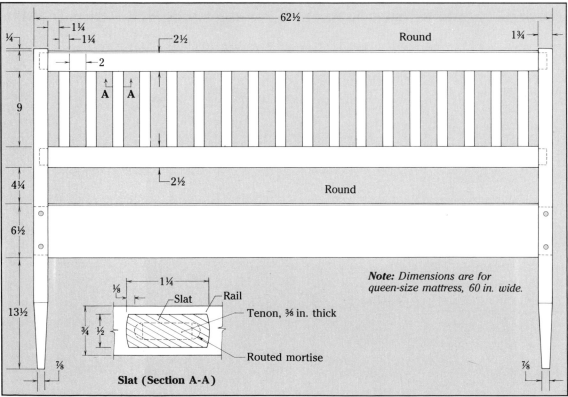

Slat (Section A-A)

Note: Dimensions are for queen-size mattress, 60 in. wide.

These headboards can be used with beds constructed as shown in the plan drawings.

boards like those shown in the drawings at left. I used the same kind of bed frame and mattress support as on the four-poster, and varied the size of the pieces slightly to obtain the most pleasing effect.

The slatted headboard is appropriate for beds of several sizes, but should not be made any wider than shown without increasing the dimensions of the supporting members. I wouldn't mind seeing this bed painted, especially if it were made for a child.

The vertical slats are stub-tenoned into the upper and lower rails. I usually make this bed with a footboard, using vertical slats half as long as those in the headboard. Machining small pieces can be dangerous, so I cut strips long enough for two slats, round the edges with a router, then cut the pieces in half. Use a rounding-over bit with a ball-bearing pilot so the wood won't burn. It's safer to mount the router upside down on a piece of plywood and use it as a small shaper than it is to try to run the router over the pieces.

I cut the tenons on a tablesaw, hooking the fingers of my hand over the top of the rip fence so they won't be in the way of the saw. It's also safer to use a table insert with a narrow throat when making the cheek cuts on small tenons. The insert will support the tenon right beside the blade. To make the insert, clamp a wooden blank in place over the lowered blade and raise the sawblade slowly to cut the opening.

The shallow mortises for the slats can be cut either with a router or a mortiser. I clamp a deep fence to the router and lower the router onto the rail, which is held in a vise. Rout to pencil marks; the shoulders on the slats will cover any slight errors. If you fit the slats snugly, there is no need to glue them, which eliminates messy cleanup. The long rails are tenoned and glued into blind mortises in the posts.

Four-Poster Bed

Scale: 1/16 in. = 1 in.

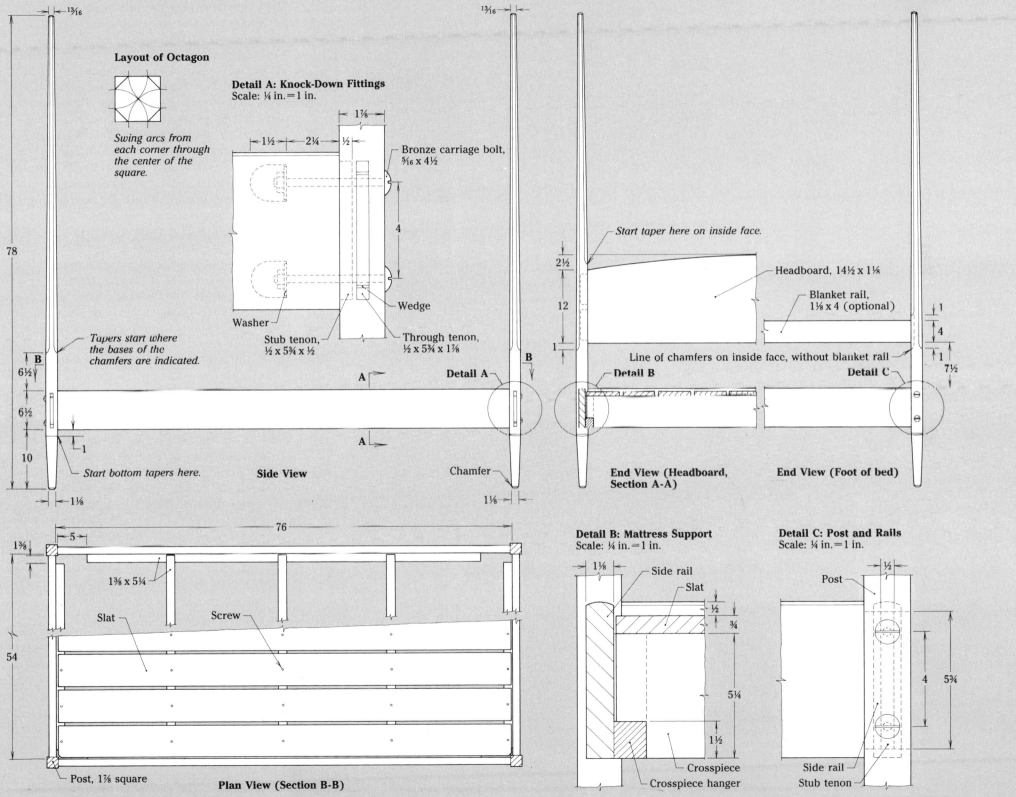

Layout of Octagon

Swing arcs from each corner through the center of the square.

Detail A: Knock-Down Fittings
Scale: 1/4 in. = 1 in.

Bronze carriage bolt, 5/16 x 4 1/2

Wedge

Through tenon, 1/2 x 5 3/4 x 1 1/8

Stub tenon, 1/2 x 5 3/4 x 1/2

Washer

78

13/16

Tapers start where the bases of the chamfers are indicated.

B

6 1/2

6 1/2

10

Start bottom tapers here.

1 1/8

A

A

B

Chamfer

Side View

13/16

Start taper here on inside face.

2 1/2

12

1

Headboard, 14 1/2 x 1 1/8

Blanket rail, 1 1/8 x 4 (optional)

Line of chamfers on inside face, without blanket rail

1
4
1

7 1/2

Detail B

Detail C

End View (Headboard, Section A-A)

End View (Foot of bed)

1 1/8

5

76

1 3/8

1 3/8 x 5 1/4

Slat

Screw

54

Post, 1 1/8 square

Plan View (Section B-B)

Detail B: Mattress Support
Scale: 1/4 in. = 1 in.

1 1/8

Side rail

Slat

1/2

3/4

5 1/4

1 1/2

Crosspiece

Crosspiece hanger

Detail C: Post and Rails
Scale: 1/4 in. = 1 in.

Post

1/2

1/2

4

5 3/4

Side rail

Stub tenon

Bunk Beds

Bunk beds, or stacking beds, are much enjoyed by children as a place to climb, play fort and talk to adults at eye level. They have to be strong so no amount of jumping or acrobatics can make them shaky. These bunk beds can be used singly or stacked in pairs. The two beds in each pair are identical. To stack them, one is turned upside down and its long posts placed on the other bed's short posts. When the beds are stacked, the ends form a solid ladder for climbing into the top bunk. I made eight pairs of these bunk beds for The Putney School in Putney, Vt. In one room at the school, two girls placed a desk under the upper bunk, as shown in the drawing at left—an arrangement I hadn't envisioned.

The school's architect cleverly designed the building so that it's impossible to get furniture wider than 20 in. into the rooms. I was reluctant to make knock-down beds because I was afraid that with the hard use they were going to get, the beds would loosen up. So I made the beds in the shop, took them up in pieces and glued them together in the rooms.

Now, twelve years and three generations of students later, the beds are all in use and still service-able. However, some of them have developed cracks that could have been avoided by a more careful selection of wood and by slightly altering the joints. In the original beds, the through mortises are too long and too close to the edge of the post. Where the grain is not quite straight, a crack running out to the edge of the post can develop. In the plan drawings, I've corrected this fault by positioning the mortise further in from the edge and doubling the tenon; the wood bridging the two mortises also helps strengthen the post. (A knock-down version, using bolts and captive nuts, as in the four-poster bed, is also shown in the plan drawings.) The only other change I would make is to finish the beds with lacquer or varnish—the children's hands and feet on the oil finish I used soon made the beds look grubby.

The original beds were made for young adults and take 36-in. by 76-in. mattresses (leaving ¾-in. clearance all around). These beds are too high off the floor and too large for young children. Use the dimensions in brackets to make smaller beds; these will take 30-in. by 60-in. mattresses and stack to a height of 5 ft. rather than 6 ft. I have also indicated where to put a removable retaining bar for the upper bunk.

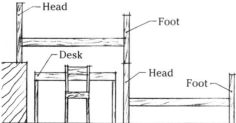

Bunk beds can be stacked in several ways. The arrangement shown creates a little nook for a desk.

Construction

The beds for the school were made of oak, but you could use any reasonably strong wood, such as ash, maple, cherry or Douglas fir.

The first step is to make and mortise the posts. They must be of straight-grained stock, free from checks or shakes. Each post has three mortises. Make the blind mortise for the long rail first and then the two double through mortises for the wedged, double-tenoned short rails, working in from both faces so you don't chip out the faces. (If you are making the knock-down version, the long rail is stub-tenoned and needs only a shallow mortise.)

To make wedged tenons more effective, taper the mortise; the wedges spread the tenon slightly and lock it so it cannot pull out. I leave a small bridge of wood between each pair of tenons. The bridge is housed in a shallow mortise that connects the two through mortises, as shown below. There are a lot of mortises in a pair of bunk beds, and the fastest way to cut them is with a slot mortiser (a vertically mounted routing machine), but you will then either have to round the tenons or square the ends of the mortise.

After cutting the mortises, make a slot in the top end of each post. These slots house crosspieces, which align the stacked beds. Lay out the slots, then

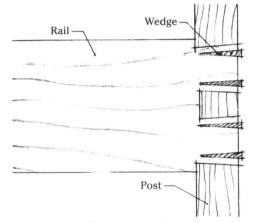

Taper the mortise for wedged tenons to correspond to the taper of the wedges.

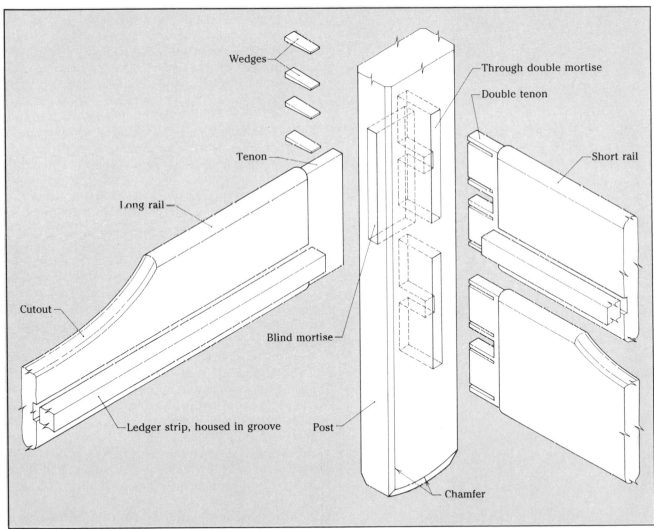

The double tenons on each short rail are wedged into the mortises in the post, and the long rail is blind-mortised. (This is a stronger joint than the one shown in the photos of the bed.)

Crosspieces at each end position the beds when stacked. The crosspieces shouldn't fit too tightly into the slots in the posts because the beds will be hard to disassemble.

bore a ¾-in. hole to make the bottom of each slot (use a backing piece to prevent tear-out). Two cuts on the tablesaw will remove the waste. You can leave the bottom rounded because it's covered by the cross-piece. The crosspieces shouldn't fit their slots too snugly because it will be hard to get the beds apart.

Lay out and cut the tenons next. Mark the distance between the double tenons directly from the mortises so that the spacing will be exact. The mattresses of the original beds were supported by a sheet of ¾-in. plywood glued into a groove on the inside of all four rails, but the plywood made assembly cumbersome and the beds heavy. Resting a loose sheet of inexpensive ⅝-in. plywood or pine slats on the ledger strips shown in the plan drawings is a better method. (Run pine slats across the width of the bed.)

After cutting the groove to take the ledger strips, I make the cutouts on the rails. Remember that bare feet will be clambering over them—the straight edges of the rails need to have an almost semicircular round, and the arrises of the cutouts are rounded. I mark the cutouts using a Masonite template, and rout the heavy rounds in two passes, using a rounding-over bit with a ball-bearing pilot. The next step is bandsawing the cutouts. Then I finish them with a plane and spokeshave.

Before assembly, chamfer the four long edges and the top end of each post. The other end, which will be on the floor when the beds are used singly, is curved—a job best done on the disc sander. The long chamfers can be quickly machined on the jointer. Set the fence at 45° and set the infeed table so that the chamfer can be cut in one pass. I'm not sure about the need for retaining bars; I have never fallen out of bed, but I know people who have. If you are adding retaining bars, rout the grooves for them now. (I only rout them for one bed and I use that bed on top.)

Finish-sand the rails and posts, glue up the end frames, and then glue the long rails in place. If you're making the knock-down version, put the long rails in place dry and bore the holes for the carriage bolts as described on p. 6. I would bore the holes for the captive nut clear through the rail. The rails are not thick enough to hide the nut, and exposing this detail would be in keeping with the straightforward construction of the bed.

Finally, you might want to paint one side of the plywood a bright color to improve the view from below when the beds are stacked.

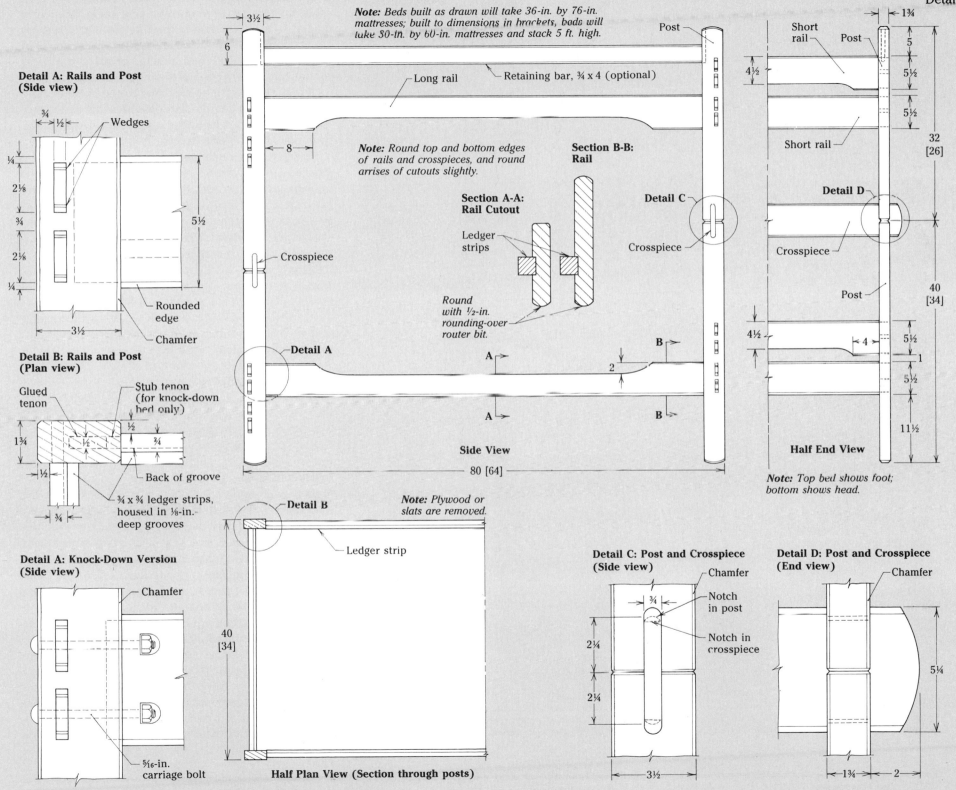

Bunk Beds

Scale: 1/16 in. = 1 in.
Details: 1/4 in = 1 in.

Note: Beds built as drawn will take 36-in. by 76-in. mattresses; built to dimensions in brackets, beds will take 30-in. by 60-in. mattresses and stack 5 ft. high.

Detail A: Rails and Post (Side view)

- Wedges
- ¾
- ½
- ¼
- 2⅛
- ¾
- 2⅛
- ¼
- 5½
- 3½
- Rounded edge
- Chamfer

Detail B: Rails and Post (Plan view)

- Glued tenon
- Stub tenon (for knock-down bed only)
- ½
- ½
- ¾
- 1¾
- ½
- ¾
- Back of groove
- ¾ x ¾ ledger strips, housed in ⅛-in.-deep grooves

Detail A: Knock-Down Version (Side view)

- Chamfer
- 40 [34]
- 5/16-in. carriage bolt

Side View

- 3½
- 6
- Long rail
- Retaining bar, ¾ x 4 (optional)
- 8
- Crosspiece
- Detail A
- A
- A
- 2
- B
- B
- Post
- 80 [64]

Note: Round top and bottom edges of rails and crosspieces, and round arrises of cutouts slightly.

Section A-A: Rail Cutout

- Ledger strips
- Round with ½-in. rounding-over router bit.

Section B-B: Rail

- Detail C
- Crosspiece

Half End View

- 1¾
- Short rail
- Post
- 5
- 4½
- 5½
- 5½
- Short rail
- 32 [26]
- Detail D
- Crosspiece
- Post
- 40 [34]
- 4½
- 4
- 5½
- 1
- 5½
- 11½

Note: Top bed shows foot; bottom shows head.

Half Plan View (Section through posts)

- Detail B
- Ledger strip
- *Note: Plywood or slats are removed.*
- 40 [34]

Detail C: Post and Crosspiece (Side view)

- Chamfer
- ¾
- Notch in post
- Notch in crosspiece
- 2¼
- 2¼
- 3½

Detail D: Post and Crosspiece (End view)

- Chamfer
- 5¼
- 1¾
- 2

Bed with Drawers

Ever since I was a child, I have disliked the dark space under a bed. I always jumped into my bed very quickly so whatever was lurking beneath had no chance to get its teeth into my ankles. When we lived in Cornwall, our cat had a habit of catching young rabbits at night and eating them under our beds, leaving grisly remains to be removed in the morning. The cat's activities gave my sister nightmares and sometimes she would refuse to get up until someone had first looked under her bed.

Perhaps because of these early memories, in my designs I usually raise the mattress well above the floor or, as in this bed, enclose the space below the mattress and fill it with drawers. The bed is designed to be made in pairs, so you can push two together side by side to make a king-size bed. (Together, two standard twin-size mattresses will take fitted sheets.) I haven't made this style bed any wider because it would be too awkward to move. A frame-and-panel version of this bed is shown at lower left.

The bed with drawers can be placed against a wall and used as a sofa or daybed. Wedge-shaped cushions (made like those used with the sofa on p. 84) will reduce the width of the bed and slope the back, making it more comfortable for sitting. I experimented with stacking these beds as bunk beds, but decided they were too heavy. I'm suspicious of any piece of furniture for which too many functions are claimed—it often turns out to do nothing very well.

Construction

Mahogany is an ideal wood for these beds because it's stable, available in large sizes, and looks well with the brass pulls. If you make a pair of beds, the boards for the ends should be chosen for grain pattern and color so the beds look pleasing when placed together. One way to do this is to use several 7-ft. or 8-ft.-long boards to make a pair of ends, one for each bed. Glue the boards together edge to edge, then cut them in half across the grain—pushing the two beds together will reassemble the boards.

The rails should be straight-grained and, if possible, made from one wide board. I cut the drawer fronts out of the rails to maintain a consistency of grain and also to economize on wood. One way to do this is to rip the rail into three strips (the center one being the width of the drawer), joint the edges of the

Here is a frame-and-panel version of the bed with drawers. The rails on the sides and ends are tenoned into the four corner posts. Glue up the long sides first, taking care to make them perfectly flat, then add the ends. The drawers are made and hung in the same way as for the dovetailed bed shown above.

strips carefully, cut the drawer fronts out of the center strip, then glue the remaining pieces back together to form the rail. You must do this before the rail is cut to final dimension and planed to final thickness, or the glued-up rail will be too narrow. If you want to cut out the drawer fronts but leave the rail intact, lower the rail onto the tablesaw to make the long cuts and cut the drawer front free with a keyhole or coping saw. (Make sure you have a secure stop so the board won't kick back.) Clean the ends of the openings by chiseling to a knife mark.

Cut and fit the dovetail joints on the ends and rails next. (Dovetailing long, unwieldy pieces is discussed on pp. 30-32.) The bed can be glued up before making the drawers, but be sure it's perfectly square. To check for square, set the assembled frame on a flat surface, or parallel sawhorses, and measure the diagonals. If the measurements are not exactly the same, the bed is out of square. Clamping across the longest diagonal can twist a frame made of wide pieces, so force the shortest diagonal apart with a stout piece of wood, wedging its ends in the corners at about the middle of the frame's depth.

After planing the dovetail joints flush, shape the arrises with a ½-in. rounding-over bit. I usually prefer crisp, right-angle arrises, but these pieces are so thick that shaping accents the transitions from the edge of a piece to its face and the end of the bed to the rails. Set the router to cut a partial arc rather than a complete quarter circle. The two new arrises formed where the arc meets the face and edge give a pleasing highlight.

The drawers are large and their joints must be carefully made. The ancient Egyptians are credited with inventing the hand-cut dovetail joint, and no one has improved upon it yet. I never use router-cut dovetails because I have little faith in their strength and I don't like their appearance. The pins and tails do not vary according to the scale of the drawer, although several new dovetail jigs for routers can be adjusted to vary the spacing and width of the pins. However, in my view, machined dovetails have no place in a craftsman's work.

I won't describe the techniques for making dovetailed drawers in detail, as these have been well covered by various experts (see the bibliography). But here are some things to keep in mind. The drawer front must be flat—if there is any twist at all, the sides will not be parallel and the drawer will never

run smoothly. Large, side-hung drawers like these need drawer sides that are ½ in. to ⅝ in. thick, so the runner groove won't weaken them. The drawer sides should be made of a stable wood (one with a low shrinkage value, as discussed in Appendix 1).

You will save time marking out if the tails on both ends of the drawer sides are the same length. In these drawers, the back is ⅝ in. thick, the front is ⅞ in. thick and the sides are set back ¼ in. from the front face. Therefore, the tails can be ⅝ in. long for both the front and back ends of each side.

I usually add a small tail at the edges of the drawer to reinforce the weakest part of the joint, as shown in the photo at bottom left. The accompanying photo shows what is liable to happen if you don't add this tail. I think these small dovetails are essential for drawers of any size, but they are often omitted even by experienced furniture makers. If you position the groove for the drawer bottom so it falls within the width of the bottom tail, you won't have to stop the groove in either the drawer sides or the front—the groove in the front will be hidden by the tail, the groove in the sides by the front.

The bottom should be stiff enough not to sag. I've used ¼-in. plywood here, though ⅜ in. (beveled to fit ¼-in. grooves), might be preferable. Whether the bottom is of plywood or solid wood, its grain should run side to side, not front to back.

Side-hung drawers are despised by some purists, but they have a considerable advantage over drawers that are supported top and bottom by runners: They can swell in damp weather without jamming and can shrink in dry weather without rattling. For a between-runners drawer 3 in. or 4 in. deep, this movement is of little consequence; for drawers 8 in. deep or more it becomes a factor to be reckoned with. If drawer sides are made of laminated wood, they can't move, so there will be no movement problem. However, if they are of solid oak, 10 in. deep, and you fit them closely between runners in dry weather, you had better leave town at the first sign of rain.

I rout the grooves for the runners in the drawer sides before assembling the drawer. I use a router mounted upside down under a table and a thick, dead-straight fence—the groove must be exactly perpendicular to the drawer front or the drawer will bind. The groove falls within the top third of the drawer side and is no more than half as deep as the drawer side is thick. It is stopped at its front end and

Relieving the sharp arrises with a rounding-over bit gives a pleasing highlight, accenting the transition from one surface to another.

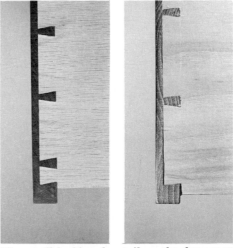

The small locking dovetail on the drawer at left prevents the drawer front from pulling away from the side, as shown at right.

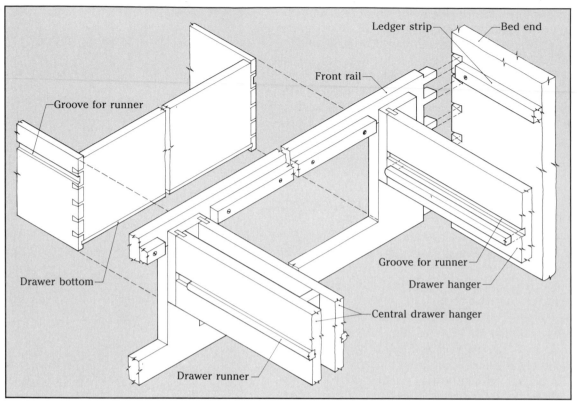

Ledger strip — — Bed end

Front rail

Groove for runner

Groove for runner

Drawer bottom

Drawer hanger

Central drawer hanger

Drawer runner

Though it may seem more complex, the bed with drawers is just a dovetailed box. The hangers are attached to the rails, and the drawers slide on runners housed in the grooves in the hangers.

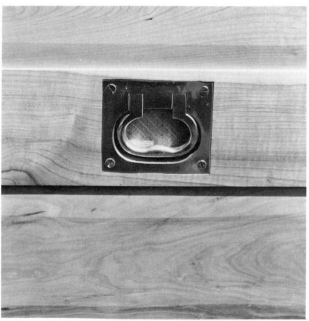

Recessed drawer handles are less likely to be damaged by feet or cause injury if the bed is used by a child.

runs through a tail at the back end of the drawer side. (You should always feed so the rotation of the router bit tends to pull the work into the fence. On one of a pair of drawer sides, you will have to begin the cut at the stopped end of the groove by lowering it onto the cutter.) It's a good idea to redraw at full size the section through the drawer and runner shown in the plan drawings, and then set the router up accordingly; the relative positions of the rail, hanger, drawer and grooves are crucial.

The hangers should be made of stable, straight-grained wood, and the runners of beech, maple or another hard, fine-grained wood. Rout the groove after the hanger has been glued together and squared up—the groove must be exactly perpendicular to the faces of the hanger's end blocks. This groove needn't be stopped at either end.

If you have cut the drawer fronts out of the rails, there is little or nothing left to trim off, so the drawers must be hung precisely. I do this by positioning the hangers approximately, holding them in place with C-clamps. Then I push the drawer in and move the hangers fractionally until the drawer runs smoothly. Make sure the gaps around the drawer front are equal and the front is flush with the rail, then screw the hangers in place and glue the runners in the hanger grooves. The runners can act as drawer stops if you position them so that they strike the stopped end of the groove in the drawer side. Or you can place a stop block at the back of each runner, as shown in the plan drawings.

These drawers are heavy and need substantial pulls. Knobs would soon be broken off by people's feet, so I use brass handles called chest lifts. A handle recessed in a brass plate, often used for ship's bunks, also works well; you should let the plate into the drawer front so that it lies flush with the surface. If the bed is to be used mostly by children, I would put two pulls on each drawer to make it easier for young arms to manage. (Sources of supply for both types of handle are given in Appendix 5.)

The mattress is supported on solid-wood slats or a single piece of plywood, screwed to the drawer hangers and ledger strips. The mattress should lie flush with the face of the rails, so there will be no gap when two beds are placed together.

Bed with Drawers

Scale: $\frac{1}{16}$ in. = 1 in.
Details: $\frac{1}{4}$ in. = 1 in.

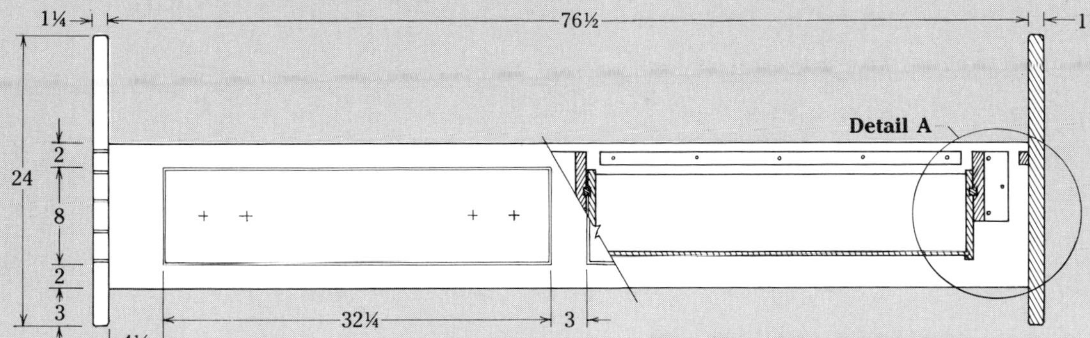

Front View (with Section A-A)

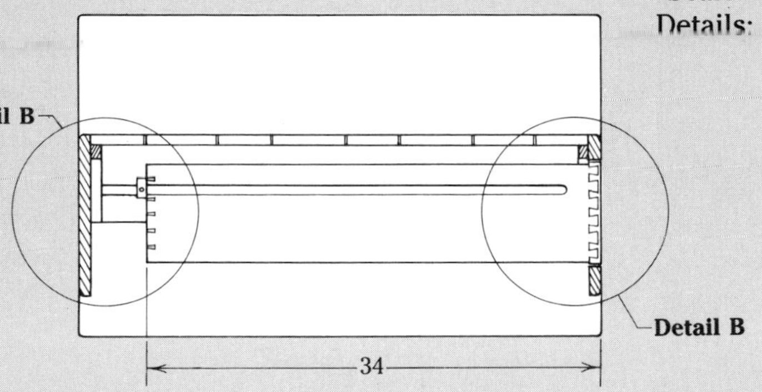

1¼   76½   1¼

24

2

8

2

3

4½

32¼   3

Detail A

End View (Section B-B)

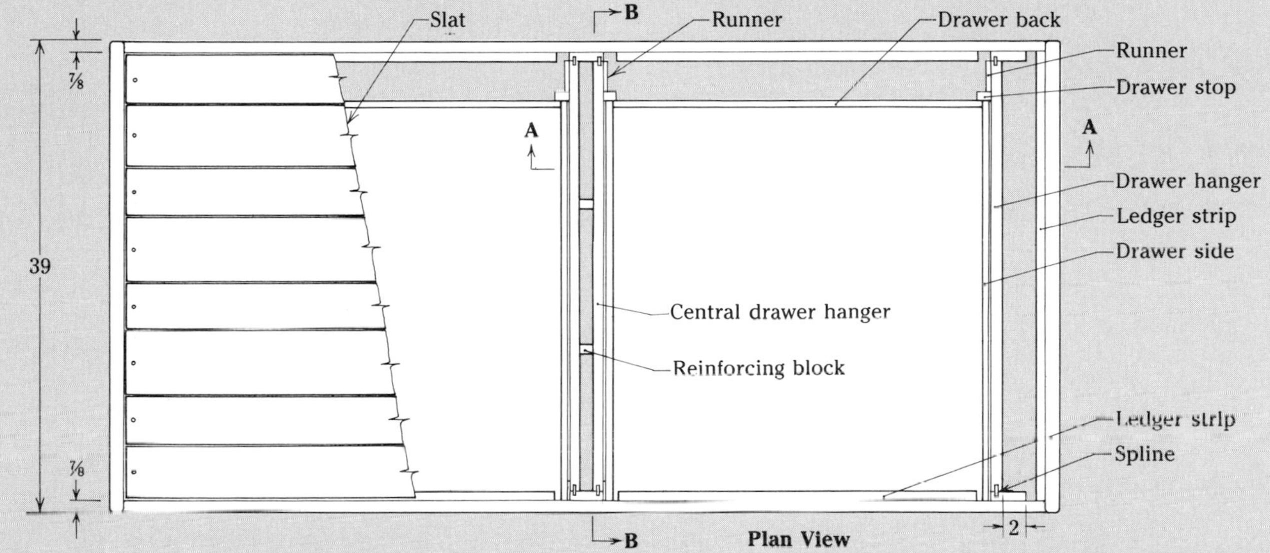

Detail B

Detail B

34

Plan View

Slat

Runner

Drawer back

Runner

Drawer stop

Drawer hanger

Ledger strip

Drawer side

Central drawer hanger

Reinforcing block

Ledger strip

Spline

⅞

39

⅞

A

A

B

B

2

Dovetail Layout for Carcase Ends

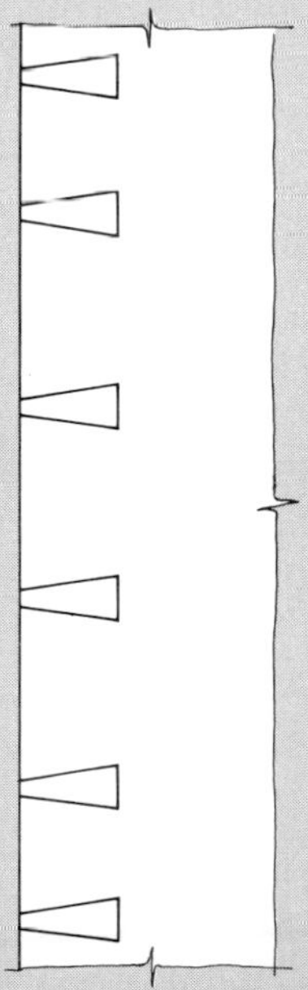

Detail A: Drawer and Drawer Hanger

Ledger strip, ¾ x 1

Runner, ⅝ x ⅝

Drawer hanger, ⅞ x 5¾

Drawer side, ½ in. thick

Bed end

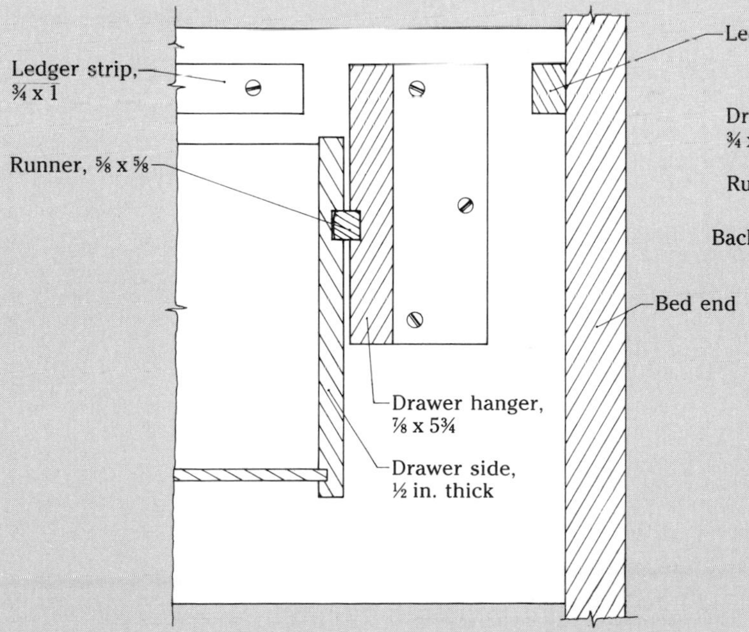

Detail B: Drawer and Drawer Hanger

⅞

Slat

Ledger strip

Drawer stop, ¾ x 1 x 1½

Runner

Back rail

Drawer hanger

Drawer back, ⅝ in. thick

Groove for runner, ⁵⁄₁₆ x ⅝

Drawer bottom, ¼-in. or ⅜-in. plywood

2

7¾   8

2

1½

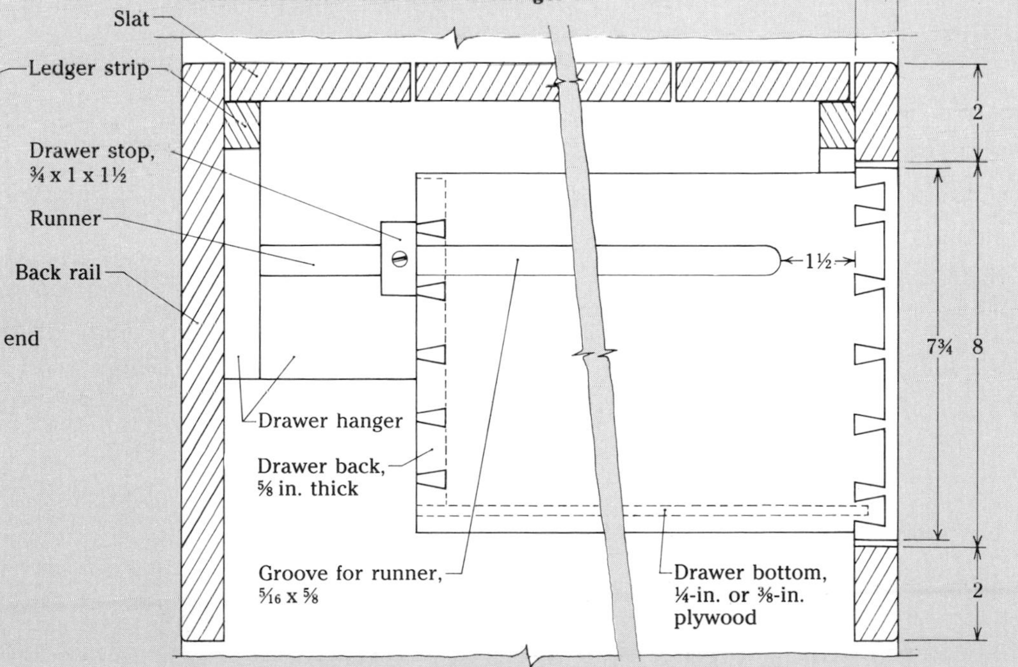

Platform Bed

Scale: ¹⁄₁₆ in. = 1 in.
Details: ¼ in. = 1 in.

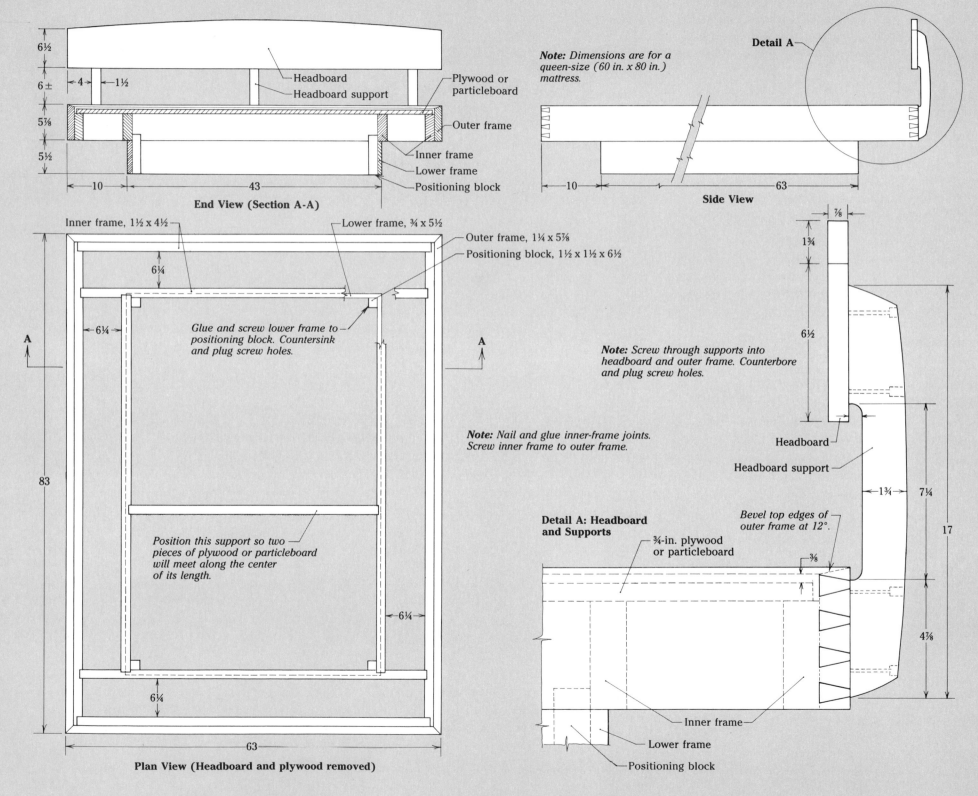

End View (Section A-A)

Headboard
Headboard support
Plywood or particleboard
Outer frame
Inner frame
Lower frame
Positioning block

6½
6 ±
5⅞
5½
4
1½
10
43

Side View

Note: Dimensions are for a queen-size (60 in. x 80 in.) mattress.

Detail A

10
63

Plan View (Headboard and plywood removed)

Inner frame, 1½ x 4½
Lower frame, ¾ x 5½
Outer frame, 1¼ x 5⅞
Positioning block, 1½ x 1½ x 6½

Glue and screw lower frame to positioning block. Countersink and plug screw holes.

Position this support so two pieces of plywood or particleboard will meet along the center of its length.

Note: Nail and glue inner-frame joints. Screw inner frame to outer frame.

A
83
6¼
6¼
6¼
6¼
63

Note: Screw through supports into headboard and outer frame. Counterbore and plug screw holes.

⅞
1¾
6½

Headboard
Headboard support
1¾
7¼
17

Detail A: Headboard and Supports

¾-in. plywood or particleboard

Bevel top edges of outer frame at 12°.

⅜
4⅞

Inner frame
Lower frame
Positioning block

Platform Bed

This platform bed is only one step up from a mattress on the floor. The dovetailed outer frame encloses a softwood inner frame that supports the mattress. The weight of the bed and its occupants is carried by the lower frame, which is set back from the bed's edge.

I once made a knock-down version of this bed for a local doctor by substituting through mortises and long tenons with loose wedges for the dovetail joints. The doctor was often called to the hospital at night and, rising in the dark, he would scrape his shins painfully on the projecting tenons—until he learned to swing wide around the foot of the bed. He remained both friend and client, and I never again used that detail on a bed.

Though the outer frame bears no weight, I made it of thick stock to give the impression that the bed is a floating slab. The corners of the lower frame are simply mitered and then screwed to blocks that project up 1 in. to position the inner frame. The separate frames make the bed a little easier to assemble and to move. The bed also looks well with a headboard, and one is shown in the plan drawings.

This design readily adapts to take a waterbed—just set the dovetailed frame directly on the floor. Water-filled mattresses are slightly different sizes than regular mattresses—alter the dimensions to suit the one you have. Don't forget that a queen-size waterbed can weigh half a ton and a king size, 1500 lb. Waterbeds can impose a load of over 40 lb. on each square foot of floor, which could cause the ceiling below to crack—or worse.

Construction

The dovetailed frame can be made of almost any hardwood or softwood, but very soft woods, such as white pine or butternut, do not dovetail cleanly. I think the bed would look well in clear Douglas fir, a durable wood available in large sizes, but often overlooked for furniture use. The lower frame and headboard should be made of the same wood as the dovetailed frame.

This is a straightforward piece of furniture, except for the mitered, through-dovetail corners. They are not especially difficult to make, but like any joint, take practice to make well. If you have not attempted a mitered through dovetail before, try it first on scraps from the boards you are using. You will then have an

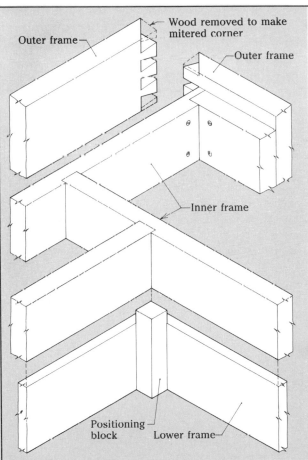

The outer, inner and lower frames of the platform bed fit together like this. The broken lines on the dovetails indicate the wood to be removed when cutting the miters on the edges of the outer frame.

Labels in diagram: Outer frame • Wood removed to make mitered corner • Outer frame • Inner frame • Positioning block • Lower frame

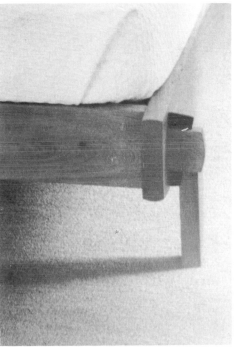

Through-mortise-and-tenon joints, held by a loose wedge, substitute for the dovetail joints in this knock-down version of the platform bed. The protruding tenons could be a hazard to the owner's shins.

The through-dovetailed corners are mitered on their top and bottom edges. When setting out the joint, take care to identify on the edges the waste wood that needs to be cut away to form the miters.

exact pattern to go by, and something to keep for future reference.

A mitered through dovetail is laid out and cut in almost the same way as a regular through dovetail. First, pencil the tails on each end of the long rails. You can cut them on a tablesaw if your ceiling is high enough, but it's awkward to do. I cut them out by hand, clear the waste with a coping saw, and chisel to the gauge lines. The half tail on each edge is mitered; knife-mark the 45° angle, but don't cut the miter yet—you have to mark the pins first.

Knife-marking the pins on such long pieces is difficult to do; I have a trapdoor in the floor of the shop, so the end of even a 10-ft. board can be worked on at bench height. Lacking this convenience, stand the short rail vertically at the end of the bench and build up a surface on the benchtop to support the long rail at a right angle to the short one. You could clamp the rails to the bench for stability while knife-marking and cutting the pins. Don't forget to number or letter each joint as you mark it.

Now cut the miters on the half tails, sawing just outside the knife mark. By placing the two mating pieces of each joint together, you can see where the waste must be removed to make the miters on the pin pieces. Knife-mark the miters, cut just outside the marks, and try the joint—the shoulders of each miter should just meet. After all the miters are cut to this stage, saw and finish-plane the 12° bevel on the top edge of all four rails.

Now do the final fitting of the miters. I use the boat carpenter's trick of pushing the joint almost together, then running a fine saw down through the mitered shoulders to make the joint close. (This practice is frowned on by old-world cabinetmakers—chiseling will work, but it takes longer.) You'll need some long clamps to pull the joints together while gluing; once they're tight, you can remove the clamps. Measure the diagonals to check that the frame is square.

The inner frame has simple rabbet and dado joints, which are nailed and glued together. The inner frame should fit snugly inside the outer frame and be screwed in place from the inside, not glued. Place ¾-in.-thick particleboard or an inexpensive plywood floor underlayment on the inner frame to support the mattress—this need not be screwed down.

The mitered lower frame is also a straightforward construction, but you may need an assistant to support the pieces if you cut the miters on a tablesaw.

There's no structural need for the miter—I just didn't want the end grain to show. Counterbore and plug the holes for the screws that fasten the frame to the corner blocks.

If you want to add a headboard, it should be a single piece of wood at least 8 in. wide and as long as the width of the bed. The top edge can be left straight, or curved as shown in the plan drawings. Using two supports, the headboard should be at least 1⅛ in. thick, but if you add a third support in the middle, you can get away with a thickness of ¾ in. The exact height is a matter of preference, but if you leave a gap of more than 6 in. between the top of the mattress and the bottom edge of the headboard, pillows are liable to fall through (which defeats the purpose of a headboard). With this bed, you could also use a wall-hung headboard, as shown on the opposite page.

To make the cutouts on the headboard supports, plane the stock to its final dimensions, clamp the two inner edges together and then bore 1-in. holes to form the tight curves of the cutout. Bandsaw the rest of the waste away and clean up with a spokeshave.

Headboard with Night Tables

Many people like to have a small table or shelf beside their beds on which to keep a lamp, books, papers and perhaps a clock. This headboard has tables that are attached to fit on each side of a double bed. It's designed for use with ready-made bed frames that have no headboard or footboard. When made of angle iron, these frames are called, for some obscure reason, Hollywood beds. I prefer to fasten the headboard to the wall rather than use the flimsy support brackets provided with these frames.

Construction

One long, wide board looks best for this headboard, but may be difficult to find and machine. If you edge-join two boards together, try to match color and figure. The headboard should be flat, so buy stock thick enough to allow for planing out wind or warp. Plane one side flat, join the boards together and plane to thickness. If you don't have a thickness planer, a local millwork shop might plane the headboard for you.

The headboard is hung on a beveled strip of wood fastened to the wall with screws or expansion bolts. I cut 1½-in. strips off the ends and edges of the headboard and glue them to the back face. Cut the strips off the ends first, then the edges. (Because the grain of the end strips runs in the same direction as the headboard, shrinkage or expansion won't be a problem.) Bevel the top strip at a 45° angle and fit the end strips to close the gap. Hang the headboard on a beveled strip screwed to the wall, as shown in the sketch.

The two little night tables are simply dovetailed boxes, each with a small drawer that slides on runners above and below the drawer sides. The runners should be slot-screwed at the back and middle to allow the carcase to shrink and expand. The back rail fits into a rabbet in the carcase top and housings routed or chiseled into the sides. If you want to add a back to the night table, cut a groove in the sides and rail for a free-floating panel. When I finish-sand the headboard and night tables, I knock off the sharp arrises with fine sandpaper.

The drawer front is wider than the drawer sides and it hides the ends of the runners from view. The lower lip of the drawer front makes a convenient finger hold, so no pulls are needed. The only difficulty with this piece might be in blind-dovetailing the drawer sides into the sloping front. The plan drawing

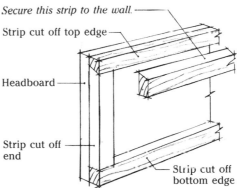

Cut 1½-in. strips off the ends and edges of the headboard stock and glue them on its back face. Bevel the top strip so you can hang the headboard on another beveled strip that is screwed to the wall.

and the photo below show the dovetail layout I used. I made the pins larger than the tails because it looks nice (the usual layout is the opposite). Whatever layout you use, the centerlines of the tails must be parallel with the grain of the drawer side; if they were perpendicular to the faces of the drawer front, the tails would be weak and soon break off. Skewed dovetails are best cut by hand, not on the tablesaw. (Making skewed dovetails is described on pp. 167-168.)

I usually wax all inside surfaces of the drawers because it makes them much easier to keep clean. If you wax them before assembly, glue squeeze-out will be easier to clean up—but don't wax the surfaces to be glued. After assembly, I like to put finish on the ends of the drawer fronts, covering the dovetails, but not extending further on the sides. The finish darkens the end grain of the front, which contrasts with the lighter tails. I wax all bearing surfaces of the drawer to make it slide better.

The drawer is stopped by small blocks glued to the underside of the carcase top so they catch the inside of the drawer front. (The back of the drawer, therefore, must clear the blocks.) It's not acceptable to use the ends of these runners as drawer stops, because if the drawer is slammed, it's possible that the impact will force the front away from the sides. Drawer stops glued on the carcase sides behind the drawer are acceptable for plywood or particleboard construction, but will not do for solid wood. This is because the drawers will begin to project as the solid-wood carcase shrinks.

The night tables are attached after the headboard is in place, so it's easy to position them at a convenient height. I position them 6 in. to 12 in. higher than the top of the mattress, about the level of the pillows. If the tables are too high, it's difficult to set things on them while sitting in bed; if they're too low, a table lamp won't shed light where you want it.

Both the night table and drawer use a dovetail construction. The large pins and small tails of the drawer stand tradition on its head, but they don't sacrifice strength.

Headboard with Night Tables

Scale: 1/16 in. = 1 in.
Details: ¼ in. = 1 in.

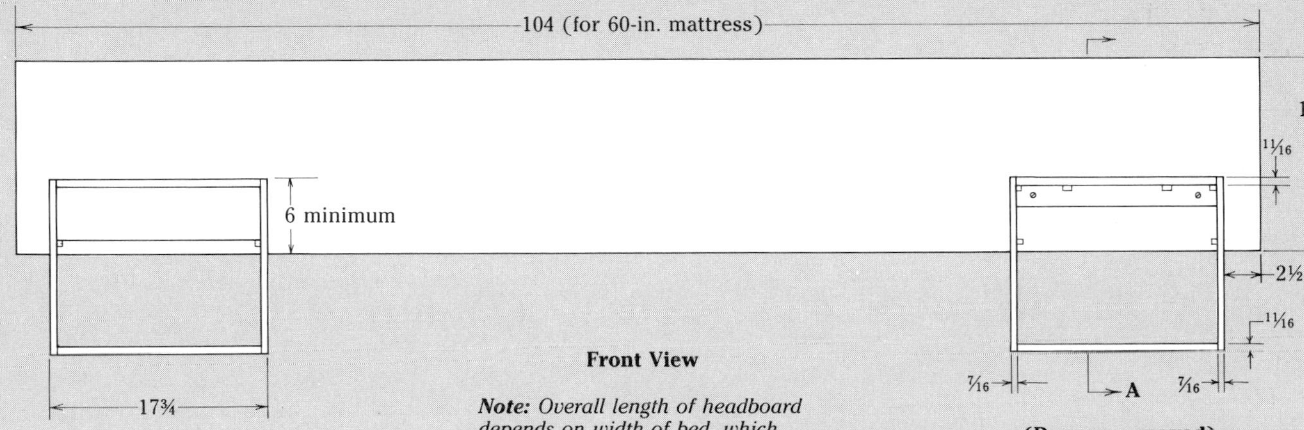

104 (for 60-in. mattress)
16
6 minimum
11/16
2½
11/16
17¾
7/16
A
7/16

Front View

Note: Overall length of headboard depends on width of bed, which must fit between night tables.

(Drawer removed)

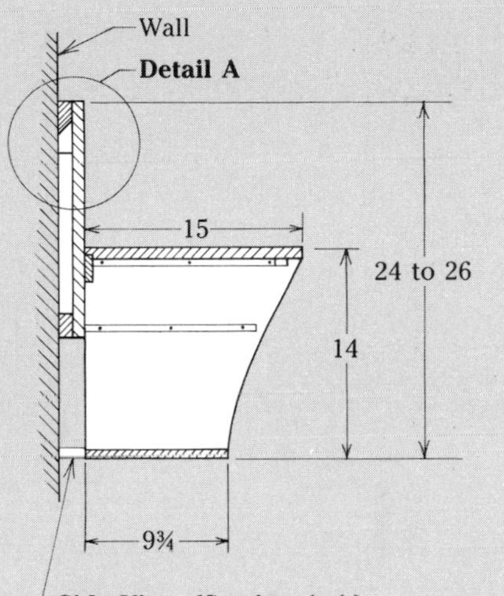

Wall
Detail A
15
24 to 26
14
9¾

Side View (Section A-A)

Add block in middle of bottom to keep night table level.

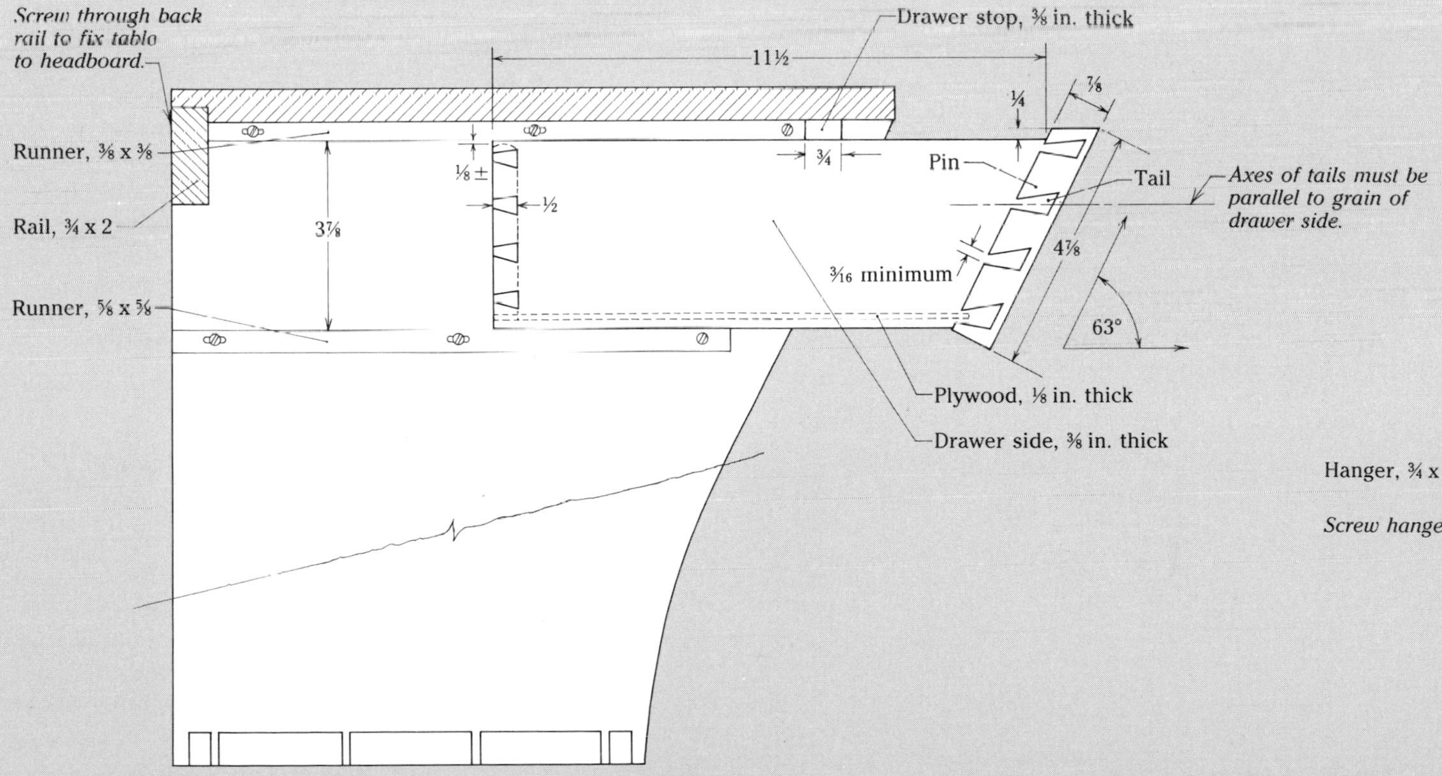

Screw through back rail to fix table to headboard.
Drawer stop, ⅜ in. thick
11½
¼
⅞
Runner, ⅜ x ⅜
⅛ ±
¾
Pin
Tail
Axes of tails must be parallel to grain of drawer side.
½
Rail, ¾ x 2
3⅞
4⅞
3/16 minimum
Runner, ⅝ x ⅝
63°
Plywood, ⅛ in. thick
Drawer side, ⅜ in. thick

Night Table (Cutaway side view)

Detail A: Section Through Headboard and Hanger

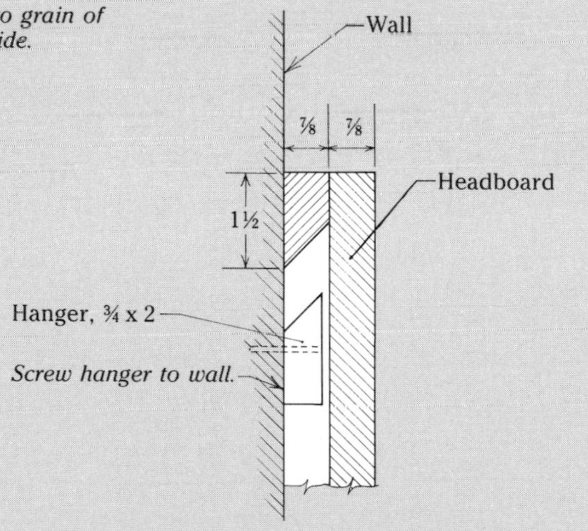

Wall
⅞
⅞
Headboard
1½
Hanger, ¾ x 2
Screw hanger to wall.

Cradle

Cradles are more common today in boatyards (where they are used to hold up boats) than they are in the nursery. The traditional wooden cradle, handed down within a family for generations, is practically a thing of the past. There is great joy and satisfaction in making a cradle for one's own child, and it's a pity more parents don't have that experience.

A few years ago, I sold the prototype of this cradle to a mass-circulation women's magazine. They simplified the design by substituting plywood for the solid-wood bottom, and dowels for all the mortise-and-tenon joints. To everyone's surprise, 18,000 plans were sold at fifty cents each. (As I was paid $180 for the original idea, the magazine did all right.)

Unlike most cradles, this one can still be used after the baby has outgrown it. Turned upside down, the cradle becomes a bench—its rockers form armrests and the mattress can be used as a seat cushion. There is thus no need to retire the cradle to the attic until the next child or grandchild comes along. Children become very attached to their cradles and, as they get older, may like to put the cat or a stuffed animal to bed in them (cats seldom cooperate for long). One of my children would even take uncomfortable naps in her cradle, her feet sticking awkwardly out at one end. To survive this kind of use, a cradle requires quality hardwood and proper joinery.

A traditional cradle such as this one has a few drawbacks that I should point out. It is usually placed on the floor, which makes picking up and laying down the child awkward and increases the chance of accidentally knocking the child's head on the wooden edge. A cradle at floor level is inviting to animals; newborn babies have been smothered by large, friendly cats making themselves at home in cradles (a piece of netting hung over the cradle is a sensible precaution). It's also colder and draftier in a cradle at floor level, particularly in older houses, than at standing or sitting height.

Construction

This cradle is relatively simple to make; the angles of the head, foot and sides are the only complications. Start by selecting and planing the stock for the four posts. If you have a lathe, you can turn the upper portions of the posts cylindrical. If not, simply make them octagonal by chamfering with a chisel and spokeshave, but be sure to remove all sharp arrises to protect the baby.

Now mark and cut the mortises in two adjacent faces of each post. The mortises are at right angles to the faces, as usual. These long, shallow mortises have a ½-in. bridge of wood centered in their length. This double mortise will not weaken the post as much as a continuous mortise will, and should be used whenever the length of a mortise is more than about eight times its width. Also, the mortises must not meet inside the post or it will be seriously weakened.

Next, choose the wood for the head, foot and sides, and machine it to correct thickness and width and to rough length. Try to find a board wide enough to make each in one piece, but if that's impossible, edge-join narrower boards. To cut the pieces to size, first lay out the angles on the ends of the pieces, as shown on the plan drawings (remember to add the length of the tenons), then saw close to the lines. To ensure that each pair (the head and foot and the two sides) is angled exactly the same, clamp them together and plane the paired ends to the lines.

Cut the tenons to fit the mortises. The tenons are offset, as shown in section A-A in the plan drawings, so that they can be of maximum length without meeting in the posts; the head, foot and sides are centered on the faces of the posts. Lay the tenons out and cut them just as you would any other tenons—the adjustment of the shoulders to compensate for the angle will be worked later. I cut the tenons on the tablesaw, taking care to set up accurately. The tenons are only ½ in. long, so they must fit tightly in the mortises for the joint to be strong.

After fitting the tenons to their mortises, assemble the cradle without glue. You will notice a very slight gap between the posts and the inside shoulders of the tenons. This gap is the result of the posts not being vertical—the greater the slope, the larger the gap. Close it by chiseling the outside shoulders at a slight angle by the same amount as the gap. Clamp a metal straightedge along the shoulders to use as a guide for the chisel.

Now cut the tenon for the rocker on the lower end of each post. To establish the angle for the shoulders, dry-assemble the head and foot of the cradle. Mark each post ½ in. from the bottom edge of the head or foot. Connect the marks on each pair of posts with a straightedge and extend the mark across each post— this line establishes one shoulder line. Use a square

to carry these shoulder lines around the posts, lay out the cheeks of the tenons with a mortise gauge and cut the tenons.

A full-size pattern of stiff paper, plywood or Masonite is a great help and cuts down on waste when laying out and cutting the rockers. I use full-size patterns whenever the design calls for two or more identically shaped or angled pieces. (Using one piece as a pattern for the next doesn't work. I once built a small planked boat by fitting the starboard plank first and then using it as a pattern for its mate on the port side. After seven or eight planks, I was embarrassed to find that the planking was 1½ in. higher on the port side than the starboard. I hadn't realized how quickly the thickness of a pencil line adds up.)

Select the pieces for the rockers and plane them to the correct thickness. If possible, place the pattern to follow the natural curve in the grain pattern of the wood. It's easier to lay out and cut the mortises while the pieces are still rectangular. Dry-assemble the head and foot and lay the rocker blank in place under the tenons to mark both the position and the slope of the mortises. It's best to bore out and chisel the mortises by hand—the angle makes it awkward to use a mortising machine. Now bandsaw the rockers to shape and finish them with a spokeshave.

Although plywood is amply strong for the bottom of the cradle, it doesn't make a nice-looking seat for the bench. I make the bottom out of solid-wood slats housed in grooves cut in the sides, head and foot. The grooves are angled to the face of the side, head or foot, not perpendicular. I cut them on a tablesaw using a ⅜-in. dado head, set to the proper angle. The grooves in the head and foot and the rabbets on the edges of the two end slats must be deep enough to allow for swelling and shrinkage. I round the edges that butt against each other, as shown at top right. (This is a precaution: If the slats swell more than is allowed by the grooves, the rounded edges will crush slightly to accommodate the expansion.) You can make the cutouts on the long edges as described on p. 20 for the platform bed's headboard supports.

Round the top edges of the sides, head and foot, knock the sharp arrises off the posts with sandpaper, and the bed is ready to assemble. First glue the head, posts and rocker; then the foot, posts and the second rocker. (This method of assembly is awkward because of the angles, so make a dry run first.) Now lay the head assembly flat on the bench and glue the two

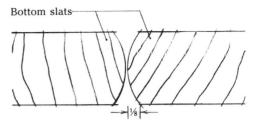

Round the meeting edges of the slats as an added precaution against seasonal movement. Rounded edges will compress a little to allow for swelling.

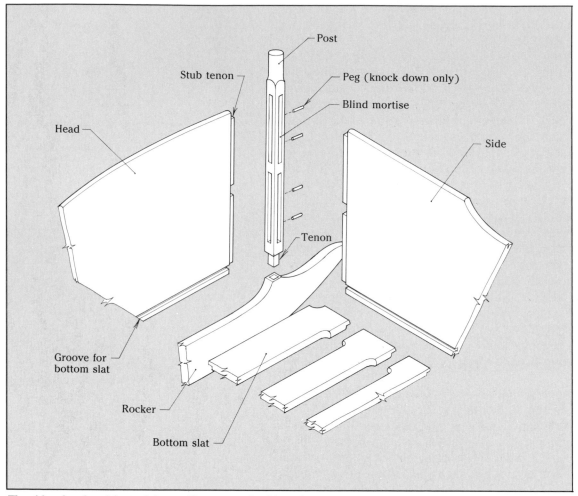

Post

Stub tenon

Peg (knock down only)

Blind mortise

Head

Side

Tenon

Groove for
bottom slat

Rocker

Bottom slat

The sides, head and foot of the cradle are mortised into the posts, and the posts are mortised into the rockers.
The loose bottom slats are housed in grooves in the sides, head and foot.

long sides into the mortises. Slide all the slats into place, glue the foot assembly, and clamp. This is best done with the cradle upside down, so the clamps don't fall off the angled sides.

Alternatively, you can assemble the sides dry using pegs, as shown in the plan drawings. Make the pegs from a contrasting wood. To make the pegs, saw $\frac{3}{16}$-in. square strips, 2 in. long, from straight-grained stock left over from the cradle, and shave them approximately round, leaving one end square. Put the bottom slats in place and clamp the sides between the head and foot. Bore four $\frac{3}{16}$-in. holes in each post, right through the post and tenons, and about $\frac{1}{8}$ in. from the edge of each post. Tap the pegs into place with light blows of a hammer until the square head is well into the wood. Trim off the surplus inside and out. If you ever need to take the cradle apart, the pegs can easily be punched out from the inside.

The pad can be a piece of 1-in. polyurethane foam, cut to size and covered with a washable, impermeable material. (A slipcover can be added later when the cradle is turned over and used as a bench).

To make the cradle easier to pick up, you may want to add a rope handle at the head and foot. Run a length of rope through holes bored in the piece and splice its ends together. The cradle could be hung from these handles, too, and swung. Brass chest lifts at the head and foot could also be added. Attach them with brass machine screws and countersink the nuts and washers on the inside. Wooden screws could pull out and "down would come baby, cradle and all."

Cradle

Scale: ⅛ in. = 1 in.

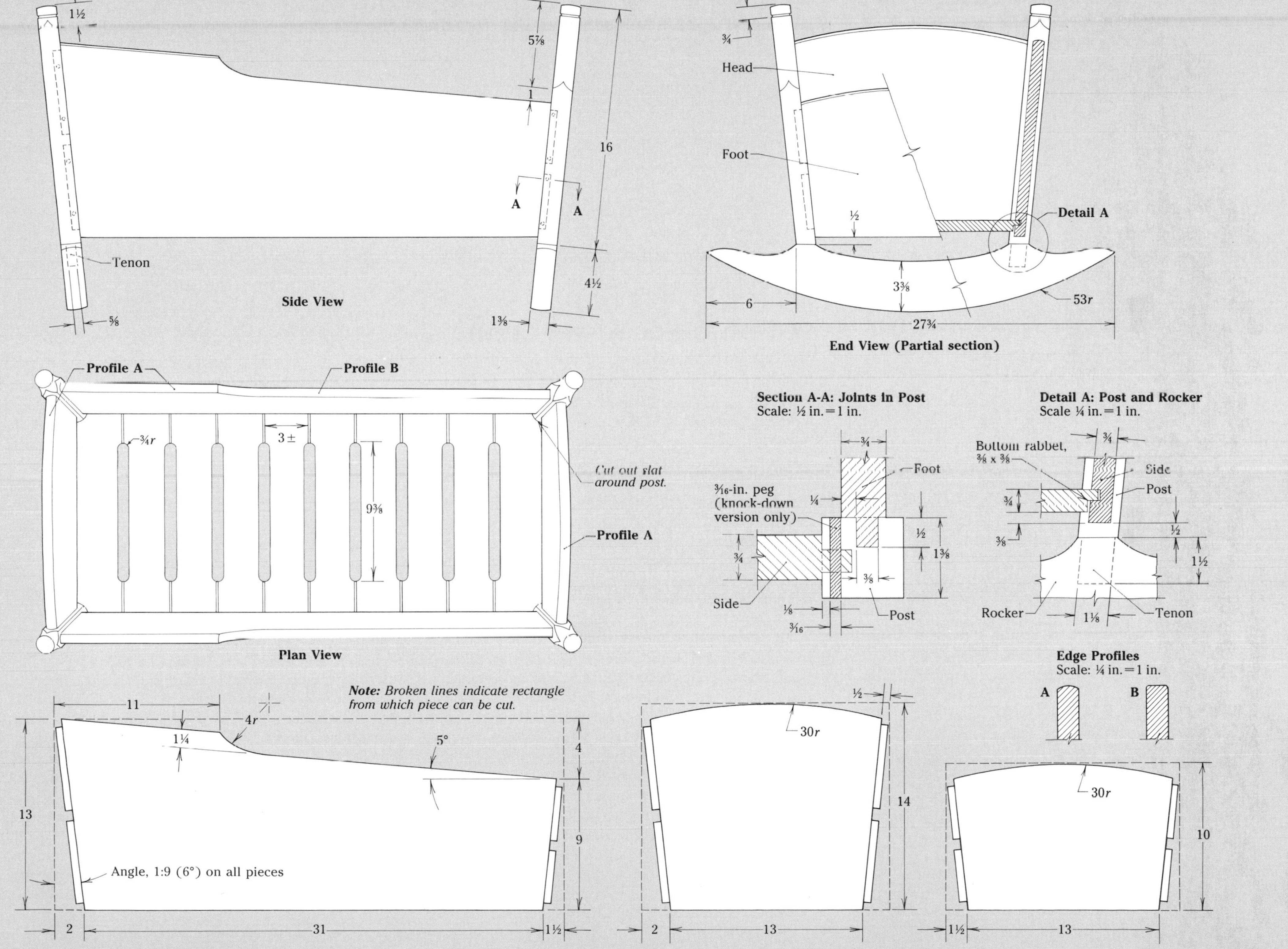

1½
5⅞
1
16
A
A
Tenon
4½
⅝
1⅜
Side View
¾
Head
Foot
½
Detail A
3⅜
6
53r
27¾
End View (Partial section)
Profile A
Profile B
¾r
3 ±
9⅜
Cut out slat around post.
Profile A
Plan View
Section A-A: Joints in Post
Scale: ½ in. = 1 in.
¾
Foot
³⁄₁₆-in. peg (knock-down version only)
¼
½
1⅜
¾
⅜
Side
⅛
³⁄₁₆
Post
Detail A: Post and Rocker
Scale ¼ in. = 1 in.
¾
Bottom rabbet, ⅜ x ⅜
Side
Post
¾
½
⅜
1½
Rocker
1⅛
Tenon
Edge Profiles
Scale: ¼ in. = 1 in.
A
B
Note: Broken lines indicate rectangle from which piece can be cut.
11
4r
1¼
5°
4
13
9
Angle, 1:9 (6°) on all pieces
2
31
1½
½
30r
14
2
13
30r
10
1½
13

Layout for Sides, Head and Foot

Chests and Bureaus 2

A Few Words About Chests

Throughout the Middle Ages, chests were a common item of furniture in Europe. Because of their rugged construction, and the protection afforded by a church, monastery or castle, many chests have survived. The owner might have succumbed to the plague or fallen victim to civil strife, but his chest and its valuable contents remained.

The twelfth or thirteenth-century chest at bottom left on the opposite page was simply hollowed out of a squared-up log, strapped with iron bands and fitted with a lid. The chest is enormously heavy and originally had three locks to make sure that at least two witnesses were present when it was opened.

As the art of joinery developed, the massive crudity of these early strongboxes gave way to more sophisticated construction in which riven or sawn boards were tenoned into corner posts. These lighter chests, like the one at top left on the opposite page, stored valuables such as books, money and silver plate, and were transported in ox carts, on packhorses or slung on poles between two mules. I particularly admire this late thirteenth-century chest. The vigorous, geometrical chip carving and the mortise-and-tenon structure, although still heavy, shows a tremendous technical advance from log chests.

The sturdy coffer at center right has a domed lid, which was able to withstand the hazards of travel and English weather better than a flat lid. Such chests were often covered with leather (probably to keep their contents dry), reinforced with iron at the corners and fitted with iron rings or handles. Stay-at-home chests, no longer needed as movable safes, became larger and lighter. Often, the frame-and-panel construction of such chests lended elegance to pieces used in a domestic setting, as in the sixteenth-century chest at top right.

Chests were also made by nailing four boards together and adding two more for the lid and bottom, as shown at bottom right. Although these chests were made in large numbers, few have survived, perhaps because they could easily be converted back into usable boards. Chests with dovetailed sides, which are much stronger than nailed chests, appeared at the end of the fifteenth century when the technique of dovetailing was rediscovered. Feet or a plinth were added to dovetailed chests to raise them off the floor.

In summary, the traditional methods of chest construction fall into the following categories: hollowing out a log; tenoning solid boards into corner posts; surrounding loose panels with mortise-and-tenoned frames; nailing or dovetailing together board sides and ends. Several of these methods were often combined in one chest—frame-and-panel sides with a solid lid, for example, or a dovetailed chest with a paneled lid. Excluding the hollowed-out log, today's methods of making chests have changed little from medieval times, and I can think of no new ones of equal durability.

The three-board sides of this thirteenth-century chest are tenoned and pegged together, and the ends are crudely frame-and-paneled. The chip carving might have been done with a simple knife.

Early chests, like early boats, were just hollowed logs. This one, made in the twelfth or thirteenth century, is fitted with iron bands and three locks.

Frame-and-panel construction was refined for chests that stayed at home. This chest was made during the sixteenth century.

This coffer was built to travel. The iron bands protected the chest and contents from rugged highways—and highwaymen.

Simple, nailed chests were common in the Middle Ages. The long, iron strap hinges reinforced the sides and top. The straps appearing on the far side were part of a hasp-type lock.

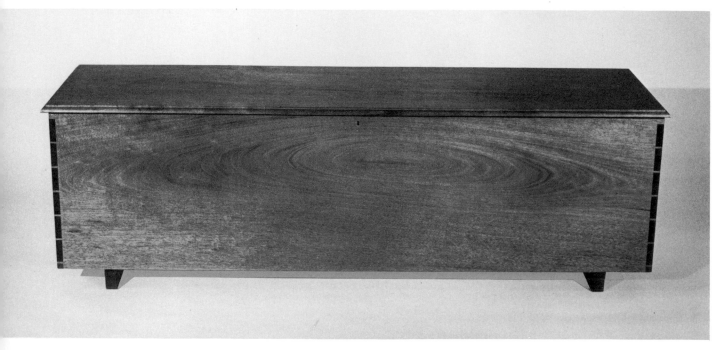

Blanket Chest

When I made my first large chest in 1969, the client required that it be 80 in. long and of solid teak. He also insisted that it not look like a coffin. I am still baffled by this—how can a 6-ft.-long box with handles at each end avoid looking like a casket?

The chest shown here is smaller and was made to store blankets and winter clothes; it has an aromatic cedar bottom to discourage moths. The sides, ends and lid are all single, wide boards. The dovetail joints keep the carcase pieces flat, but the lid should be stiffened with slot-screwed battens. The chest rests on runners instead of feet, so that it won't make deep impressions in the carpet and can be easily slid around when cleaning.

Sliding trays and dividers make it much easier to organize the contents. Customarily, a small till or shelf was put on one side to hold small objects or sweet-smelling herbs, such as lavender, to scent stored blankets and clothes. Carving the date and the owner's initials in the lid or front was often done and added a nice touch.

Construction

The dimensions of this chest were determined in part by the widths of the mahogany boards that I had. There's no reason why you couldn't use a different wood or alter these dimensions. If you have to edge-join boards for the sides and ends, I recommend using two boards each for the front and back sides and three each for the ends, so that the glue lines are staggered at the corners.

After you've planed the pieces to thickness, plane one edge of each true and rip them all to width. When you cut to length, make sure the ends are square to the planed edge and the face.

Lay out the tails next. After making the chest shown here, I decided that the tails look better on the sides, rather than on the ends. In addition, it's easier to clamp across the ends when gluing up. I have also added small tails at the top and bottom to help lock the joint and to act as visual punctuation of the long runs of dovetails. (These changes are shown in the plan drawings.) Set a marking gauge to 1/32 in. more than the thickness of the stock and mark around the ends of each piece.

The gauge lines were left on many pieces of fine, old, country furniture. On those pieces, the lines give

Carving the date, initials or other inscription in the chest lid is a nice touch.

a sense of the craftman's presence, but I don't think they're appropriate on elegant, expensive pieces of modern furniture. This chest is somewhere in between styles; make the lines very light if you plan to remove them. Cut them in neatly and firmly with a sharp cutting gauge if you want them to show.

Mark out the tails on the faces of the sides with a pencil sharpened to a fine, chisel point (not a knife), and a dovetail template or sliding bevel. Use a small square to extend the lines across the ends of the sides (it's unnecessary to draw them down the other face). Mark the waste with a red pencil, then saw right to the lines with a backsaw, making sure the kerf is on the red side. Cut out most of the waste with a coping saw, making sure to keep ⅟₁₆ in. to ⅛ in. clear of the gauge mark.

Lay the piece on the benchtop with the tails over a leg of the bench so that the tails are well supported for chiseling out the rest of the waste. (You can clamp the piece down, but I usually sit on it.) Clamping a straightedge to the work to guide the chisel is not necessary—just place the chisel's edge in the gauge mark. Use a sharp chisel and a mallet to undercut the end grain slightly—if the surface is convex, there will be gaps between the tails and pins. Chisel half to two thirds of the way through, turn the piece over and complete the cut from the other face.

When all the tails have been cut, mark the pins on the carcase ends from the corresponding tails. Letter or number each joint so the mating pieces can be identified for assembly. Marking can be awkward when a carcase is as wide as this one. Clamp the carcase end in the vise so its end is a little bit above and parallel to the surface of the bench. Place the chest side on the end, and shim up between the side and the bench with scrap until the two pieces form a right angle, as shown in the drawing at top right. The edges of the two pieces should be aligned and you should see only a glimmer of light between the end grain of the tail sockets and the inside face of the chest end.

Leaning on the chest side to hold it firmly in place, knife-mark the position of the tails into the end grain of the end. (If an end is bowed, you can clamp a batten with a shallow reverse curve to it to flatten it while knife-marking the pins. When the carcase is assembled, the joint will fit tightly along its full length and will pull the end flat.) I use a knife with a thin, flexible blade or a scratch awl with its point bent over. Keep the blade bearing tightly against the tails.

Remove the chest side and deepen the marks in the end grain with the knife if necessary. Use a small square to extend the knife mark down the face side to the gauge marks. The knife marks will be easier to see if you run a chisel-pointed pencil lightly in them.

Saw out the pins with a backsaw. Mark the waste with the red pencil and make sure the kerf is in the waste. Saw carefully—"Save me the line," as Nova Scotian boatbuilders would put it. Split the knife mark in half, and the tails and pins will fit perfectly. Cut out the waste with a coping saw or bandsaw, and chisel to the gauge marks as before.

Because the tails and pins can be damaged, it's not advisable to assemble the joint to check the fit. Tap the pins into their sockets slightly—if they enter without forcing, and if you've sawn square, they will come home all right when clamped.

Saw or rout the grooves for the bottom next. A groove in the end that falls between two pins will be covered by the tail on the side, but you'll need to stop the groove in the tail so it won't show on the end. The bottom supports the weight of the carcase, so make it at least ¾-in. thick. Rabbet the bottom with the tablesaw or router—remember to allow for the movement of the wood.

I finish the inside surfaces of the carcase with wax before assembly because it makes cleaning up the squeezed-out glue easier. Masking tape across the tails will prevent wax from getting on them accidentally. I use wax on the front, back and ends, but I leave the bottom unfinished so that the wax won't interfere with the sweet smell of the cedar.

Gluing up a dovetailed carcase can be a frustrating business, but if you're organized and proceed methodically, frustrations will be less likely. First, make four clamping strips of hardwood scrap, as shown in the drawing at bottom right. These should be about 1 in. by 1¼ in. and notched to fit over the pins, so pressure can be applied without bearing on the pins.

Clear a space to work in and lay out everything you will need to glue up. Use a glue that permits plenty of assembly time. A plastic resin glue, such as Weldwood, will work well. Titebond and other aliphatic resin glues set up too quickly. The small, metal brushes sold for applying soldering flux make ideal glue brushes.

Apply glue to the pins and tails and on the outside arrises of the socket bottoms as a filler. Fit a side to two ends, slide in the bottom, and then add the other

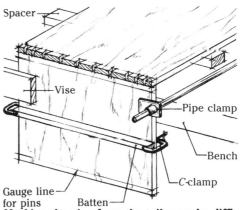

Marking the pins from the tails can be difficult on wide pieces. Clamp the pin piece so that its end is parallel to the benchtop. Support the tail piece on scraps so that it forms a right angle with the pin piece. Lean on the tail piece to hold it in place and mark the pins with a sharp knife. You can straighten a bowed piece for marking by clamping a stiff batten across it.

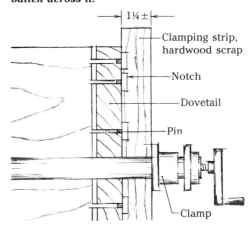

To assemble the carcase, make clamping strips, notched to fit over the pins. Use the clamping strips and a pipe or bar clamp to pull each tail tight to the bottom of its socket.

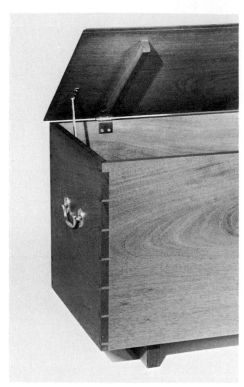

Stays prevent the lid from falling over backward, and wooden battens keep the lid flat.

side. Drive the joints together as far as possible with a rubber mallet or dead-fall hammer, which has a head filled with lead shot and won't bounce. Then pull them tight using the clamping strips and bar or pipe clamps. (It helps to have an assistant—each person positions clamps and clamping strips at each end.) If you've cut the joints accurately, you'll probably need to place a clamp over each tail and pull it home. Put the clamping strips directly over the tails, or you'll distort the carcase. Don't leave the clamps on—once the tails are seated, they shouldn't move.

Check for square by measuring from corner to corner diagonally across the carcase—a more accurate method than using a framing square or trysquare. If the carcase isn't square, I wedge out the shortest diagonal with a stout piece of scrap, pointed at both ends to fit into the corners and placed at about the midpoint of the carcase depth. (Pulling in the longest diagonal with a clamp can distort a deep carcase like this one.) You could also clamp a piece of scrap to each jaw of a wooden hand screw and spread the diagonal by spreading the clamp jaws. This method takes more time, but gives greater control.

The runner feet are heavily chamfered, which keeps them from chipping out if the chest is dragged across the floor. They are screwed to the bottom—the center screw is fixed, the other two are slot-screwed to allow the bottom to move. I use a washer with an elongated slot rather than chopping a slot in the wood.

Make the lid next. You can work the decorative rule-joint molding on the ends and front edge with a router or molding plane. (If you make a long chest, the lid will be heavy and you may wish to make it in two halves, each hinged separately, like a Dutch door.) The lid is fixed only along its hinge edge, so it needs to be stiffened with battens to keep it flat. Battens are not an elegant detail, but can be avoided only by making a frame-and-panel lid. Place the battens slightly back from the front edge so that the lid can open. I use three screws per batten, slot-screwing the ones at the batten ends. The movement will occur on either side of the center screw, so you only have to figure the movement for 6½ in., rather than the full 13-in. width of the lid. You can plug the holes to hide the screws.

Old chests were fitted with wrought-iron, offset hinges with long straps that reinforced the top and back. They're difficult to find now, so I used brass-plated, ¾-in. offset hinges made for kitchen cabinet doors. One flange of the hinge is let into the top edge of the back so it lies flush; the other flange is planted on the lid. Positioning the hinge like this leaves a little clearance between the lid and the back, which keeps the lid from binding.

Stays are essential—they prevent the chest lid from falling over backwards. The sliding, solid-brass stays shown at left work well, but a pair of them are quite expensive (see Appendix 5 for sources of supply). Lightweight brass chains attached to brass screw eyes, Dacron or cotton cords, or wooden arms that fold like wooden rules will also work. The lid will move too much with seasonal changes to permit the use of a conventional chest lock or catch.

The brass chest lifts are fastened through the ends with brass machine screws and nuts because regular wood screws might pull out.

Blanket Chest

Scale: 1/16 in. = 1 in.
Details: ½ in. = 1 in.

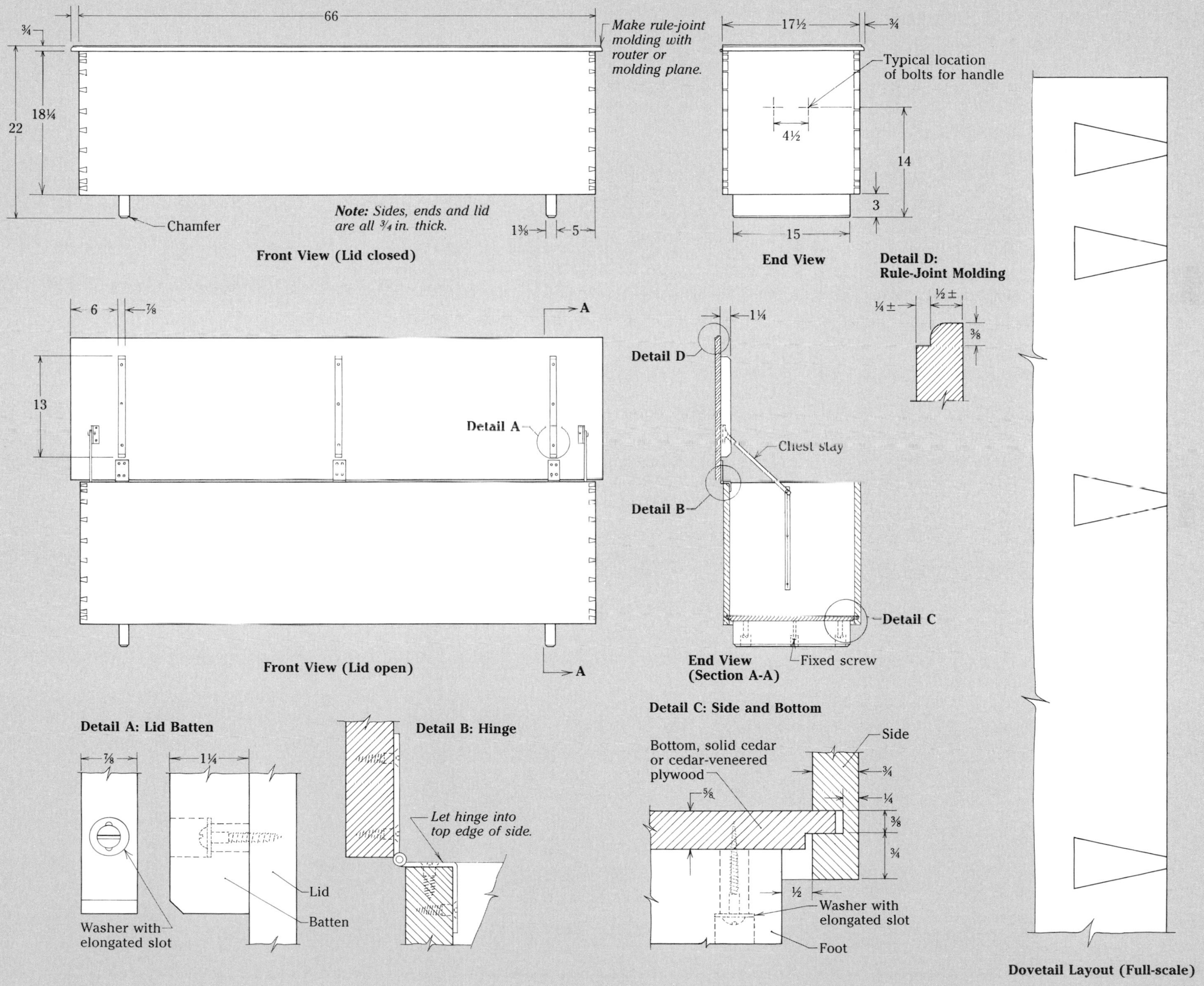
66
¾
22
18¼
Make rule-joint molding with router or molding plane.
Chamfer
Note: Sides, ends and lid are all ¾ in. thick.
1⅜
5
Front View (Lid closed)
17½
¾
Typical location of bolts for handle
4½
14
3
15
End View
Detail D: Rule-Joint Molding
¼ ±
½ ±
⅜
6
⅞
A
13
Detail A
Front View (Lid open)
1¼
Detail D
Chest stay
Detail B
Detail C
End View (Section A-A)
Fixed screw
Detail A: Lid Batten
⅞
1¼
Washer with elongated slot
Lid
Batten
Detail B: Hinge
Let hinge into top edge of side.
Detail C: Side and Bottom
Bottom, solid cedar or cedar-veneered plywood
Side
⅝
¾
¼
⅜
¾
½
Washer with elongated slot
Foot
Dovetail Layout (Full-scale)

Paneled Chest

Scale: 1⁄16 in. = 1 in.
Details: ¼ in. = 1 in.

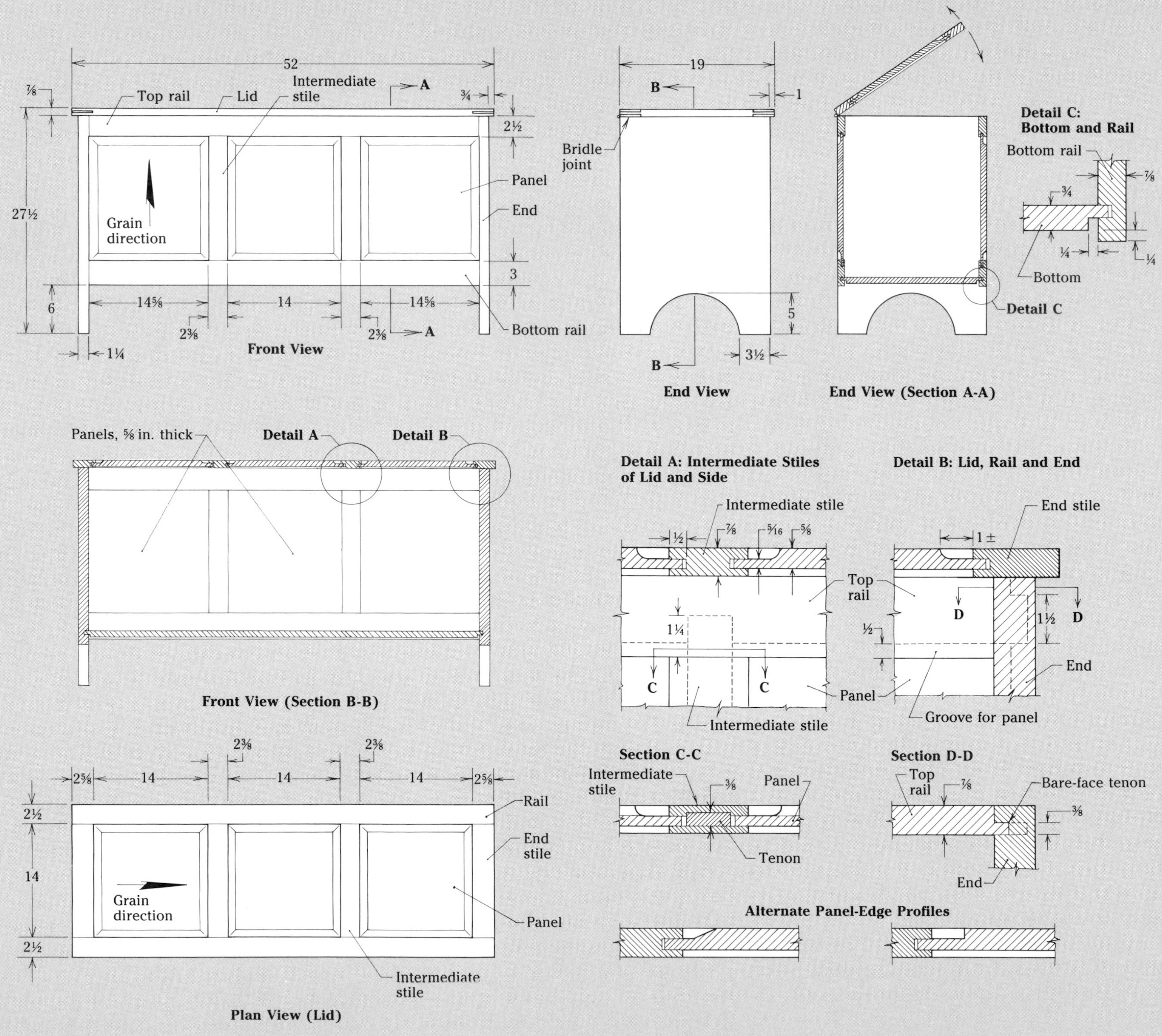

52
Top rail
Lid
Intermediate stile
A
⅞
¾
2½
27½
Grain direction
Panel
End
3
6
14⅝
14
14⅝
2⅜
2⅜
A
1¼
Bottom rail
Front View
19
B
1
Bridle joint
5
3½
B
End View
End View (Section A-A)
Detail C: Bottom and Rail
Bottom rail
⅞
¾
¼
¼
Bottom
Detail C
Panels, ⅝ in. thick
Detail A
Detail B
Front View (Section B-B)
Detail A: Intermediate Stiles of Lid and Side
Intermediate stile
½
⅞
5⁄16
⅝
Top rail
1¼
C
C
Panel
Intermediate stile
Detail B: Lid, Rail and End
End stile
1 ±
D
1½
D
½
End
Groove for panel
Section C-C
Intermediate stile
⅜
Panel
Tenon
Section D-D
Top rail
⅞
Bare-face tenon
⅜
End
Alternate Panel-Edge Profiles
2⅜
2⅜
2⅝
14
14
14
2⅝
2½
Rail
End stile
14
Grain direction
Panel
2½
Intermediate stile
Plan View (Lid)

Paneled Chest

This chest combines two traditional methods of construction. The ends are solid boards and the front, back and lid are paneled frames. For a decorative effect, I used red birch panels with walnut frames and ends. (Red birch is the heartwood of yellow birch.) The warm colors of the two woods complement each other, though the effect might be too dramatic for some people's tastes. Walnut frames with butternut, cherry or quartersawn white oak panels, or teak frames with walnut panels might also look well. If you want a quieter chest, make the whole thing of Honduras mahogany, a wood that ages with charm.

The frames and panels can be treated in many different ways. Some eighteenth-century panels were beautifully carved and inlaid. A molded frame and raised panels create a subtle interplay of shadows that can enrich a piece. On the other hand, medieval chests often had plain, flat panels and heavily chamfered frames. If your tastes are simpler, you might leave the frame unmolded, and the panels flat, with the raised face on the inside. (Books on furniture history often show various frame-and-panel treatments.)

The proportions of each panel and the relation of the panels to each other and to the whole chest are very important. These proportions are difficult to visualize on a scaled-down drawing, so I always draw the panels and framing full-size on a large sheet of paper, hang it on the wall and live with it for a bit—ungainly proportions soon become apparent.

The chest shown here was made fifteen years ago. I have since made slight changes in the dimensions and the construction details, and have changed the plan drawings accordingly. The most obvious changes are adding the bridle joints (a mortise and tenon that is open on two sides) on the corners of the lid, and making the lower rails on the front and back slightly wider than the upper rails.

Construction

The ends are 1¼ in. thick to support the tenons of the frame rails. (The rails are the long pieces, the stiles are the short ones.) A single, wide board for each end is attractive, but if you can't find boards wide enough, join up ends from several boards. Avoid centering a glue line, however, as a glue line bisecting the arch will draw attention to the joint. Cut the ends to their correct length and width.

The frame members should be fairly uniform in grain and color so they don't detract from the panels. They will match nicely if you cut them from the same wide board, or you could resaw a thick piece and book-match the pairs of rails and stiles on each frame. Plane the material for all three frames (lid, front and back) to ⅞ in. thick.

Lay out and cut the mortises in the ends, then cut the bare-face tenons (tenons with only one shoulder) on the rails of the front and back frames. The bareface tenon allows you to leave as much wood as possible between the mortise and the edge of the chest end. Even so, be careful not to move the rails from side to side when fitting the tenons, because you could break out the mortises.

Next, cut the mortises and tenons that join the stiles to the rails on the front and back frames. When you lay them out, make sure that one side of the mortise cheeks and tenon cheeks will line up with the groove, as shown in the plan drawings and isometric drawings. This way, you can be sure the grooves for the panels will fall within the thickness of the mortises and tenons. (The groove doesn't line up with the

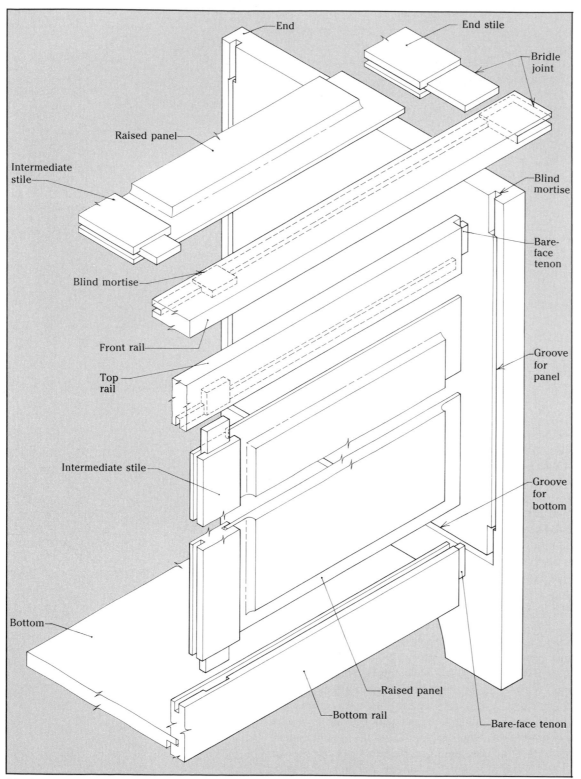

bare-face mortise-and-tenon joint that joins the rails to the ends.)

You can now push the carcase together dry while you work on the lid. Because the lid is held by hinges only along the back edge, it must be flat, so it's important to cut the joints accurately. The intermediate stiles are tenoned into the rails as for the other frames; the end stiles and rails are bridle-jointed.

I make the bridle joints using the tablesaw and a good carbide blade. A 10-in. ATB blade (one with alternately beveled teeth) with fifty or sixty teeth is often used for making cross-grain cuts because there is less tear-out than with a combination blade. Lay out the bridle joint for one corner (the saw is set to this layout so you needn't mark the rest). Use a marking gauge or knife and a square to mark the tenon shoulders on the stile—the tenon should be 1/16 in. longer than the width of the rail. The width of the tenon equals the width of the stile minus the depth of the groove for the panel. The thickness of the tenon is customarily two fifths of the thickness of the stock— 3/8 in. here. You can mark the cheeks of the mortise and the tenon with one setting on a mortise gauge; remember to gauge both pieces from the outside face (the one that will show).

Cut the tenons first, holding the stiles vertically against the rip fence. I use a homemade wooden table insert with an opening just a saw kerf wide for the saw, so the pieces will be supported right next to the blade, and I screw an 8-in.-high wooden fence to the rip fence. Set the saw 1/8 in. below the shoulder lines, and adjust the fence to cut right to the cheek lines. Cut the shoulders next, using an accurately set miter gauge. You can use the rip fence as a stop block— don't saw through the waste or it will come whistling back at you. The remaining waste is easily cleaned up with a chisel or shoulder rabbet plane.

Next saw the cheeks of the mortises in the same way as the tenon cheeks. The tenons should fit into the mortises snugly, without forcing. It's helpful to use a piece of scrap to position the rip fence exactly—try the tenons in the mortised scrap. Remove the waste by boring a hole in from both edges, or cutting it out with a coping saw. Chisel to the gauge mark to complete the mortise.

To lay out the grooves for the panels, I assemble the frames without glue and mark the four inside edges of each panel opening with a crayon—a groove in the wrong place, even when repaired, looks terri-

The front, back and lid of the chest are frame-and-panel construction. The ends are solid boards.

ble. Disassemble the frames and cut the grooves. I use the tablesaw and dado head, but several passes over a single sawblade will do the job, as will a router. Set the rip fence so that the outside face of the rail or stile will run against it. (Remember that one side of the groove lines up with one cheek of the mortises and tenons on all but the bare-face tenons, as shown in the plan drawings.) I make the grooves about ½ in. deep to allow for movement of the panels. Using the same setting, cut the panel grooves in the ends, and stop the grooves at the mortises.

Make the panels next. The grain of rectangular panels, whenever possible, should run parallel to the panel's longest dimension to minimize the effects of shrinkage. The grain of the square panels on the lid runs along the length of the top, which is customary for paneled chest lids.

It's quick, easy and most accurate to make all the panels at one time. I make the three panels for each frame from a long board, and this gives each set of panels a consistency of grain and color that's difficult to obtain any other way. A single, wide board would be ideal, but I usually have to edge-join two or three boards to obtain the width.

Plane the long piece as flat as possible and ⅝ in. thick, then cut the panels to size. Their widths and lengths depend on the size of the frame openings and the depth of the grooves. I left about ⅛ in. clearance between the edges of the panels and the bottoms of the grooves. The ends of the panels should almost make contact with the grooves. Check the table in Appendix 1 to estimate the panel shrinkage for the species of wood you're using and make the panels so that the shrinkage will be taken up inside the groove.

I make the raised center on the face of each panel using a router with a ⅝-in. corebox bit and a tablesaw. Use a sharp bit and sawblade—you'll save time later when sanding. Mark the outline of the raised center on the panels and on a few pieces of panel scrap with a pencil gauge (a marking gauge with a pencil instead of a metal point; you can make one from an old marking gauge). Now set the router fence so the widest part of the corebox bit just touches the line. Check the setting on a scrap piece, then rout four grooves on the face of each panel. It is best to take a heavy cut almost to full depth, then a light, final cut, which won't burn or chatter.

Saw off the waste on the tablesaw, holding the panel vertically with its back to the fence. Set up the ta-

blesaw as described previously for tenoning, using the wooden table insert and high fence. Check the setup on a piece of scrap to make sure the panels will fit snugly in the grooves. If the panel is slightly bowed, you can clamp it to a stiff batten while sawing, as shown in the sketch at right.

I use aromatic cedar for the bottom to keep the moths at bay. You could attach ledger strips to the rails and rest the bottom on them, but I prefer to rabbet the bottom into grooves in the ends and bottom rails, and glue the bottom to the ends. The ends and bottom will shrink and expand in the same direction so there will be no problems with movement.

Before gluing the carcase together, sand the pieces. The end of an orbital sander will conform to the curve on the face of the raised panel and will remove any router marks. You should also sand and put a light chamfer on all the edges of the frame that surround the panels, because this is difficult to do after the panels are in place. It's not a bad idea to put the finish on the panels now, so the subsequent shrinkage won't expose unfinished wood. Also, glue won't adhere to most finishes, so there will be less chance of the panel sticking to the frame and cracking with seasonal movement.

Glue the lid together, pull the shoulders of the joints tight with pipe or bar clamps, and then C-clamp the bridle joints to squeeze the cheeks tight. Place wooden pads between the clamp jaws and the wood to distribute the pressure and protect the surfaces. I glue the whole carcase together at once. Assemble it dry first to determine the positions of the clamps and to make sure that the panels aren't too large, which would prevent the joints from closing. Use a plastic resin glue so you will have enough assembly time. Center the panels in the openings and, after the clamps are off, peg through the back of the rail into the center of each panel end, so that the panels will shrink equally in each stile groove.

I use the same hinges and brass sliding stays for this lid as for the blanket chest (see p. 32; also see Appendix 5 for sources of supply). Instead of the stays, you could attach a length of brass chain or nylon cord to the lid and chest at each end. I don't put handles on this chest because they detract from the appearance, and the arch cut in each end makes a good handhold. Because the ends can shrink and expand, the width of the chest will alter enough to make it impractical to fit a conventional chest lock.

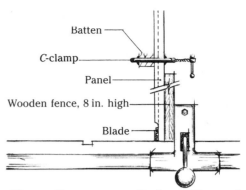

After routing grooves on the face of the panel to define the raised center, cut away the waste on the tablesaw. You can straighten a bowed panel by clamping it to a stiff batten as shown here.

Small Bureau

Scale: ⅛ in. = 1 in.

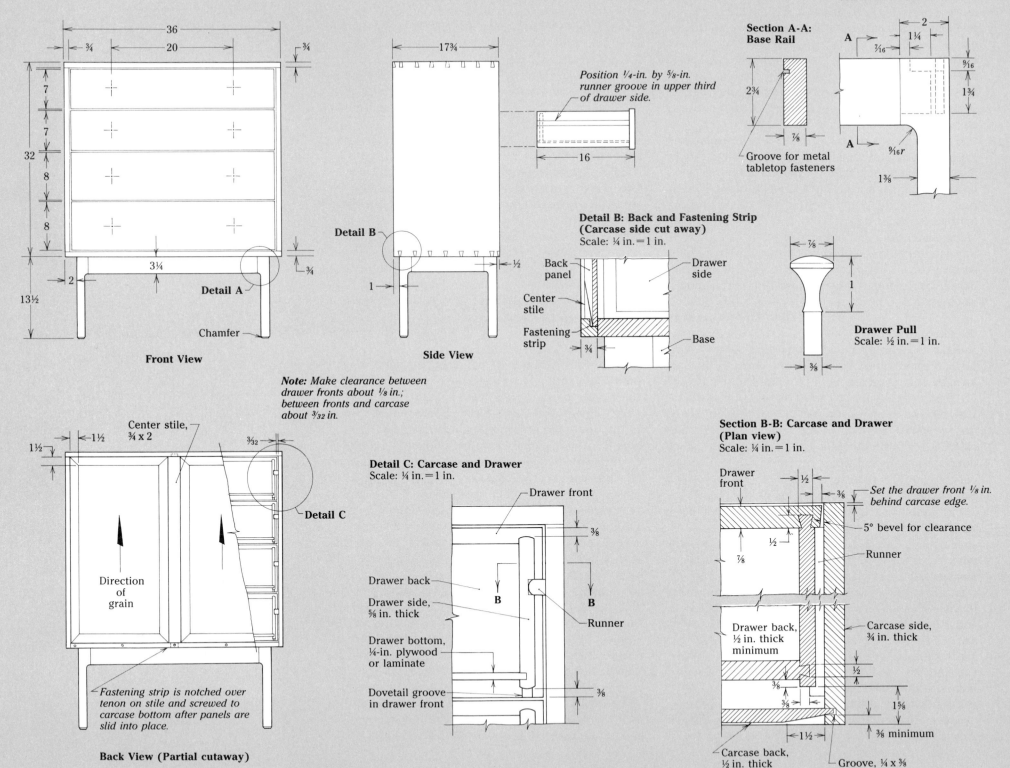

Front View

Side View

Detail A: Leg and Rail of Base
Scale: ¼ in. = 1 in.

Section A-A: Base Rail

Groove for metal tabletop fasteners

Position ¼-in. by ⅝-in. runner groove in upper third of drawer side.

Detail B: Back and Fastening Strip (Carcase side cut away)
Scale: ¼ in. = 1 in.

Back panel
Drawer side
Center stile
Fastening strip
Base

Drawer Pull
Scale: ½ in. = 1 in.

Chamfer

Detail A

Detail B

Note: Make clearance between drawer fronts about ⅛ in.; between fronts and carcase about 3/32 in.

Center stile, ¾ x 2

Direction of grain

Fastening strip is notched over tenon on stile and screwed to carcase bottom after panels are slid into place.

Back View (Partial cutaway)

Detail C

Detail C: Carcase and Drawer
Scale: ¼ in. = 1 in.

Drawer front
Drawer back
Drawer side, ⅝ in. thick
Drawer bottom, ¼-in. plywood or laminate
Dovetail groove in drawer front
Runner

Section B-B: Carcase and Drawer (Plan view)
Scale: ¼ in. = 1 in.

Drawer front
Set the drawer front ⅛ in. behind carcase edge.
5° bevel for clearance
Runner
Drawer back, ½ in. thick minimum
Carcase side, ¾ in. thick
Carcase back, ½ in. thick
Groove, ¼ x ⅜

Small Bureau

Anyone who has kept possessions in a deep chest knows how very inconvenient this can be. Whatever one wants is always at the bottom, and the books, gloves, letters and plants that collect on the lid all must be removed before anything can be taken out of the chest. Around the year 1600, some exasperated householder must have ordered a chest with a drawer in it; soon another drawer was added, then three or four more. By 1700, the chest of drawers, or bureau, had arrived.

Unfortunately, bureaus can be tedious to make—all that work, much of it hidden from view, just to make a box with smaller boxes sliding into it. And if you're not careful, the drawers will swell and jam in the springtime, and you won't be able to get your tennis shorts out. Still, I think there is a need for bureaus. Chests are best used for storing bulky items, such as winter sweaters and feather comforters, or other things that are seldom used. Articles of everyday use, such as socks and underwear, belong in a bureau.

I've included two bureaus in this book: I'll describe the smaller, simpler one here, and the tall bureau on pp. 43-45. The small bureau is designed to be made in pairs, which can then be stacked or placed side by side, as well as used separately.

Construction

Any wood that is reasonably stable will do for the carcase and drawer fronts, though I find oak difficult for dovetailed carcases because its open grain doesn't cut cleanly. The side-hung drawers are just two sizes and are made with sliding slot dovetails. Ideally, the sides of drawers should be made of a stable, hard-wearing, fine-grained wood. For drawers that are small and light, almost any wood will do, even white pine. For the large, deep drawers of a bureau, mahogany would be my first choice, then hard maple or ash. Oak, because it moves a great deal, would be a poor fourth choice, followed by poplar, yellow birch, beech and cedar. The drawer backs can be made of the same wood as the drawer sides. The best wood to use for the drawer runners is hard maple. (Rock maple, sugar maple and hard maple are all interchangeable names in the lumber trade.)

I use ¼-in. plywood or Masonite with a thin plastic skin for the drawer bottoms (the plastic is easy to clean). Baltic birch plywood works well, or plywood veneered with a light-colored wood like yellow birch. I don't use uncoated Masonite or rotary-cut fir plywood because I think those materials cheapen the whole piece.

Large drawer bottoms are liable to sag if they're too thin. As a rough guide, bottoms for drawers less than 1 sq. ft. in area should be ⅛ in. to ³⁄₁₆ in. thick and beveled or rabbeted to fit into ⅛-in. grooves. For drawers between 1 sq. ft. and 5 sq. ft., make the bottoms ¼ in. to ⁵⁄₁₆ in. thick, and fit them into ¼-in. grooves. If the drawer is over 5 sq. ft., the bottom should be ⅜ in. thick and also fit ¼-in. grooves. (These same rules apply to solid-wood bottoms.)

Begin by selecting the boards for the carcase, then join them up edge to edge and plane them to their finished thickness. Avoid glue lines meeting at a corner—they look bad. I try to make glued-up boards less than 18 in. wide so they will fit my 18-in. planer; if you don't have a planer, or only have a small one, local millwork shops will usually plane boards for a reasonable fee.

Lay out and cut the dovetail joints next, as discussed on pp. 30-32. Take care to make the ends of the sides, top and bottom square to their front edges; if they're not square, the carcase will taper and the drawers won't fit properly. There are small, locking dovetails on all but the back bottom corners of the carcase sides. They have been omitted there so the sides will cover the strip that is screwed to the edge of the bottom to hold the back panels in place.

Rout the grooves for the back panel in the carcase sides and top, and chop the blind mortise for the center stile that divides the back. Glue up the carcase—make sure that it's square by measuring the diagonals, because if it's out of square, the drawers will not fit properly.

The next step is to make the drawers, shown in the drawing at right. Rough-cut the drawer fronts slightly oversized and then plane or joint one face flat before running them through a thickness planer. Trim them long enough to fit the carcase opening, but not so long that they cause the sides to bow out. Cut the drawer fronts about ³⁄₁₆ in. wider than the dimensions shown in the plan drawings—the clearance will be worked later.

The drawer sides are about ¾ in. narrower than the drawer front, and 15⅝ in. long, which allows for the dovetail tenon and about ⅝-in. clearance at the back. Make ten sides so you'll have spares if you make a

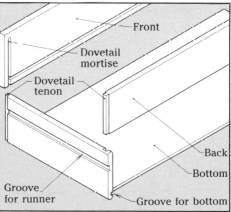

Slot-dovetail construction is simple and sturdy. The grooves for the runners and drawer bottom can also be routed.

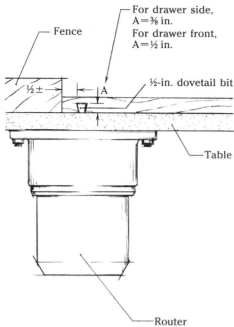

Mount a router upside down under a table to cut the mortises in the drawer front and sides for the slot-dovetail joints.

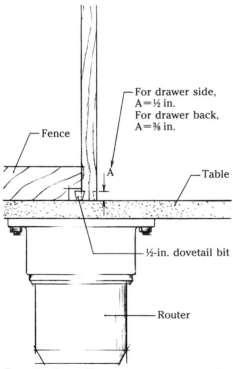

Rout the dovetail tenons on the drawer sides and back. Check the router bit and fence setup on a piece of scrap first.

mistake. I rout a light round on both edges of each drawer side—these look and feel nice.

You will need a ½-in. dovetail router bit to cut the slot-dovetail joint. Carbide-tipped bits are more expensive than high-speed steel bits, but the carbide cutting edge stays sharp much longer, especially when routing abrasive woods, such as teak.

Rout the dovetail mortises (the slots) in the drawer fronts first. The mortises should be as close as possible to the ends, but far enough away to ensure that the joints won't break—I set them about ½ in. in from the ends, which leaves about ⅜ in. of material after the clearance has been worked. I mount the router upside down under a table and run each end of the fronts against a fence, as shown in the sketch at top left. Stop the mortises so they won't show on the top edge of the front. To do this, it's necessary to rout with, rather than against, the bit's rotation on one end of each front; the bit will tend to push the end away from the fence. Practice on a piece of scrap, holding it firmly and feeding it slowly. With the same fence setting, reduce the depth of cut to ⅜ in. and mortise each drawer side for the back. I don't stop these mortises.

Next, cut the dovetail tenons on the ends of the drawer sides. Set the fence as shown in the sketch at lower left. Use scrap pieces the same thickness as the sides to get the setup just right. The dovetail tenon should slide easily into the mortise without forcing, but without any slop. (Feed against the direction of the bit's rotation so the bit won't grab.) Saw a shoulder on the top edge of each tenon to cover the rounded end of the stopped mortise.

To determine the length of the backs, assemble two sides and a front and measure the distance between the bottoms of the dovetail mortises in the sides. (Make sure the sides are parallel by measuring across the front and back.) Adjust the router setup and make the dovetail tenons on the ends of the backs.

Assemble all four drawers without glue and identify each joint with a penciled letter or number. Using a red crayon, mark the approximate position of the runner groove in each side, as well as the ¼-in. grooves for the drawer bottom. (I mark these grooves because it is easy to make a mistake when working with so many similar parts—and a groove in the wrong place is hard to move.) The drawers seem to work better if the runner grooves are positioned within the upper third of each drawer side, as shown in the photo on the opposite page.

I rout all the grooves on the table-mounted router. Always place the bottom edge of each side against the fence, so the groove will be in the same position on both sides of each drawer. The runner grooves and drawer-bottom grooves on the sides don't need to be stopped. Stop the drawer-bottom groove in the drawer front in the dovetail mortises.

Do all the finish-sanding and give the inside surfaces of each drawer a good waxing before gluing up. Put glue in the dovetail mortises only—glue will swell the tenons and might keep them from sliding into place. The bottom edge of the drawer backs must align with the top edge of the groove for the bottoms so the drawer bottom can be slid into place later.

Make sure the drawers are square before the glue sets. Check for twist or wind by standing back and sighting over the top edges of the drawer sides, which should be exactly parallel, or try them on a machined surface such as the saw table. If a drawer is twisted, put blocks under the two opposite high corners and bear down on the other two. Remove the blocks and look again. Don't clamp the corners down—they'll usually spring back up when the glue has set and the clamps are removed. Set the drawers on a flat surface while the glue cures.

Slide the drawer bottoms in place next. They can be a close fit across the width of the drawer because the plywood won't swell or shrink, but they must not be so long that they force the sides apart. Put a dab of glue in the groove in the drawer front, slide the bottom into place, and screw or tack the back edge to the drawer back. (You can add the bottoms after fitting the drawer runners to make it easier to see what's happening with the runners.)

Now make the drawer runners. These must be dead straight, because they will not be housed in grooves and kept from moving, like the runners in the bed with drawers (p. 14). Cut at least ten oversized runners from a rough board (the extras are for insurance). Plane or joint two adjacent surfaces of each runner straight and square to each other. Plane a third surface so each runner is just thick enough to slide easily in the drawer-side grooves. Rip the remaining surface to make each runner about ¾ in. wide, and plane a slight round on this surface, as shown in the plan drawings. Clamp a pair of runners in the carcase from the back and try a drawer. Trim the width of the runners until the drawer slips in easily, with no sideways movement. (I trim them on the tablesaw using a sharp carbide-tipped blade, which leaves a smooth surface requiring no further jointing or hand-planing.) Repeat for each set of runners. Before installation, bore and countersink screw holes in each runner, a single hole near the front end and slots in the middle and near the back end.

Position the runners for the bottom drawer next. Measure the distance between the bottom edge of the runner groove in the drawer side and the bottom edge of the drawer front. Cut four strips of scrap wood for spacers; they should be thin enough to slip between the drawer side and the carcase, to this length. Tack two of the spacers to each side of the carcase, as shown in the sketch at right. Rest a runner on each pair of spacers, clamping the runner to the carcase at the back. (Large spring clips are handy for this.) Try the bottom drawer on the runners—it should slide easily—then push the drawer in. The lower edge of the drawer front should just touch the bottom of the carcase. If this edge is too high or too low, trim the spacers or cut new ones.

Because the runners are also drawer stops, they must be placed to stop the drawer about ⅛ in. behind the front edge of the carcase. Cut two more strips of thin scrap 1 in. wide and as long as the carcase opening is tall. Tack these spacers flush with the front edge of the carcase. Butt the front ends of the runners against the spacers and screw the runners in place.

You'll need four more spacers to place the runners for the next three drawers. Calculate the length of these spacers as shown in the sketch at bottom right. Place these spacers on the bottom-drawer runners and tack them to the carcase sides as before. Rest the runners on the spacers, clamp them at the back and try the drawer. The bottom edge of its front should just touch the top edge of the drawer front underneath it. Butt the runners against the 1-in.-wide spacers and screw the runners in place. Trim 1 in. off the spacers and repeat the procedure for the last two drawers. (Measure first to make sure that there is enough room for these drawers. If not, you will need to adjust the spacing of their runners and trim the drawer fronts narrower to fit.)

When all the drawer runners are installed, and the drawers slide easily on them, trim the ends of each drawer front to clear the carcase sides by about ³⁄₃₂ in. Trimming is easily done on a disc sander with the table set for a 5° bevel. The bevel, which slants away

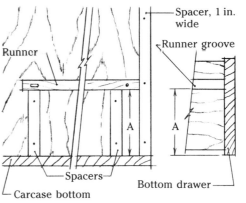

The runner groove should fall within the upper third of the drawer side. Because of the slot-dovetail construction, the groove need not be stopped.

from the face side, ensures that the fronts won't strike the carcase sides as the drawers slide in. Plane the lower edge of the bottom-drawer front so it clears the carcase bottom by about ³⁄₃₂ in. Then plane the remaining fronts so there is a uniform gap of about ⅛ in. between them.

The next step is to make the drawer fronts flush with each other, so that they are all in the same plane. Lay the carcase on its back on low sawhorses—make sure it isn't twisted. Slide the drawers in, placing small pieces of ⅛-in.-thick scrap between the back face of the drawer fronts and the ends of the runners. The scrap pieces will raise the drawer fronts flush with the front edges of the carcase. Go over the entire surface (the drawer fronts and carcase edges) with a cabinet scraper or finely set plane, and then finish-sand. The fronts should be set back a uniform distance of ⅛ in. from the carcase edges when you remove the spacers.

I put a back with solid-wood panels on this bureau. The piece is too large for a single, wide panel, because the grooves in the carcase sides would have to be excessively deep to allow for seasonal movement. I add a center stile, stub-tenoned into the carcase top as a divider, then I slide the panels into place after the carcase is glued up and the drawers are fitted. The bottom strip is rabbeted for the panels, notched

Position the drawer runners for the bottom drawer on the carcase sides using a thin spacer, cut to length, as shown here. The 1-in.-wide spacer, tacked flush with the front edge, positions the runners to act as drawer stops.

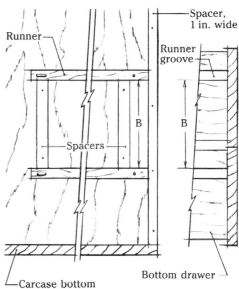

Position the remaining drawers as shown here using thin spacers cut to length.

over the tenon on the stile and then screwed in place, preferably with oval-head brass screws, as shown in the sketch below.

The base is a straightforward mortise-and-tenon construction. Machine the legs 2 in. square, cut them to length and lay out and cut the mortises. The tight curve of the relief on the leg is best made with a Forstner or a spade bit. Clamp two legs together and center the bit where the two surfaces meet. I bandsaw the rest of the waste and clean up with a cabinet scraper and a little drum sander mounted in my drill press. The rails are grooved for metal tabletop fasten-

ers (see Appendix 5 for sources of supply) or wooden buttons you can make yourself (p. 98).

The turned wooden pulls are through-tenoned and wedged into the drawer front from behind. You could use ceramic or metal pulls, like the brass handles on the bed shown on p. 14.

Any type of wood finish will do for this piece, though the top may be subject to some wear. The drawer sides can be left unfinished on their outside faces, but I give the grooves and runners a good waxing to keep the drawers running sweetly and to cut down on wear.

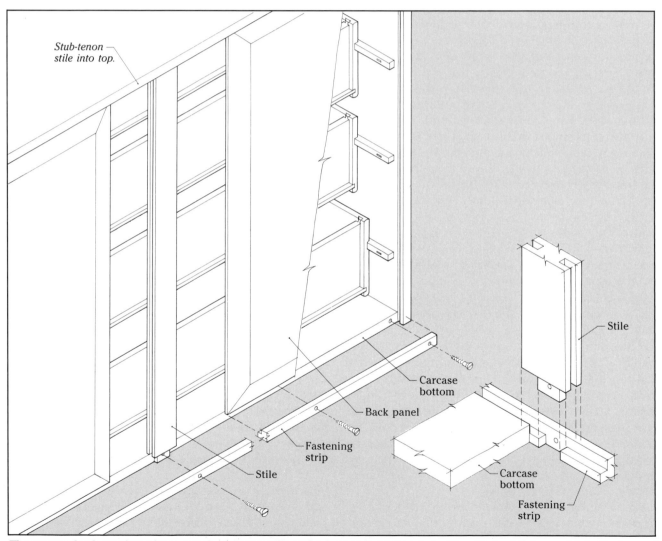

The carcase back consists of two panels, a center stile and a bottom fastening strip. The stile is stub-tenoned into the top and the panels housed in grooves. The fastening strip is notched to take the tenon on the stile and rabbeted for the panels. Position the stile, slide the panels in and screw the fastening strip in place.

Tall Bureau

This bureau is more elegant than the small one on p. 39, and more of a challenge to make. The drawers have a traditional, lap-dovetail construction, and they slide between frames attached to the carcase sides. The depths of the drawers decrease from the bottom of the case to the top, and this has both a practical and an aesthetic purpose. The practical purpose is obvious: The deep drawers at the bottom are for sweaters, the shallow ones at the top for socks and scarves, and those in between are for shirts and underwear. A tall bureau with drawers all the same depth looks top-heavy; graduated drawers lower the visual center of gravity and make a subtle but important improvement in the appearance of the bureau. The increments should be between ½ in. and 1 in. If the increments were any smaller, you wouldn't have useful variations in the drawers. In addition, there would be an irritating doubt as to whether the drawers are in fact different sizes. Attempting to add variety by making insignificant changes is a common fault of beginning designers. When I was an architecture student, this was known as M.F.V.—the Monotony of Faint Variation.

Construction

I make the carcase first, attach the frames, and then make the drawers to fit the openings between the frames. The carcase back and the base are made last. The carcase is a larger version of the one for the small bureau. (See pp. 30-32 for advice on making large, dovetailed carcases.)

The frames keep the carcase sides parallel, which helps prevent the drawers from rattling around or, worse, jamming. The frames must be square and flat—and identical. Bridle-joint the corners (p. 36); tenon the long pieces (the rails) into the short pieces (the runners), so there will be continuous grain under the drawer sides, and the drawers will run smoother. Stub-tenon the center divider to the front and back rails. (You could also groove thin dust panels into the frames—an old-fashioned touch.)

Before gluing up the frames, bore a single clearance hole for a No. 10 screw at the front of each runner (the closer to the front rail, the better), and cut slots for No. 10 screws in the middle and back. The screws at the front will fix the front rail so it can serve as a drawer stop; the slots will allow the carcase sides to

move across the grain. (Traditionally, these frames were housed in dadoes in the carcase sides. If you expect to keep books or records in the drawers, you should use dadoes.) Trim the frames to length to fit the carcase opening near the top or bottom, so that they won't force the sides in or out.

Before positioning the first frame, you'll need to make four ⅜-in. by 1¾-in. strips for runners below the bottom drawer and above the top one. Fasten one pair of the ⅜-in.-thick runners to the carcase bottom with No. 6 flat-head screws. They should also be slot-screwed at the middle and back, and all the screws should be countersunk.

The frames serve as drawer stops and must be positioned accurately back from the front edge of the carcase. Make two spacers of plywood scrap 1 in. wide and as long as the inside carcase height. Tack one spacer on each side, flush with the front edge.

The frames are also positioned by spacers to create the openings for the drawers. Make six spacers for the two bottom drawers of 1-in. by 2-in. scrap hardwood, 7¾ in. long—the nominal width of the drawer sides. (The clearance will be worked on the sides later.) Set the spacers on the bottom runners, three on each side, then set the first frame on them, as shown in the sketch at right. Butt the frame against the 1-in. strips and clamp it lightly in place while being fastened. In the center of each slot, bore pilot holes for No. 10 round-head screws, and screw the frame in place. (The front screw is added later, when the frames have been adjusted front to back.)

Attach the next frame by resting the same spacers on the first frame. Repeat the procedure for the third and fourth frames, but the third drawer is 1 in. narrower than the first two, so cut 1 in. off the spacers. Cut another inch off to fit the last frame. After each frame is installed, measure the remaining space between it and the top of the carcase to make sure you will have room for the rest of the drawers. If you are gaining or losing space, adjust the spacing of the frames accordingly.

Make the drawers next. Remember that the fronts and sides must be flat, or the drawers will jam in their openings. Cut the drawer fronts to length so they just fit the opening in the carcase. Rip them a fraction over their finished width. Wood expansion and contraction is more important for drawer sides that fit between runners than for side-hung drawer sides. The upper drawer sides can be cut to an easy sliding

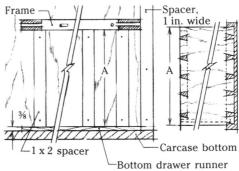

Position the bottom frame by placing spacers on the bottom runners. Place the spacers for the second frame on the first and so on. Trim the spacers for the narrower drawers.

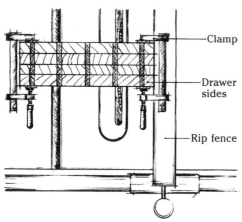

Clamp

Drawer sides

Rip fence

Dovetails in several drawer sides can be cut on the tablesaw at once. Align their edges and ends, clamp them together and adjust the rip fence for each cut.

fit between the runners, but the lower ones, which are almost twice as deep, must have more clearance, or they'll be sure to jam in damp weather.

It is particularly easy for me, a former engineer, to fit things too precisely. In the workshop, drawers can be fitted in the carcase so precisely that closing one creates air pressure inside the case. But will they remain that way? One winter when the shop was very dry, I made a large bureau of kiln-dried red oak. When I delivered the bureau, the drawers fit snugly and ran beautifully, but a wet spring followed, and by April the drawers were frozen in place. The owner was annoyed. She could neither put her winter clothes away nor get her summer ones out. I had to shut the bureau up in a room with a dehumidifier for several weeks before the drawers would budge. By then, my reputation with this client was damaged beyond repair.

There are many variables affecting drawer clearance: the depth of the drawer; the species, cut and moisture content of the wood; and the climate in which the piece will live. It is impossible to prescribe clearances without determining those variables for a particular piece. (The discussion, table and chart in Appendix 1 will help you calculate the clearance for your wood and climate conditions.)

This tall bureau has drawers of three different depths, a pair of drawers at each depth. I clamp the four sides of each pair of drawers together and cut the dovetails with a carbide-tipped blade on the tablesaw. Tilt the blade and run the pack of sides against the rip fence, as shown in the sketch at left. (You can, of course, cut the dovetails individually by hand.) The pins must be marked from the tails and cut by hand with a backsaw.

Gauge the dovetail sockets on the end of the drawer front a fraction deeper than the thickness of the sides. When fitting the drawers in the carcase, this extra amount will be planed off the end of the drawer front to give clearance.

I think solid-wood drawer bottoms suit this formal bureau better than plywood bottoms do. Use a wood that is light both in color and weight. Aromatic western cedar is ideal for clothes storage—but leave it bare, no wax or finish. The bottoms should be ⅜ in. thick to prevent sagging, and beveled or rabbeted into ¼-in. grooves. Solid-wood bottoms shrink and swell, so you must allow for this movement. Run the grain parallel to the front, so that all movement will

take place front to back. Pin or glue the bottom into the groove in the drawer front and slot-screw it to the drawer back with round-head screws.

When the drawers have been made, slide them into their openings. Plane the ends of the drawer fronts so that each drawer enters the carcase easily. Then fit the edges of the drawer fronts to the carcase and to each other so that the clearance around them is uniform—about ⅟₁₆ in. to ⅛ in., depending on the shrinkage value of the wood. Adjust the frames by tapping them lightly with a hammer until all the drawer fronts are exactly ⅛ in. back from the front edge of the carcase. Screw through the single hole at the front of each runner to fix the frame in place. If the drawer fronts are at all uneven, block them out and scrape them as described on p. 41.

The back can be solid wood or plywood. Because of the height of the carcase, I use four panels. The rails are stub-tenoned into the center stile and carcase sides. Make the stub tenons to fit the groove for the panel, so they can be slid into the grooves after the center stile and top panels are positioned. Pin through the tenons to hold them in place. The bottom panels and bottom tenon on the stile are fixed by a fastening strip, as shown in the drawing on p. 41.

The base looks and is sturdy. It also makes a satisfying transition from the horizontal plane of the floor to the strong vertical of the carcase. Screw the carcase to the front rail and attach it to the side and back rails with wooden buttons (p. 98) or metal tabletop fasteners, so that all movement has to take place at the back. The molding can be of any profile, but it should cover the dovetails and be mitered at the corners. Fix the molding after the carcase is attached—make sure the molding is glued only to the base. Use panel pins to hold it in place, then set or remove the pins and fill the holes.

Pulls like those on the small bureau look well on this bureau, too. You might consider using brass pulls—they relieve the severity of the design, contrast with the dark wood, and also twinkle pleasantly in the firelight.

Tall Bureau

Scale: ⅛ in. = 1 in.

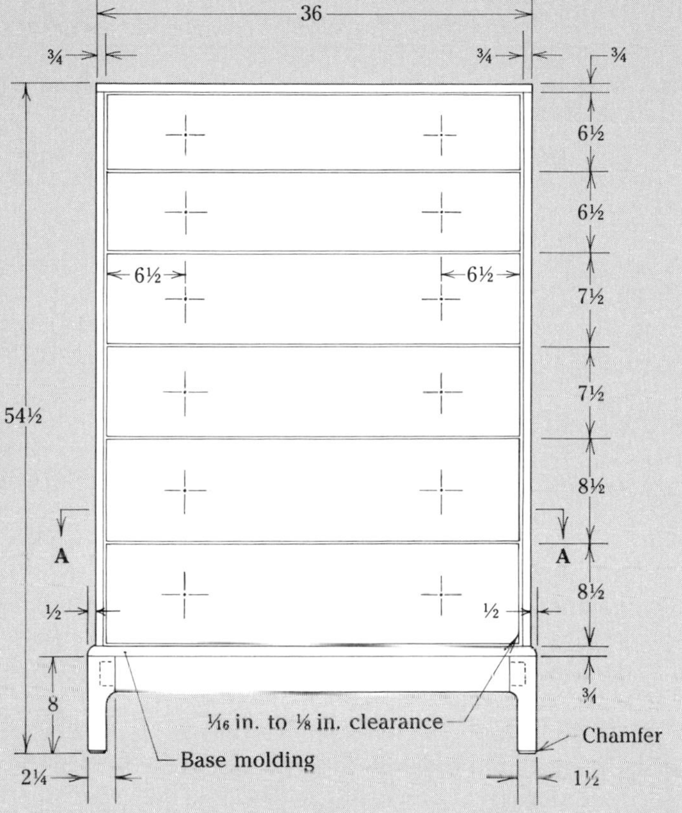

36
¾
¾
¾
6½
6½
6½
6½
7½
7½
54½
8½
8½
A
A
½
½
¾
8
⅟₁₆ in. to ⅛ in. clearance
Chamfer
Base molding
2¼
1½

Front View

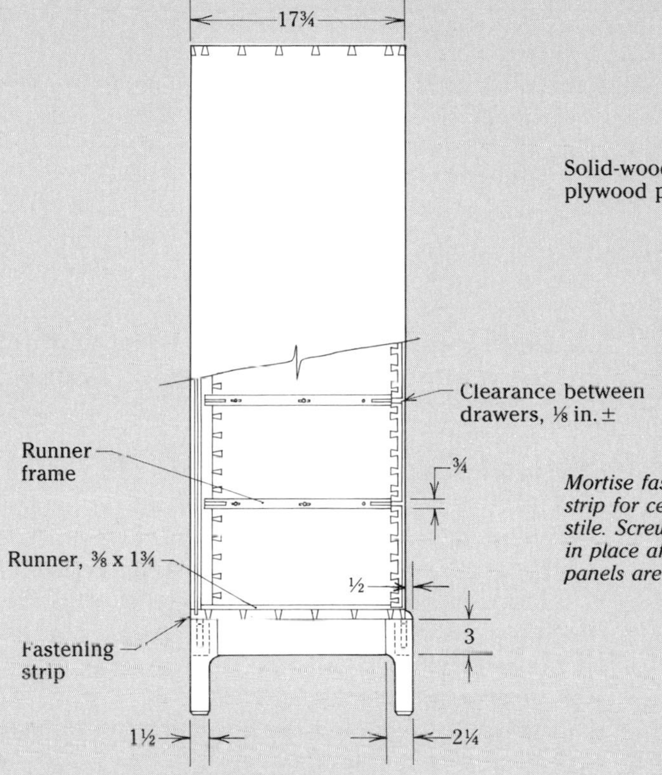

17¾
Clearance between drawers, ⅛ in. ±
Runner frame
¾
Runner, ⅜ x 1¾
½
3
Fastening strip
1½
2¼

Side View
(Carcase side and base molding cut away)

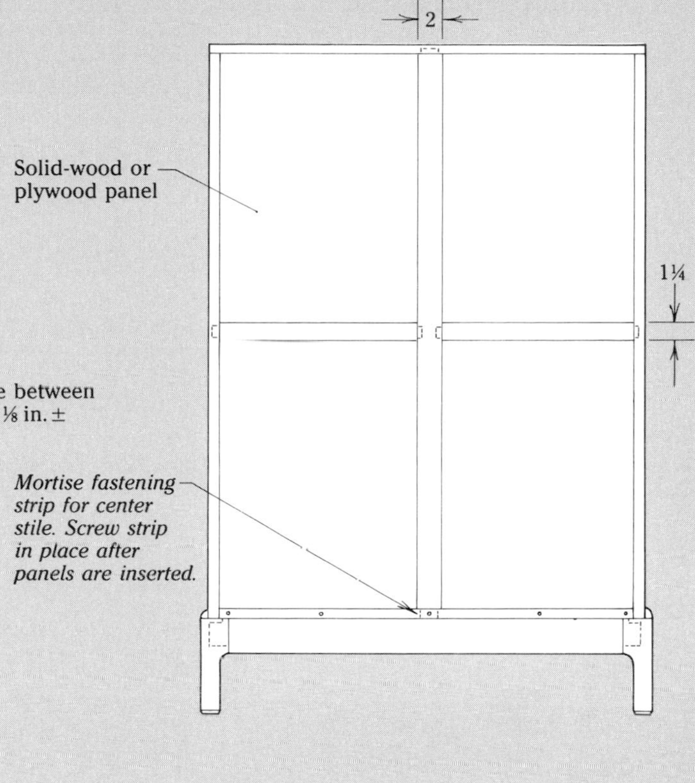

2
Solid-wood or plywood panel
1¼
Mortise fastening strip for center stile. Screw strip in place after panels are inserted.

Back View

Section A-A:
Runner Frame (Drawer removed)

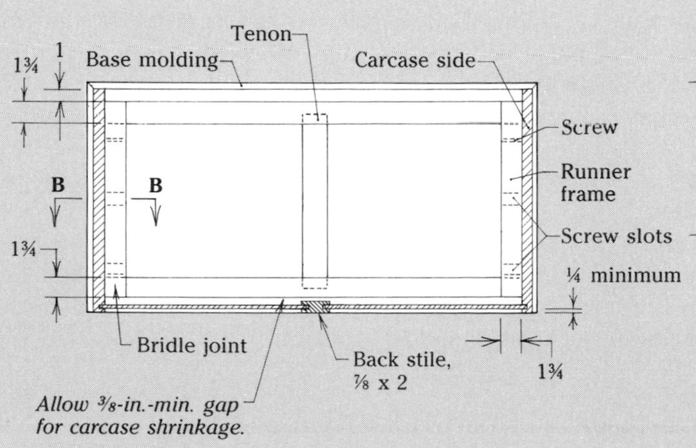

Tenon
1¾
1
Base molding
Carcase side
Screw
Runner frame
B
B
Screw slots
1¾
¼ minimum
Bridle joint
Back stile, ⅞ x 2
1¾
Allow ⅜-in.-min. gap for carcase shrinkage.

Section B-B:
Slot-Screwed
Runner Frame

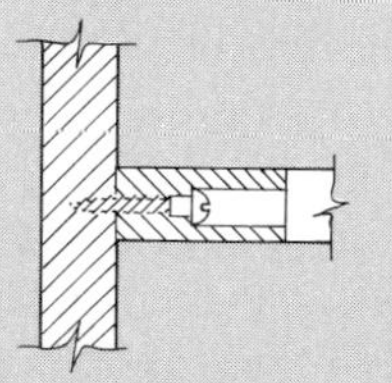

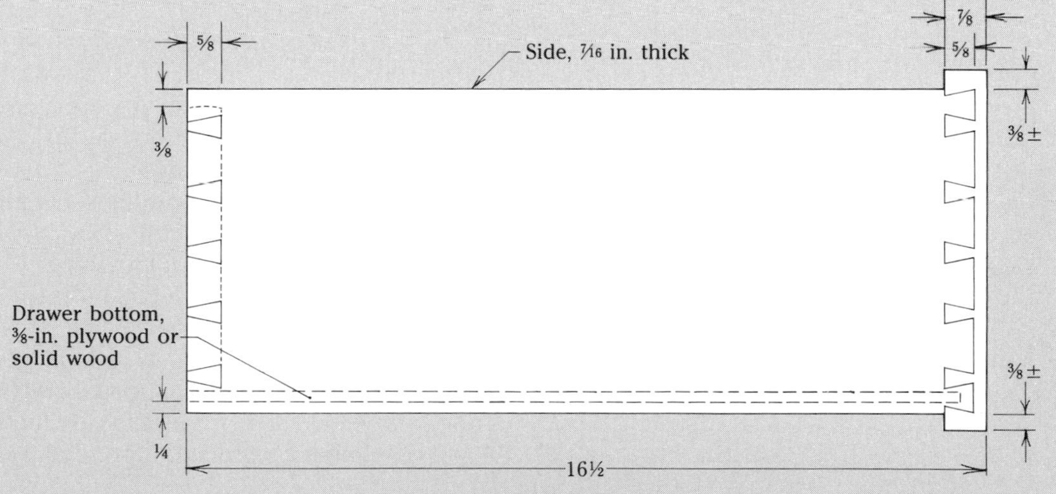

⅞
⅝
Side, ⁷⁄₁₆ in. thick
⅝
⅜
⅜ ±
Drawer bottom, ⅜-in. plywood or solid wood
⅜ ±
¼
16½

Drawer (Side view)
Scale: ¼ in. = 1 in.

Accessories 3

Night Table

This freestanding night table is a dovetailed box with a single drawer that slides between runners. The table stands on a simple base and has a solid-wood panel back to prevent things from falling out. The overall height (30 in. in the plan drawings) should be 4 in. to 8 in. higher than the mattress.

Some people might wonder about going to the trouble of putting a solid-wood back on a piece of furniture that will almost certainly be stood against a wall. Why not use veneered plywood, Masonite or painted particleboard? I feel that the back of a piece of furniture, like the back of a building, should be treated as if it were meant to be seen. We've all encountered a building with a pompous facade that extends around the corner and stops after a few feet—the shoddy backs of many commercial cabinets provide the same disagreeable surprise. I think the same attention to detail and standard of workmanship should prevail throughout an entire piece. Also, a second-rate back severely limits the placement of the piece in a room, because it *has* to stand against a wall.

Construction

The table carcase is a 15-in. cube. Lay out and cut the through dovetails (pp. 30-31). When laying them out, make sure that the groove for the back panel falls within the socket for the last tail. That way, only the grooves in the carcase sides need to be stopped; those in the top and bottom can run through because they will be hidden by the tails once the case is assembled. I rout the grooves, lowering the router onto the sides for the stopped grooves, because it is easier and safer than lowering the sides onto the tablesaw blade. You can cut the tails on the tablesaw, clamping the two sides together and holding them vertically against a miter gauge fitted with a long, wide fence for extra support.

The grain of the back panel runs vertically in the carcase. The ends of the panel can fit snugly in the grooves in the top and bottom because wood moves very little along the grain. Allowance must be made, however, for the panel to shrink across the grain. The table that is shown in the photo on p. 48 is made of American cherry, which shrinks about ⅜ in. per foot as its moisture content reduces from 20% to 10%. This means that the panel will have a maximum seasonal movement of ½ in. If the wood is at 10% moisture content, almost all of the movement will be expansion; at 20%, it will be shrinkage. Most kiln-dried or air-dried wood is somewhere in between, so I allowed for ¼-in. movement either way and made the groove depth and the panel width so that all movement would occur within the groove. (Calculating shrinkage is discussed in Appendix 1.)

The back panel is planed ½ in. or ⅝ in. thick and is beveled to ¼ in. at its edges and ends. The bevel can be cut on the tablesaw or planed by hand. Fit the back panel to the grooves in top, bottom and sides

Night Table

Scale: ⅛ in. = 1 in.
Details: ¼ in. = 1 in.

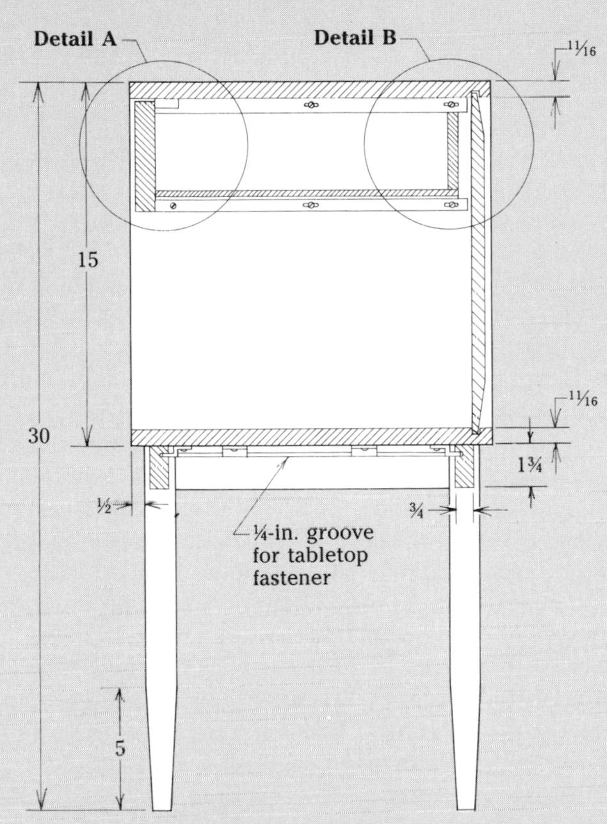

Detail A
Detail B
11⁄16
15
30
11⁄16
1¾
½
¾
¼-in. groove for tabletop fastener
5

End View (Section A-A)

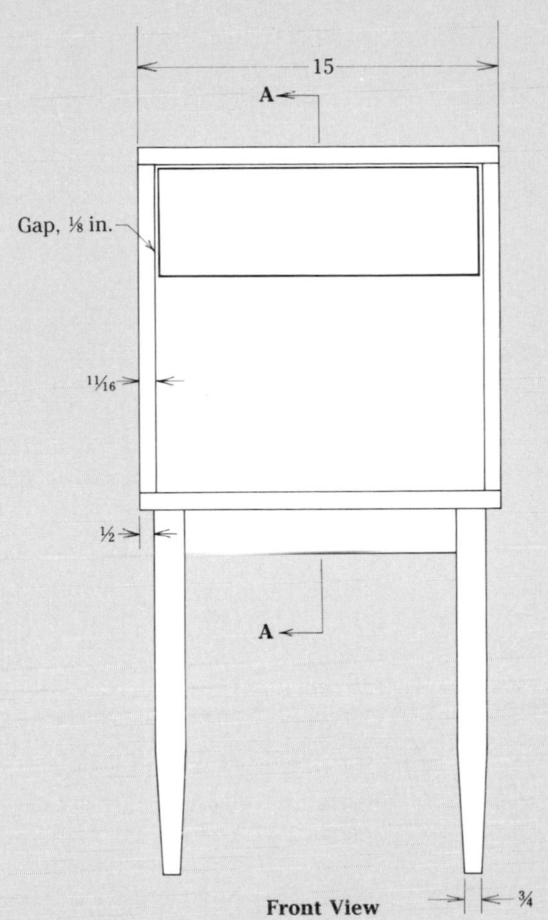

15
A
Gap, ⅛ in.
11⁄16
½
A
¾

Front View

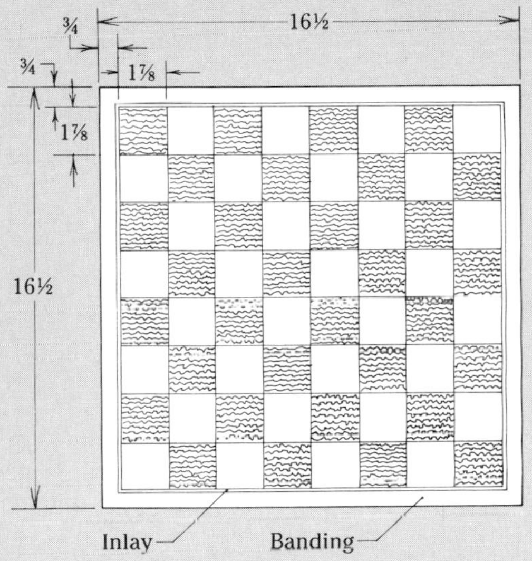

¾
16½
¾
1⅞
1⅞
16½
Inlay
Banding

Chessboard (Plan view)

Note: *Chessboard is ¾ in. thick. Grain direction of squares and banding must be the same.*

Details A and B: Drawer and Runners

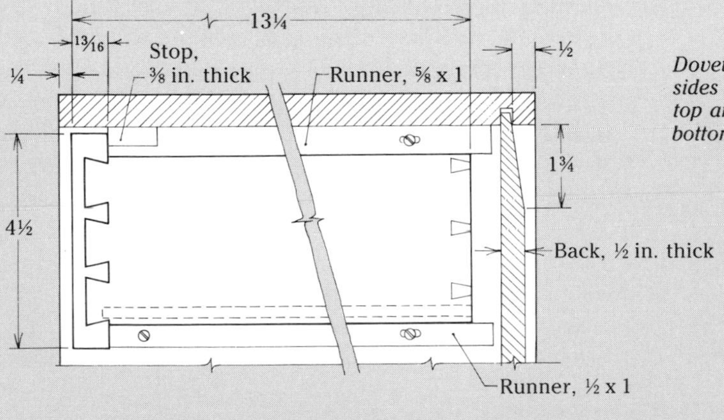

13¼
13⁄16
Stop, ⅜ in. thick
¼
Runner, ⅝ x 1
½
1¾
4½
Back, ½ in. thick
Runner, ½ x 1

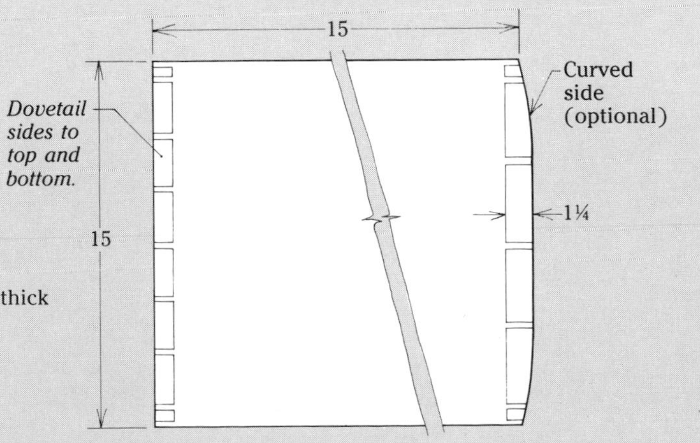

15
Dovetail sides to top and bottom.
Curved side (optional)
15
1¼

Plan View (Carcase)

Note: *Fix carcase to base with tabletop fasteners (shown here) or wooden buttons.*

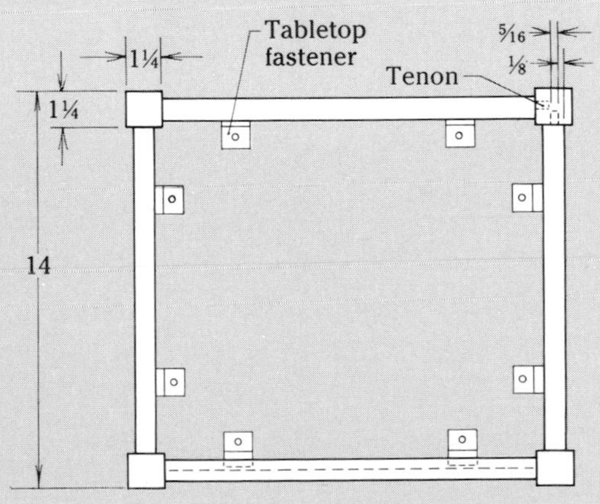

1¼
Tabletop fastener
5⁄16
Tenon
⅛
1¼
14

Plan View (Base)

separately. Make sure that the panel isn't too large, so it won't cause trouble at assembly.

Don't push the carcase together completely until you glue it up—if the pins enter the tails a short distance and you've sawn square, the carcase will go together. I usually glue up the carcase with the panel in place, after prefinishing all the interior surfaces. You can slip the panel in after the drawer has been hung if you cut the carcase bottom narrower and fix a batten to it (p. 42). Pin the ends of a panel in the middle and at the top and bottom, so that the panel shrinks and swells around its centerline. A dab of glue in the middle will serve the same purpose.

This drawer is easier to make than the one in the night table that is attached to the headboard (p. 21) because it doesn't have a slanted front. Otherwise, both drawers are of dovetail construction, made and supported in the carcase in the same way.

The base is quite straightforward. You should offset the tenons so they can be as long as possible without meeting inside the leg—the bridge of wood between the mortises helps strengthen the leg. Dowel joints could also be used, in place of the mortise-and-tenon joints. Setting the face of the rail back from the face of the leg provides a nice shadow line, which accents the joint—it also saves time because you don't have to plane the two surfaces flush after assembly. The carcase is attached to the base with wooden buttons or metal tabletop fasteners (see Appendix 5 for sources of supply). Groove the inside faces of the rails to take whichever you use.

I have made several removable chessboard tops for these tables to please night birds who like to play chess in bed. (The chessboard shown in the plan drawings can be made as described on pp. 66-67.) The grain of the borders on the board must run in the same direction as the squares, or the board will self-destruct. If you fasten the board to the top of the night table, make sure the grain of the top and board run in the same direction.

Don't forget to put the white square on the player's right. I didn't know this when I made my first chess table and not only had to remake it, but I got a stern lecture from the client as well.

Table Lamp

A table lamp must fill only a few requirements. Its base must have a fair amount of weight and a large-enough diameter to be stable. A table lamp will be moved from place to place, so it should have either a neck or bulb holder sturdy enough to be picked up. The lamp should be at a convenient height for its purpose—providing reading light, area light or whatever—but its shape is almost entirely a matter of what pleases.

I think turned shapes are better gauged by eye than by working from a pattern or template. In this respect, turning wood is like throwing pottery on a wheel. Gauging by eye allows an intimate connection between the hand, the eye and the forming of the shape. You can use the shape shown in the plan drawings as a point of departure to develop your own distinctive, individual shapes. The photo on p. 50 shows another of my favorite lamp shapes.

Construction

A table lamp can be made of short pieces glued together, so it is a good project for using the hardwood scraps that accumulate in the shop. Use any wood that turns well, or combine several different woods. If you mix different colored woods, one color should predominate, or the result is likely to resemble a high-school shop project.

The lamp shown in the plan drawings is 6⅛ in. in diameter and 11 in. tall. If you don't have a dry block of wood that size, you'll have to laminate. Draw a 6⅛-in.-dia. circle on a piece of plywood and arrange the pieces so they overlap the circle by at least ¼ in. Only the center piece has to be a full 11 in. tall. The rest can be shorter, depending on the shape you have in mind. You can edge-glue narrow stock to make wide pieces, but leave out the dowels—they might be exposed as you turn the lamp. I usually arrange the pieces on one side of the center piece so that they are a mirror image of those on the other. (If your lamp will have a long, slender neck, make the center piece a little thicker than the diameter of the neck to avoid unsightly glue lines.)

The throats of most C-clamps or quick-action clamps are too small for a block this size, so I use bar clamps and heavy bearers. (Bearers are pieces of hardwood scrap at least 2 in. thick, 3 in. wide and 8 in. long, used to put the pressure where it's needed.)

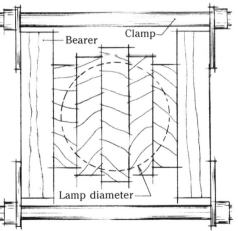

Arrange the pieces for the lamp blank on a circle with a diameter as large as the lamp's will be. Glue up the blank using bar or pipe clamps and wooden bearers.

Two pairs of clamps and bearers are enough for this lamp base, but you'll need more for a taller one. It is difficult for one person to glue up this kind of assembly quickly, so get some help and dry-clamp the pieces first. Arrange the clamps and bearers as shown in the sketch at right.

When the glue has set, clean off the excess and mark the centers of both ends by drawing diagonals. Bandsaw the top end of the center piece to approximate the shape of the neck. Draw a 6⅛-in.-dia. circle on the base end with a compass, and trim the blank close to this circle with a drawknife or plane or, if you are handy with one, you can use a small ax. Trimming will help to balance the blank and keep it from jumping off the lathe.

Mount the piece between centers, or screw a small faceplate to the base and use the tailstock center to steady the neck. Rough-out the shape with a gouge,

To avoid unsightly glue lines, use a thick center piece for a lamp with a slender neck.

using the lathe's slowest speed, until the decreasing vibration tells you the blank is balanced. Then shape the blank to conform to what your eye finds pleasing, using the plan drawing as a rough guide. Hollow the bottom of the base slightly—it will be more stable if it sits on a narrow rim.

I sand and finish the lamp next, holding it in the lathe while working. Sand with the grain to remove concentric turning marks, but be careful not to destroy crisply defined shapes. Most wood finishes are appropriate, but I don't use wax on lamps because it makes them too slippery to grip.

When the shaping is completed, bore holes for the cord. You can bore the vertical hole on the lathe using a shell auger pushed through a hollow dead center. I don't have a shell auger, so I remove the lamp from the lathe and bore the hole on the drill press. Start from the top end, boring as far as you can with a ⅜-in. twist bit. I finish the hole with a ⅜-in. spade bit brazed to a ¼-in. steel rod about 16 in. long. (You will have to clear the waste from time to time.) Enlarge the hole on the bottom slightly to house the nut on the end of the threaded tube.

Hold the lamp in a padded vise to bore the horizontal hole that will intersect the vertical one. To ensure that the holes intersect, draw a diameter on the bottom and keep the bit in line with it. Lightly chamfer the outer ends of the hole with a countersink.

Insert a ⅜-in. threaded metal tube into the vertical hole, and fix it with nuts on both ends. (You can buy tubing at most hardware or electrical supply stores.) The tube should project ½ in. above the top nut and should lie flush with the base. If you have a twist bit that is long enough, run the bit into the horizontal hole and through the wall of the tubing to make a hole for the cord. If your bit is too short, mark the location of the hole and remove the tubing to bore it. Remove the metal burr and ease the edges of the hole so there is no danger of their cutting through the cord's insulation and causing a short circuit.

With the tube in place, insert the cord in the horizontal hole and push it out through the center of the base (10 ft. to 12 ft. of cord is plenty). Pull 1½ ft. of cord through the base, then double it back into the tube, up through the vertical hole and out the neck until you can grasp the end. Pull until the loop projecting from the base disappears and about 3 in. projects from the top of the lamp.

Attach the harp (the frame that supports the shade) and the bulb holder. The bulb holders available in most hardware stores are rather flimsy, so don't count on one to support the harp. Instead, attach the harp to the top end of the threaded rod and secure it with a second nut. Connect the cord to the bulb holder and screw the holder on. The final step is to cut out a circle of felt (green seems to be a tradition) a little smaller than the diameter of the base, and stick it on with white glue.

Harps come in several different sizes, and it's best to buy one when you buy the shade so that you can make sure they match. The harp used for the lamp shown in the plan drawings was 9 in. high. The shade was 10 in. high, its lower diameter 10 in., and its upper 9 in. (Don't forget to get the finial that attaches the shade to the harp.)

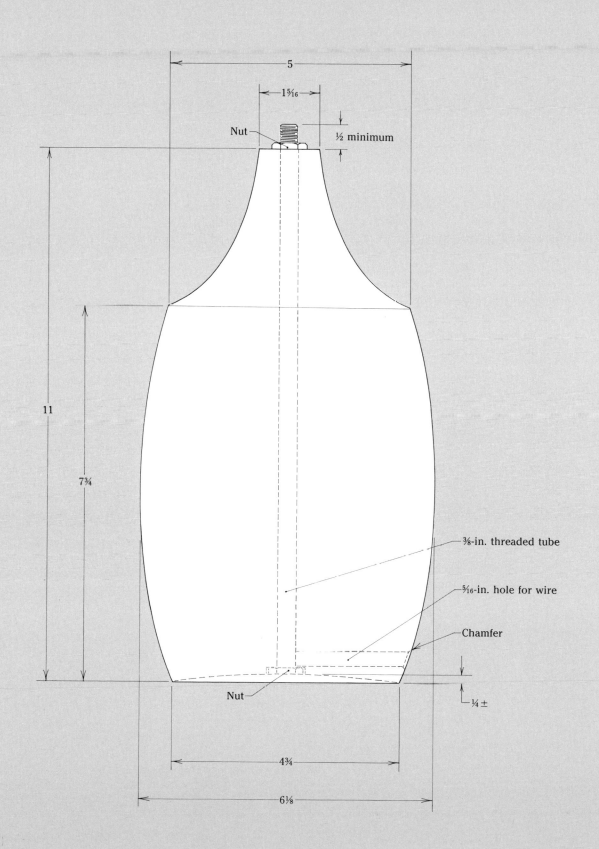

5

1⁵⁄₁₆

Nut

½ minimum

11

7¾

⅜-in. threaded tube

⁵⁄₁₆-in. hole for wire

Chamfer

Nut

¼ ±

4¾

6⅛

Rush-Seat Stool

Scale: ⅛ in. = 1 in.
Details: ½ in. = 1 in.

Section A-A: Rail and Leg

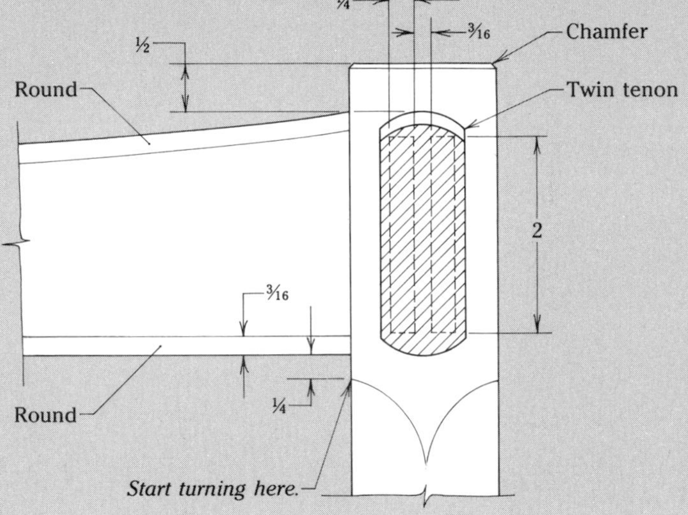

¼
3/16
Chamfer
½
Round
Twin tenon
2
3/16
¼
Round
Start turning here.

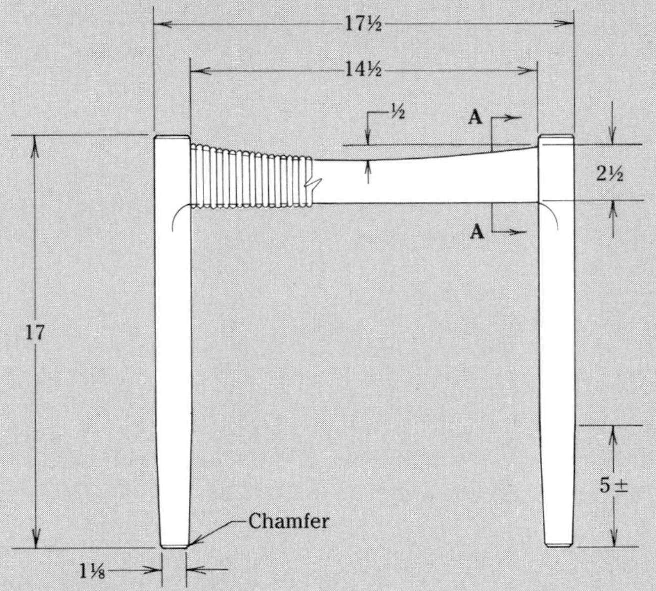

17½
14½
½
A
A
2½
17
5 ±
Chamfer
1⅛

Front View

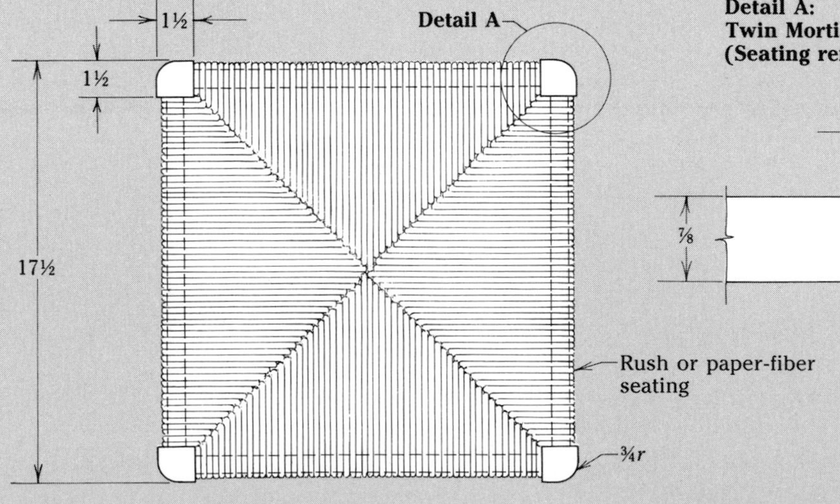

1½
1½
Detail A
17½
Rush or paper-fiber seating
¾r

Plan View

Detail A:
Twin Mortise-and-Tenon Joint
(Seating removed)

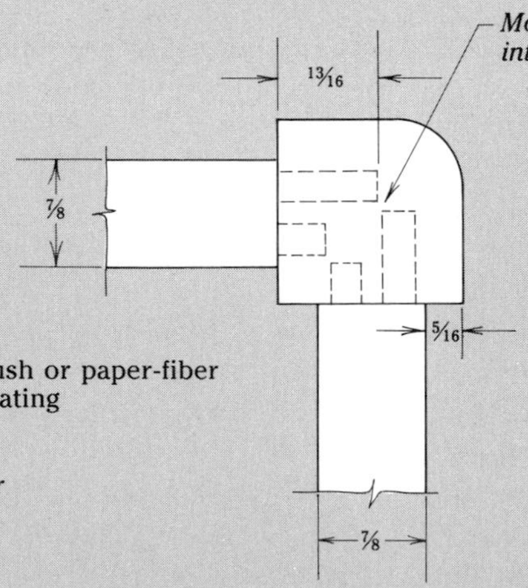

Mortises shouldn't intersect in leg.
13/16
⅞
5/16
⅞

Alternate Detail A:
Dowel Joint

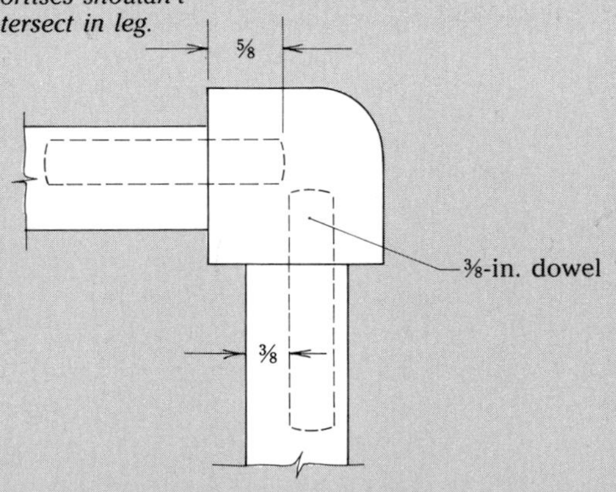

⅝
⅜-in. dowel
⅜

Rush-Seat Stool

This is a handy stool for the bedroom or bathroom and is an excellent trial project before attempting more complicated chairs. This stool can be seated with natural rush, as shown in the photo, or with a paper-fiber substitute, which is less attractive but more durable. You could also screw ledger strips to the inside of the rails and use an upholstered, drop-in seat. (See Appendix 5 for sources of supply, and the bibliography for books on seating.)

Construction

You'll probably want to match or contrast the wood for the legs with the other furniture in the room. Any sturdy, inexpensive wood, such as oak, ash or maple, will do for the rails of the stool, because they'll be hidden by the rush.

Cut the legs 1½ in. square and 1 in. over the finished length. Then cut the joints before turning the legs. You can attach the rails to the legs using mortise-and-tenon or dowel construction. Either way, leave the additional 1 in. at the top end of the legs for extra strength during mortising. I use twin mortises and tenons, which double the gluing surface of a single mortise and tenon without weakening the legs too much. Mark both mortises of each pair by running the mortise gauge against the same face of the leg, which will ensure that the spacing of each pair is uniform. Mortises at right angles to each other should not intersect—a small bridge of wood between them will make the leg stronger.

Make four identical rails and cut the tenons to fit the mortises. Laying out should be simple because all the mortises will be the same. If you cut tenons by hand, it's not a bad idea to lay out and cut a sample twin tenon in scrap to check the fit. If you cut by machine, check each setup by making a trial cut in a spare rail and trying the rail in a mortise.

A dowel joint is quicker to make, and when accurately done, as strong as a mortise and tenon. Use ⅜-in. by 2-in. spiral-grooved, hardwood dowels—smooth dowels have less withdrawal resistance. Bore the dowel holes in the rails first, using a doweling jig or drill press. (Turn the drill-press table vertically and clamp the rail to it.) Position the holes off center on the ends of the rail, so that the holes in the leg can be deeper without meeting. (You will have to shim one jaw of the dowel jig to make offset holes.) Place

dowel centers in the holes in the rails to mark the leg. Use a piece of thin scrap under the rails when marking the legs so that the rails will be set back a uniform distance from the faces of the legs.

Bandsaw the curve on the upper edge of each rail, and rout or spokeshave the round on both edges. Without the round, the rush will soon wear through on the sharp corner. Assemble the stool dry, and mark ¼ in. below where the bottom edge of each rail joins the legs—this is where the turning will begin. Draw two diagonals on the ends of the leg to find the centers, and mount the leg on the lathe, the lower end in the headstock center. Turn the leg to a cylinder, beginning at the marks near the mortises. It's easy to tear the fibers where the section changes from square to round, so I cut on the marks with a chisel or knife before turning.

When the leg is turned, use the lathe as a vise while rounding the last few inches of the outside corner of each leg with a hand plane. Sand while the leg is on the lathe, then trim and chamfer the top ends and glue up the stool.

Unless the legs are braced by stretchers, this stool should not be more than 17 in. high. The same construction can be used for making smaller and lower stools, and they don't necessarily have to be square.

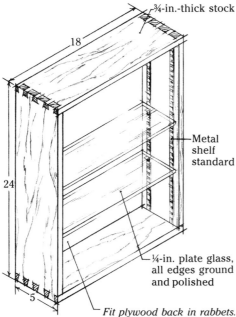

¾-in.-thick stock

18

24

Metal
shelf
standard

¼-in. plate glass,
all edges ground
and polished

Fit plywood back in rabbets.

5

You can use the mirror as a door on a medicine cabinet. Hang the mirror with drawn-brass hinges or a continuous hinge.

Mirror

I think that the things most used around the house should also be the handsomest. This mirror is simple but attractive, and would suit a bathroom, entrance hallway or bedroom.

The frame is bridle-jointed, and rabbeted for the rectangular, ¼-in. plate-glass mirror and the cardboard backing that protects the silver on the back of the glass from abrasion. I don't recommend doweled miter joints because the miters will inevitably open as the wood shrinks. The plate glass and cardboard backing are held in place with a piece of ⅛-in. plywood that is screwed to the back of the frame with round-head brass screws. I prefer to make the frame of dark wood, so it stands out visually on light-colored walls.

Construction

Plane the wood for the frame to thickness and cut it to width and length. (If you want to make a larger mirror, be sure to increase the width of the frame members.) Cut the bridle joints (p. 36), clamp the frame together dry and mark out the rabbets. You'll have to stop both ends of each rabbet, or gaps will show on the edges of the mirror. Cut the rabbets before cutting the curves on the inside edges of the frame. You could rout the rabbets, but I prefer to cut them on a tablesaw using stop blocks.

Make the first cut in the edge of each piece. Set the blade as high as the rabbet is wide, and the rip fence ⅜ in. from the blade. Because of the length of the frame pieces, you'll need to attach a long, wooden fence to the rip fence. Clamp stop blocks to the wooden fence before and after the blade to stop the cut. Hold the end of the piece firmly against the near stop while lowering it onto the sawblade. Running the front face against the fence, cut to the far stop, turn the saw off and remove the piece. Remember to reposition the stops to rabbet the shorter pieces.

Lower the blade, and reposition the fence and stops to make the shoulder cuts for the rabbets—the back faces will now run against the table. The waste will still be attached at the ends of each rabbet, so sever it with a chisel—clean up the corners after the frame is assembled.

Make a pattern for each curve and trace them all on the dry-assembled frame. I bandsaw the waste, clean up the saw marks and round the arrises with a spoke-

shave. Be careful not to run the curve or the round into the shoulders of the bridle joints.

Glue up the frame on a flat surface. Pull the shoulders tight with pipe or bar clamps; position two clamps parallel to the rails and two parallel to the stiles. With these clamps in place, *C*-clamp the bridle joints to squeeze the cheeks together. Use wooden pads to distribute the pressure and protect the surfaces. (You can remove the bar clamps after the *C*-clamps are added.) I've never had to square up a bridle-jointed frame—if the shoulders are cut square, the frame will be square.

If the mirror is hung in the bathroom, a polyurethane finish will be vastly superior to any other clear finish because of its water resistance. Whatever finish you use, apply it before installing the glass. Use steel chain and a plate fastener to hang the mirror—screw eyes and wire made for hanging pictures are not strong enough. Brass-plated steel chain, once used with old-fashioned bath plugs, is usually available at hardware stores, as are the plate fasteners.

This mirror was not designed originally as a door for a medicine cabinet, but is about the right size and works well on cabinets I've made. The sketch at left shows a dovetailed cabinet with a ¼-in. plywood back, glued into rabbets in the back edges. Hang the door on sturdy drawn-brass hinges or a continuous hinge. The ¼-in. plate-glass shelves rest on brackets in metal shelf standard housed in the cabinet sides. (Have all four edges of the plate glass ground and polished to dull the sharp edges.) You can fasten the cabinet to the wall through the back with screws or toggle bolts. One of my clients glued his cabinet to the wall and, when moving time came, had to choose between leaving the cabinet and taking the wall.

Mirror

Scale: ¼ in. = 1 in.
Details: ½ in. = 1 in.

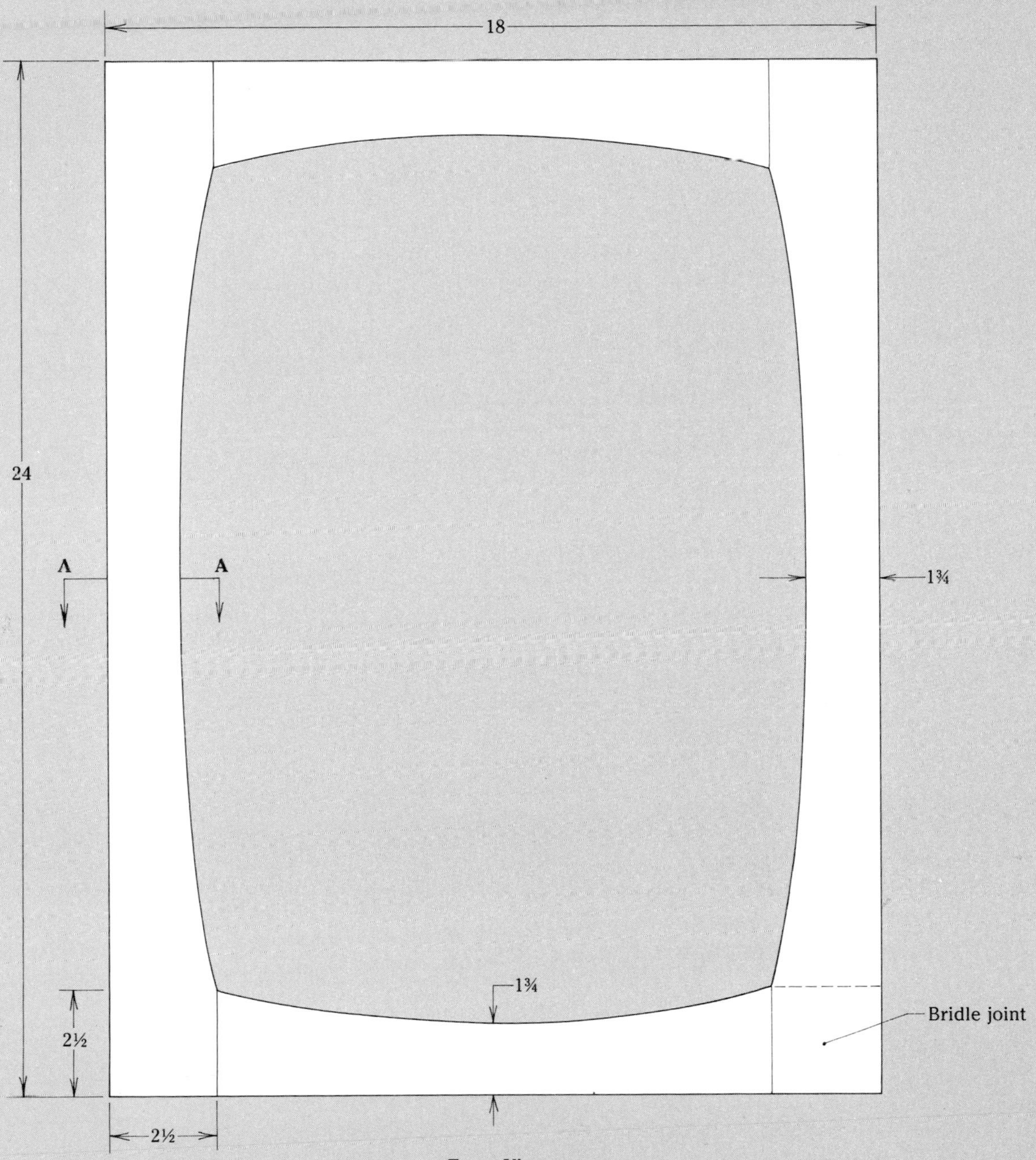

18
24
A
A
1¾
1¾
2½
2½
Bridle joint

Front View

¾

Plan View

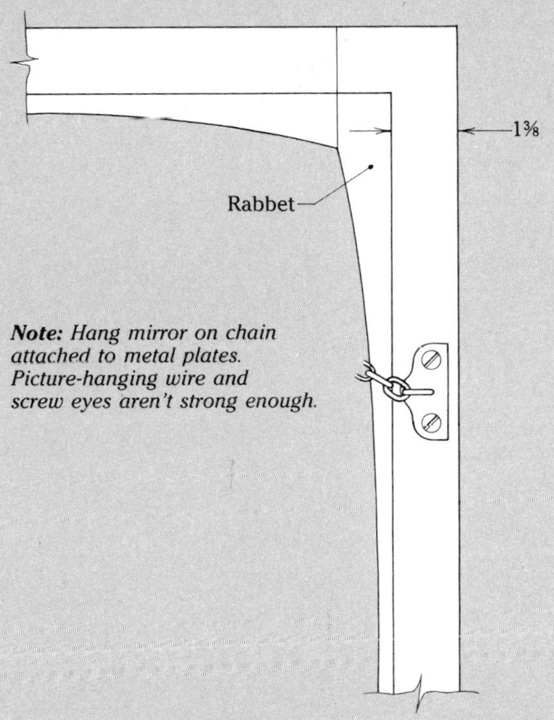

1⅜
Rabbet
Note: Hang mirror on chain attached to metal plates. Picture-hanging wire and screw eyes aren't strong enough.

Partial Back View

Section A-A: Frame, Mirror and Backing

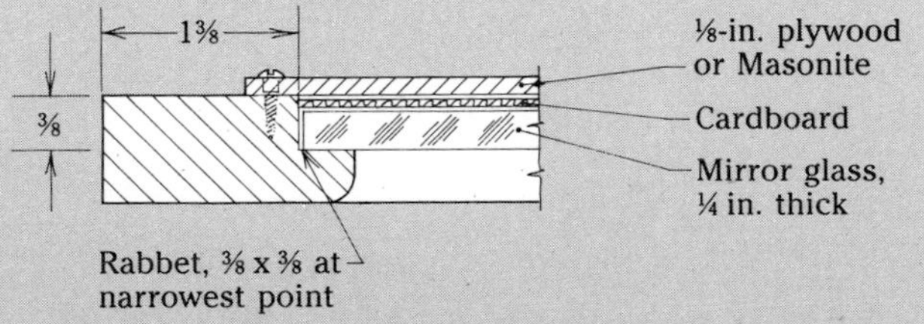

1⅜
⅜
⅛-in. plywood or Masonite
Cardboard
Mirror glass, ¼ in. thick
Rabbet, ⅜ x ⅜ at narrowest point

The Living Room

Occasional Tables 4

Notes on Occasional Tables

Most furniture has a clearly defined function. Beds are for sleeping, dining tables for eating and chairs for sitting. The purpose of an occasional table, however, is much harder to pin down. Is a coffee table for coffee or for displaying magazines and newspapers? Can you sit on one or put your feet up on it?

I tend to leave the rails when I am asked to design and make a piece of furniture with an ill-defined purpose. Helping clients clarify their needs, both real and imaginary, is an important part of a furniture maker's job. For example, I was once asked to make a dining table for a couple that maintained two Manhattan apartments. For his apartment, the man wanted a 7-ft.-long drop-leaf table to seat eight, a demand that provoked considerable argument.

"But Arnold," said the woman, "you so seldom entertain."

"I know," replied Arnold, "but I have a rich fantasy life."

An occasional table's size usually depends on its position in the living room. If the table is to be placed in front of a couch, I find that a length between one-half and two-thirds that of the couch looks right. A height of 2 in. or 3 in. above the seat cushions is comfortable, and tables less than 14 in. wide can be too easily knocked over. I like oval or boat-shaped coffee tables. They are graceful and complement a rectangular couch—they are also less of an obstruction in the room than a rectangular table.

A magazine or newspaper rack below the tabletop can help to keep down the clutter that inevitably accumulates on any free surface. (The rectangular slat-top coffee table, p. 60, is the best candidate for the addition of such a rack.) I moved my cluttered coffee table behind the couch, to give an unobstructed view of my fireplace. Now the table is almost useless, and I have to put coffee cups and newspapers on the floor. (With practice, however, I may learn to live with very little furniture, as the Japanese have been doing for centuries.)

When making occasional tables, I typically make them stronger than necessary to support coffee cups and magazines. Ill-mannered people have a habit of perching or putting their feet up on low tables—glue lines fail, joints open up and before long the table has an annoying shake. Though most of the tables in this chapter are strong enough to sit on, they are not intended for that purpose.

Reading lamps are often placed on tables at the ends of a couch or next to a chair. Set the lamp on boxes first to find the height you need—about 12 in. to 18 in. above eye level when you're seated is about right for most people. For stability, place the legs of the table as far apart as possible; alternatively, a central support or pedestal is particularly suited to round tables. Table surfaces also take a lot of abuse, so a tough, protective finish such as polyurethane or lacquer may be required.

Slat-Top Table

I made this table as a dining table for a Japanese family. The design has the apparent simplicity of a lot of Oriental furniture and is one of my favorites. It works equally well as a coffee table, whether square or rectangular. Altering the construction slightly, I made a pair of little tables with handmade tile tops, like the one shown on p. 60, to sit at either end of a sofa. (These alterations are shown in the plan drawings.)

Construction

I wanted the square dining table to appear restful and not be distracting to the eye, so I used western cedar, which has almost uniform grain, for the top. The rectangular coffee table on p. 60 needed to withstand rougher use, so I made the top of Honduras mahogany. Both these tables have a walnut base, as does the tile-top table. Other combinations of woods, such as maple and walnut or teak and rosewood, are also attractive for the top and base. If you want to make a rectangular table, proportions of length to width of 3 to 1 or 2½ to 1 are pleasing. A table 20 in. wide, 60 in. long and 16½ in. high is suitable for use with most couches and easy chairs.

It's best to make the base first, then fit the top to it. The legs should be made of straight-grained stock—highly figured wood competes with the simple design. Cut them from the same board, if possible, so the color will be uniform.

I mortise the apron rails into the legs, but doweled joints might be stronger, because less wood is removed from the legs. Both joints are shown in the plan drawings. If you use mortise-and-tenon joints, the tenons should come below the rabbet in the upper edge of the rails, and the mortises shouldn't meet inside the legs.

The rabbet makes the rail appear thinner and serves as a guide for positioning the ledger strips. Notch a corner of each leg to line up with the rabbets in the rails by making three cuts on the tablesaw, as shown in the sketch at right. Then clear the waste with a chisel. Raise the blade to full height and set the rip fence to make one of the two cuts in the end grain. Make that same cut in all four legs, with the leg horizontal and a face tight against the fence. (Clamp a stop on the fence so the cuts won't go too deep.) Then place the fence at the same distance from the blade on the other side, and make the other end-grain

cut. The last cut, across the corner, is made using the miter gauge—use a stop here, too.

If you're making a tile-top table, the rabbets are replaced by grooves that hold the ½-in. plywood or particleboard underlayment. Place the underlayment so that the surface of the tile will be about ¹⁄₁₆ in. above the top of the rails. Notch the legs and dry-assemble the base with the underlayment in place, to make sure everything goes together.

Before gluing the base together, do as much sanding as possible and cut a neat chamfer around the bottom of the legs. Glue up one pair of legs at a time, making sure that the legs are parallel and exactly square to the apron. When the glue has cured, add the remaining two rails, checking the squareness of the opening for the top. (Glue the underlayment in place if you are making a tile-top table.) Screw the

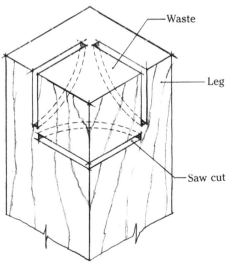

You can notch the legs by making three cuts on the tablesaw, then chiseling the waste.

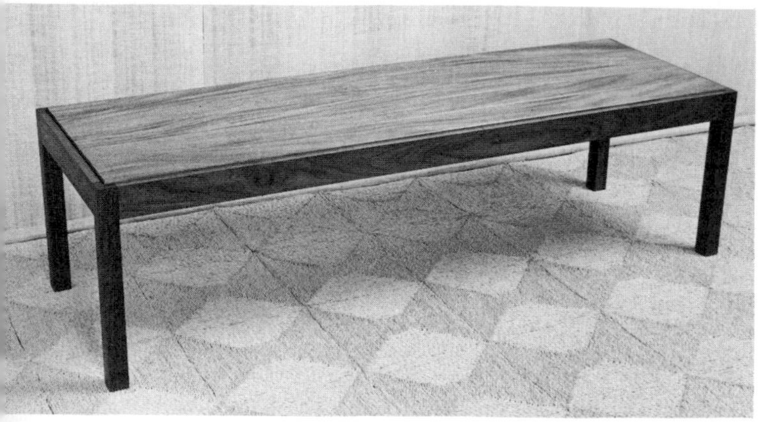

This Honduras mahogany coffee table is 60 in. long, 20 in. wide and 16½ in. high. It's made like the square table in the plan drawings.

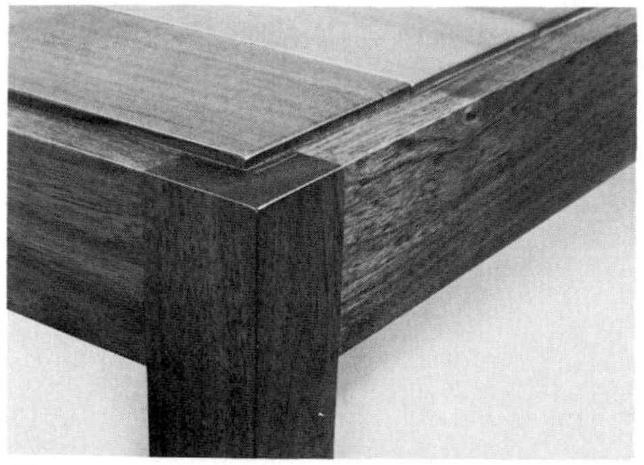

Fit the strips tightly to the rails. Round the arrises carefully—such details are highly visible on simple designs.

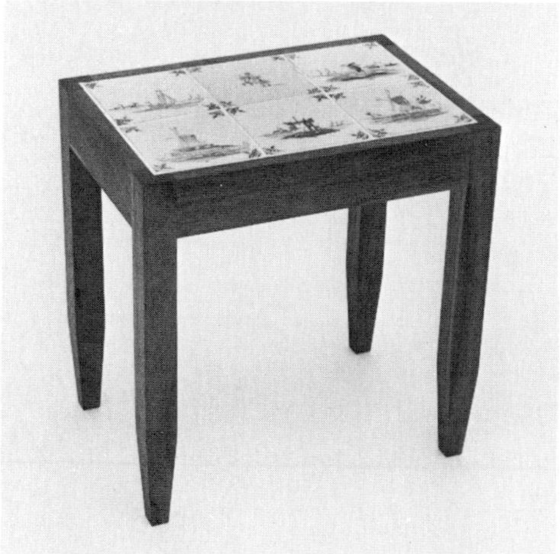

Tile can be laid on a plywood ground that is grooved into the rails of the table base. This table is 17 in. long, 12 in. wide and 18 in. high, and the tiles are 5 in. square.

ledger strips to the rails after you have bored the clearance holes for the screws that fasten the strips to the top. Clean up the joints and put a slight round on the top outside arrises of the base. Leave the inside arrises sharp.

A 2½-ft.-wide, solid-wood top would push the frame apart in wet weather and show gaps in dry. To avoid this problem, I bandsaw thick, solid-wood veneers and glue them to both faces of particleboard strips. These particleboard sandwiches won't move like solid wood, but you must veneer both faces of each strip. If you veneer only one, the strip will cup as the solid wood expands and contracts; veneering both faces prevents this. Even if this weren't true, I would still veneer the bottom face as well as the top—I don't like to leave raw, unfinished surfaces anywhere on a piece of furniture.

I made the veneers for the square table from cedar clapboards, picking the ones that had the least variation in grain and color. Other woods can be resawn from thicker stock on the bandsaw or tablesaw. If you can get all the veneers from one thick piece, the top will have a consistency of grain and color that is impossible to get any other way. The grain patterns of veneers cut from a single piece vary slightly—rather like the variation of adjacent frames of movie film. I find this subtle variation particularly appropriate for simple tables like this.

Plane the veneers ⅜ in. thick, then cut them into strips about ⅜ in. wider and 1 in. longer than their final dimension. Cut the particleboard strips and one piece of thick solid wood the same size as the veneers. (The solid wood will be used as a clamping board when gluing up.) Select the veneers for the top surface and mark their good faces; the remaining veneers will make the bottom surface.

I glue up the pieces in stacks, clamped to a flat benchtop. Cut about a dozen sheets of wax paper about 1 in. larger all around than the veneers to separate the sandwiches in each stack. Put a piece of wax paper on the benchtop and a top veneer, good face down, on the wax paper. Spread a film of Titebond or other aliphatic resin glue on the veneer, add a particleboard strip, spread glue on the strip and add a bottom veneer. Add a piece of wax paper and repeat the procedure. Work quickly and remember to glue veneer only to particleboard, not to other veneers. You should get four or five sandwiches made before the glue begins to set. Put a sheet of wax paper and the clamping board on the last veneer. Clamp the stack to the bench—large C-clamps are best, but bar clamps or pipe clamps will work, too.

When the glue has cured on all the veneered pieces for the top, plane the veneers on each face ¼ in. thick. Thicker veneers that are not thoroughly dry are likely to develop surface checks. Woods with high shrinkage values (see Appendix 1) will check more readily than others, so plane veneers made of these woods ⅛ in. thick.

Next, plane or joint one edge of each piece, and rip and crosscut it 1⁄32 in. or less over final width and length. I bevel the ends of all the pieces and one edge of each outside piece 5° to its faces, as shown in the plan drawings. This bevel butts against the rails to make a tight, clean joint.

Fit each piece to the opening, trimming the ends on a disc sander with its table set at 5°. The last piece will be too wide, so use the tablesaw, jointer or hand plane to take a shaving off one edge of the first three or four pieces. Put all the pieces in the opening again to see if they drop in. If not, keep trimming a little off the edges until they do.

Saw grooves for ⅛-in. plywood or Masonite splines in all but the outside two edges. When sawing, always put the top face against the rip fence. Make the splines about ¾ in. wide. The pieces aren't glued together, and the splines help keep the faces aligned. Complete the pieces by chamfering the edges and ends on the tablesaw, jointer or by hand. Take care not to expose the particleboard.

Finish the top pieces and the base before fastening the top. Don't use a hard finish, such as polyurethane or lacquer, on a soft wood like cedar—the surface is likely to get dented and the finish will be difficult to repair. Whatever finish you choose, apply the same number of coats to both the top and bottom faces of the top pieces, so that the rate of moisture gain and loss will be the same on both faces. If the rate is not the same, the pieces are more likely to cup or twist.

If you're making a tile top, glue it to the underlayment with mastic and grout between the tiles, as you would for bathroom tiles. Instead of ceramic or metal tile, a stone such as slate or marble could be used, but keep it thin—⅜ in. or less—to prevent the table from becoming top-heavy. The same construction and design can be used for larger tile-top tables. Determine the size and shape from the number and arrangement of the tiles.

Slat-Top Table

Scale: ⅛ in. = 1 in.
Details: ½ in. = 1 in.

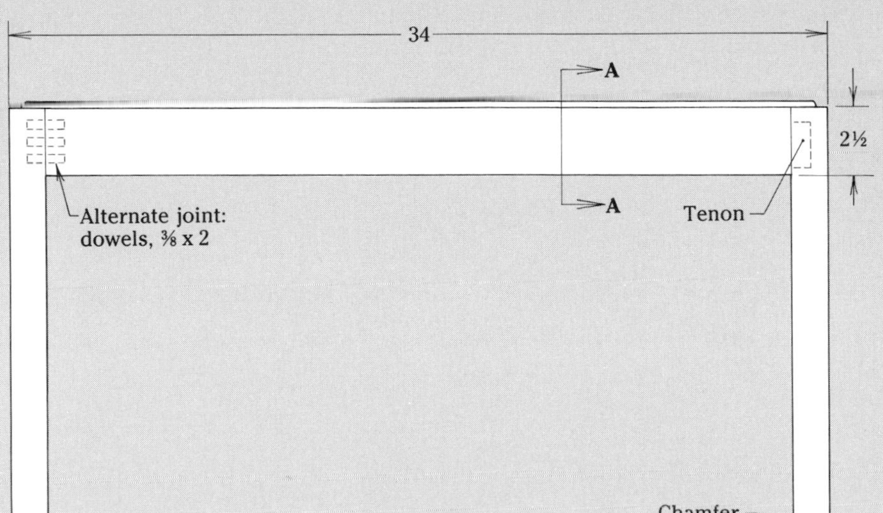

34
A
A
2½
Alternate joint:
dowels, ⅜ x 2
Tenon
Chamfer
1½

Front View

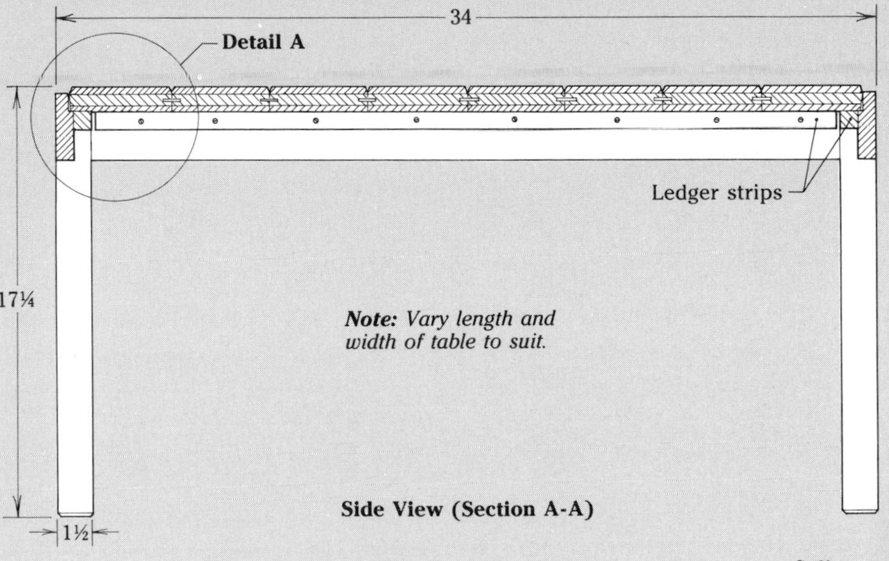

34
Detail A
Ledger strips
17¼
Note: Vary length and width of table to suit.
1½

Side View (Section A-A)

Tile-Top Alternative of Detail A

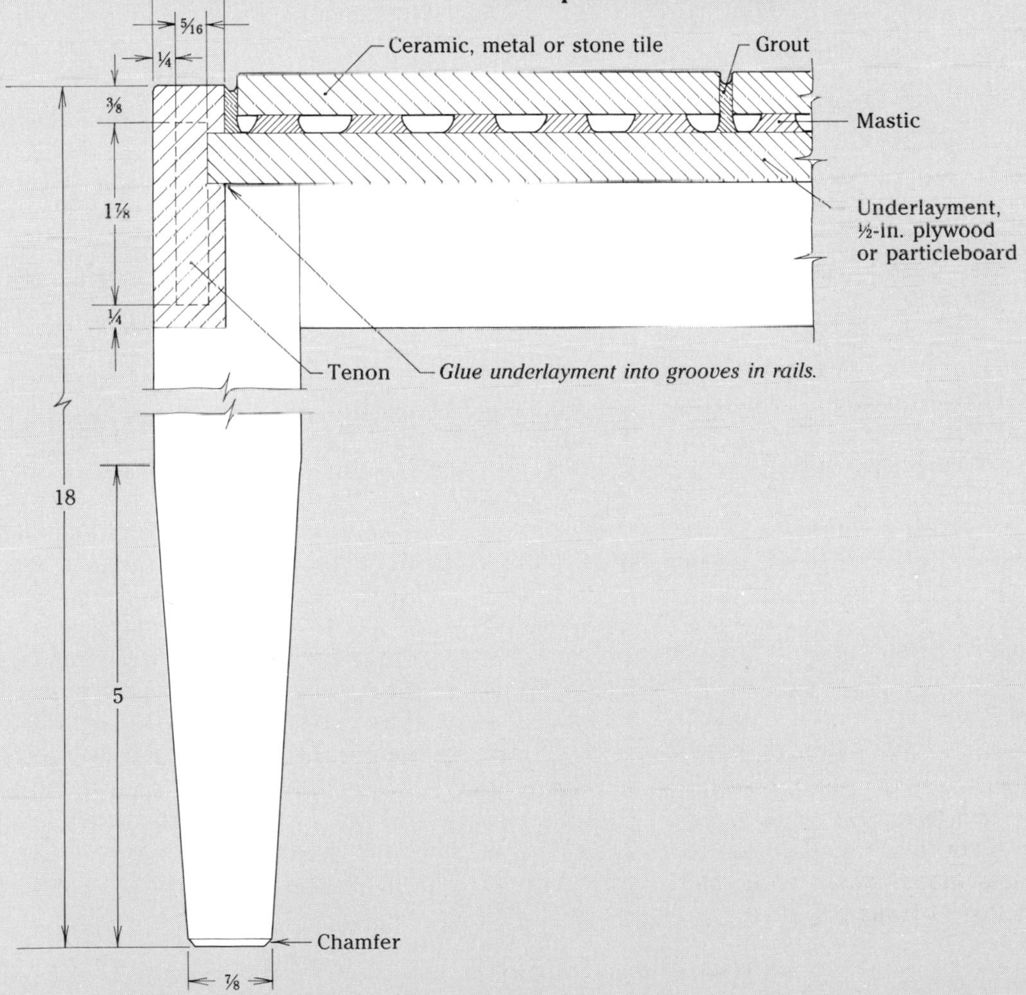

¾
5⁄16
¼
Ceramic, metal or stone tile
Grout
⅜
Mastic
1⅞
Underlayment,
½-in. plywood
or particleboard
¼
Tenon
Glue underlayment into grooves in rails.
18
5
Chamfer
⅞

Detail A: Leg, Rails and Top

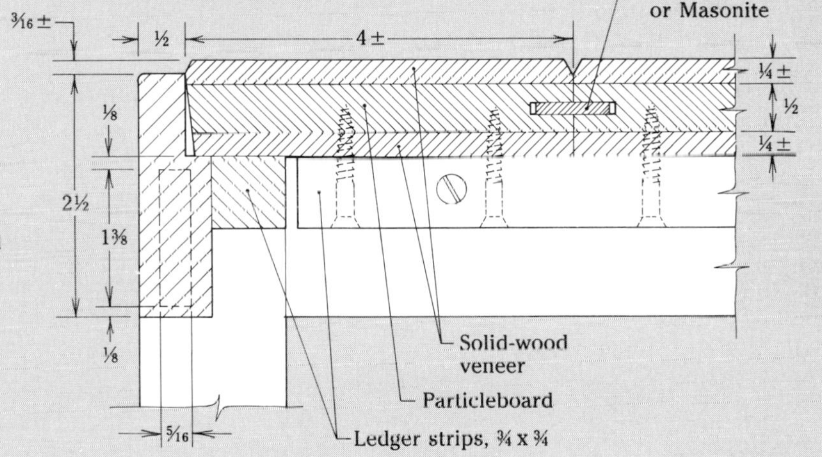

Splines,
⅛-in. plywood
or Masonite
3⁄16 ±
½
4 ±
¼ ±
½
¼ ±
⅛
2½
1⅜
⅛
Solid-wood
veneer
Particleboard
5⁄16
Ledger strips, ¾ x ¾

Plan View of Detail A (Top removed)

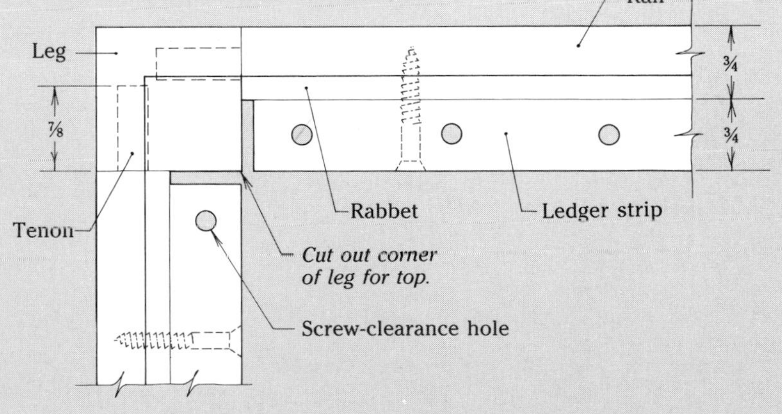

Rail
Leg
¾
⅞
¾
Tenon
Rabbet
Ledger strip
Cut out corner
of leg for top.
Screw-clearance hole

Rosewood and Teak Table

Scale: ⅛ in. = 1 in.

Partial Front View

1⅝

15/16

End View

16

⅞

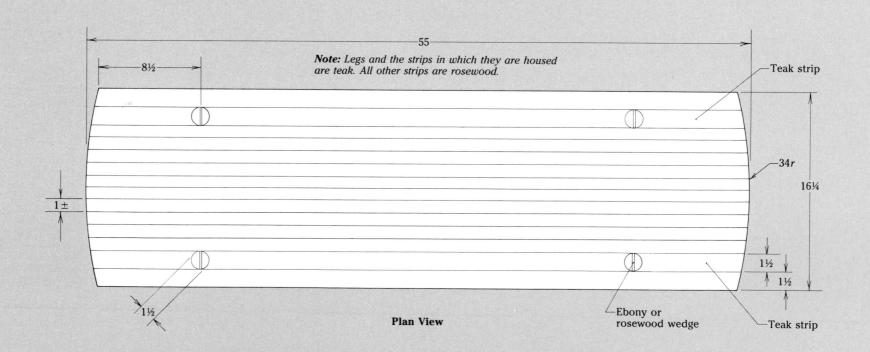

55

8½

Note: *Legs and the strips in which they are housed are teak. All other strips are rosewood.*

Teak strip

34r

16¼

1±

1½

1½

1½

Plan View

Ebony or rosewood wedge

Teak strip

Rosewood and Teak Table

This table is almost stark in its simplicity, so its proportions are crucial. If a curve is too flat or the taper of the legs too abrupt, it is immediately obvious because there are no fussy details to distract the eye. I made several full-size models in pine before I found proportions that looked right. "Looking right" may sound like a subjective yardstick, but I think anyone can develop the ability to see with discrimination.

Construction

The top of this low table is made of a dozen narrow rosewood strips and two teak strips. The turned legs, also of teak, are tenoned through the teak strips and fixed with rosewood wedges. You could, of course, combine different woods than these, but the contrast between the colors should be distinct—not too harsh, like walnut and ash, or too subtle, like mahogany and cherry. Color can vary widely within a species, so successful combinations always depend on the actual boards chosen.

This table should be made of edge-joined strips, even if you have a single board that would be wide enough. This is partly a matter of design and partly of structure. There isn't an underframe in this table to prevent the top from warping, and narrow, glued-up boards are less likely to cup or twist than single, wide boards. Seasonal swelling and shrinking across the width of the top, however, won't be reduced by gluing up strips.

Rip the strips to width and plane them a fraction over final thickness. Note any tear-out and mark all the strips with arrows indicating the direction they should be hand planed or fed through the planer to minimize tear-out. Make the rosewood strip and the teak strip on each edge 1½-in. wide, the same as the diameter of the tenons on the legs.

Glue the strips together so all the arrows are pointing in the same direction. If you cut the center strips from one board, don't glue them up in the same order—this will not look good nor will it reduce warpage as much as positioning them in random order will. I usually dowel edge-joined boards to prevent them from sliding on each other, but for a small tabletop like this, I just C-clamp pairs of slightly convex bearers across the width of the top when gluing up. Place a piece of wax paper between each bearer and the strips to prevent them from sticking together.

If possible, run the glued-up top through a thickness planer, in the direction of the arrows. If not, plane and scrape it by hand. Mark out the curve on each end with a beam compass, and bandsaw the curves. Remove the bandsaw marks and work the round on the ends with a finely set spokeshave. The long edges are flat, and I round their arrises just slightly with sandpaper.

Bore the round mortises for the leg tenons with a Forstner bit or a hole saw from the face side, using a backing board to prevent tear-out. Make sure each mortise is at a right angle to the top surface. Turn the legs, cut the slots in the tenons, and glue and wedge the tenons in the top as described on pp. 95-96.

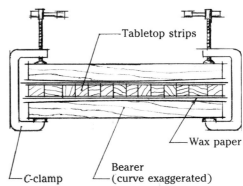

Clamp bearers on the strips to keep them aligned while edge-gluing. Arrange the end grain of the strips in random order so each strip will move in a different direction, reducing the risk of the top warping.

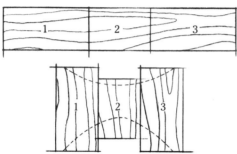

Make each side of the base from the same board to ensure that the grain pattern and the color will be consistent.

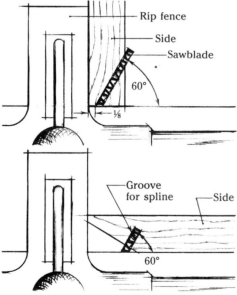

Cut the miters and the grooves for the splines on the tablesaw, with the rip fence to the left of the blade.

Slate-Top Table

I designed the base of this table with the shallow arch at the bottom, but once it was made, I decided the base looked better upside down. The top is Pennsylvania slate. I would have preferred a slightly thicker top, but I got this piece of slate cheap—the dark band I thought so attractive was flawed in the quarry's view. Slate's layered structure (geologists call it *foliated*) makes it strong enough to be supported on just three points of the base.

You could make the top of plywood or particleboard laminated with wood, mosaic, tile, slate or leather, or of tempered plate glass or marble. Many different kinds of marble are available, but marble isn't as strong as slate, so it should be at least 1¼ in. thick. Don't use solid wood—it's unlikely to stay flat when supported on only three points.

Construction

The base shown in the photo at left is made of solid walnut, but any reasonably hard wood will do. Make a full-size cardboard or stiff-paper pattern from the plan drawings, so each side will be identical. Establish the curves by bending a thin batten, or scale-up the drawing by superimposing ⅛-in. squares on it and then reproducing the curve in each small square in a corresponding 1-in. square.

To make each side of the base, I edge-join three boards, cut from one 9-in.-wide board and glued together as shown in the sketch at top left. This method gives each side consistent color and grain pattern, which makes the glue joints less noticeable. Running the grain of the sides horizontally would overcome the weakness inherent in the narrow center of each vertical-grain side, but a horizontal-grain side would look wrong. (A favorite dictum of mine is "what looks right is right.")

After dimensioning the sides, bandsaw the curves and round their surfaces with a finely set spokeshave. Next, miter the edges of the sides on the tablesaw. Set the blade 30° from vertical and put the fence to the left side of the blade so that the blade angles away from the fence. The miters are cut with the wood held vertically, edge on the table, with the outside face against the fence, as shown in the sketch at bottom left. Adjust the fence by making trial cuts in scrap wood of the same thickness as the sides until you can saw a miter and leave a small flat on the edge. If you

miter completely across the edge, the thin apex of the miter won't support the weight of the side against the saw table as you saw.

Adjust the fence and height of the blade to cut grooves in the miters for ⅛-in.-thick plywood or Masonite splines. Run the edge against the fence and the inside face of the side on the table. For maximum joint strength, these grooves should be near the inside face of the side, as shown in Detail B on the plan drawings. You'll need to reset the fence and cut the grooves in two passes if the saw kerf is too thin. Once assembled, the base is awkward to handle, so do all finish-sanding now.

The base is difficult to assemble without some form of band clamp. Make three softwood blocks to protect the mitered corners and distribute the clamping pressure evenly. Each block should be the same height as the base, and have a 60° notch running along its length to take the corner. Wax the notch to prevent the glue from adhering to the block. Dry-assemble and clamp the base—if you haven't got a band clamp, loop nylon cord around the base and tension it by twisting a stick of wood in the slack.

Check the joints. If one is open even a whisker, take the base apart, plane a little off the heel of the miter and try again. Persevere until all the miters close completely. Glue up with a plastic resin glue, which will give plenty of assembly time to tighten and adjust the band clamps. When the glue has cured, hand-plane the apex of each corner. I like to leave this surface flat, but it might suffer less damage from stray feet if you round it.

The top is positioned on the base by three brass pins epoxied into the slate. To mark the holes for the pins in the slate, drive finish nails into the base, centered where the pins will go. Clip off the nail heads, leaving ⅛ in. or so protruding. Carefully place the base in position on the underside of the slate. A light hammer blow on each foot will mark the slate. Bore holes in the slate with a ⅜-in. masonry bit. Pull the nails out of the base and bore holes for the pins centered on the nail holes. (For pins, you can use ¼-in. brazing rod, available at most machine shops). Push the pins into the base. Lay the slate upside down, fill the holes in the slate with epoxy and set the base gently in place. A small piece of wax paper will prevent the epoxy from adhering to the base. When the glue has set, remove the base. The pins epoxied in the slate and the holes in the base will be perfectly aligned.

Slate-Top Table

Scale: ⅛ in. = 1 in.
Details: ½ in. = 1 in.

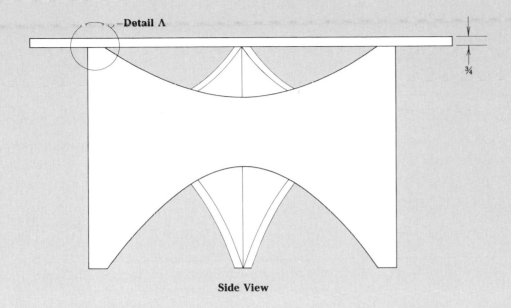

Detail A

¾

Side View

25½

1½

1½

18¼

4¼

Grain
direction

8½

Side Layout

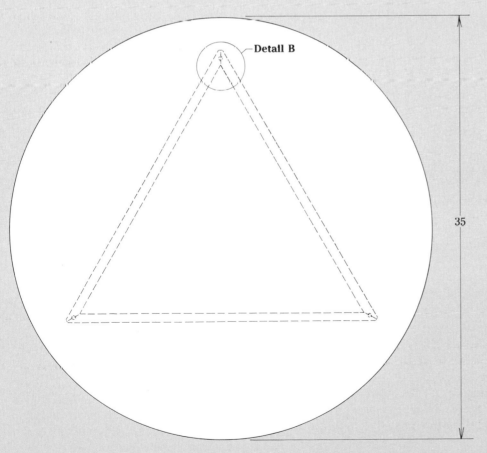

Detail B

35

Plan View

**Detail B: Corner Joint
(Top removed)**

¼ ±

⅝

¼-in. hole for brass pin

Spline, ⅛-in. plywood
or Masonite

60°

¾

A

A

**Detail A: Top and Base
(Section through top)**

*Glue ¼-in. brass
pin into top with epoxy.*

⅜ ±

Slate top

Base

**Section A-A:
Edge Profile
(Typical of all curves)**

Coffee Table with Chessboard

This occasional table, which is also a game table, looks good in front of a long couch or against a wall. As the tabletop swells and shrinks with seasonal changes in humidity, the *U*-shaped base frames will flex slightly. The frames are proportioned to do this, but to minimize strain on the joints, you should use a stable wood, such as mahogany. The chessboard in the photo is veneered with ebony and mahogany, but maple and walnut or ebony and rosewood would work equally well. Some woods, such as mahogany and cherry, darken noticeably with age, so they should be combined only with much darker or lighter woods.

Construction

The tabletop is made of five pieces: the chessboard, one wide piece glued to each end of the chessboard, and two narrow strips that run the length of the top. The base frames are bridle-jointed together and dovetailed into the top. Make the chessboard first.

I once glued up sixty-four separate squares to make a chessboard. It was an exasperating job—the whole mess slips and slides around when you clamp up, and unless you work very fast, the glue begins to set before the last block is in place. It's much easier to do the gluing in two steps. First, alternate strips of light and dark wood; then, cut this assembly into strips and glue up again for the checkerboard effect. Because I used ebony, an expensive wood, for the dark squares, I veneered the strips first. The veneer construction can be easily adapted to solid-wood-strip construction using less expensive woods.

To make the veneered chessboard, cut nine strips 2 in. wide and 18 in. long from the same wood that you're using for the rest of the top. Joint one face of each strip and plane the strips 1⅛ in. thick. Next, cut eight light and ten dark strips of veneer, ³⁄₁₆ in. thick, 2 in. wide and 18 in. long. Glue veneer strips of the same color on both faces of each thick strip. You don't need a veneer press, just clamp the sandwiches to the benchtop, two or three at a time, using a heavy bearer on top to distribute clamping pressure. Use Titebond glue and put wax paper between each laminate to prevent the pieces from sticking to each other or to the bench.

When the glue has cured, joint or plane one edge of each laminated strip and rip them 1⅞ in. wide using a good carbide-tipped blade. (An alternate-top-bevel carbide blade cuts cleanly, so you can glue up without having to plane the edges.) Glue all nine strips edge to edge, alternating light and dark. Plane the glued-up board 1⅜ in. thick, taking about 1/16 in. off each face so the thickness of the veneers remains equal. Crosscut one end, then crosscut the rest of the glued-up board to make eight new strips at right angles to the original strips, running against the same 1⅞-in. fence setting.

Offset every other strip by one square to create the checkerboard pattern. (Turning the strips end for end reverses the grain direction and makes any subsequent planing more difficult.) Glue the strips together, making sure that the corners of the light and dark squares meet exactly. I usually do this on the tablesaw table to ensure flatness. These end-grain joints don't need reinforcement—the long strips of the tabletop will provide that. Clamp thick bearers on the edges to distribute the clamping pressure evenly.

Clean up the faces, edges and ends of the board. I glue a 1/16-in. to ⅛-in.-wide banding of contrasting wood around the board to set the chessboard off from the tabletop. Plane a piece about ¼ in. thick and rip the bands off an edge, jointing the edge before each cut. Saw or rout a rabbet on the edges and ends of the board and glue the planed surface of the bands to the rabbets. Hold the bands in place with masking tape. Flush all the surfaces after the glue has dried.

Now make the rest of the top. The chessboard should be about 15 in. square. Machine a single board (or edge-join two or more boards) a fraction wider than the chessboard, 4½ ft. long and 1⅜ in. thick.

Crosscut this board in two, and glue the pieces on either end of the chessboard. Make sure that the grain of all three pieces runs in the same direction and that a light-colored square will be to each player's right. Chess players become enraged (as I accidentally discovered) when presented with a dark square on their right—it upsets all their favorite gambits.

When the glue has cured, plane the edges of the two end pieces flush with the edges of the chessboard. The end-grain joints are fragile, so handle the top carefully. Cut the long edge pieces and glue them on, using dowels to position them. I have run tops like this through a thickness planer, but it's risky unless the grain is very straight. Hand-planing or scraping is safer and is also better exercise.

Mark the dovetail sockets with a knife and marking gauge on the top and bottom surfaces of the tabletop. Saw them by hand or on a tablesaw with the blade set at the correct angle. If you use the tablesaw, you'll

Narrow banding defines the chessboard within the tabletop. The banding is glued into a ¼-in.-deep rabbet around the board before the tabletop is glued up.

The legs are joined to the tabletop by a large dovetail. The arrises on the outside edge of the legs and the bottom arris on the tabletop are rounded.

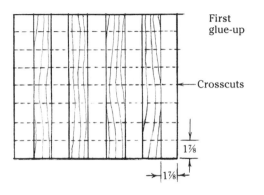

First glue-up

Crosscuts

1⅞

1⅞

Note: Dark strips are grained.

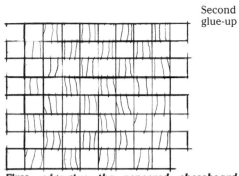

Second glue-up

First, edge-glue the veneered chessboard strips, alternating dark and light. Then cut new strips across the grain and glue these up, offsetting every other strip by one square. Make sure the corners are exactly aligned.

This cherry pedestal table has a cherry and ebony veneered chessboard. The column is wedge-tenoned into the turned base and top support.

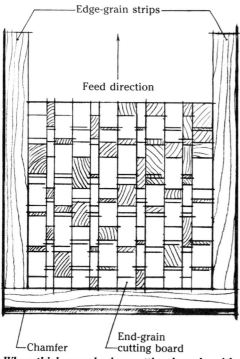

Edge-grain strips

Feed direction

Chamfer

End-grain cutting board

When thickness-planing cutting boards with end-grain surfaces, glue edge-grain strips to the sides and end of the cutting board to prevent it from jamming in the planer. Chamfer the end piece so it won't splinter.

End-grain cutting boards with interesting surface patterns can be made using the same strip-gluing techniques used for making the chessboard.

need help to handle the large top safely. Clear the waste with a coping saw and chisel to the marking-gauge line without undercutting.

Cut out rectangular blanks for the legs (each *U*-shaped frame consists of two vertical legs and a horizontal rail). It's easier to mark and cut the dovetail pin before tapering the leg. Position each blank under a socket and mark it with a knife exactly as you would a dovetail. Saw out the pins and fit them so the shoulders rest squarely against the underside of the table.

Cut the bridle joints on the tablesaw, as described on p. 36. Insert the legs into the top and clamp the rail in place to establish the shoulder lines of the tenon. Cut and fit the joints, then taper the outside edge and both faces of each leg. Glue up the legs and rails, and plane the faces of the rails so they're flush with the tapered faces of the legs. Then glue the completed frames to the tabletop.

I round all arrises on the outside edges of the *U*-shaped frames, otherwise they'll get rounded by the constant wear of people's feet. I also round the bottom arris of the tabletop. A carbide rounding-over bit with a ball-bearing pilot works well, but you can also work the rounds by hand with a spokeshave and files.

The chessboard can be omitted from the tabletop or placed differently, though I think it would look awkward centered. The chessboard top of the table in the photo at top left was made using the technique I've described. The pedestal table is a bit unstable, so I'd make a larger base next time. You can make the chessboard without the table. A folding board can be made by cutting it in half and joining the halves with Soss hinges, which will be invisible when the board is open (see Appendix 5 for sources of supply).

The technique of edge-joining strips of different woods, crosscutting them and regluing has many decorative possibilities. Cutting boards can be made so that the end grain forms the top surface. A board like this can be used as a tabletop, as shown at bottom right. The base is made and proportioned like the night table (pp. 46-48). Make sure you give ample allowance for expansion and contraction when you fasten an end-grain top to a base.

A word of caution: Never feed an end-grain cutting board through a thickness planer unless you have glued edge-grain strips to three sides as shown in the sketch at left. I broke some bones in my left hand when a cutting board jammed in the planer and came flying out backward.

Coffee Table with Chessboard

Scale: ⅛ in. = 1 in.

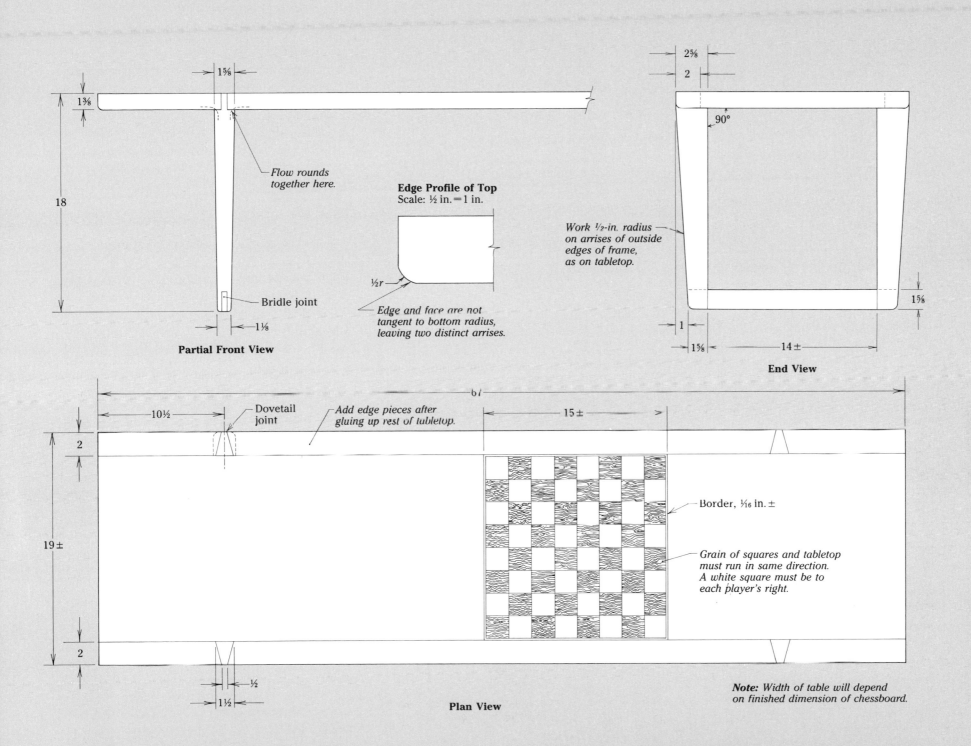

1⅝

1⅜

18

Flow rounds together here.

Bridle joint

1⅛

Partial Front View

Edge Profile of Top
Scale: ½ in. = 1 in.

½r

Edge and face are not tangent to bottom radius, leaving two distinct arrises.

2⅝

2

90°

Work ½-in. radius on arrises of outside edges of frame, as on tabletop.

1⅝

1

1⅝

14±

End View

61

10½

Dovetail joint

Add edge pieces after gluing up rest of tabletop.

15±

2

19±

2

Border, 1/16 in. ±

Grain of squares and tabletop must run in same direction. A white square must be to each player's right.

½

1½

Plan View

Note: Width of table will depend on finished dimension of chessboard.

Low Trestle Table

Scale: 1/8 in. = 1 in.
Details: 1/4 in. = 1 in.

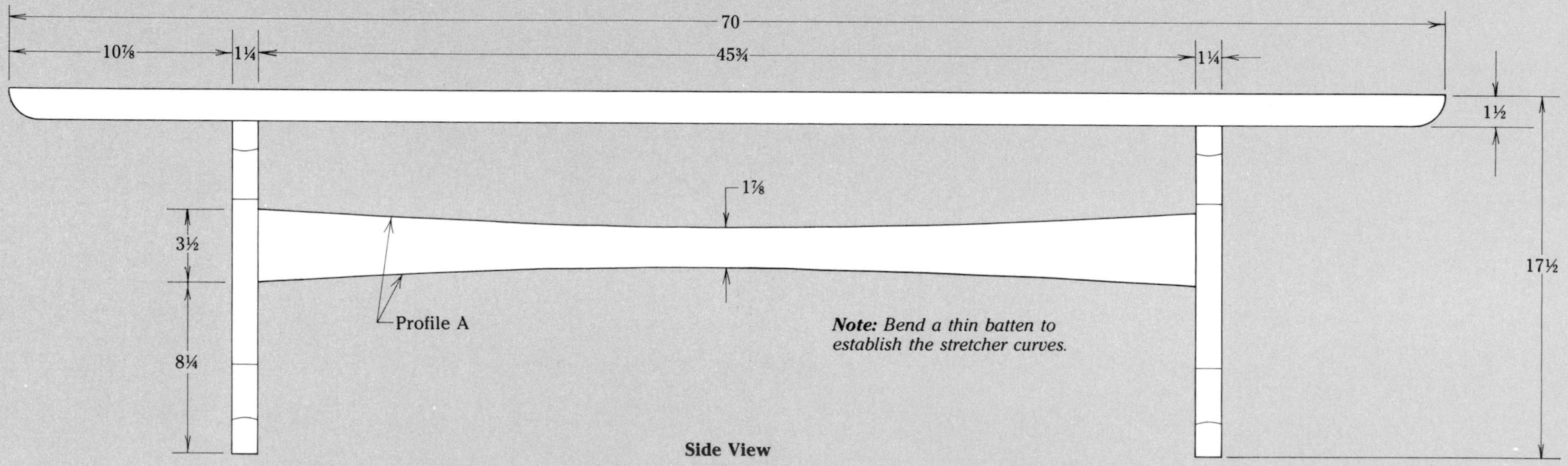
70
10⅞
1¼
45¾
1¼
1½
17½
1⅞
3½
8¼
Profile A
Note: Bend a thin batten to establish the stretcher curves.

Side View

Edge Profiles

Profile A
Profile B

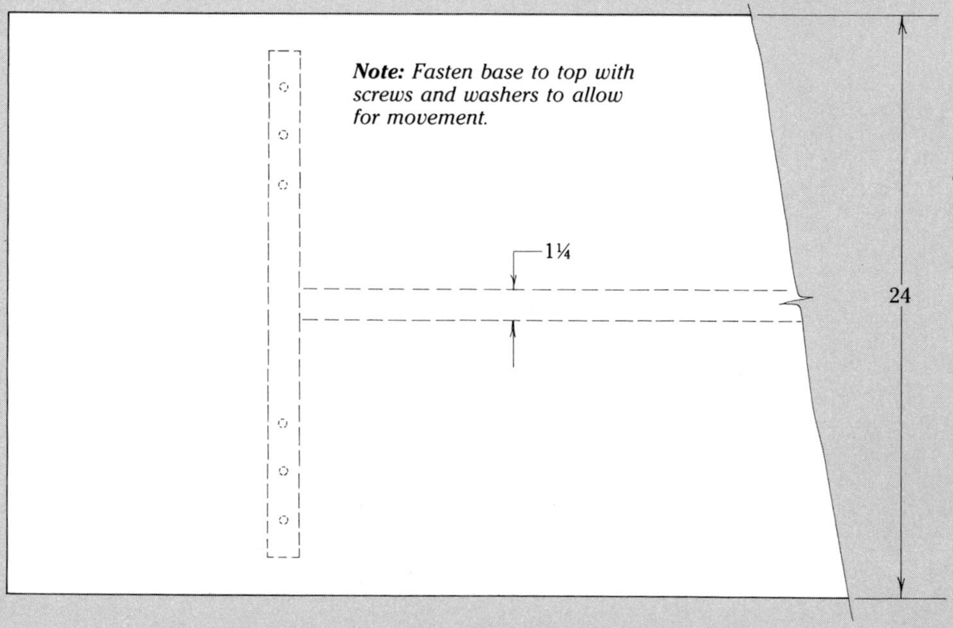
Note: Fasten base to top with screws and washers to allow for movement.
1¼
24

Half Plan View

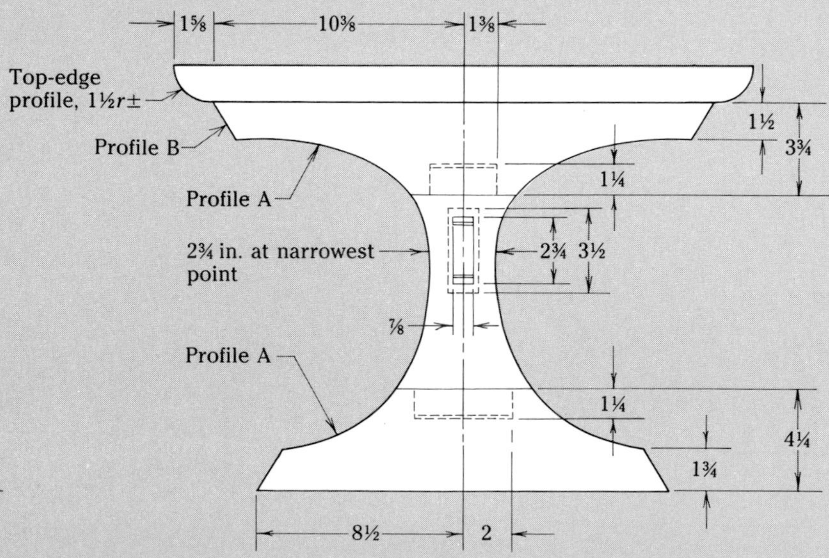
1⅝
10⅜
1⅜
Top-edge profile, 1½r±
Profile B
Profile A
2¾ in. at narrowest point
⅞
Profile A
1½
3¾
1¼
2¾
3½
1¼
4¼
1¾
8½
2

End View

Low Trestle Table

This is a rather formal table that I made for a spot in front of some low windows overlooking a lake. Embedded in the surface of the dark, walnut top is a lead bullet, a relic of some long-forgotten forest fracas. I have made three of these tables, all in walnut. I think the design would also look well in mahogany, but not in a very blond wood such as ash or maple.

Construction

The structure of the table is simple. The trestle is made of two ends connected by a stretcher. Each end consists of a leg that is tenoned into a foot and a top support; the stretcher is through-tenoned and wedged to the legs. The top is screwed to the trestle through the top support.

I think a three-board or five-board top looks better than a two-board top. A two-board top with a central glue line looks bad unless the grain patterns are symmetrical around the glue line. The symmetry then becomes a deliberate design feature of the table. The quickest way to shape the edges and ends of the top is to set the tablesaw blade at 45° and cut off the waste, then finish the profile with a spokeshave and block plane. Make sure that all the arrises—especially where top meets edge—are crisp. Nothing spoils the look of furniture more than blunt arrises that look as if they've been sandblasted.

Plane the parts for the trestle 1¼ in. thick and cut them to length and width. Cut the mortises and tenons while the pieces are still rectangular. The tenon shoulders of the legs must be flat, not undercut—any gaps will be exposed when the ends are sawn to shape. Knife-mark the through mortises for the stretcher on both faces of each leg. Clear the waste by boring in from both faces and chisel to the lines.

Glue the legs to the feet and the top supports before cutting the curve to ensure a more even, continuous curve than you would get by cutting each piece separately. To mark the curves, use a Masonite half-template. The template should register on the centerline of the trestle end, so each end will be symmetrical and both will be identical. Bandsaw the curves, then spokeshave the profiles on the edges of the curves—a spokeshave with a convex sole works best. (A small sanding drum mounted in a drill press will also do a fair job.) Plane the ends of the top supports and feet flat, and slightly round the arrises of these ends.

Next, bore the holes for the fastening screws in the top supports. To allow for seasonal movement, the screws are housed in oversized clearance holes and bear on washers, as shown in the sketch at right. Bore the holes for the washers first, then bore the clearance holes for the screw shanks. These should be as large as possible while leaving a ledge for the washer to rest on. Use a standard washer, with a hole just smaller than the head of whatever size round-head screw you're using. (I recommend at least a No. 10 brass screw.) Or use a washer with a hole the size of the screw shank and file it to form a slot. An elongated slot allows for more movement, and is advisable to use with less stable woods.

Now make the stretcher. As with the legs, cut the tenons before sawing the curves. Saw the tenons by hand or on a tablesaw (p. 5), then saw-kerf them for the wedges.

To assemble the base, pull the stretcher tight to the legs with clamps, and drive in the wedges, striking them alternately with a steel hammer so they penetrate the tenons equally. You may remove the clamps when the wedges are set. Sand and finish the base and top, then screw them together.

This trestle construction is also appropriate for a bench. The top should be narrower and about 18 in. to 20 in. high for sitting. A bench seat shouldn't overhang the ends as much as a tabletop, otherwise a person sitting on the end might tip over.

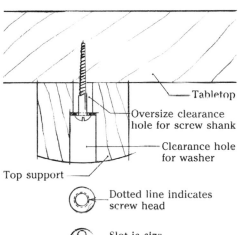

The screws that fasten the base to the top pass through oversized clearance holes and bear on a washer. Use a standard washer, or file an elongated hole in a standard washer.

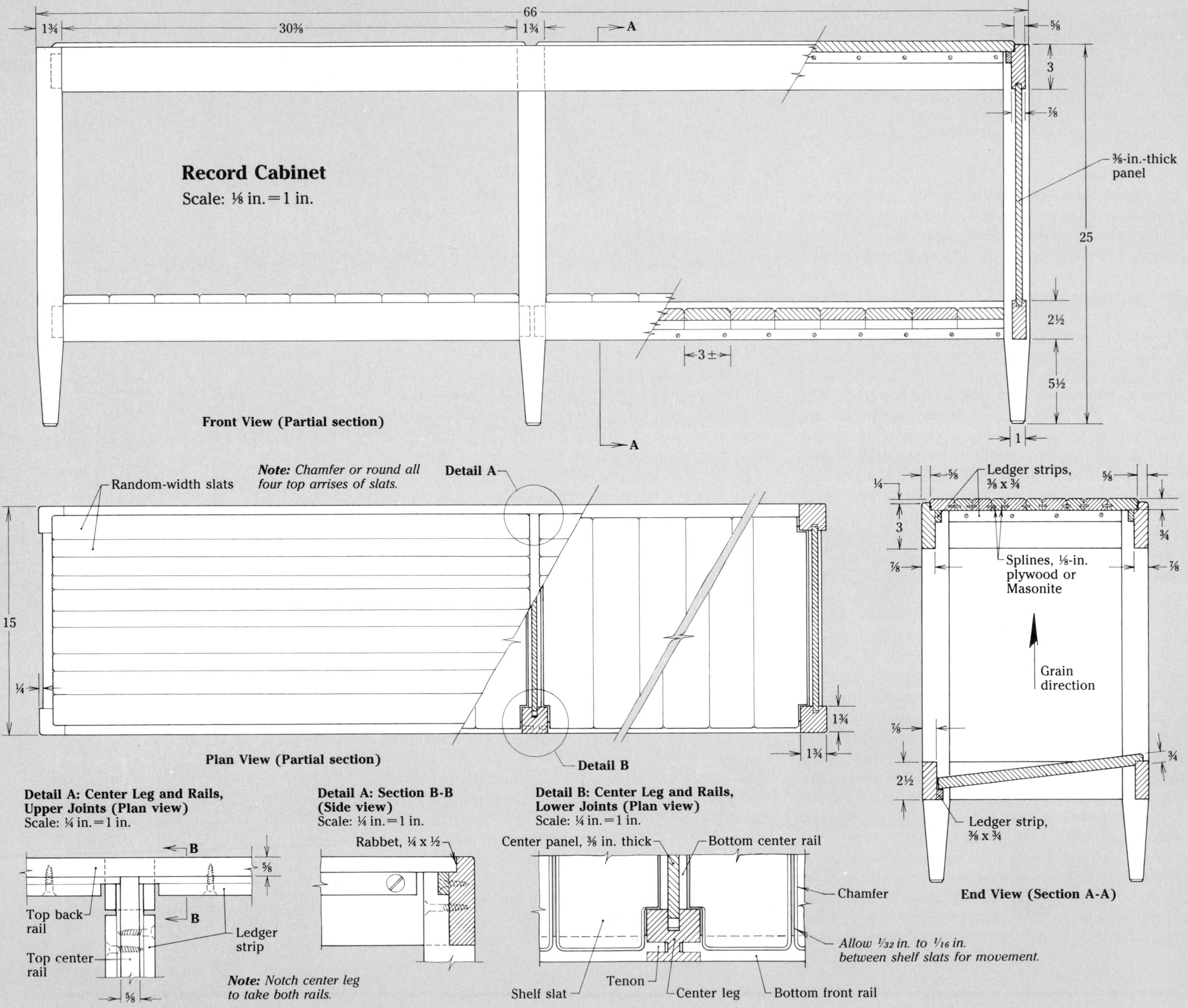

Record Cabinet
Scale: ⅛ in. = 1 in.
66
1¾
30⅜
1¾
A
⅝
3
⅞
⅜-in.-thick panel
25
2½
5½
3 ±
1
A
Front View (Partial section)
Note: Chamfer or round all four top arrises of slats.
Random-width slats
Detail A
15
¼
1¾
1¾
Detail B
Plan View (Partial section)
Ledger strips, ⅜ x ¾
¼
⅝
⅝
3
¾
⅞
⅞
Splines, ⅛-in. plywood or Masonite
Grain direction
⅞
¾
2½
Ledger strip, ⅜ x ¾
End View (Section A-A)
Detail A: Center Leg and Rails, Upper Joints (Plan view)
Scale: ¼ in. = 1 in.
B
⅝
Top back rail
B
Ledger strip
Top center rail
⅝
Detail A: Section B-B (Side view)
Scale: ¼ in. = 1 in.
Rabbet, ¼ x ½
Note: Notch center leg to take both rails.
Detail B: Center Leg and Rails, Lower Joints (Plan view)
Scale: ¼ in. = 1 in.
Center panel, ⅜ in. thick
Bottom center rail
Chamfer
Allow 1/32 in. to 1/16 in. between shelf slats for movement.
Shelf slat
Tenon
Center leg
Bottom front rail

Record Cabinet

As a child, I played records on the solidly built, mahogany wind-up gramaphones of the 1930s. The steel or thorn needle had to be changed after every two or three records were played, and the spring-loaded turntables ran only at 78 rpm. After the spring had run down, my sister and I found that we could twirl the record backward and turn the King's English into Polish—or so we thought. When my mother brought a recording of folk songs back from Poland, we were disappointed that we could not make it sing in English.

Until recently, high-fidelity audio equipment was always enclosed in cabinets. Glowing tubes, condensers, transformers and tuners, though marvelous pieces of electrical engineering, were unsightly and hot. The transistor has changed all that—modern amplifiers and turntables are elegant and compact. Today, cabinets are needed to store records and to display, rather than hide, the equipment.

The walnut record cabinet shown in the photo is designed to stand behind a couch. The turntable, amplifier and so on, are placed on the top surface, and below is space for about 300 records. The lower shelf is sloped toward the back to keep the records in place and make it easier to see the name on the spine of each record jacket. The center legs are needed to support the weight of the records. The cabinet shouldn't be lifted at its ends when loaded, because this strains the lower mortise-and-tenon joints.

Construction

This cabinet may look more difficult to build than it is, so I'll summarize its parts before telling how they're made. The two ends and center section are simple frame-and-panel constructions—in each, two legs and two short rails surround a solid-wood panel. These three sections are joined by long rails—four bottom rails are tenoned into the end and center legs, two top rails run from end to end, notched into the center legs. The narrow-slat top is supported on ledger strips screwed to the top rails. The shelf, made of wider strips, rests on the front bottom rails and ledger strips screwed to the back bottom rails.

I prefer a dark, straight-grained hardwood for this cabinet, though any reasonably strong wood will do. Cut all the legs and rails to length, width and thickness, then lay out and cut the mortises and tenons.

Center all the tenons on the rail ends. I made them ⅜ in. thick, with ¼-in.-wide shoulders—a thicker tenon would put the mortises too close to the face of the legs.

To avoid misplaced mortises, first mark the faces of the legs that are to be mortised. Then place the legs together with the marked faces up, align their ends and mark the positions of the mortises across those faces with a square. Do the same for the other mortised faces. Mark the mortise cheeks with a marking gauge or a mortise gauge. Make the front and back rails flush with the faces of the legs, and set the end rails back from the faces.

The cabinet ends are simple frame-and-panel construction, Setting the face of the rail back from the faces of the legs adds a little depth to the end.

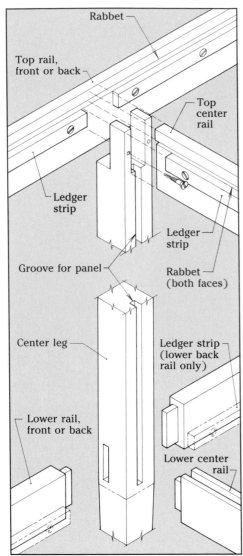

The joints at the center leg are more complicated than those at the ends of the cabinet. Cut the notch for the long top rail before cutting the bridle joint for the short rail.

The joints of the rails and center legs are rather complicated. As shown in the drawing at left, the top of each center leg is notched twice. One notch takes the long rail, which finishes flush with the face of the leg. The other notch forms a bridle joint for the short rail. Both notches can be cut on the tablesaw using the techniques described for tenons (p. 5) and bridle joints (p. 36). The bottom center rail and two long bottom rails are tenoned into each center leg—make sure the three mortises don't meet inside the leg, because that will weaken it.

When all the mortises and tenons have been cut and fitted, rabbet the top rails. (The rabbets position the ledger strips that support the slat top, and make the rails appear to be thinner.) Cut ¼-in. by ½-in. rabbets on the inside faces of the front, back and both end rails; cut a ⅛-in. by ½-in. rabbet on both faces of the center rail. The top center rail butts into the front and back top rails, and its ends must be notched into the rabbets in those rails or a gap will show.

Dry-assemble the whole cabinet frame. Mark the notches for the slat top on the corner legs. Mark where to cut off the top ends of the bridle-jointed center legs even with the rabbets of the rails. At the same time, mark with a crayon the position of the panel grooves in the legs and rails. (The panel between the center legs provides two more surfaces for records to lean against.) Trim the center legs to length and saw or rout the grooves—be sure to stop the grooves in the legs in the mortises. (See p. 59 for how to cut the notches in the corner legs on the tablesaw.)

Glue up the ⅜-in.-thick panels, running the grain parallel with the long dimension (vertically in the cabinet). Cut the panels long enough to fit the grooves snugly at top and bottom, but leave room for expansion and contraction from side to side.

Sand the legs, rails and panels. Use a sanding block carefully to round or chamfer all the arrises of the legs and rails. I finish-sand all the pieces before gluing up, because it's difficult to get into the corners of the assembled piece.

After sanding the rails, align the ledger strips with the rabbet on the top rails and screw them in place. (I didn't screw the top down; if you wish to do so, make the ledger strips at least ¾ in. wide.) Screw the ledger strips for the shelf along the bottom edge of the back bottom rails. Bore and countersink clearance holes in the center legs for the screws that will fix the long top rails to the notch.

It's easiest to glue the frame-and-panel ends and center section together first. Protect the wood from the clamp jaws with softwood pads. Set the cabinet on a flat surface while gluing and clamping the remaining rails to prevent twisting. Make sure the openings for the slat top are square. Clamp the long top rails tight to the notches in the center legs, then screw them in place and remove the clamps.

The top can be made and fitted the same way as for the slat-top coffee table (p. 60). Instead of veneering solid wood to a particleboard core to make the slats, I used narrow slats of solid walnut. A stable wood, such as walnut, teak or mahogany, when cut in very narrow strips and left loose in a narrow top like this, won't expand enough to destroy the top. The wood will compress to absorb the expansion that will occur in wet weather. If you live in a climate with extremes of wet and dry, or if you're using oak or another unstable wood, veneer the slats.

Bevel the ends of all the slats and one edge of each outer slat at 5° to give a better fit (beveling all the edges would also allow the slats to compress a bit more in damp weather). Groove the edges of the slats for splines, which will keep the surfaces of adjacent slats even. The splines shouldn't be glued in. After fitting the slats to the openings, put a light round or a small, neat chamfer on all four top arrises of each slat. A crisp chamfer can be made with a plane or jointer, but not with a sanding block. Finish all the surfaces of the slats before final installation. If you want to fasten the top to the ledger strips, one screw in each end of the slats will be sufficient.

Cut the shelf slats to dimension and rabbet their front ends to fit over the front bottom rails. These slats are wider than the top slats, and their combined widths run the length of the cabinet. Allow ¹⁄₃₂ in. to ¹⁄₁₆ in. per slat for movement when fitting them, otherwise they could push the frame apart when they swell. Finish all the surfaces of these slats, too, before final installation. You needn't fasten the slats—the weight of the records will keep them in place. The shelf slats are short and stiff, so splining for alignment is also unnecessary.

You could make a liquor cabinet with only slight alterations to this design. Place the bottom shelf flat to hold bottles and glasses, add doors and 5 in. or 6 in. to the legs. Replacing the slat top with slate or another impermeable material would provide a good surface for mixing drinks.

Floor Lamp

People hesitate to make floor lamps because they think it's necessary to bore a 5-ft.-long hole through the stem for the cord. The proper method is to join two grooved pieces to make the stem, so that the combined grooves make the hole. When neatly done, the joint is almost invisible.

A floor lamp for general illumination should have a stem 55 in. to 60 in. long. If the lamp is to be placed beside a chair or couch for reading, the stem should be 48 in. to 55 in. long. The filament in the bulb will be about 5 in. higher than these dimensions and should be roughly centered in the lamp shade.

I will describe how to make the lamp, shown at right, on the lathe, but you can also shape the stem and base with a bandsaw, spokeshaves and planes, and substitute a square mortise-and-tenon joint for the round one. If you don't turn the lamp, you could make an eight-sided or sixteen-sided base and stem to match, or shape a round base using a spokeshave. The two-piece stem construction I'll describe will work regardless of how the lamp is shaped.

Construction

The stem is fitted to the base, so I make the base first. If you glue up the base, join two or three pieces so that the center of the base won't fall on a glue line, which doesn't look good. Mark the center of the bottom face, draw a circle a little larger than the finished diameter on that face, then bandsaw to the line. Screw a faceplate to the bottom face, centered on the disk, and turn the base to shape. The concave and convex bases shown in the plan drawings echo the gentle curve of the stem, but you may wish to experiment with other shapes. Sand the base on the lathe, rounding the arrises slightly with sandpaper.

Before removing the base from the lathe, mark the center of the top face. The mortise in the base must be exactly perpendicular to the bottom face, so I remove the faceplate and bore the hole on the drill press. I use a 1½-in. Forstner bit and a backing piece for a clean exit on the bottom. (If you have a large-enough chuck for your tailstock, you can bore the hole while the base is on the lathe.)

The glue joint of the stem will be least noticeable if you bandsaw a straight piece of 2-in.-thick stock in half and glue the halves back together after grooving for the cord. Lacking thick stock, you can rip a 1-in.

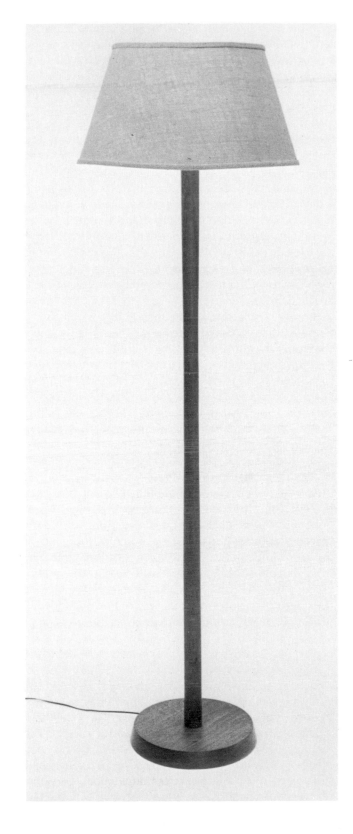

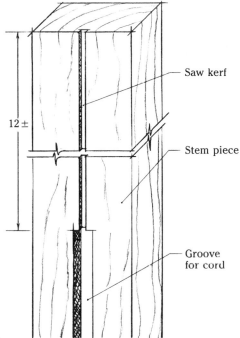

A saw kerf in each stem piece guides the point of the bit when boring the hole for the threaded tube that takes the bulb holder.

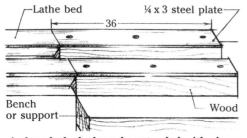

A short lathe bed can be extended with pieces of mild-steel plate. Make sure that the extensions are perfectly in line with the bed.

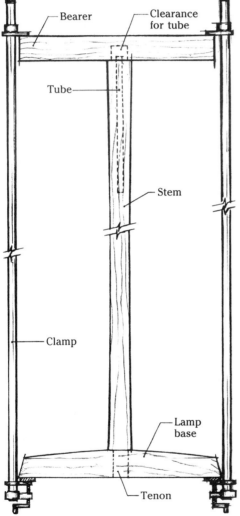

Pull the stem tight to the base with a heavy bearer and two pipe or bar clamps.

by 4-in. board in half and glue the pieces together face to face. Regardless of the method, make sure you end up with a turning blank a bit larger than the largest diameter of the completed stem. Cut the two halves to length, rip them to the same width, and plane or joint the faces that will be glued together.

Before gluing the halves together, you need to cut the grooves for the cord and bore a hole for the threaded metal tube at the top end of the stem. First, cut a ⅜-in.-wide by ³⁄₁₆-in.-deep groove down the center of each inside face. Do this on the tablesaw using a dado head or making several passes over a single blade, or use a router. (It's important that the grooves be exactly centered, so that when you glue up, aligning the edges of the pieces will also align the grooves inside.) Stop the grooves about 12 in. from one end of each piece, and square up the stopped end of each groove with a chisel.

Now make the hole for the metal tube. With a single blade in the tablesaw, make a saw kerf ¹⁄₁₆ in. deep, centered on and running through the end of the groove in each stem piece, as shown in the sketch on p. 75. Clamp the stem pieces firmly together without glue, aligning the saw kerfs and the edges, and bore a ⅜-in.-dia. hole in the kerfed end, all the way to the groove. I use an electric drill and a ⅜-in. spade bit with an extension shank. The saw kerf will guide the spur on the bit so the hole for the threaded tube is centered exactly on the groove.

Now take the stem apart and chisel a notch in each piece for the threaded tube's lower nut, which should bear against the stopped end of the groove. Glue the pieces together after inserting the tube with nuts at the top and bottom. Leave 1 in. of tube projecting from the top of the piece—it will be cut down later. Clamp with *C*-clamps or quick-action clamps, aligning the edges of the pieces so the groove will be aligned inside. To distribute the clamping pressure evenly, I clamp the stem to the benchtop, placing a heavy bearer on the top half. To prevent squeezed-out glue from blocking the groove, run a thin, square piece of wood up and down in the groove while the glue is still wet. Pass a piece of rod or doweling through the tube to clear its ends of glue.

The stem is 5 ft. long, and my lathe is only 3 ft. long, so I extended the lathe bed with two 3-ft.-long pieces of ¼-in. by 3-in. mild-steel plate, as shown in the sketch at top left. An extension need not be elaborate—just make sure that it is sturdy and that the tail-

stock center is centered over the lathe bed at exactly the same height as the headstock center.

Before you mount the stem between centers, saw off its corners so that it approximates an octagon. Also, fit a wooden block over the projecting metal tube so it won't chew up your tailstock center and put a temporary wood plug in the hole in the other end. Turn the round tenon at the bottom end first to fit it snugly in the mortise. If you've turned a base with a convex top surface, you can undercut the shoulder of the tenon slightly so it will seat on the base without gapping.

Shape the stem next. Turning anything this long and thin is tricky because it whips around and chatters. Some turners support the stem with a steady rest or with their hand. I usually just rough-out the shape with a turning gouge, and do the final shaping with a spokeshave and block plane, using the lathe simply to hold the work. This is a more peaceful procedure than struggling with a chattering tool, and doesn't take much longer.

Finish-sand the stem and cut two slots for the wedges in the tenon. Assemble the stem and base so that the wedge slots are at right angles to the grain direction of the base. The pieces are awkward to clamp, so I use two long bar or pipe clamps and a heavy bearer as long as the diameter of the base. Bore a ½-in. hole in the center of the bearer and place it over the protruding tube at the top of the stem, as shown in the sketch at lower left. Make sure the bearer runs parallel to the grain of the base, or the clamping pressure might split the base. Pull the joint tight, drive in the wedges and remove the clamps.

Now bore the horizontal hole in the base that meets the groove in the stem. I do this by eye, lining up the shaft of the drill bit with a diameter drawn on the bottom of the base. Trim the tube to length so that the harp (the lamp-shade support), nut and bulb holder can be screwed onto it. Thread about 16 ft. of cord into the tube and out through the horizontal hole in the base. (If you have trouble pulling the cord through the base, use a hooked piece of wire coat hanger.) Plug the square groove in the bottom of the stem with wood.

Attach the harp securely to the tube with a nut and then screw on the bulb holder. Don't attach the harp to the bulb holder, because it isn't strong enough to support the shade. Small rubber or felt pads on the bottom of the base will raise it above any irregularities in the floor.

Floor Lamp

Scale: ⅛ in. = 1 in.

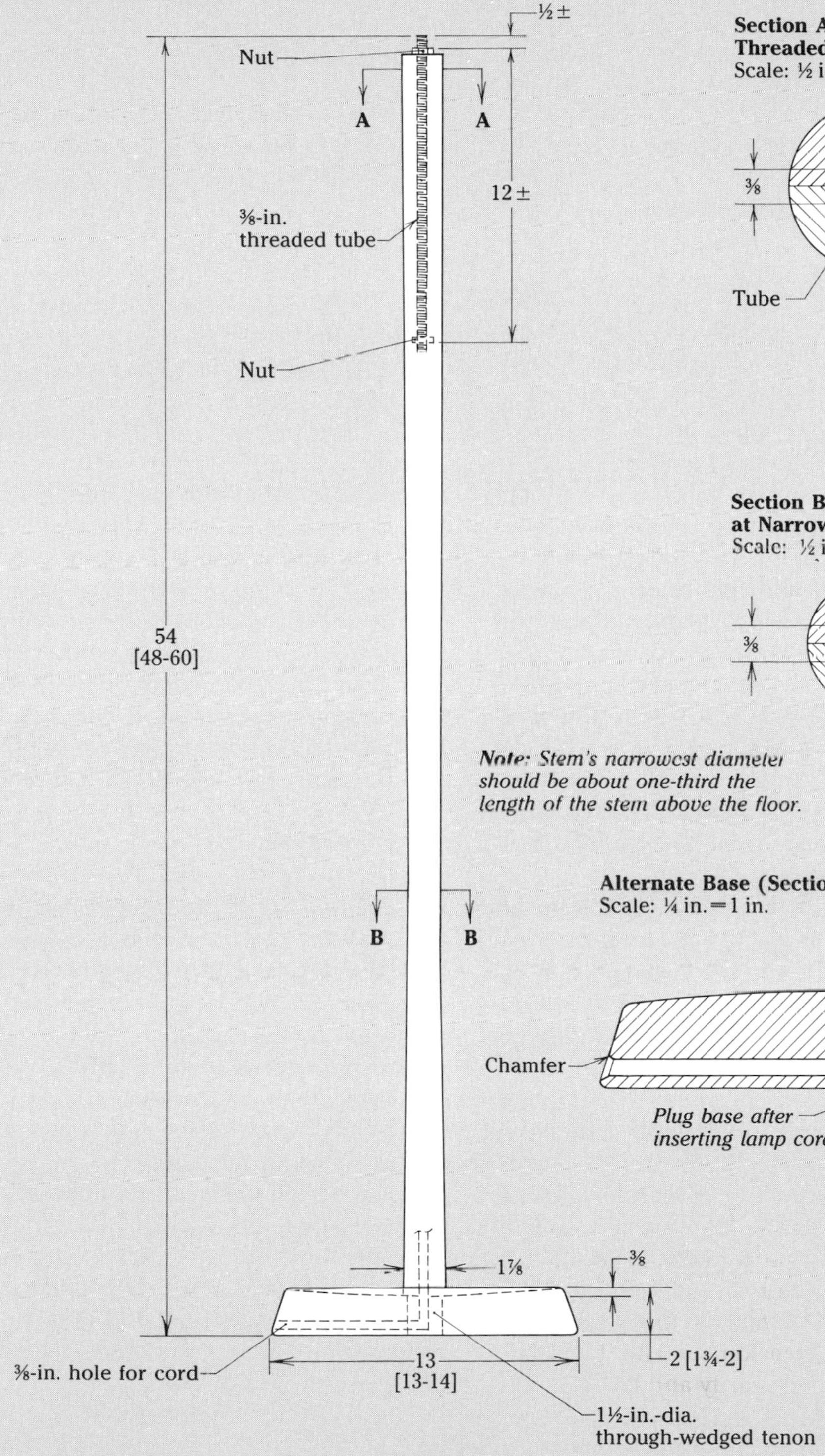

½ ±
Nut
A
A
12 ±
⅜-in.
threaded tube
Nut
54
[48-60]
B
B
1⅞
⅜
2 [1¾-2]
⅜-in. hole for cord
13
[13-14]
1½-in.-dia.
through-wedged tenon

Side View

Section A-A: Stem and Threaded Tube
Scale: ½ in. = 1 in.

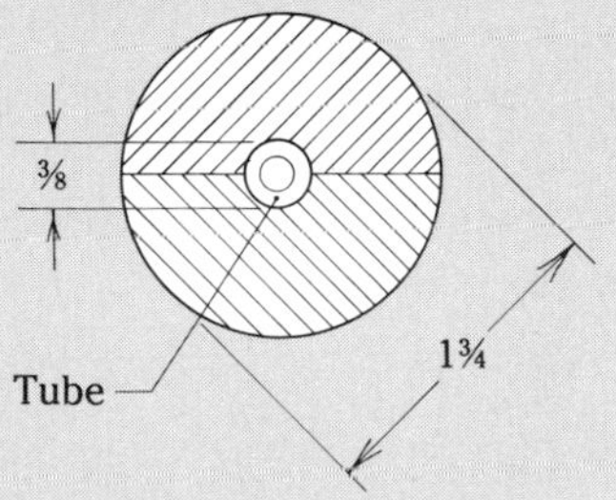

⅜
Tube
1¾

Section B-B: Stem and Groove at Narrowest Point
Scale: ½ in. = 1 in.

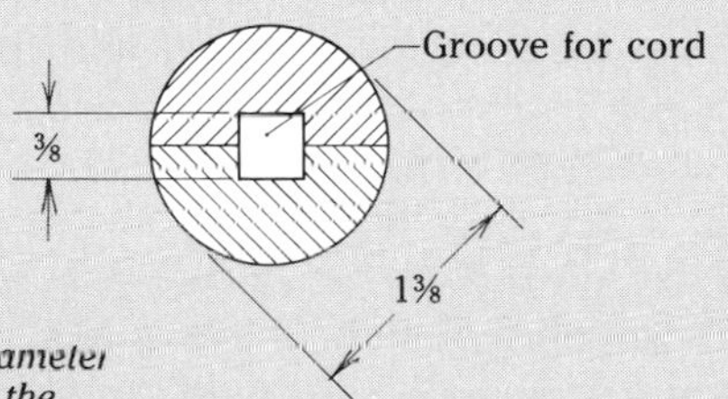

Groove for cord
⅜
1⅜

Note: *Stem's narrowest diameter should be about one-third the length of the stem above the floor.*

Alternate Base (Section)
Scale: ¼ in. = 1 in.

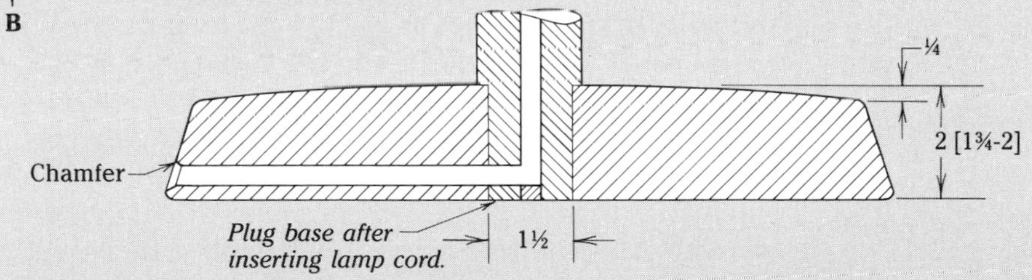

¼
2 [1¾-2]
Chamfer
Plug base after
inserting lamp cord.
1½

Living Room Seating   5

Chair and Sofa

This chair and sofa are two variations on one simple theme: a wood frame spanned by tensioned canvas that supports loose cushions. The canvas is kept taut by nylon lacing running through brass grommets. Both pieces are light and easy to make and don't require much wood.

I designed the chair as a project for my apprentices in their first few weeks of training. It teaches the mortise-and-tenon and bridle joints, and by following the plan drawings, the chair can be made with minimum supervision. Because little material is involved, a poorly cut joint can be made again correctly without feeling badly about the waste.

I'm often tempted to adapt a workable design for other purposes, but this is risky, because only a few adaptations succeed. For example, I was able to expand the chair to make the two-seat sofa shown on the opposite page, but when I tried to shrink the dovetailed sofa on p. 84, the result was an ugly box. A three-seat version of the sofa shown in the photo was also a failure—it was strong, but it looked weak because the end frames were too far apart.

I mention my failures not to discourage people from modifying the designs in this book, but to point out the pitfalls of modification. Remember that the *proportions* are what matter. It is hardly noticeable in the photos, but the parts of the sofa frames are ⅛ in. thicker than those of the chair, in proportion to the increased length of the sofa. Changing one dimension inevitably leads to changing others, and before you realize it, the force of the original idea has evaporated and been replaced by a cloud of uneasy compromise.

Even a small sofa can be awkward to move or store, so a knock-down detail is shown in the plan drawings. The chair and sofa constructions are so similar that I'll describe the chair here, and mention the sofa alterations briefly where appropriate. (The dimensions of the sofa are indicated in brackets on the drawing.)

Construction

Any straight-grained hardwood or strong softwood such as Douglas fir, is suitable for the chair or sofa, but consider how the wood will look combined with both the canvas and the fabric for the cushion covers. I like black canvas because it doesn't show dirt, goes with any wood (except walnut) and looks well with brass grommets and white lacing.

Starting with rough-sawn 6/4 stock, cut out the pieces for the end frames and seat-support frame. If you are making the knock-down version, be sure to add 3 in. to the long seat-support rails for the tenons. Plane all these pieces 1¼ in. thick for the chair, 1⅜ in. thick for the sofa.

The end frames are bridle-jointed at each corner. Bridle joints are best cut on the tablesaw using a carbide blade to ensure accuracy. (See p. 36 for how to cut a bridle joint on the tablesaw.) A mitered-dovetail bridle joint does the same job, but more elegantly. I'll describe how to make this joint by hand.

Begin by marking the faces and edges of each pair to be joined (shown by the dotted lines in the sketch at right). Knife-mark the lines of the mitered shoulders on both faces of each piece and pencil them across the edges, but don't saw the miters yet. Next, mark the socket for the pin on both edges and the end of the horizontal piece *(A)*. Make the cheek cuts with a tenon saw, clear the waste with a coping saw and chisel in from the line *Y-Y* on both edges. Lay piece *A* firmly on the end of *B* and mark the pin with a scribe or thin-bladed knife. Carry the lines down the inside edge and make the cheek cuts on piece *B* with the tenon saw. Angle the sawblade parallel to the miter lines—be sure not to cut beyond the miter lines on the edges.

Saw the mitered shoulders on both pieces and assemble the joint without glue. I saw a little to the waste side of the line, push the joint together and then run a fine saw into the joint, on both sides, until the miter closes. You can also use a chisel or shoulder plane to fit the joint.

The middle rail of each end frame is stub-tenoned into the two verticals. When those joints have been cut and fitted, you're ready to glue up the end frames. When gluing mitered-dovetail bridle joints, put glue on the miters as well as on the pins and tails. Pull all the joints together with pipe or bar clamps. Clamp the cheeks of the bridle joints lightly with padded C-clamps. Then remove all the clamps, check the frame for square and make sure the joints are tight. Before the glue is bone-hard, flush off the surfaces with a sharp plane.

The long rails of the seat-support frame are through-tenoned to the middle rail of each end frame. Mark the positions of the through mortises accurately on both faces of each middle rail with a knife. Bore out the waste, then chisel to the knife marks working from both faces. Cut the through tenons on the long rails to fit the mortises. Remember that the knock-down version requires long tenons.

The short rails of the seat-support frame are stub-tenoned into the long rails. Dry-assemble the long rails and end frames—the distance between the long rails equals the shoulder-to-shoulder length of the short rails. Glue the short rails in place, making sure the support frame is square.

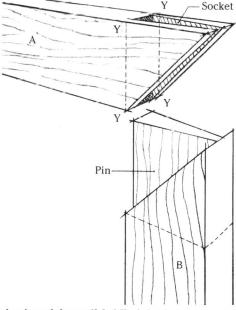

A mitered-dovetail bridle joint is a more elegant alternative to a simple bridle joint for the corners of the end frames.

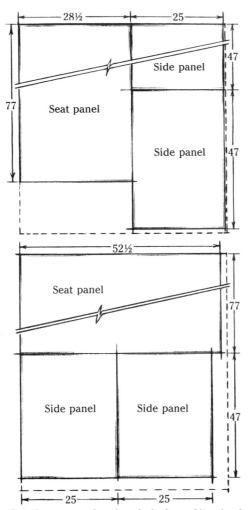

Cut the canvas for the chair from 2¾ yd. of 54-in. or 60-in.-wide material, laid out as shown at top. For the sofa, you'll need 3½ yd. of material, laid out as shown at bottom.

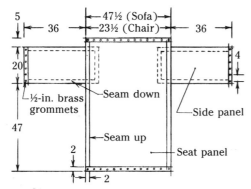

Sew the three pieces of canvas together as shown so only the smooth side of the seams will show on the chair.

The back rail rests in semicircular cutouts in the end frames and is held in place by the tension of the canvas. I now prefer the lacing pattern shown in the drawing on the opposite page because it doesn't pull the corners in toward the center.

The top rail at the back of the chair, is not fastened, but rests in semicircular cutouts in the end frames and is held in place by the tension of the canvas. To make the cutouts, clamp the top rails of each frame together, edge to edge, and bore a single 1¼-in. hole. (Remember to use a backing piece to prevent the wood from splintering as the bit exits the hole.) The top edge of the top back rail is a half round along its whole length. Saw off the waste and shape the two round ends of the rail with a rasp or file so they fit loosely into the cutouts.

The arrises on the end frames and seat-support frame must be rounded to keep the canvas from wearing. I use a router with a carbide rounding-over bit that is fitted with a ball-bearing pilot. (I like to set the bit to cut an arc, rather than a full round. This leaves two arrises where the arc intersects the flat surfaces. These arrises catch the light and give a crisper appearance.) If you make the rounds by hand, use a block plane or a wood file and sandpaper. Stop the rounds where the long rails will join the middle rails—otherwise, the round will go right through the joint when the chair is assembled.

The two end frames are glued to the seat-support frame, and the through tenons wedged. The wedges should be vertical, at right angles to the grain of the middle rail.

For the knock-down version, you'll need to make wedges and tapered mortises in the long through tenons. Make the wedges 1 in. overlong so they can be trimmed later. Assemble the seat-support frame and end frames, lay a wedge on the protruding tenons and mark the slope with a pencil. Disassemble and mark the end of the mortise that extends into the rail, as shown in the plan drawings. Mark the openings on the top and bottom of the tenon with a marking gauge. Bore out most of the waste, working from both edges of the tenon, and chisel to the lines. Assemble the chair, drive in the wedges and mark them for trimming. The top of each wedge should project slightly more than the bottom—they invariably get driven lower.

The frame is complete now, but you need to add canvas and cushions to sit on. The canvas is wrapped around the frame and laced across the back and under the seat. Cushions are then placed on top of the canvas panels, and can be covered with removable slipcovers of wool, linen or heavy cotton, depending on the climate and your personal preferences.

Canvas—For the chair, you will need about 2¾ yd. of 54-in. or 60-in.-wide canvas. I use 18-oz. treated chair duck, but this is too heavy a material for a domestic sewing machine, especially when doubled or tripled, so I would recommend having the canvas sewn by an upholsterer, tent and awning manufacturer, or a sail maker. For the sofa, you will need 3½ yd. of fabric of the same width.

Use the layout patterns in the sketch at the top of the facing page to cut out the canvas pieces. All dimensions allow for a 2½-in. hem allowance. Once the pieces are cut out, finish the edges by turning under ½ in. of the edge and machine-basting it to hold it in place. Then turn the edge 2 in. under and stitch the hem, making sure to secure the loose threads at each end by backstitching or tying knots.

Now attach the three pieces as shown in the sketch at the bottom of the opposite page, making sure to sew with the seams of the side panels facing down, those of the seat panel facing up. Position the side panels 5 in. from the top edge of the seat panel. The seat panel should overlap the ends of the side panels by about 6 in. Tape or baste the pieces together to prevent shifting while sewing.

To make reinforced holes for the nylon lacing, you'll need a ½-in. punch-and-die set and about three dozen ½-in. brass grommets (five dozen for the sofa). Use the punch-and-die set to insert the grommets through the hemmed edges of the canvas pieces. The grommets should be positioned at a distance of 4 in. on center, as shown in the sketch.

You'll also need 45 ft. of ¼-in. lacing (90 ft. for the sofa) to secure the canvas across the back and under the seat of the chair frame. The lacing must be made of nylon or an equivalent. Don't use cotton clothesline or sash cord because neither is strong enough. The sketch at top right shows the lacing pattern.

Cushions—The cushions are made of 4-in.-thick, medium-density polyurethane foam, 1-in. Dacron batting, an undercover of medium-weight, unbleached muslin and a slipcover. Make a full-size pattern in heavy brown wrapping paper for each cushion, as shown in the sketch at bottom right. Transfer the patterns to the foam using a soft pencil or tailor's chalk. If you don't have a bandsaw or electric hot-wire foam cutter, the easiest way to cut polyurethane foam is with a fine panel saw or hacksaw. I've been told that an electric carving knife will work, too, but I've never

tried it. Support the foam on the edge of a piece of plywood and saw with light strokes along the lines, keeping the sawblade vertical.

Dacron batting will give the cushions some extra bulk and make them less hard—both on the seat and on the eye. You will need about 5½ yd. of batting at least 40 in. wide for the chair, 8¾ yd. of the same width for the sofa. For extra comfort, the cushions are padded a little more on one side than on the other, so using the same patterns used for the foam, cut out one piece of batting for each cushion with scissors. Lay this piece on the side of the foam that a person will sit on or lean against (not the side that will be next to the canvas). Then wrap each cushion once with the batting around its narrowest width. To cover the unwrapped ends of the foam, either cut the batting overwide by 8 in. (4 in. for each side) and fold it over the ends like wrapping a parcel, or cut separate pieces of batting and spray-glue them in place with foam or fabric adhesive. You may want to keep all the batting in place with the spray glue while making the muslin undercovers.

Undercovers—Muslin undercovers are essential. Without them, it is practically impossible to remove and replace the slipcover (the outer cover) for cleaning. Undercovers and slipcovers are made in the same way: Two fabric panels are joined by another strip of fabric (called boxing) that runs around the edge of the cushion.

To undercover all the cushions for the chair, you will require 3½ yd. of muslin 45 in. wide. For the sofa, you will need 4¼ yd. of the same width. Make new patterns for the undercover panels by laying each original brown-paper pattern on a piece of newspaper and tracing around it with a felt pen. Draw a second line ½ in. outside the pattern, and a third one ½ in. outside that. Cut the newspaper pattern around the third line. (The second line allows for the extra bulk of the batting, the third line allows enough material to make the ½-in. seam).

Fold the fabric in half along the width so that, as you cut out each pattern, you will be cutting out the two pieces of fabric you need for each cushion. Pin all the newspaper patterns to the muslin, laying them out in the most efficient way to avoid waste. Next, cut the boxing strips 4 in. wide and a little longer than the perimeter of each cushion. They don't have to be one long piece.

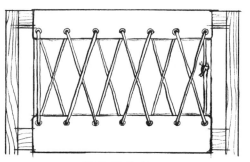

Back of chair

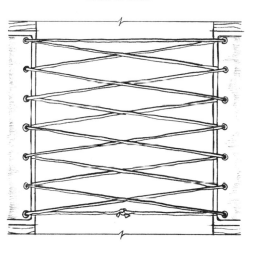

Underside of seat
Lace canvas on the frame using this pattern.

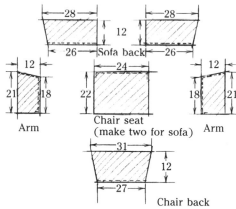

Use these patterns to cut out foam for the cushions. Muslin undercover patterns are 2 in. larger, slipcover patterns are 1 in. larger. The broken lines indicate zipper placement.

If you are an old hand with a sewing machine, machine-stitch the undercovers directly, sewing ½ in. in from the edge of the muslin (the middle line of your pattern). This is best done by putting a piece of tape ½ in. from the machine's needle, if your machine is not equipped with a seam-allowance gauge. Sew the boxing all the way around one panel, putting right sides of the fabric (the sides that are going to show) together. Then start from a corner and sew the other panel, leaving one long edge unsewn. If you are a novice, pin or baste (hand-stitch) the boxing to the panels before machining. Turn the covers inside out and insert the foam wrapped with batting. The open edge is turned under and blind-hemstitched by hand.

Slipcovers—As in choosing wood, certain criteria apply when picking fabric for slipcovers. Leaving aside matters of color and pattern, you must choose a strong fabric that will not stretch in use—which means you need a tight weave—or shrink when washed, or wear too quickly. Think of the climate, too. Wool is fine in Vermont, but it would be a poor choice for the heat and humidity of a Washington summer, where linen or heavy cotton would be preferable. Remember that light colors need cleaning more often than dark colors, blues fade in bright sunlight, and some synthetic fabrics not only can melt but are flammable. The slipcovers require roughly the same amount of material as the muslin undercovers. Make sure the fabric is preshrunk. If it is not, you must wash it once to shrink it, then iron it to make the sewing easier.

Cut ½ in. off the perimeter of the newspaper patterns used for the muslin covers (to the middle line). Then pin the patterns to the slipcover fabric and cut out the pieces, using the same layout as for cutting the muslin, and cut out enough 4-in. strips for the boxing. Fabric, like wood, has grain. The grain runs in the same direction as the selvage (finished edge) of the fabric, which is usually along the length of the fabric as it comes from the store. Position all the pieces so that the grain is running the same way. (If you are using a striped or print fabric, you will have to pay particular attention to positioning the pieces, and may need to use more fabric.) You will now be sewing on the innermost line of the pattern, leaving the excess as seam allowance.

The alert reader will notice that the muslin-covered cushions are ½ in. bigger than the slipcovers. Like putting a sausage in its skin, this helps keep the slipcovers tight and free from wrinkles. Wrinkles in the muslin will not show through the slipcover—the muslin is too thin.

The slipcovers are made exactly the same way as the undercovers, except a zipper is added to the slipcovers. The zipper must be placed where it will not show, and the best placement is indicated by the dotted lines on the sketch at the bottom of p. 81. To install the zipper, take a piece of boxing 1 in. longer than the zipper and fold it in half on its long axis, wrong sides (the sides of the fabric that won't show) together. Make a crease—ironing helps if the fabric won't stay creased. Unzip the zipper and lay one strip along the crease so that the tops of the zipper teeth are aligned with the folded edge of the boxing. Pin or tailor-tack it in place, then stitch it using the zipper foot of your sewing machine. Now take another piece of 4-in. boxing, crease it lengthwise, and stitch it to the other side of the zipper. Zip the zipper and you will have a 4-in. strip of boxing, double thickness, with a zipper running neatly up the middle.

When sewing this piece of boxing to the cushion pieces, remember to face the zipper in. Then, when the slipcover is turned inside out, the zipper will be on the right side.

Our local professional upholsterer covers the two ends of the zipper by overlapping the adjacent boxing, but he pointed out that you can simply join the zipper ends to the boxing with a neat seam.

He also said that it is a good practice to sew the seams twice, once along a line ½ in. from the edge and again as near to the edge as you can manage. This will prevent the material from unraveling at the seam if roughly laundered.

Chair and Sofa

Scale: ⅛ in. = 1 in.
Details: ½ in = 1 in.

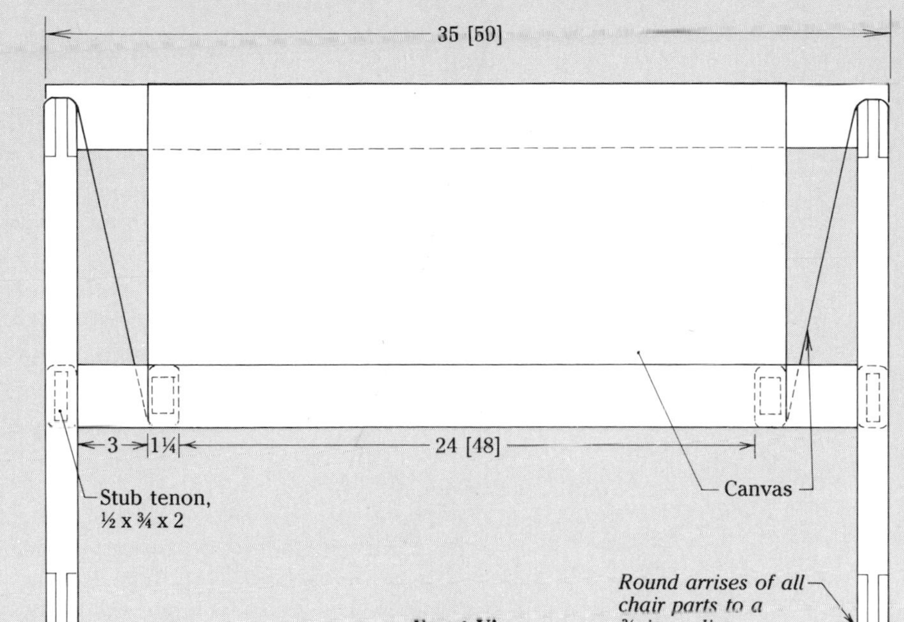
35 [59]
3
1¼
24 [48]
Stub tenon,
½ x ¾ x 2
Canvas
Round arrises of all chair parts to a ⅜-in. radius.
1¼
Front View

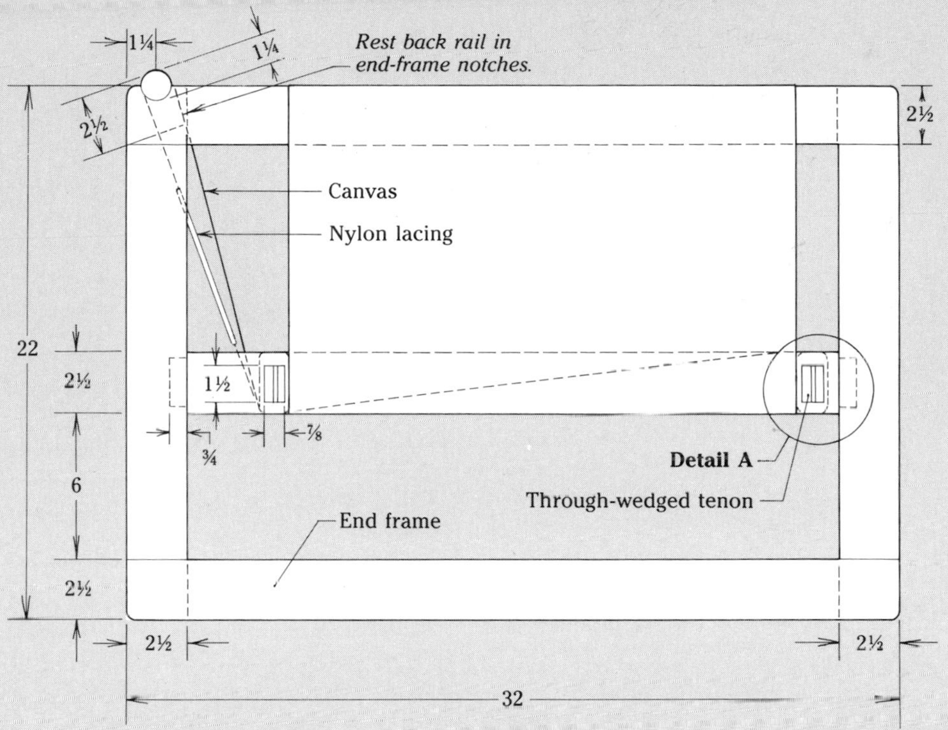
1¼
1¼
Rest back rail in end-frame notches.
2½
2½
Canvas
Nylon lacing
22
2½
2½
1½
¾
⅞
6
2½
Detail A
Through-wedged tenon
End frame
2½
2½
32
Side View

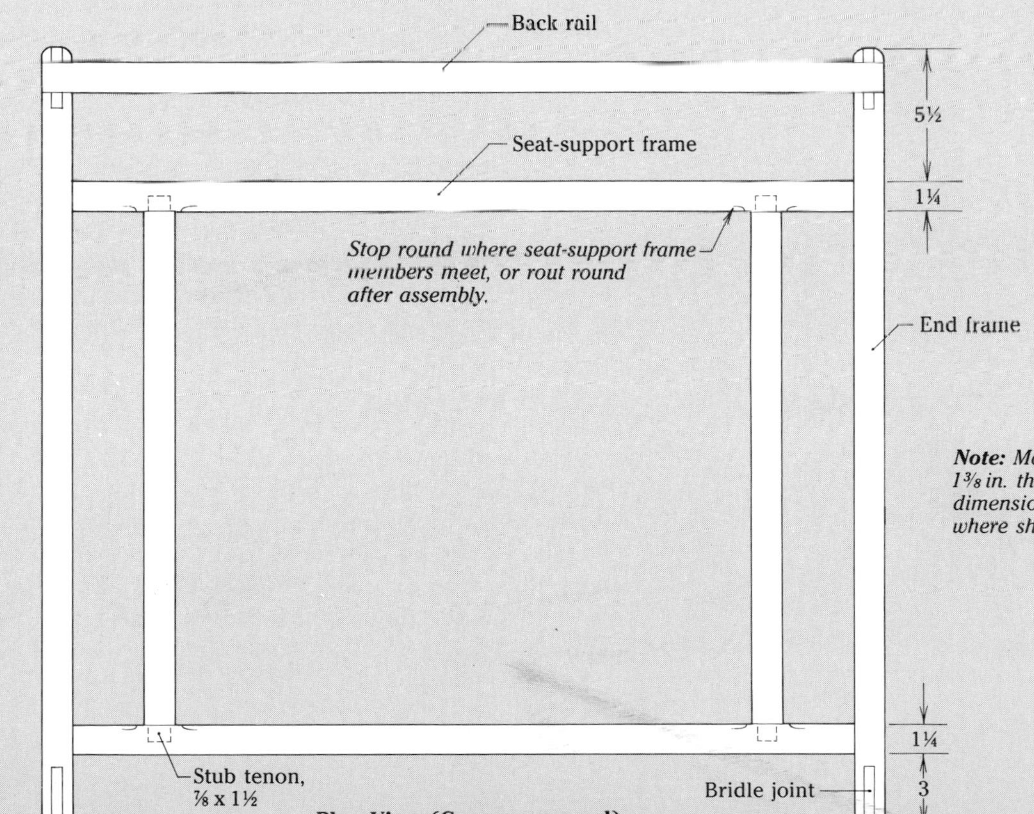
Back rail
5½
Seat-support frame
1¼
Stop round where seat-support frame members meet, or rout round after assembly.
End frame
1¼
Stub tenon,
⅞ x 1½
Bridle joint
3
Plan View (Canvas removed)

Detail A:
Knock-Down Alternative to Through-Wedged Tenon

Side View
(Section through rail)

Note: Make sofa frame members 1⅜ in. thick. Other sofa and chair dimensions are the same, except where shown in brackets for sofa.

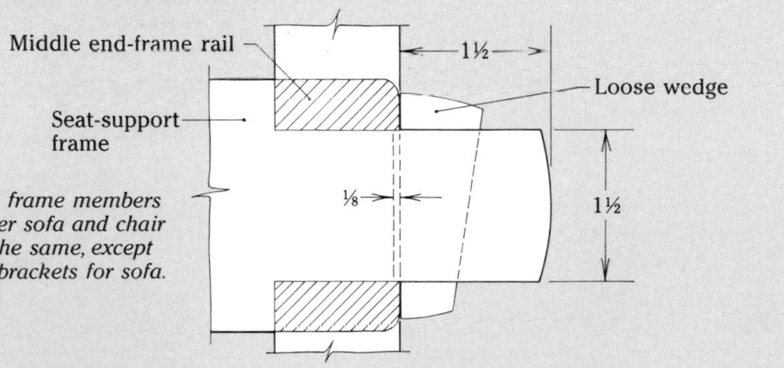
Middle end-frame rail
1½
Loose wedge
Seat-support frame
⅛
1½

Plan View
(Section through rail)

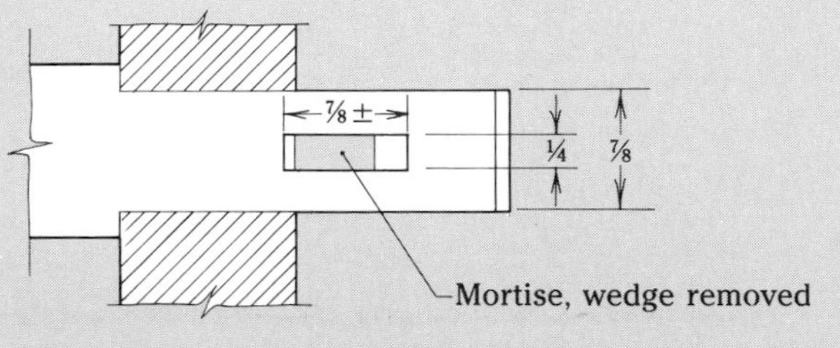
⅞ ±
¼
⅞
Mortise, wedge removed

Dovetailed Sofa

This sofa is made up of two assemblies: An internal frame is tenoned to a dovetailed carcase. The legs are attached to the frame, so the weight of the sofa's users is transmitted directly to the floor. This sofa is a heavy, bulky piece of furniture, so a knock-down alternative is included.

The sofa is long enough to be used as a bed when the back cushions are removed. The seat slopes back gently and the cushions are supported on Pirelli webbing (rubber straps reinforced with nylon) held in tension by the frame. (See Appendix 5 for sources of supply.) The clips on the ends of the Pirelli webbing engage in slots in the frame—tension in the strap and firmness of the seat can be adjusted by moving the clips to a different slot.

Construction

The back and ends of the sofa shown in the photo were made from a single mahogany board, 22 in. wide. Unfortunately, such boards are rare, so the back and ends usually have to be joined together of narrower stock.

Some woods, notably walnut, are more expensive to buy in lengths long enough for the back. I have made several sofa backs using walnut shorts, 18 in. to 24 in. long and 3 in. to 4 in. wide. (Shorts, a trade designation, are a relatively inexpensive way to buy hardwood.) This method is strong enough if you lay out the boards carefully, staggering the end-grain-to-end-grain joints as much as possible (see Appendix 2). I wouldn't join the ends up in the same way because the sofa might begin to look a bit restless. If you join long boards to make the back and ends, when gluing up, take care that the curved cutouts on the ends will not expose any dowels or splines.

The back and front are ⅞ in. thick; the ends are 1⅛ in. thick. Marking and cutting the dovetail joints is awkward because of the size and weight of the back. I have a trapdoor in the floor of my workshop and can cut the dovetails on the long pieces at bench height. You can also fix the pieces vertically in the vise and cut the tails while standing or kneeling on the benchtop. To mark the pins on the ends, clamp the front and back in place, and knife-mark all four sets of pins at the same time.

In the knock-down version, the dovetailing is replaced by through tenons with loose wedges, and the

Cutting the dovetails for this sofa may be awkward, but the result is strong and pleasing to the eye. The seat cushions can extend over the front rail, as shown here, or sit behind the rail as shown in the plan drawings.

one-piece back is replaced by two horizontal rails with vertical slats. (I have never made a knock-down sofa with a solid back, because a 22-in.-wide board is unlikely to stay flat during transit or storage, and any warping would make reassembly difficult.) Because the knock-down joints have to withstand the stress of assembly and disassembly, this sofa needs beefier ends—make them 1⅜ in. thick. The front rail and two back rails should be ⅞ in. thick, and slats ½ in. thick. (See p. 80 for how to cut and fit the mortise and loose wedge of the knock-down joints.) I make the groove for the slats in the top rail ½ in. deep so that the slats can be slipped in after the rails are in place. Round the meeting edges of the slats (as done for the cradle, p. 25). If you don't make cutouts, groove the edges of the slats and add a loose spline to keep them aligned.

The internal frame of the sofa is identical for both versions. It consists of two grooved battens screwed to the ends, and two long, grooved boards attached to three supports. The Pirelli webbing is stretched between the grooved battens and grooved boards.

The supports are mortised into the front and back (the front rail and bottom back rail for the knock-down version). Cut the mortises before gluing up the dovetailed carcase—a double mortise in the front, a single in the back. Use blind mortises as shown in the plan drawings, or through mortises for wedged tenons. The tenons will be cut to fit them later. Finish-sand the front, back and ends, and glue up the carcase. Use notched clamping blocks, as described on p. 31, to pull the dovetails tight. Remember to check for square by measuring the diagonals.

Each of the three supports consists of two crosspieces and two short blocks. Make the blocks first, cutting a double stub tenon on the front block, and a single tenon on the back block. Glue the blocks into the mortises, making sure they are at right angles to the rail and back.

Next, cut the six crosspieces to length and joint one edge. The crosspieces are wider at the front than the back so that the seat will slope back, and they are curved in between so that the cushions can't bottom out on them. Lay out and bandsaw the profile on one crosspiece and use it as a template for the others. (As a precaution, I round the arrises of the curved crosspieces; that way, there will be no serious injury if a child jumps on the sofa and strikes the arris.) Fasten pairs of crosspieces to the blocks. I glue them first and then, after removing the clamps, put in a few countersunk, flat-head screws. (The front rail, bottom

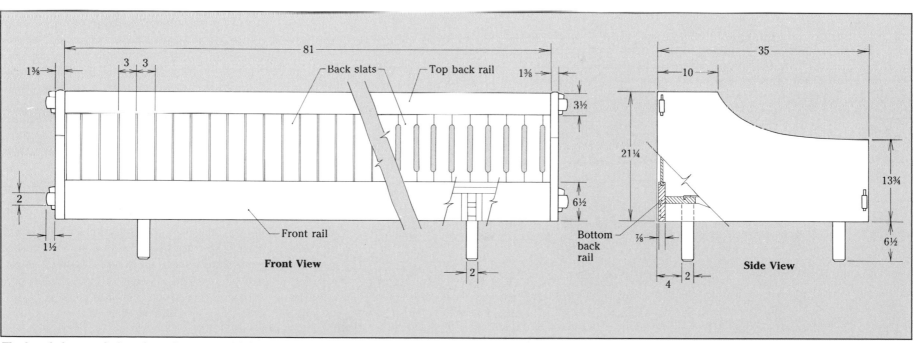

The knock-down sofa has through tenons with loose wedges, and a back made up of two rails and vertical slats. The construction of the internal frame is the same as for the dovetailed sofa. The ends are grooved to allow the slats to move with seasonal humidity changes.

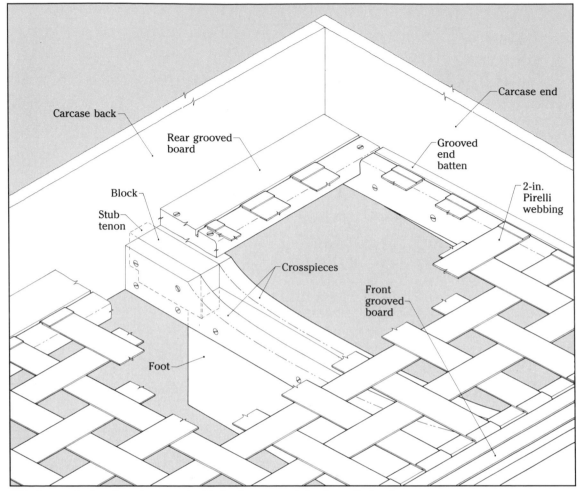

Carcase back

Rear grooved
board

Carcase end

Grooved
end
batten

Block

Stub
tenon

2-in.
Pirelli
webbing

Crosspieces

Front
grooved
board

Foot

This isometric drawing shows an inside back corner of the dovetailed sofa.

back rail and three supports make a permanent unit on the knock-down sofa.)

The long, grooved boards and end battens will be heavily stressed and must be made of strong wood such as oak or ash. The battens slope down from the front of the sofa to the back, and are screwed, but not glued, to the ends. The ends of the grooved boards are screwed to notches cut in the battens and to the support crosspieces. The grooves are single ⅛-in. saw cuts, ⅜ in. deep; angle them at about 15° to help prevent the clips on the ends of the webbing from jumping out. The long front board has three grooves 1 in. apart so the tension can be adjusted. Round the arrises of the grooved boards and battens to prevent the webbing from wearing on them.

The sofa can be supported by legs or runners—legs are shown on the knock-down version, runners on the dovetailed. Runners are less damaging to carpets and make it easier for one person to slide the sofa around. Legs, tapered or straight, make the sofa appear less bulky and heavy. Both are glued and screwed to the crosspieces of the supports at each end of the sofa. Runners have shoulders front and back that engage the support blocks. Legs should have shoulders that engage the crosspieces.

Cut the short pieces of webbing so it takes a moderate pull to get them to the first slot in the long board. Use a metal vise or a hammer and hardwood block to close the clips on the ends of the webbing. The tension can be increased by moving the clips to the second or third slots. The long straps should have as much tension as you can comfortably get and should be woven in and out of the short ones.

The cushions can be made as described on pp. 81-82, altering the sizes to suit. Filling the rectangular back cushions with down, Dacron batting or cotton batting, instead of foam makes them softer. As the cushions are highly visible, the choice of fabric is crucial. I like corduroy. It wears well, has a texture that contrasts favorably with the smoothness of the wood and is available in a range of colorfast, strong colors. Some considerations to bear in mind when choosing upholstery fabrics are mentioned on p. 82.

Dovetailed Sofa

Scale: 1/16 in. = 1 in.
Details: 1/4 in. = 1 in.

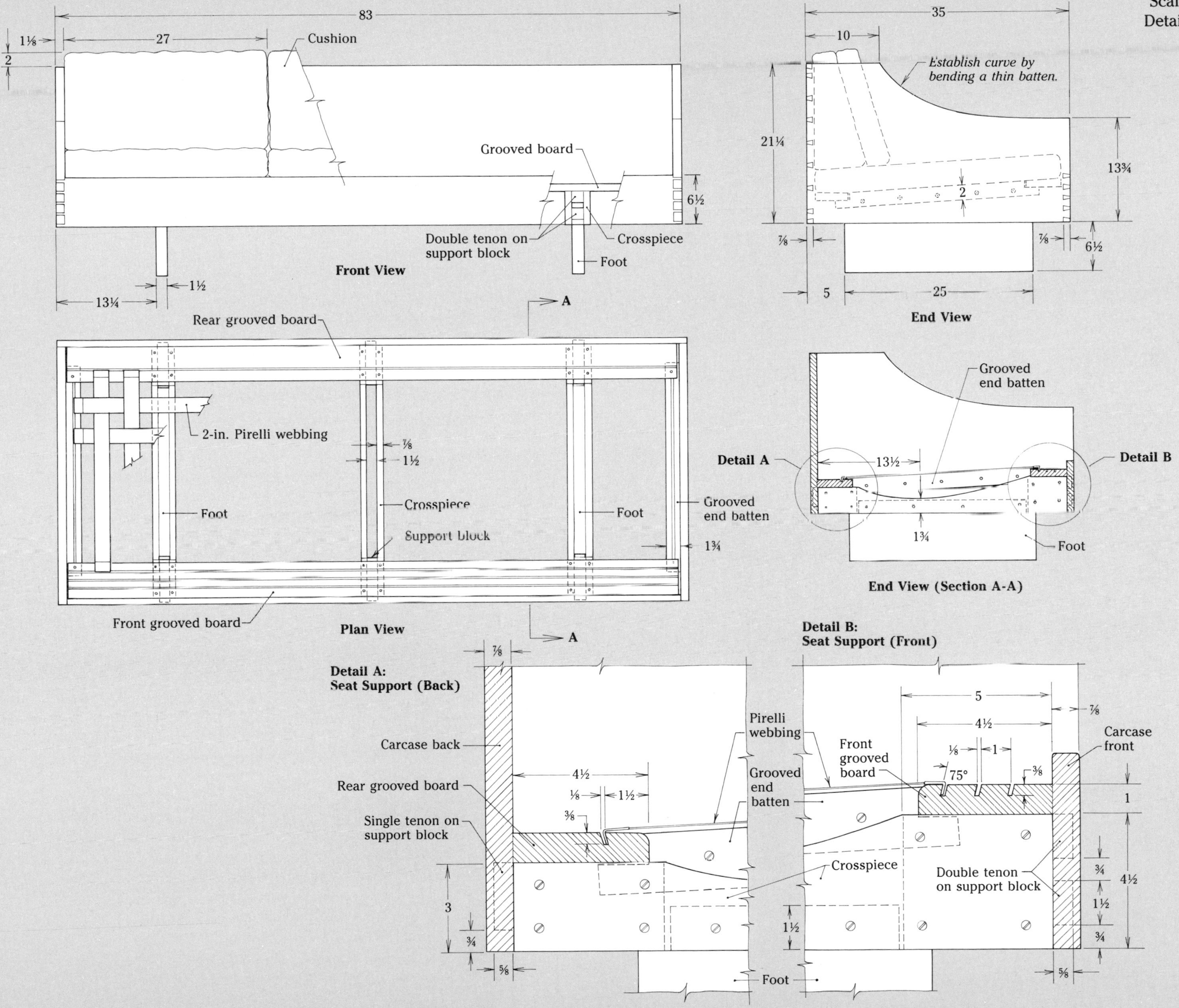

Front View

83

27

1 1/8

2

Cushion

Grooved board

6 1/2

Double tenon on support block

Crosspiece

Foot

13 1/4

1 1/2

End View

35

10

Establish curve by bending a thin batten.

21 1/4

13 3/4

2

7/8

7/8

5

25

6 1/2

Plan View

Rear grooved board

2-in. Pirelli webbing

7/8

1 1/2

Foot

Crosspiece

Support block

Foot

Grooved end batten

1 3/4

Front grooved board

A

A

End View (Section A-A)

Grooved end batten

Detail A

Detail B

13 1/2

1 3/4

Foot

**Detail A:
Seat Support (Back)**

7/8

Carcase back

Rear grooved board

Single tenon on support block

4 1/2

1/8

1 1/2

3/8

3

3/4

5/8

Pirelli webbing

Grooved end batten

Grooved end batten

Crosspiece

Foot

1 1/2

**Detail B:
Seat Support (Front)**

5

4 1/2

1/8

1

75°

3/8

Front grooved board

Carcase front

Double tenon on support block

1

3/4

4 1/2

1 1/2

3/4

7/8

5/8

The Dining Room

Dining Tables

6

Notes on Dining Tables

Faced with an unfurnished house, many people would make a bed first, then a dining table and chairs. I don't think it's accidental that the old inns advertised "Bed & Board" and not the other way around. From sleeping to eating seems a natural progression, and so I will discuss dining tables next.

Sitting down to share a meal together is an ancient custom, but sitting down on chairs to eat at a table is a relatively recent innovation. Neither the Greeks nor the Romans used dining tables, but preferred instead to be served while reclining on low couches. The Romans left their mark on Britain during their 400-year occupation of the island, but took this custom back to Italy with them.

Medieval inns and lodging houses provided the traveler with "Bed & Board for Man & Beaste." The word *board* refers to the early eating tables, massive affairs made of hewn or riven planks laid across movable supports called trestles. Known as tre-style, or trestle tables, they could be easily dismantled and set against the wall after the meal, to free the floor for dancing or other entertainment.

These trestle tables were narrow because it was the custom for family and guests to sit only along one side and be served across the table from the other side. Also, the number of persons that had to be seated for meals in a great medieval household might be very large. The oak table, shown in the top photo on the opposite page, is 27 ft. long and 3 ft. wide. Even longer tables were made—in 1373 two 40-ft.-long trestle tables were made for Argilly Castle in Scotland.

Tables with tops fixed to heavy frame bases, as shown in the photo at bottom right, were also common throughout the Middle Ages. Known as *tables dormant,* to distinguish them from the more-movable trestle tables, they indicated wealth and an open-handed hospitality. The draw-top table in the photo at bottom left evolved from the *table dormant* in the sixteenth century. This convenient table could be extended to nearly twice its length. Extending tables soon relegated the cumbersome trestle table to the kitchen and servants' quarters.

By the middle of the seventeenth century, the prototypes of most of today's eating tables had appeared, including drop-leaf tables, gate-leg tables, and various flip-top tables that converted to seats. Heavy oak furniture gradually gave way to lighter but equally durable constructions. During the eighteenth century, mahogany came into vogue, and although the same basic forms persisted, dining tables developed a refinement and grace that matched the elegance of the society.

Four oak boards, each 27 ft. long, comprise the top of this massive trestle table, which is thought to date from the fifteenth century. The table is in the Great Hall of Penshurst Place, Kent, England.

Fully extended, this draw-top table, built around 1600, could seat a sizable group for a banquet. Closed, it could be moved out of the way to make room for entertainment.

When supported by sturdy frames, tabletops can be made of thinner wood. This mid-seventeenth-century oak table, has a two-board top and its rails and legs are joined by pegged mortises and tenons.

Two Round Tables

Scale: 1/16 in. = 1 in.

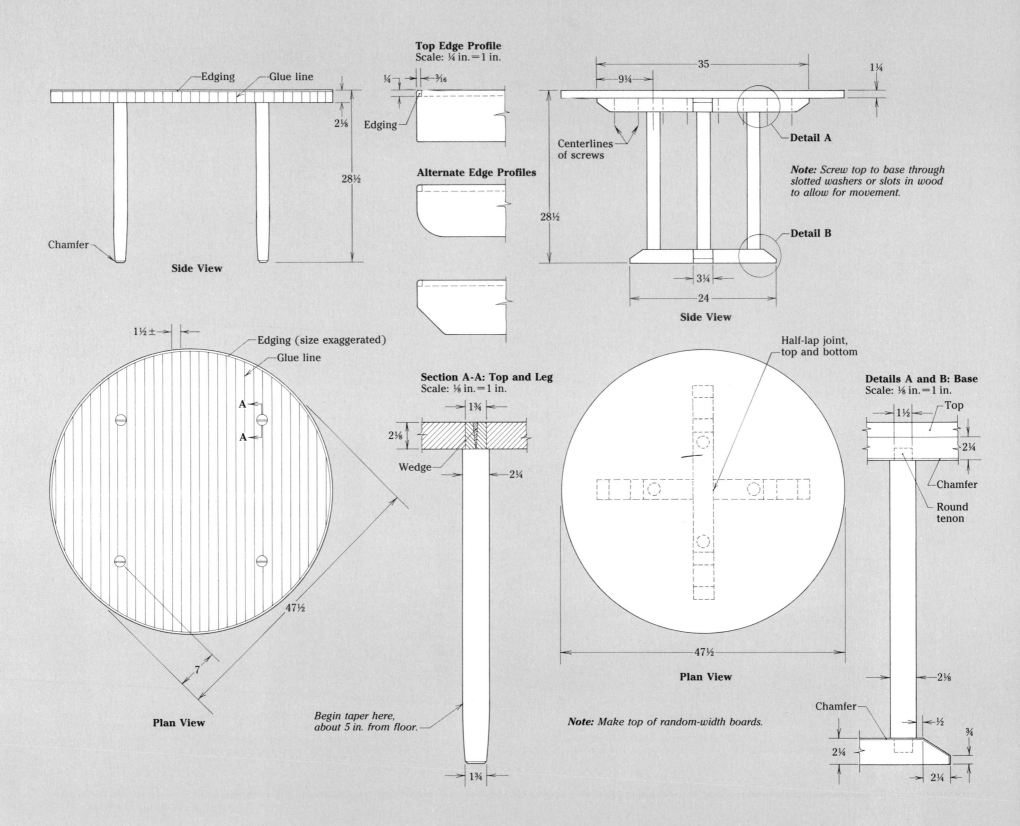

Edging — Glue line

2⅛

28½

Chamfer

Side View

Top Edge Profile
Scale: ¼ in. = 1 in.

¼ — 3/16

Edging

Alternate Edge Profiles

35 — 1¼

9¼

Centerlines of screws

Detail A

Note: Screw top to base through slotted washers or slots in wood to allow for movement.

Detail B

3¼

24

Side View

28½

1½ ±

Edging (size exaggerated)
Glue line

A

A

47½

7

Plan View

Section A-A: Top and Leg
Scale: ⅛ in. = 1 in.

1¾

2⅛

Wedge — 2¼

Begin taper here, about 5 in. from floor.

1¾

Half-lap joint, top and bottom

47½

Plan View

Note: Make top of random-width boards.

Details A and B: Base
Scale: ⅛ in. = 1 in.

1½ — Top

2¼

Chamfer

Round tenon

2⅛

Chamfer — ½

¾

2¼

2¼

Two Round Tables

I know that kitchens and dining rooms are now combined in many households, but to me there is still a real difference between the two rooms. I grew up in England in the 1930s, when it wasn't the custom for the young children of middle-class families to eat with their parents. Most of the time, we had our meals with the nanny in front of the coal fire in the nursery. We joined the grown-ups in the dining room only on special occasions, such as birthdays and Christmas, or for tea with a visiting great aunt, which was, at best, a dubious honor. We were on our best behavior, wore clean clothes, had hands and faces washed, kept elbows off the table, and didn't speak unless spoken to.

Times have changed, even in England, but a dining room to me still suggests a high degree of formality—an evening meal with guests, candles, wine and well-mannered children. The kitchen, on the other hand, suggests breakfasts and bustle, or jigsaw puzzles on a rainy afternoon. The round table in the photo at right is particularly suited to the kitchen; I think a kitchen table should be a straightforward, sturdy design, made out of solid wood, not veneer. It should be large enough to seat comfortably the number of people who usually sit down to a meal together, and must have a surface that doesn't have to be pampered. You shouldn't have to worry about ball-point pens, hot dishes or the eating habits of babies.

A kitchen is often a busy place with a lot of traffic, so tables with corners can be harmful, especially to young children whose heads are at tabletop height. Round tables are also more flexible with regard to seating than a square or rectangular table—an extra person can usually be squeezed in around the circumference. They are also very easy to move. Even a heavy round table can be laid on its edge (with suitable padding) and rolled from one place to another by one person.

Round tables, however, don't work well when they're very large or very small. A diameter less than 3 ft. doesn't provide enough room for dishes and the table settings. A diameter over 5½ ft. is awkward because things must be passed around the perimeter, rather than across the table. A table 4 ft. to 4½ ft. in diameter will seat four people comfortably and six in a pinch. A 5-ft.-dia. table will seat six people comfortably and eight in a pinch. Round tables are more

comfortable if their legs are set back at least 7 in. from the edge of the tabletop.

Construction

I made the kitchen table shown above from air-dried oak and I used dark walnut for the thin strip of edging. It is a very simple table—just four turned legs, through-tenoned into the top, which is 4 ft. in diameter. The top is glued up of narrow strips, which won't cup or twist as wide boards might—if one wide board twists, the whole table will be distorted because there is no underframe.

To make the top, start with rough-sawn boards, 1¼-in. thick or thicker. Joint one edge of each board, then rip off as many 2½-in.-wide strips as the width allows. (The top is made by gluing these strips face to

This dark walnut edging strip contrasts with the golden brown of the oak top. The tenon wedge, which must be at a right angle to the grain of the top, is also walnut.

face, making a 2⅛-in.-thick top when it is planed to final thickness. The thick top is necessary because the legs are tenoned directly into it.) When you have enough strips, joint one of the 2½-in.-wide faces of each strip, then plane the opposite face until it is clean and the strip is uniformly thick. The finished thickness of the strips may vary, but a little variety here is nothing to be afraid of.

Lay all the strips, edge up, on a bench, and arrange them so that the different colors and grain patterns will be evenly distributed on the tabletop. I cut the strips for this particular table from boards that had been sawn out of one log, so there is little color variation. If a strip is noticeably different from its neighbors, it can spoil the look of a large surface. (Furniture makers call such boards strangers.) Once the strips are arranged, mark them with a colored crayon so they can be glued up in the right order—a large *V* that crosses all the edges works well.

Glue the strips together in three or four sections, depending on the width of your planer (mine is 18 in. wide, so I glued up three sections, each 16 in. wide). Dowels aren't needed—they lengthen assembly time, and the strips that slip a little will be planed flat later. Remember that the wide faces form the joints, the narrow edges form the top and bottom surfaces.

Plane the glued-up sections 2⅛ in. thick, and joint the edges that will be glued together. I put a few dowels in these edge joints, because if a section slides up or down, a great deal of hand-planing will be necessary to level the top. Keep the dowels well away from the ends so there is no danger of finding one when bandsawing the top round. It's almost as disconcerting to saw through an unexpected dowel as to bite into an apple and find half a worm.

Clean off the hardened, squeezed-out glue with a plane and scraper, then draw a circle on the underside of the tabletop with trammels or a beam compass. If the circle touches one edge, it will be easy to start the bandsaw cut. Mark the center with a punch so it can be easily located later.

I bandsaw circular tops of all sizes with the aid of an auxiliary table. Rig up a flat surface next to, and even with, the bandsaw table. A heavy table raised to the correct height will work, or a piece of plywood or particleboard laid across two sawhorses—weight the sawhorses with concrete blocks so they're stable. Drive a 12d or 16d common nail into the surface of the auxiliary table, perpendicular to the bandsaw

blade and the radius of the tabletop away from the blade. Cut off the head of the nail about ⅜ in. above the surface and file a point on the nail. Pivoting the tabletop on the nail as you turn it into the bandsaw blade will accurately cut a circle.

When working alone with a heavy tabletop, it's difficult to position the center of the top on the nail, so I make a template to help. Drill a hole of the same diameter as the nail in a small piece of light sheet metal. Tack the metal to the underside of the tabletop so that the hole coincides with the center of the circle. The metal protects the wood from the nail as you slide the top around to get the nail positioned in the hole. Press the point of the nail into the wood and cut the circle. For a thick top like this, use your widest bandsaw blade. (If you don't have a bandsaw, cut the circle with a bowsaw or saber saw.)

You can use the same type of auxiliary-table-and-pivot setup with a stationary disc sander to clean up the bandsaw marks on the edge of the tabletop. A spokeshave will also do the job. You can leave the edge square, or shape it as shown in the plan drawings. The shaped edges are more graceful, and make the top appear thinner.

The edging strip, shown in the photo at left, isn't essential, but it relieves the plainness of the design and, by contrast, enhances the color and grain pattern of the top. Be wary, however, of too strident a contrast. The two woods must complement and not shout at each other. Oak with dark walnut edging, ash with light walnut edging, and cherry with walnut, rosewood or ebony edging are pleasing combinations. Edging should be straight-grained or it will break before making the bend.

For a 4-ft.-dia. table, you'll need about 13 ft. of edging. Plane a board to ⅜ in. thick, joint one edge and rip a strip ¼ in. wide off that edge on the tablesaw. This is a very narrow strip, so I use a wooden table insert with an opening just wide enough for the blade, and a push stick to finish the cut. It's helpful to have an assistant pull the strip through the saw after the cut is complete. When you have enough strips, join the strips into one long piece of edging with 1-in.-long scarf joints. (A scarf is the joining of long complementary bevels on the ends of two pieces.) Place the two pieces side by side, hold or clamp them tightly together and saw the bevel across both with a fine backsaw—there should be no need to plane the bevels. Glue and clamp the beveled ends together.

Rout the rabbet in the tabletop edge with a sharp, small-diameter, straight bit. Make a fence for the router from scrap wood that is about 1 ft. long and at least ½ in. thick, and curve one edge to the same radius as the tabletop. Screw the fence to the router base, or to the adjustable fence that comes with most routers, so that the curved edge will run against the tabletop edge. Adjust the fence and bit to cut a rabbet ³⁄₁₆ in. wide and ¼ in. deep. Practice on the edge of a curved piece of scrap until you can make a clean, unwavering rabbet. Then rout the rabbet on the tabletop.

Cut a scarf bevel on one end of the edging strip and, beginning with this scarfed end, glue the strip in place. Use an aliphatic resin glue like Titebond, which is stronger than white glue. Masking tape works much better than clamps to hold the strip in place. An extra pair of hands is helpful during gluing. One person pushes the edging tight in the rabbet, while the other fastens a strip of tape, putting as much tension on the tape as possible without breaking it. Space the tape strips at intervals of 1 in. or less.

When most of the strip is in place, bevel its second end to fit the first, then finish gluing the strip up to the bevels. Glue the two bevels to form the scarf and hold them in place with light pressure from a clamp across the diameter of the table—pad the clamp jaws so you don't damage the edging. Remove the tape after the glue has set. Make the edging flush with the face and edge of the tabletop using a sharp block plane on the face and a spokeshave on the edge.

For the legs you'll need turning blanks about 2½ in. square. If you glue up the blanks, cut the two halves from the same board so differences in grain and color will be minimal. Turning a single leg is simple, but turning four identical legs isn't quite as easy. You might want to make a plywood or Masonite pattern of the leg profile. With a little practice, though, you can turn all the legs accurately by eye.

Before turning the legs, make a template for the tenon by boring a 1¾-in. hole in a piece of ¾-in.-thick hardwood scrap, about 3 in. square. Place the template over the tailstock center (so you will be able to check the tenon diameter without removing the leg from the lathe) and fix the first leg between centers in the lathe, top end toward the tailstock.

Turn the blank to a 2¼-in. cylinder and taper the bottom end. Then, while the leg is turning, mark the tenon shoulder with a pencil. The tenon should be about ½ in. longer than the thickness of the tabletop

(the extra will be trimmed after assembly). Cut the shoulder with a parting tool, then as you turn the tenon to size, check its diameter with the template. Make it a sliding fit in the template, not a jam fit, and undercut the shoulder slightly, to ensure a tight joint. You can sand and finish the legs on the lathe.

The most accurate method of boring the round mortises in the tabletop is with a 1¾-in. Forstner bit or multi-spur bit (a Forstner-type bit with saw teeth around the rim) mounted in a drill press. Bore from the top face into a backing piece on the drill-press table. If you are using a hand drill, as you turn the bit, have a friend align it with a trysquare placed on the tabletop to ensure that the mortises will be at right angles to the top.

Cut the wedges from the same wood as the edging. The wedges must have straight grain running parallel to their length or they will crumple when driven. I make a jig to cut the ⅛-in. wedge slots in the tenons

Scale down the kitchen table, and you have a coffee table. This ebony table is 38 in. in diameter and 16½ in. high. The crossed wedges are holly.

on the tablesaw. Bore a 1¾-in.-dia. hole through a piece of 2-in.-thick scrap that is about 4 in. wide and 24 in. long. Place the edge of the jig against the rip fence, and adjust the fence so the saw will cut through the center of the hole. The blade should be high enough to cut almost to the tenon shoulders. Put the tenon in the hole and cut the slot. (The slot should coincide with the glue line of a glued-up leg.)

Insert the legs dry in the tabletop to check that all the tenons fit. Run a pencil mark around the ends of the tenons protruding above the table, then remove and trim each tenon to the line—now the wedge will expand the tenon inside the mortise, not above it. Put glue on the tenons and in the mortises, and assemble the top and legs. The wedge slots should be at right angles to the grain of the top, as shown in the photo on p. 94. Stand the table on a flat surface, dab glue in the slots and on the wedges and drive the wedges in with a few blows of a 16-oz. hammer.

Wipe off the glue and saw off the wedge. I have a little backsaw with an offset handle (called a cranked handle in some catalogs) that is ideal for this job, but a coping saw will work, too. The tenon will be just a little proud of the surface, so sever the tenon's fibers around its perimeter with a chisel, then plane the tenon flush with the top. Severing the outside fibers prevents the plane from breaking the fibers off below the surface of the top.

It is essential to apply the same number of coats of finish to both sides of an unbraced tabletop, whether the finish is polyurethane, lacquer or oil. If you don't finish the bottom surface, it will absorb or lose moisture faster than the top surface when the humidity changes, and the table will not stay flat. I recommend polyurethane for oak because water will penetrate an oil finish and stain the wood.

Pedestal base—The sturdy base of the round table shown in the photo at left prevents the tabletop from warping or twisting. Because this tabletop isn't structural, as is the other round top, it needn't be thick and can be made of wide, edge-joined boards. Though it could have been thinner, I made the top 1¼ in. thick to be in proportion with the heavy base. The widths of the boards should be in scale with each other and with the overall dimension of the top. A 10-in. board next to a 4-in. board looks wrong; rip the wider one into unequal halves—4½ in. and 5½ in., for example—and separate the halves. For a table this size, I select

boards between 6½ in. and 4½ in. wide.

I didn't edge this tabletop with a strip of contrasting wood, because there's enough going on visually without it. You could chamfer the edge of the top, which would complement the chamfer on the foot of the base.

The base consists of a foot and a top support, which are joined by four turned legs. Make the foot and top support using simple half-lap joints. The legs are tenoned into 1½-in.-dia. blind mortises—the extra strength of a through-wedged tenon isn't needed here. Lay out the mortise positions so that the mortises on the foot will align with those on the top support. (An easy way to do this is to align the half laps in each top support and foot pair, and mark the mortise positions simultaneously). Bore the mortises with a drill press or hand drill, as described on p. 95. Bevel the ends of the pieces and glue up the top support and foot, then chamfer the arrises of the foot with a spokeshave or router.

Next, bore clearance holes in the top support for the screws that secure the top. If you position the top support diagonally to the grain direction of the top, all the screws will need to allow for movement. If you run one member of the top support parallel with the grain, only the other member will need to be slot-screwed. (If you position the base in this way, you could use the same system as used for the oval table, pp. 114-119.) I bore oversized clearance holes and insert the screws through washers with holes just smaller than the screw head or slotted holes the size of the shank (p. 71) to allow for movement. No. 10 screws are sufficient to hold this top in place.

Turn the legs to 1¾-in.-dia. cylinders and turn a shouldered tenon on each end, checking the diameter with a template as described on p. 95. A bar clamp or pipe clamp centered on each leg will draw the joints together when you glue up the base. Check that the legs are perpendicular to the foot and top support, not leaning or twisting.

This type of base is ideal for a carpeted floor because it distributes the weight evenly—it won't make the wrong kind of impression. Placed on a brick floor or other uneven surface, however, the table may wobble. I solve this by gluing short pieces of 1-in.-dia. dowel into shallow holes bored in the foot directly under each leg. If the dowel pieces project no more than ⅛ in., they'll get the base off the floor, but won't be noticeable.

Trestle Table

Trestle tables have a simplicity and presence that I find very appealing. In addition, they bring to mind (my mind, anyway) scenes from a fascinating period of history. Iron-bracketed torches flare on the walls of a lofty, smoke-blackened medieval hall. At a long, cloth-covered table on a dais at one end of the hall, the lord and lady entertain honored guests. Down the length of the hall stretch two rows of long, bare trestle tables at which are seated lesser guests, distant kin, retainers and hangers-on. Servants rush to and fro, occasionally tripping over the master's greyhounds, who snarl and fight for bones on the rush-strewn floor. After the meal, the minstrel is called, the servants shove the tables against the walls and clear the floor for dancing. Suddenly, hooves clatter in the courtyard, and there's a thunderous knocking at the great oak doors....

It may be entirely a matter of tradition, but I think trestle tables look best when their length is roughly three times their width: about 2½ ft. to 3 ft. wide, 7½ ft. to 9 ft. long, and 1½ in. to 2 in. thick. If you make the table smaller, pay particular attention to proportions—merely scaling down the dimensions by a constant factor might make the table too narrow for serving dishes, and the ends too narrow to seat one person comfortably. If the table is longer than 9 ft., even a thick top eventually will sag and will need some sort of support in the center.

Trestle tables can be made to be taken apart easily. The table shown in the photo can be dismantled by knocking the loose wedges out of the stretcher tenons that protrude through the trestle ends. The tabletop of a knock-down table must overhang the ends of the trestle by at least 14 in. so that people won't scrape their knees on the projecting tenons. The plan drawings show both fixed and knock-down trestles.

You may want to add a decorative touch to the table. Chamfering the trestle and tabletop can lighten the appearance of a massive table. I have also carved the date, and sometimes initials, in the stretcher. Chip carving would be in keeping with the table's medieval origins.

Construction

I have made trestle tables of practically every kind of wood available to me, and no one species seems more suitable than another. The mahogany table

shown in the photo, which is 6½ ft. long and 34 in. wide, has been so well cared for that it looks better now than when it left the shop years ago.

Make the base first. The foot and top support of each trestle end are joined to the leg with twin mortise-and-tenon joints, which have twice the gluing surface of a single mortise and tenon. Cut the feet, top supports and legs to size. (If you're making the alternate end, shown in the plan drawings, leave the pieces rectangular until the joints have been cut.) Mark the faces of the pieces that will form one face of each trestle end. Gauge the joints from only the marked faces. Scribe one mortise and one tenon of each pair on all the pieces with a mortise gauge; reset the fence and scribe the other mortise and tenon. This procedure ensures the joints will align and the faces will be flush.

Cut the mortises first, then cut the tenons by hand or on the tablesaw, as described on p. 134. (Be sure to test the tablesaw settings on a piece of scrap wood before cutting into a leg.) Clear the waste between the two tenons with a coping saw or drill a hole through the wood to separate the waste from the shoulder. If you chop out a little of the wood that separates the

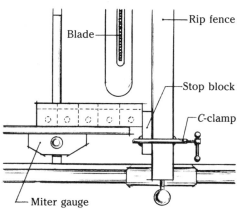

The stretcher of a knock-down trestle is held in place by loose wedges mortised through the stretcher's long tenon.

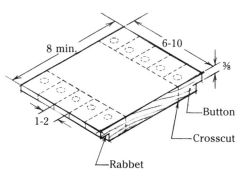

To make wooden buttons in batches, rabbet the ends of an 8-in. or longer piece of hardwood scrap. Crosscut two strips of buttons off the ends, then cut off the individual buttons and bore the screw holes.

two mortises, you won't need to chisel the space between the tenons to the shoulder line.

Lay out and cut the through mortises for the stretcher before gluing up the trestle ends. Mark the mortises carefully with a knife on both faces of each leg, bore out the waste and chisel to the knife lines. (Shape the feet and top supports if you're making the alternate design.) Glue up the trestle ends, taking care to make the top supports and feet parallel.

Next, make the stretcher and cut the tenon on each of its ends. For the fixed trestle, the through tenons will be glued and wedged in the legs. Cut the tenons $\frac{1}{32}$ in. or so longer than the thickness of the legs so they can be planed flush after assembly. (See p. 5 for hints on tenoning long, heavy boards.)

The tenons of the knock-down stretcher, shown in the photo at left, must be longer to house the loose wedge. I cut these tenons on the tablesaw and jointer. First, cut the shoulders for both tenons on the tablesaw, holding the stretcher firmly against the miter gauge and using the rip fence as a stop and guide. Then rip the tenon to width, running each edge of the stretcher against the rip fence. Place a stop to keep from cutting into the shoulders. Sever the waste with a handsaw or chisel.

Rather than trying to saw the wide cheeks, I cut them on the jointer. The stretcher is 1¼ in. thick and the tenon ⅞ in. thick, so set the infeed table for a $\frac{3}{16}$-in. cut. Set a stop on the outfeed table to prevent cutting into the shoulders. Press firmly down on the stretcher and feed it slowly into the knives until you hit the stop. Drop the back end of the stretcher to lift the tenon clear of the knives—don't slide the tenon backward over the knives. Joint the other cheek and clean up the remaining waste with a chisel or shoulder plane.

Make the loose wedges, then cut the mortises in the tenons to fit. Cut the wedges about 1 in. overlong so they can be trimmed after the mortise has been cut. Dry-assemble the trestle, pulling the shoulders of the stretcher tight to the legs with clamps if necessary. Mark the outside face of the legs on the tenons with a pencil, then position a wedge on a face of each tenon and mark the slope. Disassemble the trestle and then mark the mortise openings on the top and bottom edges of the tenon with a mortise gauge and knife. The mortise should extend into the leg about ⅛ in. so the wedge bears against the leg and not the back of the mortise. Bore in from both edges to clear

most of the waste from the mortise, then chisel to the lines. Assemble the trestle and tap the wedges in place—they should project slightly more at the top than the bottom because they'll be driven lower to tighten the trestle from time to time.

Like any other wide piece of solid wood, the top will expand and contract with changes in humidity—a 3-ft.-wide oak tabletop could move as much as 1 in. I use wooden buttons to attach this tabletop to the trestle to allow for movement, as shown in the top photo on the opposite page. The buttons are screwed to the underside of the tabletop, and their tongues engage in grooves cut on the inside face of the top support. The buttons are free to slide in the grooves when the tabletop expands or contracts. Short dowels, glued in the middle of each top support, fit into holes in the tabletop. The dowels position the top and ensure that it moves only about its centerline.

Almost any hardwood will make good buttons. To make a batch of buttons, select a piece of straight-grained hardwood scrap, about 6 in. to 10 in. wide, 8 in. long and 1 in. thick. Plane one edge and cut both ends square to it on the tablesaw. Rabbet both ends, leaving a ⅜-in. by ⅜-in. tongue, as shown in the sketch at left. Cut off each end, making two strips of 1⅜-in.-long buttons. Cut each button off the strip, using a block clamped to the rip fence as a stop. (The block keeps the buttons from wedging between the blade and the fence after they are severed and keeps them from kicking back at you.)

To bore the screw holes, clamp an *L*-shaped plywood stop to the drill-press table to position each button under the bit precisely. Countersink the holes for flat-head screws. I clean up the buttons on a disc sander—for large buttons, I usually round the ends, as shown in the top photo on the opposite page, or chamfer the arris, as shown in the plan drawings, to make them look less clumsy.

The groove on each top support of the trestle ends can be sawn or routed. Stop the grooves before the ends of the top support. The groove should be a snug sliding fit on the tongue—it should not have to be forced. Position the groove so the top of the button will be about $\frac{1}{32}$ in. from the underside of the tabletop—closing this gap will draw the top tight to the support. Be sure to use stops on the rip fence when sawing stopped grooves on the tablesaw. Bore a hole in the center of each top support and then glue the positioning dowels in place.

Ideally, the tabletop should be a single, wide board, but finding a board wide enough is seldom possible. You might find a long, wide board that can be crosscut in half and joined edge to edge for a two-board top. Otherwise, make the top of three or five boards joined together—a top made of an odd number of boards will look better than one made of an even number. (The boards should be 6 in. to 8 in. minimum in width—this tabletop doesn't look well joined up from narrow strips.)

Balance the width, color and grain patterns of the boards in the top. If one board is a stranger (a board noticeably different from its neighbors), put it in the middle or, if it's long enough, crosscut it and pair the two halves. Place bowed boards so they pull against each other—one bow up, the adjacent bow down.

Sand and finish the trestle and top (if you're making the fixed trestle, glue and wedge the two ends to the stretcher after sanding). I think an oil finish is best for this kind of table—it's durable, easily renewed and repaired. Remember, however, that oil won't protect oak from being stained by iron, especially when wet. If the top is bowed along its length, put the convex side up (if it's a good side) so that its own weight will help bring it down flat. Lay the tabletop upside down on a suitably padded surface, put the trestle in place and mark the position of the dowels. Bore holes for the dowels, reposition the trestle base and button it to the top.

Trestle desk—The photo at bottom right shows a knock-down trestle table fitted with drawers for use as a desk. The drawers hang from runners that are concealed inside the drawer by the drawer sides. The runners are screwed to the underside of the tabletop, as shown in the drawing on p. 100. The contrast of the oak drawer sides with the walnut fronts accents the through-dovetail joints. When both drawers are closed, the pins meeting in the center look like little bow ties—an unconscious comment on the formality of the Washington lawyer's office for which this desk was made.

The table is made as described above, but the top is smaller, and the trestle ends reproportioned accordingly. The height of a writing table is usually between 27½ in. and 29 in., depending on the height of the user and of the chair. The drawers are simple dovetailed boxes. They can be almost as long as the table is wide—there is less chance of pulling a long

The wooden buttons that fix the trestle to the tabletop slide in a groove and permit the top to swell and shrink with changes in humidity.

The oak pins stand between the walnut dovetails of the trestle-desk drawers like little bow ties. Use contrasting woods for drawer fronts and sides to accent the dovetails.

Add drawers to a trestle table, lower it a little, and you've got a desk. The knock-down trestle is made just like the one for the trestle dining table.

drawer off the runners than a short drawer. You can also run the sides by the back so the drawer can be completely opened, but not pulled off the runners. The drawers shouldn't be more than 3 in. deep or they will scrape the writer's knees. The bottom is housed in grooves in the front, back and sides, so it can't move and must be made of plywood.

Cut the pieces to size and plane them to thickness—the front and back are ¾ in. thick, the sides ½ in. thick. Remember to rip the back narrower than the front so the back will clear the runners. Lay out and cut the through dovetails. I like the look of the tails on the drawer front and back, but they could just as well be on the sides. Saw or rout the ¼-in. grooves for the bottom and for the runners. (Stop the drawer-bot-

tom grooves in the front and back so they won't show on the sides.) When assembling the drawers, measure the diagonals to make sure they are square. No drawer pulls are needed—you can just hook your fingers under the drawer front.

The runners should be hard maple or some other close-grained wood. To make the tongues, I rabbet the runners on the tablesaw. Make the shallow cut first, then the deep cut, so there will be enough support for the runner as the waste is severed. The tongue should be an easy sliding fit in the drawer-side groove. Turn the tabletop upside down, position the drawers and runners on the underside, and screw the runners in place. The runners serve as drawer stops, so position them accordingly.

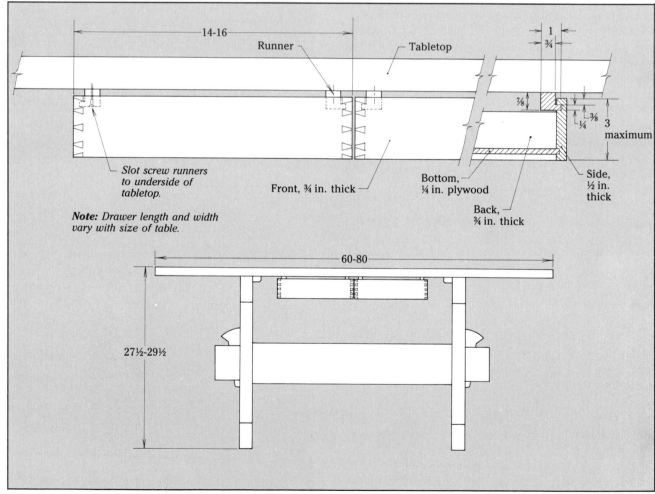

Drawers for the trestle writing desk are just through-dovetailed boxes. The length and width of the drawers will depend on the size of the table.

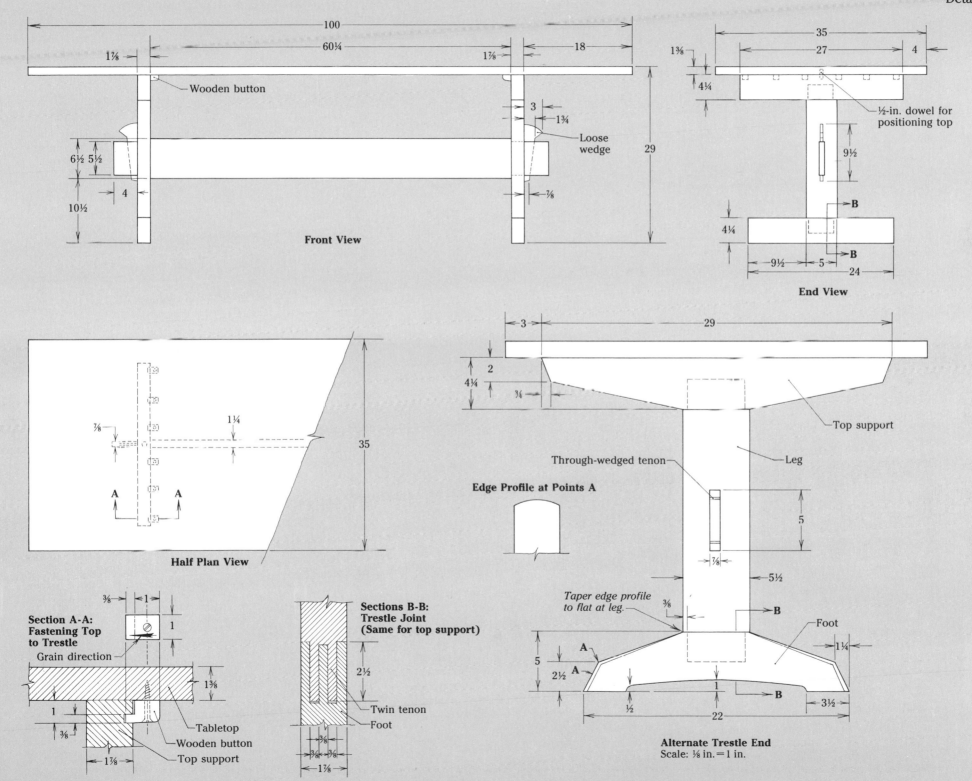

Trestle Table

Scale: ⅟₁₆ in. = 1 in.
Details: ¼ in. = 1 in.

Front View

End View

Half Plan View

Edge Profile at Points A

**Section A-A:
Fastening Top
to Trestle**

**Sections B-B:
Trestle Joint
(Same for top support)**

Alternate Trestle End
Scale: ⅛ in. = 1 in.

Wooden button

Loose wedge

½-in. dowel for positioning top

Grain direction

Tabletop

Wooden button

Top support

Twin tenon

Foot

Through-wedged tenon

Leg

Top support

Taper edge profile to flat at leg.

Foot

Drop-Leaf Table

Scale: 1/16 in. = 1 in.

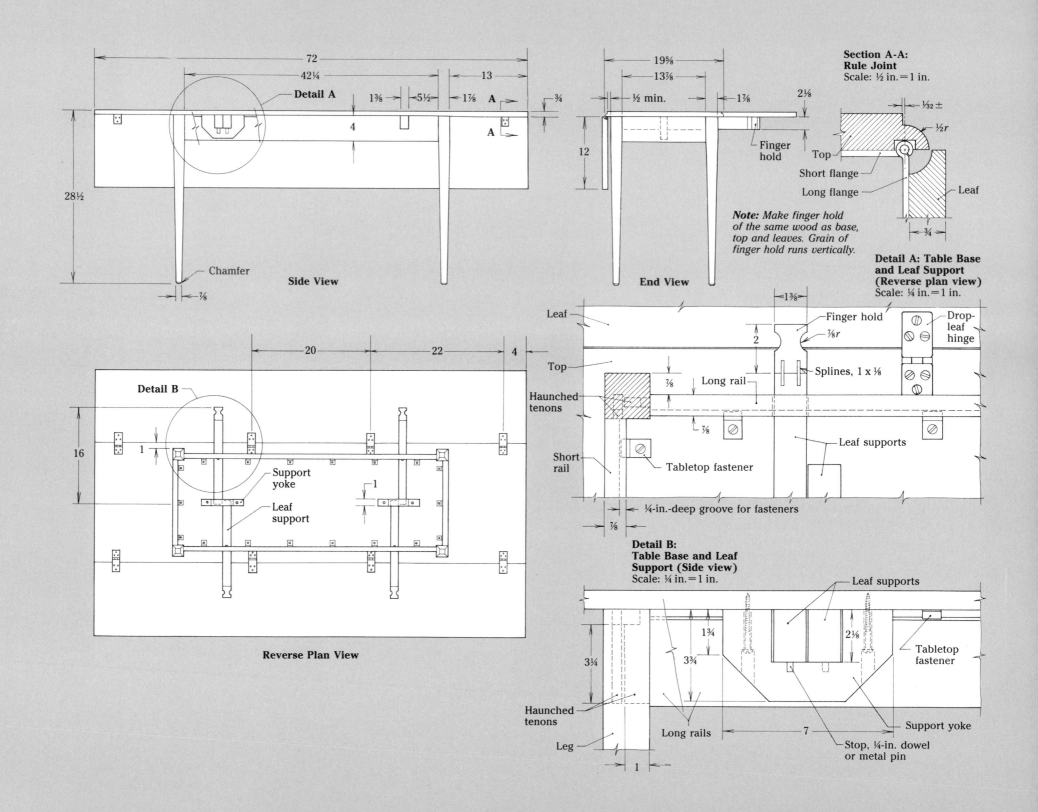

Side View

End View

Note: Make finger hold of the same wood as base, top and leaves. Grain of finger hold runs vertically.

Section A-A: Rule Joint
Scale: 1/2 in. = 1 in.

Top
Short flange
Long flange
Leaf

Detail A: Table Base and Leaf Support (Reverse plan view)
Scale: 1/4 in. = 1 in.

Leaf
Top
Haunched tenons
Short rail
Finger hold
Splines, 1 x 1/8
Long rail
Tabletop fastener
Drop-leaf hinge
Leaf supports
1/4-in.-deep groove for fasteners

Reverse Plan View

Detail B
Support yoke
Leaf support

Detail B: Table Base and Leaf Support (Side view)
Scale: 1/4 in. = 1 in.

Leaf supports
Tabletop fastener
Haunched tenons
Leg
Long rails
Support yoke
Stop, 1/4-in. dowel or metal pin

Chamfer
Detail A
Finger hold

Drop-Leaf Table

Drop-leaf tables were made in England as early as the sixteenth century, but they weren't commonly used until coffee and coffeehouses arrived during the following century. The cramped confines of a coffee-house required a table that could be easily stored and could seat a great many coffee drinkers—the drop-leaf table was ideally suited.

Though coffeehouses were a boon to joiners, who were asked to build numerous tables, the government took a dimmer view. Small groups of dissidents could meet inconspicuously in a coffeehouse around a table or in a private booth safe from eavesdroppers. This worried Charles II, whose father had lost his throne, and head, not too many years before. Charles II tried, but failed to suppress London coffeehouses.

A popular drop-leaf style of the period had only one leaf, which was folded up, not down, and leaned against a wall when not in use. The tavern table usually had two leaves, both folding down, like today's drop-leaf tables.

The two-leaf table shown in the photo at upper right is 6 ft. long and will seat eight people quite comfortably. The top overhangs each end by 13 in., so someone can sit at an end without banging the table legs. The mating edges of the leaves and top are rule-jointed, and the leaves are supported on slides that pull out through the rails, as shown in the photo on p. 105. (Brackets hinged to the rail aren't a good idea for supporting the top—the strain can warp the hinges and twist the rail.)

I made the table for a family with three small children. I suggested rounding the corners, but the parents decided that would detract too much from the appearance, so the corners were left square. By now, all three children have met a corner head-on. (I think a furniture maker should point out this kind of hazard, but shouldn't insist on doing it his way.)

The proportions of the table are important for looks and stability. If you alter the size of the table, don't make the leaves narrower than about half the width of the top. A narrow top brings the legs so close together that the table might overturn when only one leaf is up. I like to make the top 18 in. to 22 in. wide and the leaves 10 in. to 12 in. wide.

The leaves can be curved, as shown in the photo at bottom right, but this reduces the space available at the ends. I don't like oval-shaped drop-leaf tables be-

cause the curve crossing the rule joint makes part of the joint project in an unsightly way.

Construction

Choose the wood for a drop-leaf table carefully. The leaves are supported only along the hinged edge, so there is nothing to prevent them from cupping or twisting. For this reason, I like to make the table out of a stable wood, such as mahogany. For the top and leaves, I select boards whose annual rings run nearly at right angles to the board's faces. These boards are less likely to cup and twist than boards whose annual rings are tangent to the faces. If you can make the leaves and top out of boards cut in sequence from the same log, the leaves will look good whether up or down and will match the top beautifully.

The leaves of the drop-leaf table can be curved as well as rectangular. Lay out the curve by springing a thin wooden batten. Bandsaw and plane to the line.

A rule joint is elegant whether the leaves are up or down. Placing the barrel of the hinge in front of the rule-joint shoulder allows the leaf to swing clear of the round on the top when dropped.

Rout a recess in the underside of the tabletop to house the hinge knuckles. There is no need to mortise the hinge flanges into the top.

I make the table base first so that I'll have something on which to set the top while working on it. Cut and plane the rails and legs to size, then lay out and cut the mortises and tenons (taper the legs later). The entire strength of the table is in these joints, so it is crucial that they fit well and are properly proportioned. The tenons aren't centered on the rails, but are offset slightly, as shown in the plan drawings, to allow a thicker wall on the face side of each mortise. I haunch the tenons, because a mortise cut too close to the top of a leg is likely to break out, and the haunch provides extra gluing surface.

Place the mortises so the short end rails will be flush with the outside faces of the legs. The long rails are set back, so the finger holds on the slides will be readily accessible. Cut the mortises for the long rails first—if you cut them after those for the short end rails, you might break through the bridge of wood separating the two mortises.

Put the long rails side by side to lay out the notches for the leaf-support slides—remember that opposing notches are offset, as shown in the plan drawings. Gauge lines on both faces for the bottoms of the notches. I cut the sides of the notches on the tablesaw, clean out the waste on the bandsaw and chisel to the gauged lines. Next, groove the inside of the rails for tabletop fasteners, as shown in the plan drawings, or cut individual slots for buttons.

Taper the legs as described for the four-poster bed on pp. 5-6—remember to start the taper a fraction below where the bottom edge of the rails meets the legs. The amount of taper is important: Too much taper and the table looks nervous, as if it were about to get up and walk away; too little taper and the whole piece looks clumsy. There is no formula for the correct taper—what *looks* right generally *is* right. I put a substantial chamfer around the bottom end of each leg. Furniture always gets dragged around and the legs eventually wear down. If there is little or no chamfer on the ends, the legs will be sure to splinter.

Sand the rails and legs and glue up the base. I glue up the long rails first, so I can clamp across the inside face of the rail and center the clamping pressure on the joint. (You may want to cut blocks to fit in the slide notches so that they won't give under the pressure of the clamps.) When the glue has cured, add the two short rails. To keep the base from twisting, stand it on a level surface or turn it upside down on a flat surface while clamping. Check that the assembly is square by measuring across the diagonals. (I toe the legs out about ¼ in. by slightly moving the center of the clamping pressure to correct the perspective distortion that makes the legs look like they're toeing in. The closer together the legs are, the more apparent this distortion becomes.) Make the rails flush with the top of the legs after the glue has cured.

Next, cut and plane the top and two leaves to size. It's very important that the pieces be flat because any twist or bow will be conspicuous and may cause the rule joint to bind. Plane the mating edges perfectly straight, then make the rule joints.

On old drop-leaf tables, the mating edges of top and leaf were both square, which was simple, but crude. The barrel of the iron hinge could be seen through the substantial gap between leaf and top. Later, tables had a 45° angle cut on the lower edge of each board, with the hinge set in from the underside. At some point, an unidentified genius invented the rule joint (so called because of its use in wooden folding rules.) This elegant detail conceals the barrel of the hinge from view, and when the leaves are down, shows an attractive molded edge on the top.

Originally, rule joints were made with two complementary molding planes. I make them with complementary router bits—a ½-in.-radius cove bit and a ½-in.-radius quarter-round bit. These cuts can be made with the router mounted in a table and running the edges of the top and leaves against a fence, or by attaching a 10-in.-long wooden fence to the base of the router and moving the router over the pieces. Cut the cove in the leaves and the round on the tabletop, as shown in the plan drawings. (It's an excellent idea to cut and hinge a rule joint on two pieces of scrap to get router settings and hinge positions right.)

Hinges for rule joints have one flange longer than the other (see Appendix 5 for sources of supply). The long flange is screwed to the table leaf, the short flange to the top. I've found that it's a mistake to make a rule joint too snug, because crumbs and other debris tend to get ground into it. Position the center of the hinge knuckles about ¹⁄₃₂ in. in front of the shoulder of the round, as shown in the plan drawings, to allow the joint to open slightly as the leaf drops. Set a marking gauge to this distance and scribe a line on the underside of the top. There is no need to set the whole hinge into the wood, so I just rout a short recess in the top for the knuckles of each hinge, as shown in the photo at bottom left.

To attach the hinges, position the top and leaves upside down on a flat surface and clamp them lightly together. Align the ends of the leaves and top, place each hinge so the scribed line is centered on the knuckles, then screw the hinges down.

Unscrew the leaves and screw the top to the base with steel tabletop fasteners or wooden buttons (see p. 98 for how to make wooden buttons). Cut shallow notches in the top edge of the long rails for the hinges. Never screw through the rails to fasten the top because this would prevent the top from moving with changes in humidity.

Make the slides and support yokes of maple or another hard, dense wood. The notches in the support yokes should be as deep as those in the rails and wide enough to take two slides without binding. Turn the table upside down, center each yoke on the underside of the top between the rails and in line with the notches in both rails, and screw the yokes in place, as shown at bottom right.

Plane the slides so they pass easily through the rails and support yokes. Glue a 2-in.-wide block of whatever wood the table is made of to the end of each slide. I rout the finger holds with a ½-in. or ¾-in. corebox bit. The edge grain of the block is glued to the end grain of the slide, so I added two plywood splines to reinforce the joint. Cut the slides to length and fix a short ¼-in. dowel or metal pin in each as a stop, to prevent the slide from being pulled right out.

Attach the leaves, set the table upright and try the slides. Nothing spoils the look of a drop-leaf table more than drooping leaves. To cure this, I glue a block about 1½ in. long by ½ in. wide and about ¹⁄₁₆ in. thick to the tabletop under each slide just in front of the yoke. The blocks wedge the slides away from the underside of the top, angling them up slightly under the leaves. By trimming these blocks as necessary, the leaves can be made to lie in the same plane as the top. It's easy to replace the blocks if they wear down and the leaves begin to sag over the years.

I used an oil finish on the table. Oil only the fingerholds of the slides—wax the rest of the slide surfaces. Whatever finish you use, the top and bottom surfaces of the leaves must be finished in exactly the same way. I have repaired a number of drop-leaf tabletops that had been stripped and polyurethaned on one surface only. The leaves curled, spoiling the looks of the table—wood picks up moisture or dries out more readily on the surface with the least amount of finish.

Sturdy pieces of wood slide through notches in the rails to support the leaves.

One support yoke in the center of the tabletop aligns two leaf supports. The pins strike the rails to keep the supports from being pulled out too far.

Gate-Leg Table

This gate-leg table, like the drop-leaf table on pp. 102-105, is ideal for small apartments or for people who entertain groups of varying sizes. When folded, it occupies little space, but raise one leaf and three can sit comfortably. Raise both leaves to seat six or, in a pinch, eight. Each leaf is supported by a gate leg attached by wooden hinges to the rails of the table base. The fixed top and base can be narrower than would be possible with a drop-leaf table with slides, but the base shouldn't be much less than 10 in. wide, or the table will be top-heavy and liable to tip when both leaves are down.

For a table of standard height (28½ in.), the leaves shouldn't be wider than 26 in. Any wider, and the bottom edge of the leaves will be too close to the floor and will get kicked. The tabletop (fixed top and two leaves) can be square, rectangular, round or oval. If the top is longer than 60 in., two gates will be needed to support each leaf, which can interfere with seating.

Construction

The choice of wood for this table is important because both leaves are long, wide and free to twist, cup or bow. Plywood moves very little, of course, but a plywood tabletop is difficult to repair if the finish is damaged, because the face veneers are very thin. If you're going to the trouble of making this table, I think it is worth making it in solid wood. Choose a stable wood, though, such as walnut, cherry, teak or mahogany. I don't think the table looks good made of oak, maple or other blond wood.

Make the base and gates first—the less time the top sits around the shop, the less chance there is of damaging it. Each end is a single, thick board, cut in half lengthwise, shaped and rejoined. (You could make the cutouts with a saber saw or a small frame saw without splitting the board, but cleaning up the edges would be tedious.) Cut the end boards ¼ in. over finished length and width, and plane them 1¼ in. thick. Rip them in half and carefully joint the mating edges—they can't be jointed again after shaping. Mark the cutouts and bore a hole for a ⅜-in. dowel in each bridge of wood, to ensure proper alignment. Bandsaw the waste and clean up the rough edges. Glue the two halves of each end together.

When the glue has cured, square up the ends. I clean up the bandsaw marks with a small sanding

drum that fits into the chuck of my drill press. The edges can be left square, or they can be chamfered or rounded. I routed a small arc on all the arrises of the ends of the table shown in the photos with a ½-in. rounding-over bit with a ball-bearing pilot. The full arcs shown on the edges in the plan drawings can be made this way or with a spokeshave.

The ends of the base are joined by two rails, as shown in the drawing below. The long shoulders of the stub tenons are only ⅛ in. wide, to give the tenon maximum thickness. The short shoulders are wider (½ in.), so there will be enough wood above and below the mortises to prevent the mortises from splitting out. Cut these mortises and tenons carefully—the strength of the base relies entirely on them.

The top is attached to the base by screwing through the top rail, so bore the clearance holes for these screws now. There is no need to allow for movement because the screws are aligned parallel to the grain of the top. The base requires only two long

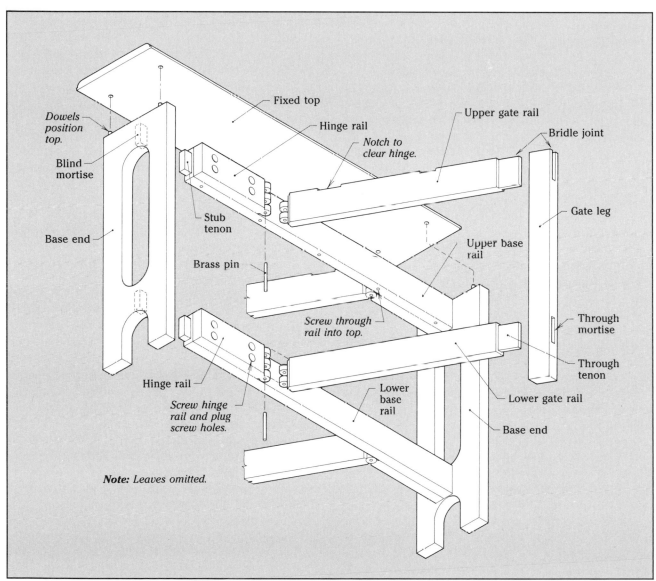

The gate legs and table base are assembled with mortise-and-tenon joints. Screw the short hinge rail to the base rails—glue is unnecessary as well as messy to use.

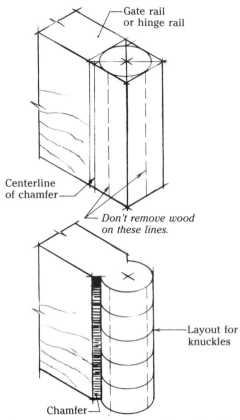

Gate rail
or hinge rail

Centerline
of chamfer

*Don't remove wood
on these lines.*

Layout for
knuckles

Chamfer

**Lay out the hinge knuckles on the ends of the
gate rails and hinge rails, as shown.**

**Cut the hinge accurately so there is little play
between the flat surfaces of the knuckles.
The pin should be a tight fit in its hole.**

clamps for gluing up. Make sure the rails are square to the ends.

The leaves of this table are heavy and require the support of gate legs, which are much stronger than the cantilevered, sliding supports of the drop-leaf table. Each gate leg consists of a vertical leg and two horizontal rails, which are attached to the base rails with wooden hinges. Two knuckles of each hinge are worked on the end of each gate rail; the other three knuckles are on the end of a short rail that is screwed to the base rails.

Make the gate legs and rails from stock that is the same thickness as the ends and rails of the base. Bridle-joint the upper gate rail to the leg (p. 36). The lower gate rail is at the same height as the lower base rail and is through-mortise-and-tenoned to the leg.

After the leg-to-rail joints have been cut (but not glued up), make the hinge. Wooden hinges are traditional on gate-leg tables, and they can be mastered by anyone with a bit of patience and the time to make one or two practice sets. Lay out the knuckles on the ends of the gate rails and short rails as shown in the sketch at left. Set a marking gauge to the thickness of the rails, and gauge around the ends of each pair. Draw the diagonals on both edges to locate the center of pivot, and scribe circles on the edges with dividers. The bottoms of the chamfers are located where the circle crosses the diagonals. Square lines around the piece at this point, so you know where to start the chamfer. (A chamfer at this 45° angle permits the hinge to pivot through 180°; varying the angle of the chamfer will increase or decrease the amount of pivot.) Square lines across the faces and the end where the circle touches them, to mark the points where no wood will be removed.

When the layout is completed, I saw the chamfers and remove the bulk of the waste with the tablesaw set at 45°, then I finish the cylinders with a rasp and sandpaper. Divide the width of the wood into five equal parts for the knuckles. Saw in as far as the bottom of the chamfers on the waste side of the lines and cut out most of the waste with a coping saw. Each socket is curved to accept the corresponding knuckle. These curved surfaces are set back slightly, as shown in the plan drawings, so that only the flat surfaces of the knuckles will rub. You can cut the curve on the open end sockets with an in-canel gouge (a gouge with an inside bevel). The curved surface between the knuckles has to be cut with a chisel, bevel down.

Finally, fit the halves together, clamping them in line with a hand-screw clamp, and bore the pin hole through both pieces at once. I usually use a piece of ³⁄₁₆-in. brazing rod for a pin.

When the hinges are cut and fitted, glue the gate legs together, making sure that the rails are in line with each other and at right angles to the legs. Protect the knuckles from the clamp jaws with scrap wood, and tighten the clamps only enough to close the joints. Screw the short hinge rails in place on the base rails. I counterbore and plug the screw holes. Sand and finish the gates and base and put them together. A little wax on the flat surfaces of the knuckles will make the hinge work easier. I flatten one end of the pin with a ball-peen hammer so it can't fall out.

Now make the fixed top and leaves. It is possible to make each leaf of one or two wide boards, but the boards should be quartersawn or rift-sawn (the faces approximately at right angles to the annual rings). If the boards are flat-sawn (faces approximately tangential to the annual rings), expansion and contraction will be more likely to cause twisting or cupping. For this reason, rift-sawn or quartersawn boards are also preferable for leaves joined of a number of narrow boards. If you must use flat-sawn boards, when gluing up, alternate the heart side and the sap side of adjacent pieces, as shown in the sketch in Appendix 2. Opinions vary among craftsmen, but I think this alternation makes a table leaf more likely to stay flat. (Appendix 2 also includes a full discussion of joining boards edge to edge.)

After the fixed top and leaves are glued up, cut them to size. Make the rule joints and fit the hinges as described on pp. 104-105. If you have young children, it's a good idea to round the outside corners of the leaves, so that bumping a corner won't cause injury.

Bore holes in the ends of the base for the dowels. Put dowel centers in these holes, taped so they won't fall out, and set the base in position on the inverted top. A smart blow with a hammer on each leg will transfer the centers. Bore holes for the dowels in the top, and glue the dowels into the base. Cut shallow notches in the upper gate rails so that the rails will clear the hinges. Screw the base to the top—a job best done with the entire assembly upside down. Finally, open the gates until they are centered on the length of the leaves. Mark this position on each leaf and screw a block of wood there to act as a stop for the gate.

Gate-Leg Table

Scale: ¹⁄₁₆ in. = 1 in.
Details: ½ in. = 1 in.

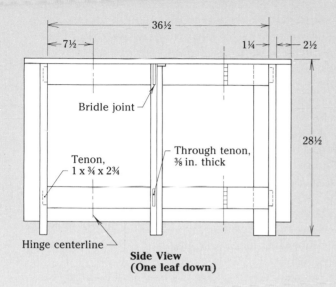

36½
7½
1¼
2½
28½

Bridle joint

Tenon,
1 x ¾ x 2¾

Through tenon,
⅜ in. thick

Hinge centerline

**Side View
(One leaf down)**

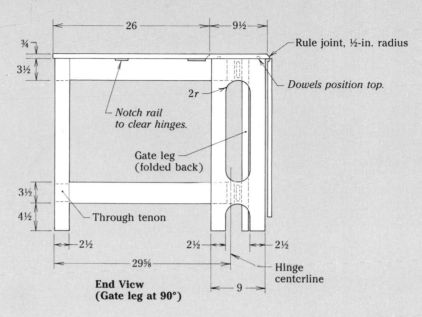

26
9½
¾
3½

Rule joint, ½-in. radius

Dowels position top.

2r

*Notch rail
to clear hinges.*

Gate leg
(folded back)

3½
4½

Through tenon

2½
2½
2½

29⅝

Hinge
centerline

9

**End View
(Gate leg at 90°)**

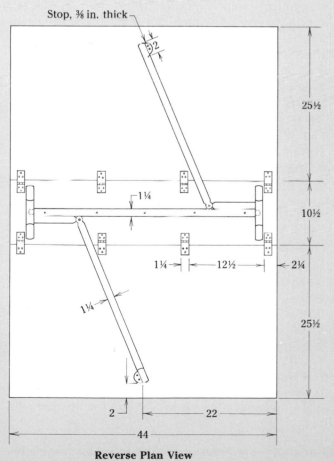

Stop, ⅜ in. thick

2

25½

1¼

10½

1¼
12½
2¼

1¼

25½

2
22

44

Reverse Plan View

Wooden Hinge

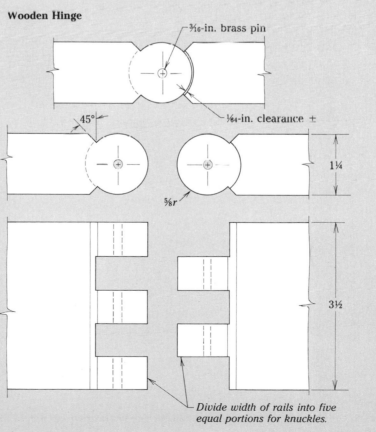

³⁄₁₆-in. brass pin

¹⁄₆₄-in. clearance ±

45°

1¼

⅝r

3½

*Divide width of rails into five
equal portions for knuckles.*

Extending Table

Dining tables that can be extended to accommodate a varying number of guests have been around for a long time. The early versions, called draw-top tables, were enlarged by sliding leaves out from either end (p. 91). Though the leaves were conveniently stored under the fixed top, such tables were awkward to operate. The table shown in the photo divides in the center and pulls apart to take a loose leaf. Sturdy maple slides tie the halves together and support the leaf. The outside faces of the apron rails are curved to echo the outline of the top.

It's difficult to design an extending table so it looks good both with and without leaves. Legs tend to look chubby when the leaves aren't in place and skinny when they are. I know of no solution to this dilemma, so I try to proportion the legs so the table will look best in its usual configuration. The table in the photo was made for a friend who most often dines alone, so the table is seldom extended, and I proportioned the legs to suit.

You can make the table slides yourself, or buy them ready-made (see Appendix 5). If you buy slides, specify their length when closed and open, and the number and size of the leaves. Two slides are sufficient for this table, but for a table that is heavy or unusually wide, it is best to use three or even four slides. You can make this table to take two leaves, but I don't recommend three. (Slides for two or three leaves have more runners than those shown in the plan drawings.) Three-leaf tables are difficult to proportion correctly, and the weight of dishes, food and elbows puts a considerable strain on the slides. Tables, like people, tend to sag when overloaded.

Construction

Select the boards for the tabletop for consistency of grain and color. The two fixed halves of the tabletop are fastened to apron rails, so you needn't worry about movement as much as you would for an unsupported top. If the leaf will be used infrequently, make the joint between the two fixed tabletop halves as inconspicuous as possible. I ripped a wide board in half down its length and joined each piece to one half of the fixed tabletop—pushing the tabletop together reassembles the board.

The leaf has no stiffening support, and though the leaf's thickness will help keep it flat, use quartersawn or rift-sawn wood if possible (see Appendix 1). If the tabletop is ¾-in. thick, it is best to slot-screw the leaf to short aprons, which prevent the leaf from curling and conceal the slides when the table is extended. (I don't object to seeing the maple slides when the table is extended, but I improve the appearance of ready-made slides by sanding and finishing them.) I don't like to see joints in leaves, so I crosscut a 10-in.-wide by 10-ft.-long board in half across its length and edge-joined the two pieces, so that the consistent color and grain would mask the joint.

After gluing up each of the halves of the fixed top, plane their mating edges. Place the halves edge to edge on a benchtop and lay out the curves with a beam compass or by springing a thin batten. I prefer using the batten because it makes a more subtle, and therefore more pleasing, curve than the arc of a circle. Use a clear, straight-grained batten about ⅜ in. square and at least 1 ft. longer than the table. Clamp the center of the batten lightly at the midpoint of an edge or end of the table and spring both ends. (Large spring clips are handy for holding them in place.) When the curve looks right, mark it with a soft pencil.

The curves on the ends and edges of the table are the same (without the leaves, the width and length of the table are equal). So if you are not confident that you can reproduce the curve each time, make a thin plywood template—or saw the first edge carefully to the line and use the offcut as a template. You can bandsaw the curve or, because the curve is shallow, you might find a sharp handsaw easier. Clean up the curved edges and ends with a hand plane, then place the leaf between the halves of the fixed top, mark its length and crosscut the ends square to the edges. When the leaf is in place, the curve of the tabletop is flattened, but almost imperceptibly.

Chamfer the edges and ends of the fixed tops and the ends of the leaf, as shown in the plan drawings. The heavy chamfer makes the top appear lighter, and makes it easier for the mating edges to meet precisely. Mark the chamfer with a cutting gauge (or the sharp point of a marking gauge) on the edges and ends, and make a pencil line on the underside. When you plane off the waste, just remove the incised gauge mark so the edges and ends will be a uniform ⅝-in. width. Keep a nice, sharp 45° arris where two chamfers intersect at a corner.

Small mortises and tenons in the mating edges of the fixed tops and leaf locate and align the surfaces.

Lay out and cut the mortises carefully in one edge of each half of the fixed top and both edges of the leaf. (If you are making a two-leaf table, mark each leaf from the same fixed top so the leaves will be interchangeable.) The tenons are best made of teak, a naturally oily wood that will slide into the mortises easily. Glue the tenons into the mortises in one half of the fixed top and one edge of the leaf; sliding the tenons on one half of the top into the open mortises on the other half aligns the two halves. Chamfer the projecting end of each tenon so it will slip easily into the corresponding mortise. If the tenons fit too snugly, it will be difficult for one person to open the table unaided, and the top won't close properly.

Now make the base. Square up rectangular blanks for the legs and aprons from 2-in.-thick rough stock. Two of the rails will be cut in half to allow for extension, but cut them after gluing up the base. (To conserve expensive wood, you can laminate the rectangular blanks. Make sure that the inner, inexpensive lamination is no more than ¾ in. thick, or it will show when the curve is cut.) Lay out the mortises and tenons by gauging from the inside faces of the blanks. The inside tenon shoulder is ⅛ in. wide, just enough to provide a bearing surface, so the outside cheek of the mortise can be as thick as possible.

Dry-assemble the base to lay out the curves on the rails and the top ends of the legs. These curves parallel those of the top and can be established with a thin batten or template. Bandsaw the waste off the rails and plane close to the line, making sure that the curved face is at right angles to the edges. Assemble the base again, and mark the position of the bottom edges of the rails on the inside faces of the legs. Lay out the tapers on the legs from these lines, bandsaw the waste and finish tapering the inside faces with a sharp hand plane.

The outside faces of each leg do not taper, but are shaped across their width to flow into the curve of the aprons. Gauge a line down one face to establish the limit of the curve on the adjacent face and plane close to the line. These curves are very shallow, and are best finished with a cabinet scraper after the base is glued up.

The tabletop is fastened to the base with screws driven through the rails. Bore the clearance holes for these screws now, before assembling the base, so you can place holes ½ in. to ¾ in. from each leg. The fixed tops must be allowed to expand and contract with

The base rails follow the gentle curve of the top. Plane the chamfers on the top carefully, maintaining a crisp arris where two meet at a corner.

Small mortises and tenons align the mating edges of the fixed tops and leaf. Each tenon slides freely into and out of a corresponding mortise in the other piece.

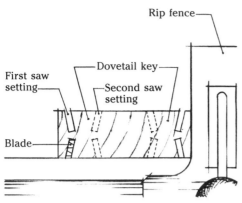

First saw setting

Dovetail key

Second saw setting

Blade

Rip fence

With the blade angle set the same as for cutting the dovetail grooves, you can cut the dovetail keys with two settings of the rip fence. Use a sharp carbide blade, set so that the keys remain attached to the waste after the second cut to prevent accidents.

changes in humidity, so I bore oversized clearance holes and pass the screws through slotted washers (p. 71). The rails that run parallel to the grain need no allowance for movement, so smaller clearance holes without washers are sufficient.

The curved faces of the legs and rails make clamping a little awkward. I find a 2-in.-wide band clamp works best, though you may need to add bar or pipe clamps to bring the joints home. Have a dry run first, to make sure that all the joints go together tightly. Use resin glue to give you time to assemble and clamp, and place wax paper over each joint so the glue won't adhere to the band. Be sure to check that the legs are parallel to each other, and that the outside faces of the legs are square to the rails.

After the glue has cured, make the curved faces of the legs flush with the curved faces of the rails using a cabinet scraper or finely set plane. Chamfer the ends of the legs, and finish-sand the base. Then cut two opposite rails exactly in half to form the half-bases for the halves of the fixed top.

If you don't want to buy slides, they aren't too difficult to make. Each slide consists of two short runners connected to a long runner by 4-in.-long dovetail keys. A close-grained, hard-wearing wood, such as maple, works best for runners and keys. Select straight-grained, thoroughly dry pieces and plane the faces and edges dead straight and at right angles to each other. I cut the dovetail grooves in the slides and the dovetail keys on the tablesaw, with the blade tilted at 75° to the table. The grooves are equidistant from both edges, so you can make cuts for two grooves with each setting of the rip fence. Cut the two cheeks of each groove first, then clear the waste by making additional cuts with the blade vertical.

The dovetail keys are ½ in. thick, 1 in. wide and 4 in. long, and the grain runs parallel to the length. A block about 24 in. long, 2½ in. to 3 in. wide and 1 in. thick will yield twelve keys 4 in. long. Using the same angle setting on the tablesaw as for the grooves, set the fence to cut two sides of each key, as shown in the sketch at left. The blade should cut about ¹⁄₁₆ in. less than halfway through the thickness of the piece. Reset the fence to cut the other sides of the keys. Bridges of wood, ⅛ in. thick, still connect the keys to the waste, so nothing will be thrown back at you. Snap the keys free of the waste and clean up with a rabbet or shoulder plane, then cut them to length. Using this method, all the keys will be identical.

Glue two keys into the grooves in each short runner and screw four keys (two at each end) into the grooves in the long runner, as shown in the plan drawings. Use a cabinet scraper to trim the keys to a smooth sliding fit. The keys in one end of the long runner must be added after both short runners have been slid into place. Bore clearance holes for the screws that fasten the short runners to the top. The screw near the mating edges of the top should be fixed, so the positions of the short runners will remain constant with respect to those edges. The other screws should run in oversized or slotted washers to allow the tabletop to move.

I finished the table with Watco oil. Even though the leaf is thick, it should have an equal number of coats of finish on both sides to help prevent warping. After finishing, assemble the table. Lay the halves of the fixed top upside down on a blanket spread over a flat surface, and push the halves tightly together. Close the slides and put them in place. Insert a ⅛-in.-thick spacer between the two short runners—the gap will allow the top to close before the ends of the runners touch. Make sure the slides are parallel to each other and at right angles to the mating edges of the top, then screw them down.

Position the half-bases next, inserting the ⅛-in. spacer between the ends of the cut rails. Align the faces of the cut rails by clamping across both of them lightly with a wooden hand-screw clamp, then screw the bases down.

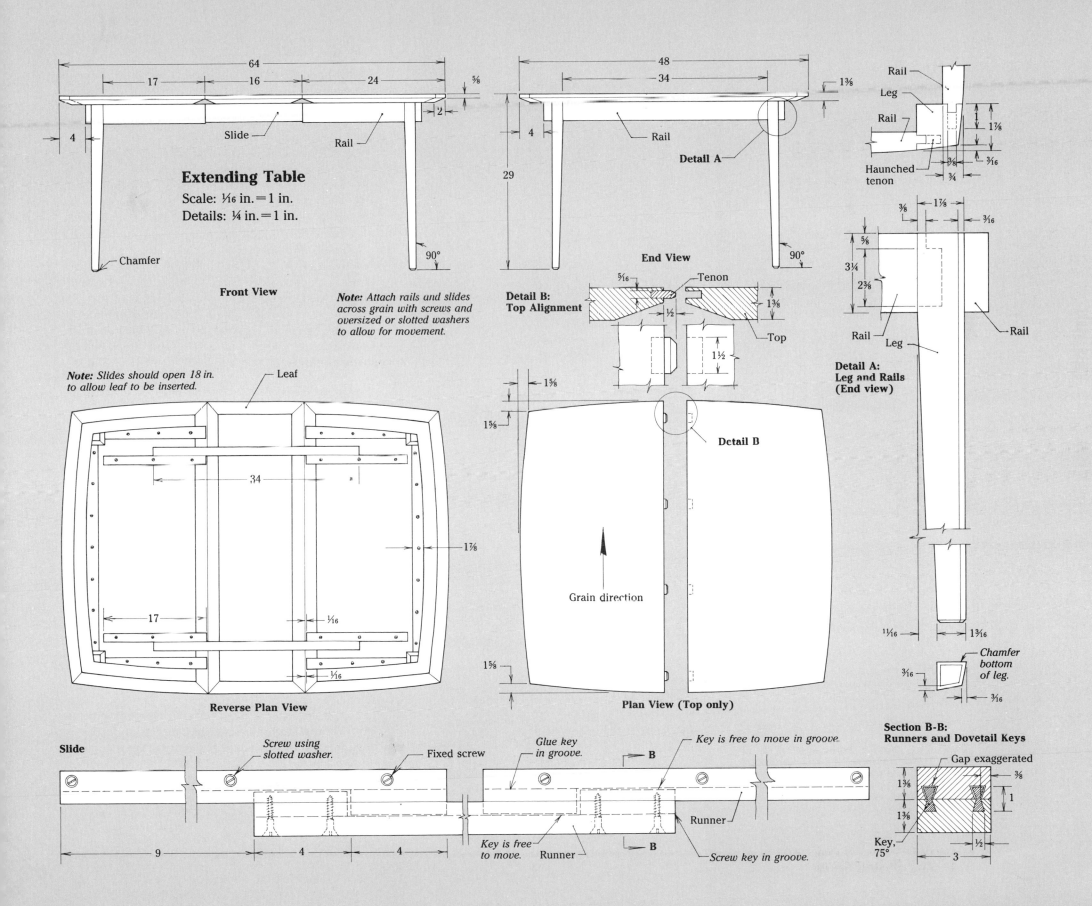

Extending Table
Scale: 1/16 in. = 1 in.
Details: 1/4 in. = 1 in.

64
17
16
24
5/8
Slide
Rail
2
4
Chamfer
90°

Front View

Note: Attach rails and slides across grain with screws and oversized or slotted washers to allow for movement.

48
34
1 3/8
4
Rail
29
90°

End View

Detail A

Rail
Leg
Rail
1
1 7/8
Haunched tenon
3/8
3/16
3/4

3/8
1 7/8
3/16
5/8
3 1/4
2 3/8
Rail
Leg
Rail

**Detail A:
Leg and Rails
(End view)**

Note: Slides should open 18 in. to allow leaf to be inserted.

Leaf

34
17
1/16
1/16
1 7/8

Reverse Plan View

5/16
Tenon
1/2
1 3/8
Top

**Detail B:
Top Alignment**

1 1/2

1 5/8
1 5/8
Detail B

Grain direction

1 5/8

Plan View (Top only)

11/16
1 3/16

Chamfer bottom of leg.
3/16
3/16

**Section B-B:
Runners and Dovetail Keys**

Gap exaggerated
3/8
1 3/8
1
1 3/8
Key, 75°
1/2
3

Slide

Screw using slotted washer.
Fixed screw
Glue key in groove.
Key is free to move in groove.
B
Runner
Key is free to move.
Runner
Screw key in groove.
B

9
4
4

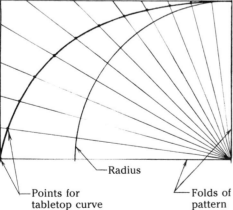

Radius

Points for tabletop curve

Folds of pattern

Draw an arc with the largest possible radius on the folded paper for the top pattern. Divide the arc into twelve equal sections, draw a radius through each of these points and plot the tabletop curve, using the dimensions in the plan view (p. 118).

Oval Table

This formal dining table is one of the more difficult pieces in the book—even an experienced woodworker could find it challenging. It seats eight people comfortably, and the pedestal base allows all to sit without fear of banging their knees.

David Powell made the first of these tables when we shared a shop in Vermont. I admired it very much. When another was ordered, I made it. I then made this one in walnut. (I think a dark wood looks best for this table, but avoid teak because its oiliness makes glue joints risky.) Finding chairs to suit the table was a problem. My client and I finally found an antique bow-back chair that looked exactly right—the curve of the back echoed that of the table without obscuring it. Making the chairs was a considerable chore. The original was pine with maple legs, and walnut doesn't bend or carve as easily as pine, so I laminated the bow backs on a form rather than bend them. However, the final result was worth all the effort.

Construction

The plan drawings on pp. 118-119 were scaled down from my original, full-scale drawings. I recommend that you scale the drawings back up. There's no substitute for full-scale plans (and sometimes mock-ups) when building complicated pieces. Start by making a pattern for the top; then draw the elevations full-scale on this pattern.

The tabletop is not a true ellipse, so it is no good trying to generate the shape by muttering mathematical formulas for ellipses or playing around with two thumb tacks and a loop of string. Here's an easy way to lay out the shape that is shown in the photos and plan drawings. You'll need a 5-ft. by 7-ft. sheet of paper—I used seamless background paper (available at photographic supply stores), but you can join lengths of brown wrapping paper with tape or rubber cement. Fold the paper in half and then in half again. Make sure that the folds are straight and at right angles to each other.

From the corner where the two folds meet, draw an arc with the largest radius the paper permits. Divide this arc into twelve equal segments using a compass or dividers. Draw lines with a straightedge from the center through the eleven points on the arc and extend them to the limits of the paper, as shown in the sketch. (The angle between adjacent lines will be

7½°.) Now mark the length of each line, as shown in the plan view. Also mark half the width and half the length of the top along the creases of the paper.

Establish the curve with a flexible wooden batten, about ³⁄₁₆ in. thick and at least 7 ft. long. Bend the batten so its edge touches the marks on the paper, but don't force it to one mark or another. Let it assume an even curve, without flat spots or kinks. The batten should extend about 1 ft. beyond the folds—make sure it crosses the folds at a right angle. Hold the batten in place with push pins or small finish nails, and mark the curve. Cut along the curve through all four thicknesses of paper. A few dabs of rubber cement will prevent the paper from sliding on itself while you are cutting. Unfold the paper and *voilà*—you have the pattern for the top. Draw full-scale elevations on the pattern or other sheets of heavy paper. It's probably easiest to scale up these drawings by measurement, rather than by using a grid.

The base—I make the base first, because a top this large is liable to get damaged sitting around the shop waiting for its base. The base is as difficult to make as it looks. If you haven't attempted anything as complicated before, making a full-size mock-up in pine is well worth the extra time. The mock-up allows you to figure out the joints and experiment with shaping techniques without the risk of spoiling expensive wood. I suggest mocking-up the stem and two legs, one long and one short.

I glue up the stem because an 8-in.-thick solid stem would be too heavy and unstable. The mitered joints coincide with the arrises and are practically invisible. You will need stock rough-sawn 2 in. thick and at least 8½ in. wide. It must be good and dry so that shrinkage won't open the miters. Cut four pieces 30 in. long, joint one face of each, then plane the pieces 1¾ in. thick. Next, cut 6 in. off one end of each piece and, without turning this cutoff over or around, glue it onto the face of the longer piece, as shown in the sketch at top right. (By making the stem pieces this way, each one will have consistent grain pattern and color.) I use resin glue for the entire project, because it permits long assembly time and won't creep in the joints, as will white and yellow glues.

Next, taper all four pieces and miter their edges. Joint one edge of each piece and rip the pieces 8½ in. wide. Crosscut about ⅛ in. off the glued-up ends to square them to the edges, then cut all four pieces to

their finished length of 22⅝ in. Because of the block glued to the outside faces of the stem pieces, it is best to lay out the tapers on the inside faces. Draw a centerline along the length of each inside face and measure from it to establish the taper, as shown in the sketch at top right. Using a miter square or combination square, extend these lines across the top and bottom ends at 45°. Draw the tapers on each front face by connecting these miter lines—the width of this face will taper from about 8 in. at the top to about 4 in. at the bottom.

Saw off the waste on the bandsaw with the table set at 45°. Lay the inside (flat) face of each piece down on the table and cut close to the taper lines on the front face. Plane to the miter and taper lines with a long plane (using a jointer could be dangerous—the bottom end is too narrow, and the inside face doesn't have enough surface to bear against the fence). There should be no gaps when you dry-assemble the miters. This is very important, because the apex of the mitered joints will be planed off when shaping the stem, and you don't want to plane into a gap.

I put a spline in each miter to prevent the surfaces from slipping when gluing up. Use ⅛-in. or ¼-in. plywood or Masonite for the splines, and cut the grooves for them on the tablesaw, with the fence to the left of the blade set at 45°. The apex of the miter bears against the fence, as shown in the sketch on p. 64.

The stem is awkward to glue up. Ideally, pressure should be applied diagonally, but only band clamps can do this easily, and they can't exert enough pressure for a good bond. I glue the stem using heavy bearers and clamps, as shown at bottom right—this is somewhat awkward, but it works. Make about fourteen bearers from 2x4s about 1 ft. long. Wax them to prevent the glue from sticking, apply the glue and assemble the stem. Align the ends of the pieces and stand the stem upright on its widest end—the accurate positioning of the mortises for the legs depends on the ends being aligned. Pencil or crayon marks meeting at the corners will help you check the alignment. Place the first pair of bearers (wide faces against the stem) and clamps at the wide end. Place the next pair at 90° to the first pair and as close to it as possible. The third is at 90° to the second, and so on. Tighten the clamps just enough to close the miters and hold the bearers in place. When all the clamps and bearers are on, check the miters for gaps and tighten the necessary clamps to close them.

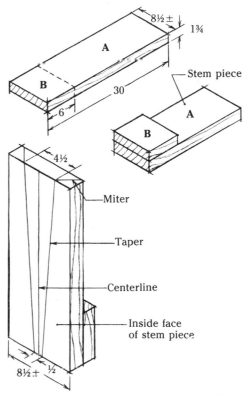

Make each stem piece from one board to maintain consistency of color and grain pattern. Lay out the taper on the inside face of each stem piece, then extend these lines across the ends at 45°. Connect these lines to establish the taper on the front face.

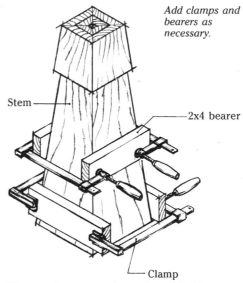

Glue up the stem using pairs of 2x4 bearers and clamps.

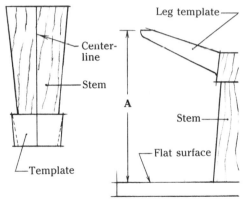

Make a template to establish the correct angles for the faces of the blocks. The broken line indicates the edges of the template. Align the template with the end of the stem and the centerline of the block. Check the angles with patterns for the long and short legs, as shown at right. The measurement (A) should be equal for each leg.

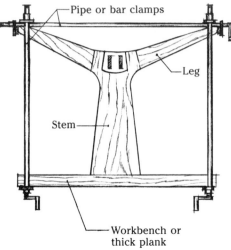

Clamp the legs in pairs—the vertical clamps bear on the horizontal clamp.

Clean glue off the stem—no shaping is done until the leg joints are cut and fitted.

Each leg is twin-tenoned into the block glued to each stem piece. The shoulders of the tenons are at right angles to the bottom surface of the leg, so the faces of the blocks must be planed to the correct angles to make all four legs sit flat on the floor. Templates are the best way to ensure accuracy when laying out these angles. Make a template for the blocks that take the short legs and one for the blocks that take the long legs from your own full-scale drawings of the front and side views of the base (or scale up from the plan drawings). The edges of the template should align with the bottom end of each stem piece and the centerline of those pieces, as shown in the sketch at top left. Mark the angles from the template for the short leg on two opposite faces and plane the two adjacent faces to the marks (those faces will take the short legs). With the other template, mark the two planed faces and plane to those marks (those two faces will take the long legs). Carefully plane to the lines, making sure the surfaces are flat.

To check the angled faces, make a Masonite pattern of a long leg and a short leg (without tenons). Turn the stem upside down on a flat surface, hold a short-leg pattern in place against a short-leg face and measure from the flat surface to the bottom of the pattern *(A)*. Repeat this procedure for the other short-leg face and with the long-leg pattern and faces. If all four measurements are the same, the angles are correct. If not, trim the angled faces until they are.

Draw a centerline on the face of each block and mark the twin mortises by measuring from it. Haunch the mortises at the bottom to give extra gluing surface. Cut the mortises by hand, or if you have a mortising machine, you can block the stem up until the chisel is at a right angle to the face of the block.

The legs can be made of 4-in.-thick stock, or glued up of thinner boards. If you glue up the legs, the joints should run parallel to the bottom surface of the leg—a vertical glue line would show. The bottom piece of a glued-up leg should be no more than 2 in. thick, otherwise shaping and tapering will expose a glue line on the top surface.

Leave the legs rectangular, so the haunched twin tenons can be marked out and cut on the tablesaw. The tenon shoulders should be 90° to the bottom surface of each leg. Cut the twin tenons in much the same way as a single tenon: cheek cuts with the legs

held vertically against a high, wooden rip fence; shoulder cuts horizontally against a miter gauge with a long fence. The waste between the tenons can be cut out with a coping saw or cleared with an auger bit, then chiseled to the shoulder lines.

When the tenons have been cut and fitted to the mortises, shape the legs roughly on the bandsaw. I hand-plane to lines drawn on each surface to indicate the tapers and rounds. Cut the flat surface that rests on the floor, but leave the ends of the legs square to provide clamping surfaces for gluing the base later.

Notch the top end of the stem to take the top supports before shaping the stem—it's easier to mark the notches on flat surfaces. The notches take the full thickness and width of the top supports, as shown in the plan drawings. (I prefer to make the top supports after the base has been shaped and legs glued on.)

It is easier to do the initial rough-shaping of the stem before gluing the legs in place. Make full-size Masonite or plywood templates of different sections of the stem, so you can check your progress and make sure the stem is symmetrical. (The concave templates should fit the convex curves of the stem.) I shape the upper portion of the stem with a spokeshave and a hand plane. The glue line of each miter is a helpful guide for keeping the shape symmetrical.

The lower part of the stem is more complicated. Insert each leg in its mortises and trace the leg profile onto the stem. Lay out the curves between adjacent legs on the bottom of the stem. I remove most of the waste with a thin-bladed bowsaw and a heavy gouge. Work the curves closer to the finished shape with a spokeshave, wood files or Surform. The final shaping will be done after the legs are glued in place.

Make a final check of the angles of the blocks now. Place the stem upside down on a large, flat surface and insert the legs in the mortises. Measure from the flat surface to the bottom of each leg, as you did with the patterns. If all measurements are not equal, plane a little off the face of the appropriate stem blocks, and check again.

The legs are most easily glued on in pairs—both long legs, then both short legs, or vice versa. (I dry-clamp first to make sure everything fits.) Place the stem upside down on a sturdy bench, or a thick plank at least 8 in. wide, as shown in the sketch at bottom left. Apply glue to the mortises, tenons and tenon shoulders and push the legs in place. Place a bar or pipe clamp on the bottom surfaces of the legs and tighten it gently against the toes, just enough to hold it in place. Place a vertical clamp at the end of each leg, hooking one jaw on the bench or plank and the other on the horizontal bar or pipe. Tighten all three clamps as needed to draw the shoulders of the joints tight. Avoid applying too much pressure, which might distort the alignment of the legs with each other and the stem. When the glue has cured, glue the other pair of legs to the stem in the same manner.

Finish the shaping of the base after the legs have been glued on. The curves should flow smoothly, but keep the arrises that mark the juncture of one curve with another crisp. Before completing the shaping of the ends of the legs, set them on a flat, level surface and make sure they all make contact—plane the bottom surfaces if they don't.

Make the top supports next. The supports are half-lapped together and housed in the notches in the stem. Make the supports so that their top edges will be about ⅛ in. above the top end of the stem. This allows the supports to shrink across grain without the top hitting the end of the stem. The half-lap joining the supports should be a sliding fit—the supports aren't glued together or to the stem, but are held in place by a threaded rod running inside the stem.

Next, bore clearance holes in the one support for the screws that will fasten it to the top. The support that runs parallel to the grain of the top needs no allowance for movement. Counterbore the clearance holes so you need only one length of screw. Because the other support runs perpendicular to the grain of the top, it must be attached with wooden buttons (or metal tabletop fasteners) to allow for seasonal movement. Chop the recesses for the buttons now. (See p. 98 for how to make wooden buttons.)

I tension the base with a ¼-in. threaded metal rod. The rod passes through the stem and is fastened to metal straps screwed to the top supports and to the bottom surfaces of the legs and stem. The straps on the legs and stem reinforce the mortise-and-tenon joints and anchor the rod. Tensioning the rod pulls the ends of the top supports up slightly, which keeps the tabletop from sagging.

Make the straps of ⅛-in.-thick metal strap, ¾ in. wide. Recess a single strap into the top supports (place it on the long support, across the open lap for extra strength). Fasten the strap with flat-head screws, countersunk into the strap. Bore a hole through both wood and metal for the rod. Screw two straps to the legs and stem, and bore through the straps into the hollow stem for the rod. You can lay the straps on the surface, as shown in the photo at bottom right, or recess them into the legs. Insert the rod, add nuts top and bottom, and tension the rod so that the top supports are bowed about ⅛ in. end to end. (You could thread the straps at the bottom to eliminate the bottom nut.) You may have to adjust the tension in the rod from season to season.

The top—Select and arrange the boards for the top by laying them on the pattern so that differences in color and grain are minimal. You should be able to appreciate the graceful shape of the top and not be distracted by its surface.

I plane the boards to finished thickness and dowel the edges to keep them from sliding while gluing—a dowel every 18 in. is sufficient. To eliminate the risk of exposing a dowel when bandsawing the top, lay out all the boards in the correct sequence after you have planed or jointed the edges. Trace around the pattern and then position the dowels well clear of the line. Leave the boards rectangular to provide a surface for the clamps, and glue up the top with resin glue.

Scrape off the glue squeeze-out and cut the top to shape on a bandsaw or by hand with a bowsaw. (I seldom use saber saws, perhaps because I'm afraid of that stabbing blade, but for a job like this, a saber saw would be useful.) You'll need a helper to steady the top if you bandsaw. Saw accurately and save yourself a lot of time cleaning up the edge. Flush the top with a finely set plane and a cabinet scraper.

The edge of the top is shaped, making a transition through seven profiles on each quadrant, as shown in the plan drawings. Make full-size templates of ⅛-in. Masonite of these profiles. Shape the edge with a spokeshave, one quadrant at a time, checking your progress with the templates, and make the profiles flow into one another. Make sure that the arrises (the lines visible where the top and bottom surfaces meet the edge) make a smooth curve all around the table.

Turn the tabletop upside down on a piece of carpet or padded sawhorses. Bore a recess in the exact center of the underside of the tabletop for the nut on the rod. Sand the top and base thoroughly, but don't lose the sharpness of the arrises. I finished the table shown in the photos with oil. Oil isn't impervious to staining, but the owner has cherished the table and it looks better now than it did when new.

Crisp arrises help to define the curves of the stem and top—don't lose them when shaping and sanding.

Metal straps across the bottom of the legs and stem reinforce the twin mortise-and-tenon joints. A threaded metal rod joins the bottom straps with a strap on the top supports. Tightening the nuts tensions the rod and springs the top supports up to keep the tabletop from sagging.

Oval Dining Table

Scale: ⅛ in. = 1 in.

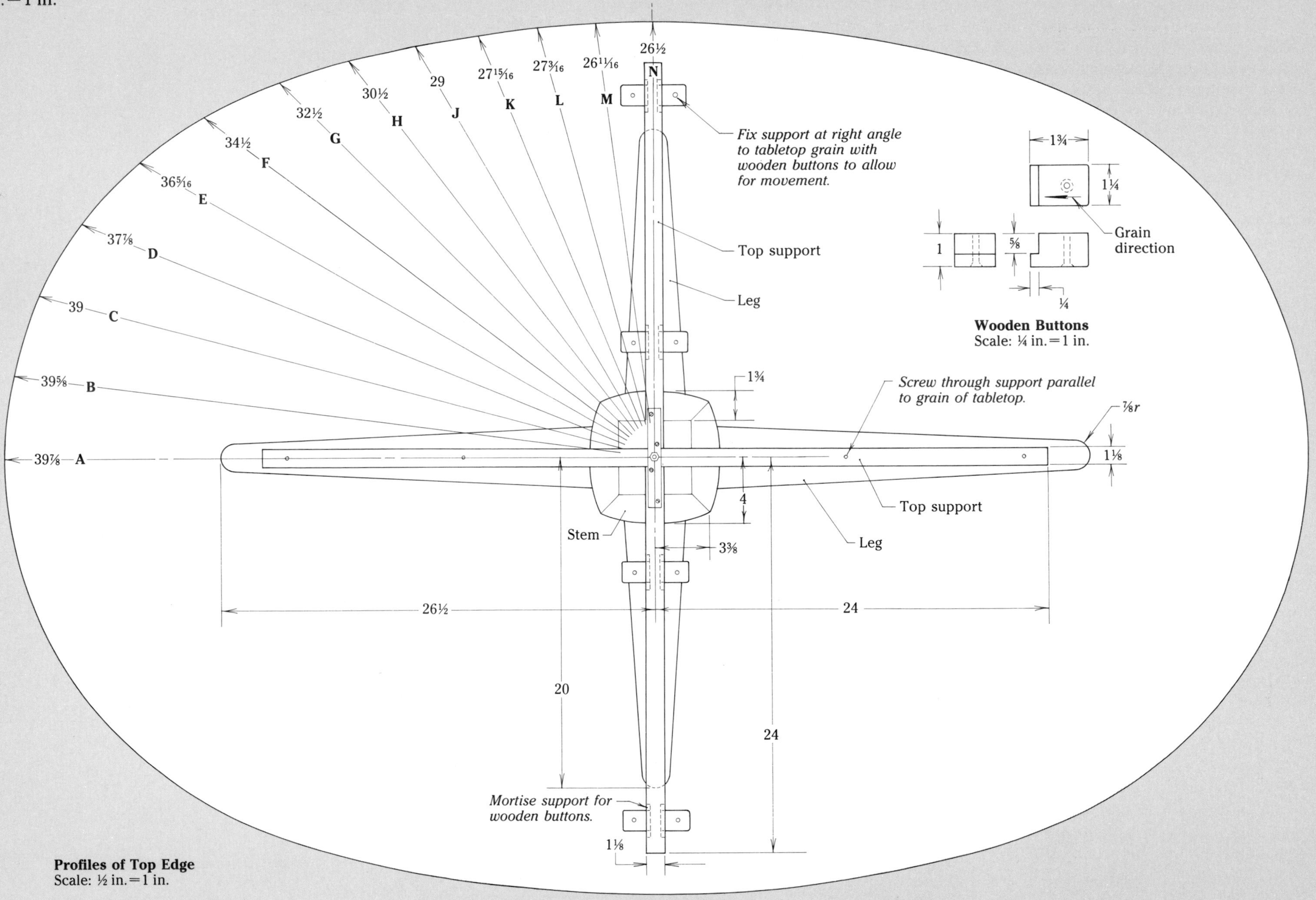
26½
N
M
L
K
J
H
G
F
E
D
C
B
A
26¹¹⁄₁₆
27³⁄₁₆
27¹⁵⁄₁₆
29
30½
32½
34½
36⁵⁄₁₆
37⅞
39
39⅝
39⅞
Fix support at right angle to tabletop grain with wooden buttons to allow for movement.
Top support
Leg
1¾
Screw through support parallel to grain of tabletop.
⅞r
1⅛
Top support
4
Leg
Stem
3⅜
26½
24
20
24
Mortise support for wooden buttons.
1⅛
1¾
1¼
Grain direction
1
⅝
¼
Wooden Buttons
Scale: ¼ in. = 1 in.

Plan View

Profiles of Top Edge
Scale: ½ in. = 1 in.

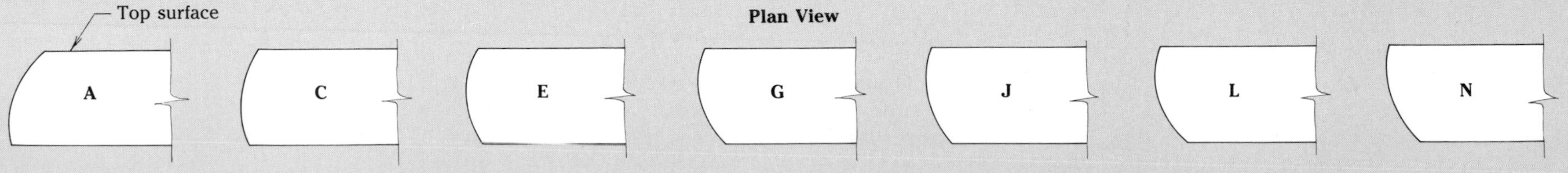
Top surface
A
C
E
G
J
L
N

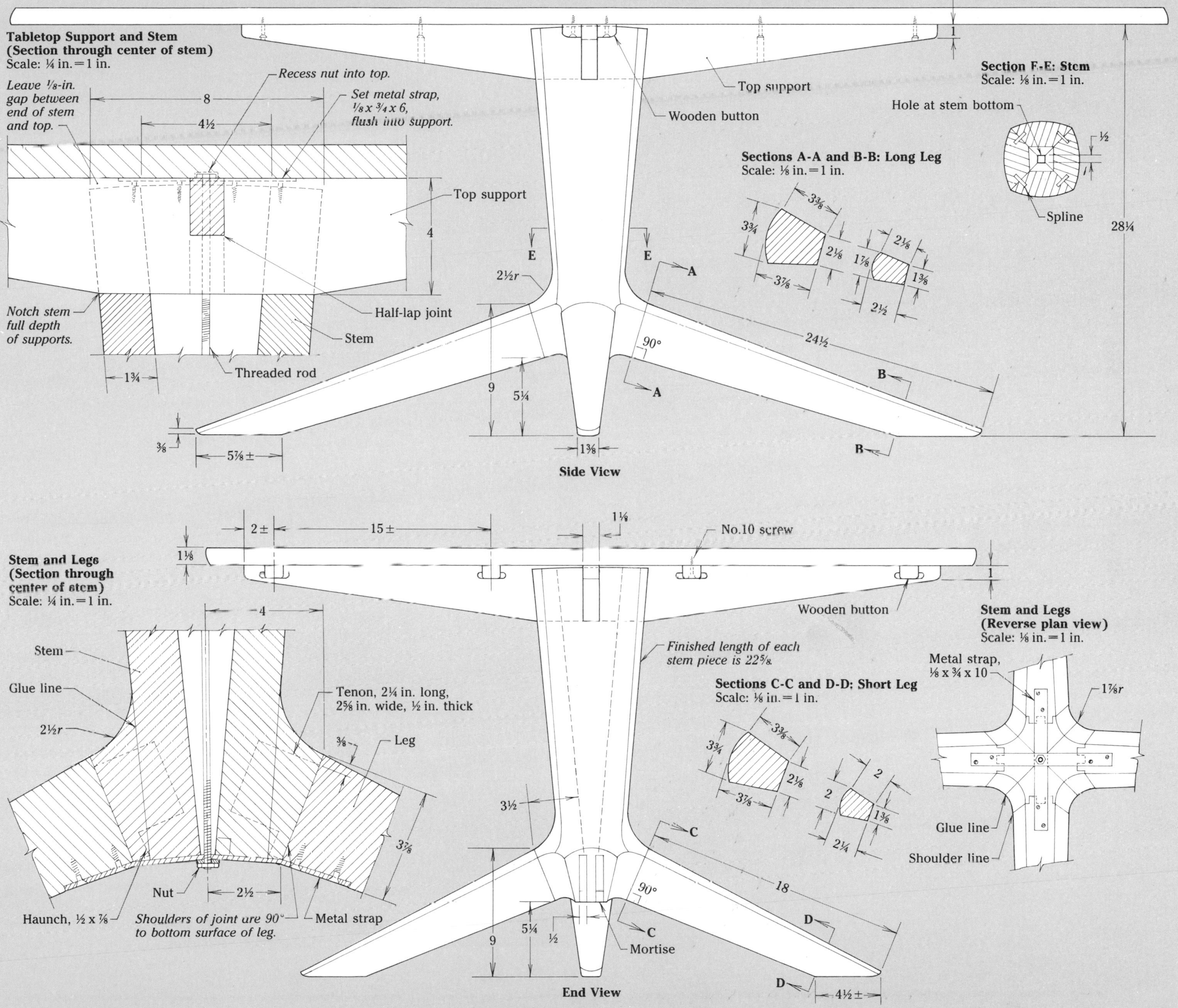

Tabletop Support and Stem
(Section through center of stem)
Scale: ¼ in. = 1 in.
Recess nut into top.
Leave ⅛-in. gap between end of stem and top.
Set metal strap, ⅛ x ¾ x 6, flush into support.
8
4½
Top support
4
Half-lap joint
Notch stem full depth of supports.
Stem
1¾
Threaded rod
Wooden button
Top support
1
Section E-E: Stem
Scale: ⅛ in. = 1 in.
Hole at stem bottom
½
Spline
28¼
Sections A-A and B-B: Long Leg
Scale: ⅛ in. = 1 in.
3⅜
3¾
2⅛
3⅞
2⅛
1⅞
1⅜
2½
E
E
2½r
A
A
90°
24½
B
B
9
5¼
⅜
5⅞ ±
1⅜
Side View
2 ±
15 ±
1⅛
1⅛
No.10 screw
1
Wooden button
Stem and Legs
(Section through center of stem)
Scale: ¼ in. = 1 in.
4
Stem
Glue line
2½r
Tenon, 2¼ in. long, 2⅝ in. wide, ½ in. thick
⅜
Leg
3⅞
Nut
2½
Haunch, ½ x ⅞
Shoulders of joint are 90° to bottom surface of leg.
Metal strap
Finished length of each stem piece is 22⅝.
Sections C-C and D-D: Short Leg
Scale: ⅛ in. = 1 in.
3⅜
3¾
2⅛
3⅞
2
2
1⅜
2¼
Stem and Legs
(Reverse plan view)
Scale: ⅛ in. = 1 in.
Metal strap, ⅛ x ¾ x 10
1⅞r
Glue line
Shoulder line
3½
C
C
90°
18
D
D
9
5¼
½
Mortise
4½ ±
End View

Serving Table

A serving table provides a convenient surface for serving buffet suppers, as well as storage space for silverware, place mats, napkins and dishes. It can also double as a liquor cabinet and bar—mix drinks on top, store liquor and glasses below. The design can be altered slightly for other pieces, such as the stereo cabinet on p. 125.

The table's top surface should be resistant to hot and cold dishes and abrasion from hand-thrown stoneware. (For twenty years I have had a running battle with potters who will not grind smooth bases on their pots.) The surface should also be impervious to the inevitable spills of food, alcohol and hot coffee. These requirements needn't add up to a prescription for Formica—tile and stone are attractive alternatives. The serving table in these photos has a top of Canadian black marble that weighs 230 lb. This top was difficult to handle, so I would suggest squares of tile or slate laid on a particleboard or plywood underlayment and surrounded by solid-wood edging as a practical alternative to solid stone.

Construction

The clients wanted a walnut serving table to match their dining table and chairs. The inside of a walnut cabinet can be very dark, which can make it difficult to find things. Because of this disadvantage, and to economize on an expensive wood, I made the carcase of oak. Then I glued walnut lippings on the carcase edges and screwed ¾-in.-thick facings of solid walnut to the carcase ends. The doors, drawer fronts, base and slatted back are also walnut (an oak back would have further lightened the interior). The result is a walnut cabinet with an oak interior. You can also use a light-colored, less expensive wood, such as cherry or birch, for the entire piece.

Though this is a large, complex piece, it needn't overwhelm you or your shop. Read through the following description and study the drawings to get a firm grasp on the construction. The piece is best built in manageable sections—carcase, base, doors and drawers, back, shelves and top. Most important, organize your work logically: Prepare the wood for the carcase sides, top, bottom and dividers at the same time, cut similar joints with the same machine settings, and so on. You can avoid errors by making a full-size mock-up of any detail you don't understand.

The carcase—The carcase is simply a large box, separated into thirds by two vertical dividers. A horizontal divider and a short, vertical drawer divider in the middle third support the two drawers. The grain of all these pieces runs in the same direction, so the carcase won't self-destruct with changes in humidity. For maximum strength and rigidity, the top, bottom and sides are through-dovetailed, and the dividers are through-tenoned and wedged, as shown in the drawing on p. 126.

Join up the boards for the carcase parts, then plane and cut them to size. Make sure that the ends of the pieces are square to the edges so that the carcase will be square when assembled. The top and bottom are 92½ in. long and 17¾ in. wide. The carcase ends and horizontal and vertical dividers are all 17⅛ in. wide. The difference in width is the allowance for the ¾-in.-thick back, which is set in ⅜ in. from the edges of the carcase top and bottom. The ends and vertical dividers are 27 in. long, the horizontal divider is 28¾ in. long, and the short, vertical divider between the two drawers is 6½ in. long. (These dimensions include the joints, but not the lippings, which are added after the carcase is assembled.)

Lay out and cut the joints. Make sure that the front edges of all the carcase parts will finish flush with each other. It is helpful to mark the front edge of each piece and to number or letter the mating parts of each joint to avoid confusion. Lay out and cut the dovetails as described on pp. 30-31. I place the tails on the top and bottom to make assembly easier—few people have 8-ft.-long clamps. If you're not facing the ends, you can lap-dovetail the carcase to hide the joints from view.

Scribe a line around the ends of the dividers to lay out the through tenons. The dividers and ends are the same length, so use the same marking gauge setting as for the dovetails. Mark a 1-in.-wide tenon ½ in. from each edge and two more tenons evenly spaced between the first two; the tenons can be as thick as the dividers. Saw the tenons with a backsaw, clear the waste between them with a bandsaw or coping saw, and chisel to the scribed line.

Now carefully lay out and cut the mortises. The dividers must be at right angles to the front edges of the carcase; the openings they create must be square, or the doors and drawers won't work properly. Bore through from both faces to clear the waste from the mortises, then chisel to the lines, working from both

faces to prevent tear-out. It is essential that these through-tenoned joints be tight, because they stiffen the carcase to help prevent it from racking. Cut a slot in each tenon for a wedge.

The wooden shelf standards shown in the photo at right are housed in ¾-in.-wide by ⅛-in.-deep grooves in the dividers. Rout the grooves, or use a dado head on the tablesaw. The standards will be made later, but it's far more difficult to cut the grooves after assembling the carcase.

Sand the inside faces of the top, bottom and ends, and both faces of the dividers. If you're lacquering or varnishing the cabinet, you can finish these faces now. (If you're using an oil finish, apply it after assembly, or put tape over the joints to keep the surfaces free of oil for gluing.)

Gluing up the carcase requires a helper and proper preparation. Don't glue up at the end of the day when you're tired—you'll need to be cool and calm to sort out any problems that may arise. Dry-assemble the carcase for a final check and determine what clamps you'll need. You'll need to push the horizontal divider tight to the two verticals. There's no need to push the rest of the joints tight, only just enough to see that all the parts align. Check that the lettering or numbering of the joints is clear, all the wedge slots are cut and the inside surfaces are sanded and finished.

It's impossible to put a clamp in the middle of the carcase to pull the top and bottom flat to the vertical dividers. I make four heavy, clamping bearers as long as the carcase is wide and slightly crowned, so that a clamp on each end of the bearers will exert pressure in the middle. If the tenons are slightly long, cut a groove down the center of the bearers' crowned edges, so the pressure will bear on the top or bottom, not the ends of the tenons. You'll also need to make clamping blocks for the dovetails (for how to make clamping blocks, see p. 31). Clear an area, set up and level two sawhorses to support the carcase, and lay out everything you'll need for gluing up.

It takes at least half an hour to assemble the carcase, so use a resin glue that sets up slowly. First, assemble the horizontal and two vertical dividers and pull them tight with the bearers and clamps. Check that the pieces are square to each other, then remove the clamps and drive in the wedges.

Spread glue on the remaining mortises and tenons and on the dovetails. Add the short vertical divider to the horizontal divider, push the vertical dividers and

Wooden standards, housed in grooves in the dividers, hold wooden pegs that support the shelves. The door is hung with a Soss hinge, which is mortised into the door stile and the lipping of the divider.

the two ends into the bottom, and add the top. Drive the joints most of the way home with a hammer and block of wood, then pull them tight with the clamps, bearers and blocks.

When all the joints are pulled home, remove the clamps and measure the diagonals of the openings (front and back) to check the carcase for square. If one diagonal is longer, push across it to bring the carcase square. (Use a clamp if necessary, but don't leave it on the diagonal while the glue is curing, because the carcase might twist.) Sight across the front and back edges of the carcase to make sure there's no twist. If you need to add clamps to pull the shoulders of the dividers tight, apply as little pressure as possible and check for square again after the clamps are placed. When you're satisfied that the carcase is square, drive in the wedges, and let the glue cure.

Lippings and facings—Next, plane the dovetails and through tenons flush, then prepare the front edges of the carcase for the lippings by planing them flush with each other and square to the adjacent faces. Make the 1¼-in.-thick lippings for the ends and dividers first. The end lippings are 1⁹⁄₁₆ in. wide; each one overlaps the outside face of the carcase end by ¾-in. and overlaps the inside face by ¹⁄₁₆ in. The overlap on the outside face will cover the walnut facing that will be attached later. The lippings on the long vertical dividers overlap both adjacent faces by ¹⁄₁₆ in. Cut these vertical lippings about ¹⁄₃₂ in. long so you can plane their ends flush with the top and bottom. The lipping on the horizontal divider is flush with both adjacent faces so that it won't interfere with the drawers. Make the lipping slightly thicker than the divider, and scrape it flush after it's glued on.

I hang the doors with Soss hinges (shown in the photo on p. 121). The hinges are set into small mortises in the edges of the door stiles and carcase lippings, and therefore can't be seen when the doors are closed. (See Appendix 5 for sources of supply.) It's much easier to mortise the lippings before gluing them to the carcase than after. The mortising can be done on the drill press with a power-bore bit, as explained in the instructions that come with each set of hinges. A template is also included, which positions the mortises so the faces of the doors will be flush with the faces of the lippings. Be sure to offset the hinges on opposite edges of a divider's lipping, so that the screws don't meet.

Dowels spaced every foot or so will help to position the lippings while gluing. Be careful not to dowel into a hinge mortise. I glue the lippings with pipe clamps and heavy bearers (about ⅞ in. by 2 in. by 27 in.). Place the bearer, edge up, on the lipping to distribute the clamping pressure evenly—a job best done with the carcase resting on its back on a pair of sawhorses.

Because the doors and drawers overlap the edges of the top, bottom and short vertical divider, the lippings for those parts are only ½ in. thick. The back edges of the top and bottom also get ½-in.-thick lippings (the dividers and ends are covered by the carcase back). Cut the lippings a fraction over ¾ in. wide so that you can scrape or plane them flush with the faces of the top and bottom after they're glued on. Dowel these lippings, too, if you're worried about them slipping, and clamp them in place using bearers. With help, it's easy to clamp the lippings on both edges of the top and bottom at the same time.

Glue up the walnut facings for the carcase ends. Remember that the back edge of the facings are flush with the back edge of the top and bottom, not the back edge of the carcase ends. Cut the facings ¹⁄₃₂ in. over finished length; after attaching them, you can plane them even with the carcase top and bottom. Plane a bevel on the mating surfaces of the facing and lipping to make a small *V*-groove to emphasize the joint. Attach the facings by screwing through the carcase ends near the edges and in the center. If glued together, the facing and end would warp with seasonal humidity changes because oak and walnut have different shrinkage values, but the screws will give enough to avoid warping. Glue the edge of the facing to the lip so that the joint won't open with movement.

The base—I make and attach the base next, so that the carcase will be fixed in position when making and fitting the doors and drawers. The base consists of two long, heavy rails dovetailed to two end rails, a center stretcher for reinforcement and four sturdy legs bridle-jointed to the long rails. Make the legs and the ¾ in.-thick short rails from solid walnut (laminate the legs if necessary). I use oak faced with ½-in.-thick walnut for the long, 2-in.-thick rails. To glue the facings, sandwich them between the rails and clamp them with *C*-clamps—the rails are thick enough to distribute the clamping pressure.

The facings extend beyond the ends of the rails to form a lapped through dovetail, so that only walnut shows on the end of the base. Cut the laps and dove-tails, stub-tenon the center stretcher to the rails, then notch the rails and the legs as shown in the drawing on p. 126 to form the bridle joints. Groove the rails for the tabletop fasteners or wooden buttons, then glue up the base. (See p. 98 for how to make wooden buttons.) Plane the dovetails flush, screw the base to the carcase, then set the cabinet on a flat, level surface while you make and fit the doors, drawers and carcase back.

Doors—Each door is made up of a bridle-jointed frame with narrow slats held in place by splines. I make the doors to fit the openings exactly, then I plane the edges for clearance when hanging them. Plane the rails, stiles and slats ¾ in. thick, then cut the bridle joints as described on p. 36. Dry-assemble the frames, then cut the slats to fit, allowing a little sideways play in the slats for expansion. Groove the edges and ends of the slats and the inside edges of the rails and stiles for ⅛-in. splines. (The splines are best made of the same wood as the doors, and finished before assembly.) Chamfer the arrises on both faces of the stiles, rails and slats to form *V*-grooves, as shown in the photo at near right.

Before assembly, mortise the edges of the appropriate stiles for the hinges. Mark the positions by placing each hinge stile in its carcase opening next to the mortised lipping. Use the hinge template to position the hinges on the stile so that the face of the door will be flush with the faces of the vertical lippings. When gluing up, make sure that the doors are flat.

Hang the doors and plane the edges, or trim them with a carbide blade on the tablesaw for a uniform clearance of ⅟₃₂ in. to ⅟₁₆ in. all around. The edges of stiles that aren't hinged should be beveled about 5° toward the inside so the doors can swing shut. (You may have the doors on and off the cabinet several times before you get the clearances right.) I mounted brass double-ball catches, as shown at far right, on the bottom faces of the top and horizontal divider.

Drawers—The drawers are dovetailed oak boxes with walnut fronts screwed onto them. This false-front construction arouses indignation in the minds of some purists, but it is a perfectly sound method for a drawer whose front is wider than its opening. Here, the false front overlaps ⅜-in.-thick runners on one end and the short vertical divider on the other, as

Brass double-ball catches, mounted here on strips of walnut, can be adjusted to give more or less resistance to opening. The door overlaps the lipped edge of the top.

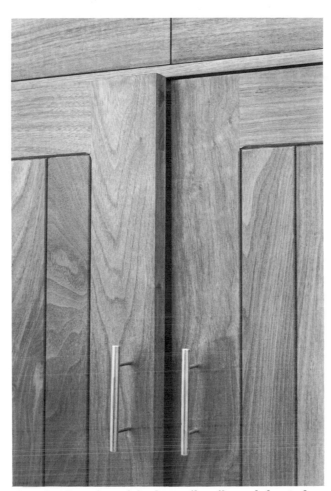

Chamfer the arrises of the door rails, stiles and slats to form V-grooves. Dry-assemble the frames and chamfer them using a router bit with a ball-bearing pilot. The simple pull is made by brazing two pieces of ⅛-in. brazing rod to a ¼-in. piece.

well as the edge of the carcase top. The slotted-dove-tail construction on p. 39 will also work.

Slot-screw the runners to the long dividers, as shown in the plan drawings, and make the boxes to fit the openings. I used ½-in. oak for the box sides, front and back. (If the bottom is plywood, it can be enclosed; if it's solid wood, slot-screw it to the bottom edge of the back to allow for movement.) Plane the edges and sides until the boxes run easily in the openings, but without much play.

I made the two false fronts from the same board, so the grain and color would be continuous. Cut the fronts slightly oversized, screw them to the drawers, then plane the edges and ends until the clearances around each front are even, about ¹⁄₃₂ in. to ¹⁄₁₆ in. If the faces of the drawer fronts extend beyond the lippings, plane them flush. If they are shy of the lippings, tap the runners forward to bring the fronts flush. You may wish to line one or both drawers with felt for silverware, and add internal divisions to keep things in place.

I made the drawer and door pulls out of ¼-in. and ⅛-in. brazing rods obtained from the local machine shop. Bore holes to seat the ⅛-in. pieces, then braze the rods together with silver solder—lead solder is too weak. An ordinary propane torch will braze small sections such as these. To install the pulls, bore holes ¹⁄₆₄-in. smaller than the diameter of the rod through the drawer front or door stile. Ease the pulls into the holes using a vise—tapping them with a hammer will probably break the solder.

Shelves—Next, make and install the wooden shelf standards that hold the pegs for the adjustable shelves. The standards in each compartment must have holes at identical heights and intervals, or the shelves will wobble. To ensure alignment, I make four standards at once. Cut a piece of ¾-in. by 2½-in. walnut as long as the grooves in the compartment, then use the drill press with a fence clamped to the table to bore ⅜-in. holes on 1-in. centers from edge to edge through the piece. Rip the piece into four standards, each ½ in. thick, and glue them into the ⅛-in.-deep grooves cut in the divisions. If you need to apply pressure to the standards while gluing, cut ¼-in.-thick pieces of wood about 1 in. longer than the width of the compartment and spring them between two opposite standards. (Piano makers call these springy devices go-bars.)

I turned the wooden shelf pegs on the lathe; you could whittle them or substitute ⅜-in. brazing rod. To make pegs with one round and one square end, as shown in the plan drawings, cut 1-in.-long pieces off a length of ⅜-in.-square oak or walnut—cut enough for plenty of pegs, because you'll always need spares. Fasten a scrap piece of hardwood, about ¾ in. thick, to a lathe faceplate. Mount the faceplate and turn on the lathe to mark the center of the scrap, then bore a ⅜-in. hole in the center. Chisel this hole square so a peg will fit it tightly. Insert a peg and turn one end round. To accommodate the length of the pegs, you may need to deepen the holes in the standards by boring into the dividers with an electric drill.

The shelves are solid oak, ⅞ in. thick. I taper the front edge to ⅝ in. thick so they don't look clumsy. Whether the front edges look better lipped with walnut is a matter of preference. Notch the ends for the shelf standards—the notches prevent the shelves from sliding off the pegs.

The back—If the carcase back is attractive, the cabinet needn't be placed against a wall, but can be used as a room divider. I made a framed back of walnut. The long rails and end stiles are bridle-jointed and the intermediate stiles are stub-tenoned. Groove the rails and stiles to house the ⅜-in.-thick slats. (The slats could be replaced by three veneered plywood panels.) Groove the edges of the slats for ⅛-in.-thick splines made of the same wood as the slats. The splines align the slats and prevent gaps from showing when the slats shrink.

When assembling the back, insert the slats in the frame and the splines in the slats without glue, so the slats are free to move. It's easiest to glue the top and bottom rails and the center stiles and slats first, then add the remaining slats and bridle-jointed end stiles. Fit the back to the opening, then secure it to the carcase ends and dividers with No. 6 brass screws.

The top—The serving table is now complete except for the top. Solid granite, slate or marble tops are so heavy that there is no need to secure them to the carcase. Stone tops should be treated with a masonry sealer to prevent stains (see Appendix 5 for sources of supply). The stereo cabinet shown on the opposite page, a variation on the serving-table design, has a solid-walnut top, which is tenoned to the ends and dividers, and thus is a part of the structure.

Another alternative to a thick, heavy stone top is ceramic tile or squares of slate glued to an underlayment (p. 60). Edge the top with solid wood, and slot-screw through the carcase top to the underlayment. Make sure to adapt the size of the top to some multiple of the size of the tile you choose, with allowance for grouting

If you choose slate, don't be tempted by the cheapness and availability of used roofing slate. These slates are split on two surfaces and are all slightly different thicknesses, which makes it difficult to obtain a level, even surface. I recommend slate sold for flooring, which is gauged (machined flat on one side) and usually averages ⁵⁄₁₆ in. in thickness. (See Appendix 5 for sources of supply.) Flooring slate can be cut on a tablesaw using a masonry blade. This creates a lot of stone dust, so use a mask when cutting it and give the machine a thorough vacuuming when you are through. Glue the machined side to the underlayment, add a dark-colored grout and protect the top with masonry sealer.

This stereo cabinet has walnut top and ends, and an oak bottom and dividers The opening cut in the top permits access to the turntable. The four lower doors, which slide on tracks, conceal stored records.

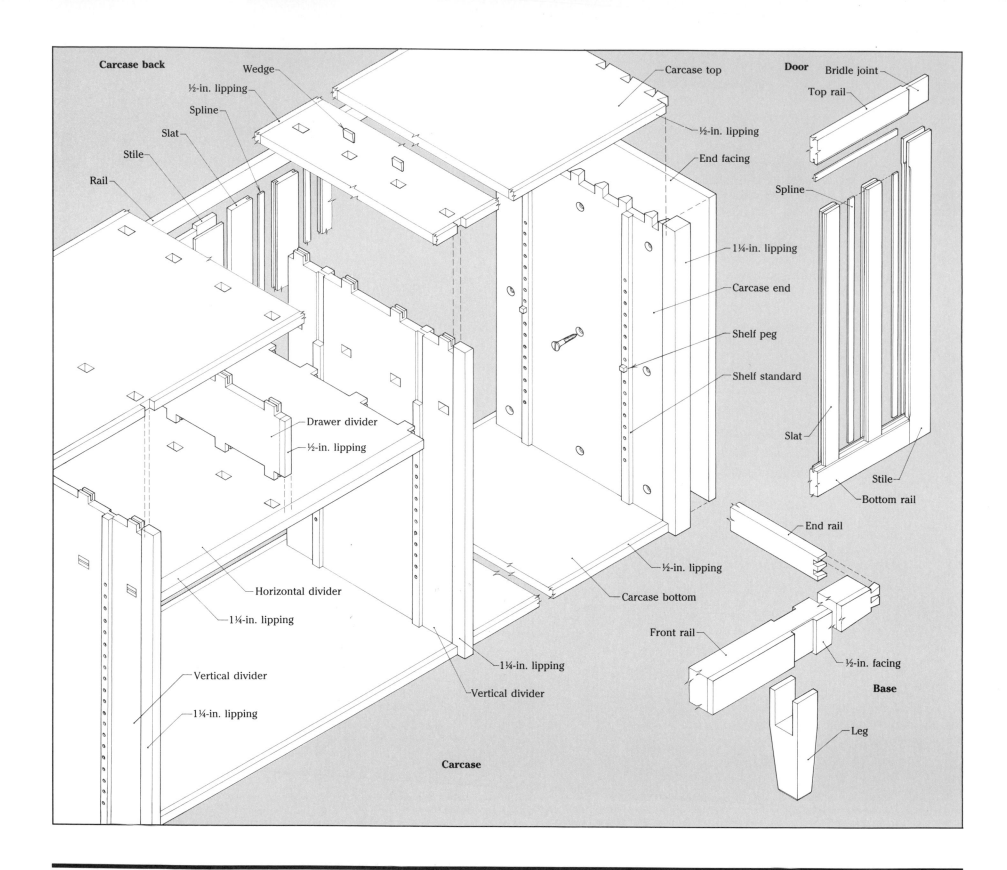

Carcase back

Wedge

½-in. lipping

Spline

Slat

Stile

Rail

Carcase top

½-in. lipping

End facing

1¼-in. lipping

Carcase end

Shelf peg

Shelf standard

Slat

Drawer divider

½-in. lipping

Horizontal divider

1¼-in. lipping

Vertical divider

1¼-in. lipping

½-in. lipping

Carcase bottom

1¼-in. lipping

Vertical divider

Carcase

Door

Bridle joint

Top rail

Spline

Stile

Bottom rail

End rail

Front rail

½-in. facing

Base

Leg

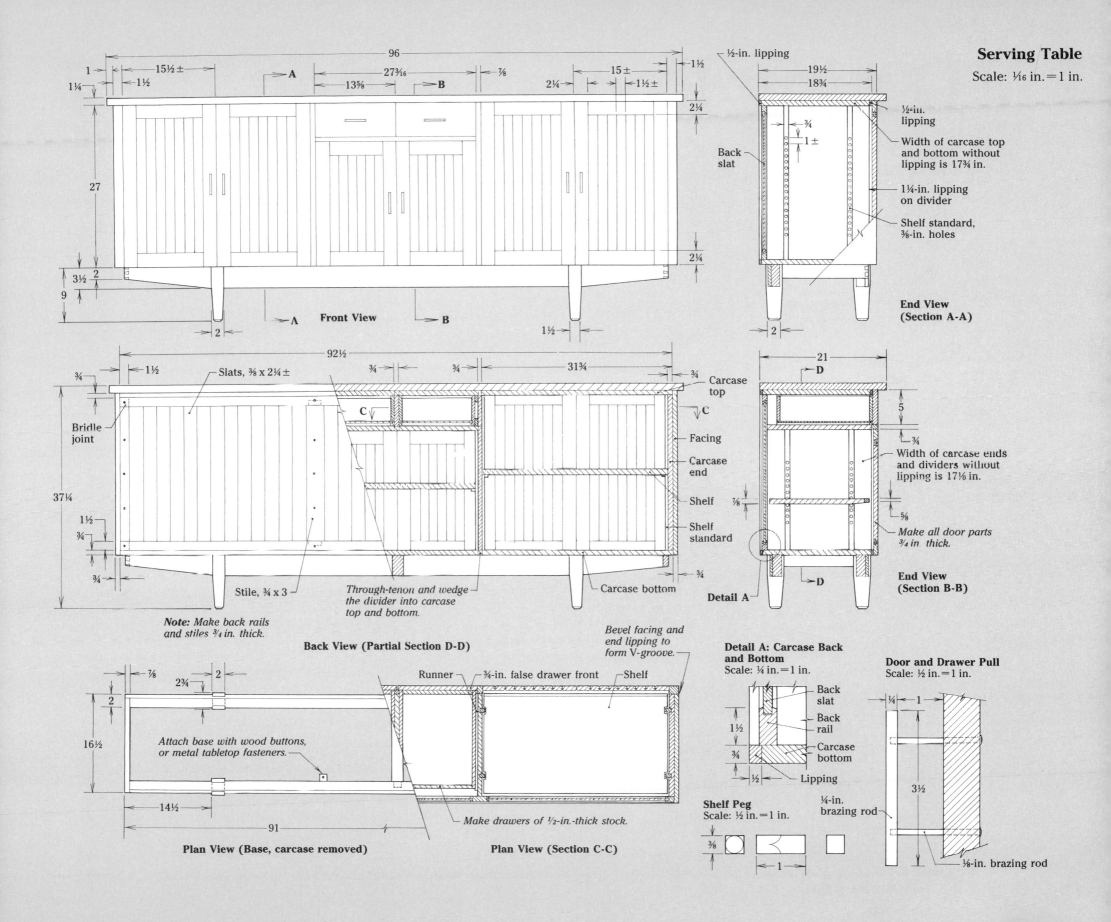

Serving Table

Scale: 1/16 in. = 1 in.

Front View

96
1
1¼
15½ ±
1½
A
13⅝
27³⁄₁₆
B
⅞
2¼
15 ±
1½ ±
1½
2¼
27
2¼
3½
2
9
2
A
B

End View (Section A-A)

19½
18¾
¾
1 ±
½-in. lipping
½-in. lipping
Back slat
Width of carcase top and bottom without lipping is 17¾ in.
1¼-in. lipping on divider
Shelf standard, ⅜-in. holes
2

Back View (Partial Section D-D)

92½
¾
1½
Slats, ⅜ x 2¼ ±
¾
¾
31¾
¾
Carcase top
Bridle joint
C
C
Facing
Carcase end
Shelf
37¼
Shelf standard
1½
¾
¾
Stile, ¾ x 3
Through-tenon and wedge the divider into carcase top and bottom.
Carcase bottom

Note: Make back rails and stiles ¾ in. thick.

End View (Section B-B)

21
D
5
¾
Width of carcase ends and dividers without lipping is 17⅛ in.
⅞
⅝
Make all door parts ¾ in. thick.
Detail A
D

Plan View (Base, carcase removed)

⅞
2
2¾
2
2
16½
Attach base with wood buttons, or metal tabletop fasteners.
14½
91

Plan View (Section C-C)

Bevel facing and end lipping to form V-groove.
Runner
¾-in. false drawer front
Shelf
Make drawers of ½-in.-thick stock.

Detail A: Carcase Back and Bottom
Scale: ¼ in. = 1 in.

Back slat
Back rail
1½
¾
Carcase bottom
½
Lipping

Shelf Peg
Scale: ½ in. = 1 in.

⅜
1

Door and Drawer Pull
Scale: ½ in. = 1 in.

¼
1
3½
¼-in. brazing rod
⅛-in. brazing rod

Dining Room Seating 7

About Chairs and Stools

Chairs have always been made in greater quantity and diversity of style than any other type of furniture. In ancient times, chairs were often used to convey the power and dignity of the sitter, and so had a symbolic importance transcending their function as furniture.

One of the oldest surviving ceremonial seats is the great ecclesiastical throne of Tutankhamen, shown in the photo at bottom left on the opposite page. In 1357 B.C., it was walled up with the god-king's mummified body and remained untouched for over 3000 years. Made of cedar with gold mounts, the chair is carved to represent the union of Upper and Lower Egypt, and its inscriptions list the attributes and achievements of Tutankhamen. With striking, but rather obvious symbolism, the pharaoh rested his feet on a matching footstool inscribed with the names of Egypt's nine traditional enemies.

A much later but more monumental throne is shown in the photo at far right. Made in 1300 A.D. for Edward I of England, this throne has been used ever since for the coronation of British kings and queens. Edward, like the Romans 1000 years before him, spent much of his time trying to put down the unruly Scots. After a successful campaign, he seized one of Scotland's national treasures, the mystical Stone of Scone, and had a shelf built for it in the base of this throne. He could then not only display the stone as a trophy, but with a symbolism even cruder than the Pharaoh's, sit on it.

The republican Greeks had no need for thrones, and used their talents to develop a peculiarly beautiful chair known as a *klismos,* shown at top center. Unfortunately, none of these elegant chairs have survived, but their forms are known from relief carvings and painted urns. No stretchers connected the curved legs, which must have been springy—well suited for use outdoors or on uneven surfaces. It is not known whether the legs were made from specially grown curved trees or branches, or if they were bent, and the nature of the joints is still being debated.

Early English chairs have a heaviness often bordering on clumsy, as shown in the photo at bottom center, but you must bear in mind that they were made during a time of constant civil strife. Armor and weapons were frequently worn inside the house and furniture had to withstand rough use. With the ending of the Wars of the Roses in 1480, chairs became lighter and the carving more delicate. It was not until the eighteenth century, however, that English chairs rivaled the Greek *klismos* in elegance and comfort.

Human anatomy hasn't changed much, and the problems of chair design that faced the Greeks still face us today. A lot of experience is needed to design and make a chair that is light, comfortable and durable. People abuse chairs as they do no other piece of furniture. They stand on them or tip them back on two legs, which imposes terrific strains on the rear joints. Most of my early attempts at chairs were failures because I simply did not realize how strong chairs must be if they are to last.

The first chairs I made did not even survive long enough to be photographed. I based the design on an old kitchen chair with a solid pine seat, turned maple legs and a steam-bent, oak back. I made four in cherry, but having no lathe, I shaped all the round pieces with a rasp and spokeshave. When I steam-bent the backs, I found that cherry, unlike oak, cracks sooner than bends. Carving the hollow in the cherry seat was tedious, and the joints didn't fit very well because the tenons were not perfectly round. After assembly, I aggravated all my prevous mistakes by driving metal brads into the joints, making it impossible to ever disassemble the chair for regluing.

Although the chairs were a disaster, the experience of making them was valuable. I realized that there were good reasons for the back to be of oak, the seat of pine and the legs to be maple and turned on a

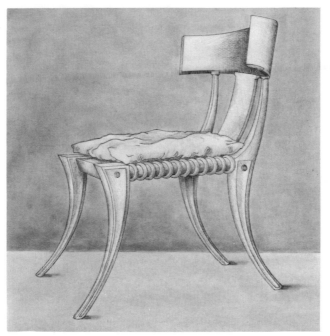

The Greek klismos dates from the sixth century B.C. The steam-bent or naturally curved legs were joined to four round rails. Plaited cord or strips of leather were wrapped around the rails to support a cushion.

The ecclesiastical throne of Tutankhamen is made of ebony with gold mounts and ivory, lapis lazuli and other precious inlays. The seat is a variant of the stools of the period, and the back appears to be a later addition.

This massive chair was made in sixteenth-century England, when joiners made chairs as well as houses, using the same techniques for both.

The throne made for King Edward I of England, now called the Coronation Chair, is kept in the crypt of Westminster Abbey in London. The lions at the base are eighteenth-century copies of sixteenth-century additions to the chair. Scotland's Stone of Scone rests on a platform beneath the seat.

The selection of materials and construction techniques for a chair is as important as the design. The chair on the left has a carved pine seat, a bow back of steam-bent oak, and turned maple legs and spindles. The one at right is a copy in walnut. Although walnut turns well, it doesn't bend easily, so the back had to be laminated.

Though a three-legged chair isn't a bad idea, this one lacked sufficient bracing for the legs and support for the back.

Unbraced, the rail-to-leg joints of this chair failed under the strain of daily use. Adding the diagonal stretcher allowed the chair to be saved without disassembling it, which would have destroyed the rush seat.

lathe. The next time I copied an old chair, I used more-appropriate materials and proper techniques. That chair, shown in the foreground in the photo at top, has lasted well.

The chair at bottom left, made in walnut with a laminated back, had two design flaws that proved to be fatal: The legs were insufficiently braced and the back support too weak. It was fortunate that I only made one chair, because it soon came apart. Although this chair failed, I still think that the idea of a three-legged chair is valid. The three legs discourage people from tipping the chair back, and will stand firmly on an uneven surface.

I once made a set of six chairs based on the design of the rush-seat stool (pp. 52-53). The stool is perfectly sound, but trying to adapt it to make a chair was a mistake. After a few years of use, the rear joints failed on all six chairs, and the client brought them back for repair, or if repair proved impossible, replacement. I couldn't take them apart for regluing without destroying the rush seats, and anyway, the trouble was in the design, not the joints. So I added a diagonal stretcher, as shown at bottom right, and put a long machine screw through the rear joints into a captive nut slotted into the inside of the rail. The screw heads were plugged with wood, and the repair actually improved the appearance of the chairs.

I have included this final disaster story to illustrate the dangers of adapting existing designs. A stool and a chair appear to be quite similar—both are sat upon—but because you can lean back in a chair, the forces imposed on the structure are more severe and call for a different design.

The dining chair shown on the opposite page is the result of further experimentation. I made several full-size versions and subjected them to family wear and tear for half a year before selling one. About fifty are now in use, and none have yet failed. I don't make chairs for the money—I couldn't charge enough. I make them because chairs should be part of a furniture maker's repertoire, and also because I enjoy the challenge.

Dining Chair

This is a sturdy, comfortable chair that can be used equally well at a dining table or a desk. The chair is square in plan, and all the legs are straight and vertical, so there are no odd angles to complicate the making. The curved back and seat and the tapered side rails make the chair just as comfortable as chairs with angled construction.

Both the seat and the back are glued up from thinner pieces, a process that requires two forms or molds. This is a considerable amount of work for one chair, and molds can be used many times over, so it makes sense to build a set of at least four chairs. You can also save time and cut down on errors by performing other operations on all the parts at once, such as laying out and cutting the tenons.

Because people tend to tip back in chairs, the back-leg-to-side-rail joint is crucial. I make the rail wider at the back and twin-tenon it to the leg. A twin tenon has double the gluing surface of a single, wide tenon, and the twin mortises weaken the leg less than a single, wide mortise. I once saw the chair-torture machine operated by the Danish Furniture Maker's Control Association in action. A 50-kg. (110 lb.) weight was strapped to the back and seat of the victim, which was then rocked back and forth on its rear legs by a steel arm. A passing grade was 30,000 cycles before joint failure, but some chairs made 50,000 before giving up the ghost. I don't know how these chairs I've made would rate if tested, but in normal use there have been no reports of failures so far.

The front rail, seat, back and back rung join the chair from side to side. I dowel the front rail, because this weakens the leg less than another mortise would. Screwing the plywood seat to the side rails provides considerable additional strength.

Construction

The wood you select must be suitable for turning, so it should be fine-grained like maple or cherry, not coarse-grained and splintery like oak. The wood must also be reasonably strong, and must make a good glue joint—for this reason I avoid teak, which is oily. (The chair shown at right is made of walnut.) When choosing the wood, also consider where the chair will be used, the prevailing tone of the room, its colors and other furniture, and the texture and color of the upholstery fabric you plan to use. If the chair is likely to

The chair is a simple shape, so the details catch the eye. It is important that the joints fit precisely and the curves flow smoothly from leg to rail. The side rails and legs are joined by twin mortise-and-tenon joints, the front rail and legs by dowels, the back stretcher and legs by round mortises and tenons. The back and seat are screwed in place.

be used by messy eaters—of any age—choose an upholstery fabric that can be cleaned easily.

The seat and back—Make the laminated back and seat first, because the curves and bevels on the frame rails are determined by the curve of the seat. You can continue to make the chair while waiting for the glue to cure on the laminated parts in the molds—I always leave them for at least twelve hours.

I tried to make the curve of the seat the same as the back so I would need only one mold, but I was defeated by human anatomy, which decrees that these curves be different. Because I expected to use the molds for several dozen chairs, I made them of Douglas fir. Laminated particleboard or fir plywood would do as well—it just depends on what kind of scrap you have most of.

The back mold requires convex and concave halves, as shown in the bottom photo on the opposite page. Make the mold about ½ in. thicker than the width of the back so that you have something to trim after gluing. Glue up a single, rectangular block and bandsaw it to form two halves, following the outside curve of the back. Bandsaw ½ in. off the curved edge of the convex half to allow for the thickness of the veneers. Clean the curved surfaces with a spokeshave or Surform; be careful to keep the curved surfaces perpendicular to the faces of the molds. (You can cut deep slots in the back of one part of a mold to allow it to flex slightly under pressure.) Then, give the surfaces a thorough waxing to prevent the glue from adhering.

You can buy veneer for the back laminations or cut them yourself. I bandsaw ³⁄₁₆-in.-thick veneer off 2-in.-thick stock using a wide blade and a fence clamped to the table. Then I plane them ⅛ in. thick—any thicker and they will be hard to bend. Select straight-grained wood for the veneers. Run them through the planer on a thick backing board, or the planer will tear them up. I use a piece of 1-in. birch plywood for a backing board and feed it through the planer under the veneer. You can cut the veneer on a tablesaw with a carbide blade, but this usually leaves a slight step in the middle of each piece, which must be removed before gluing up. The back is made up of four veneers, but cut a few extra for insurance. (Because the grain of each veneer runs in the same direction, there is no need to use an odd number for balance.) Cut the veneers about ½ in. wider and 3 in. longer than the final dimensions of the back.

It's not a bad idea to dry-clamp to determine the number and placement of clamps required to pull the joints tight and to make sure the veneers will bend. I found that ten clamps, five on each side of the mold, were sufficient. Plastic resin glues are best for laminating. The assembly times of Titebond and the other polyvinyls are too short, and these glues tend to creep when heavily stressed over a period of time.

The seat requires only a convex mold and heavy bearers to distribute the clamping pressure, as shown at top right. The mold is glued up and bandsawn to shape. Unless you have a large bandsaw, you will have to saw two or more sections and glue them up side by side. When the mold is assembled, plane out any irregularities in the curved surface, and wax heavily to prevent the glue from sticking. I added four dowel legs to the mold to make placing the clamps easier. Plane the bearing edge of each hardwood bearer to a slight crown (about ⅛ in. in length) so pressure will be applied in the center of the mold.

I use four pieces of ⅛-in. plywood for the seat, arranged so that the grain of the face plies runs at right angles to the curve—from front to back of the seat. Cut the plywood slightly oversized so it can be trimmed after gluing. A small, short-nap paint roller is useful for spreading glue on large surfaces like these.

Trim the seat and back to size after gluing. The curves can be bandsawn, but be sure that the piece touches the bandsaw table near the blade. Clean up and round the edges of the back with a plane and spokeshave, and then sand the faces.

The chair frame—Start with the legs. Cut the blanks for the legs out of 2-in. stock with the straightest grain you can find. Joint two adjacent surfaces and saw or plane the other two to make the blanks exactly 1½ in. square. Cut the blanks to length, two long and two short for each chair. Make the short legs about ½ in. overlong, so the end grain won't split out while mortising. (If you are making a set of chairs, select and mark the four legs of each chair now.)

It's best to cut and fit the joints for the rails before turning the legs—square legs are more easily held in a vise or clamped to the bench while you work on them. Cut the twin mortises first. You need mark only one pair of legs if you have a mortising machine with a sliding carriage; set the carriage stops to the limits of the marked mortises on the front leg and cut the mortises on all the front legs, then do the same for

A single, convex mold and heavy bearers shape the four ⅛-in.-thick plywood laminates of the seat. Small gaps in the glue joints won't matter because the seat is upholstered.

The curved back is glued up in a two-part mold (consisting of convex and concave halves), made of solid wood, scrap plywood or particleboard. The inner surfaces of the mold should be smooth, even curves.

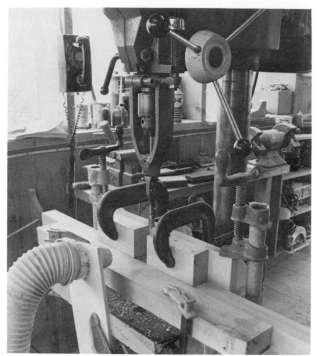

Fences on both sides position the leg for mortising on the drill press. An air compressor blows the shavings away.

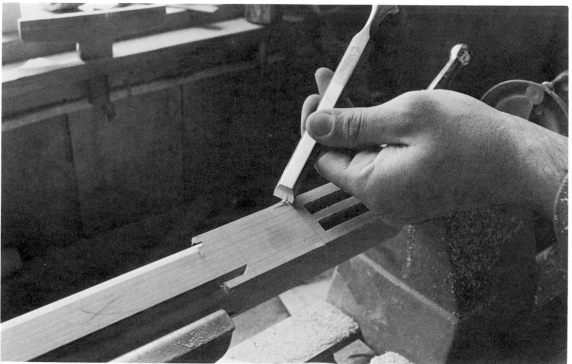

To avoid tear-out where the leg makes the transition from square section to round, remove most of the waste with a chisel before turning.

the back legs. I used a mortising attachment on the drill press, as shown at top left. A fence on each side of the leg kept the leg positioned under the mortising chisel, so I only needed to mark the top and bottom limit of each mortise with a knife. Remember to haunch the mortises in the front legs.

Make a full-size template for the side rails, including the tenons at each end. The shoulders will be perpendicular to the floor, but not to the edges, which taper from front to back, so it's important that the template be accurate. I cut the twin tenons on the tablesaw, using a high fence for the cheek cuts and the miter gauge (set at the proper angles by trial and error on scrap wood) for the shoulder cuts, using the rip fence as a stop. Clear the waste between the tenons with an auger bit or coping saw and chisel to the lines. The tenons must fit snugly in the mortises, but shouldn't need to be forced.

As you fit the tenons to each leg, mark with a pencil line the point where the edges of the rail meet the leg—the legs are turned to these lines. Number or letter each joint in a place where it will not be accidentally erased.

To counterbore the side rails for the seat screws, set the depth stop on the drill press so a ⅜-in. bit will stop 1 in. above the table. Place the top edge of each rail on the table, and bore all the clearance holes for the screw heads to this depth. (You can then use the same length of screw in each of the four holes.) Change the bit and the stop setting and bore shank-clearance holes for a No. 8 screw centered in the larger holes. I bevel the top edge of the rails on the tablesaw to take the seat. To determine this bevel, place the rails about the right distance apart on the benchtop, lay the seat on the rails and set a sliding bevel to the correct angle.

Make the front rail next. Cut it rectangular and saw the ends of the rail square to its edges. Bore the holes for the dowels in the ends using a self-centering doweling jig or a drill press with the table set vertically. When positioning the dowels, remember that the top edge of the rail will be cut down later to meet the side-rail bevels. Bore clearance holes for the seat fastening screws in the rail.

Mark the positions of the dowel holes in the legs using dowel centers set in the holes in the rail. Lay the rail and the leg face down on a flat surface, such as a tablesaw, and position them so the joint is correctly aligned. Then give the rail a single, smart blow with a hammer. (The dowel holes in the leg are bored and the top edge of the rail is curved after the legs and side rails have been assembled.)

Turn the legs next. Mark the diagonals on each end of the legs to find the centers. These centers must be accurate—if they're off, the flat surfaces of each leg won't be tangent to the turned cylinder. To remove waste before turning, I set the tablesaw blade at 45° and I fix stops to the rip fence. Then I saw the outside corners of the legs to within 2 in. of the shoulder marks, and cut the waste free with a backsaw. It's easy to tear the wood fibers near the shoulder mark with the turning gouge, so start the curve with a chisel before turning, as shown in the bottom photo on the opposite page. All the legs are tapered at their bottom ends; the back legs are also tapered at their top ends. Finish-sand the legs on the lathe, up to where the leg changes from round to flat. Those transitions will be trimmed and sanded after assembly.

Glue up the side rails and legs, making sure that the legs are exactly parallel. If they taper in or out, change the clamp's center of pressure. When the glue has cured, plane the faces of each rail flush with the flat faces of both legs. (If necessary, deepen the dowel-center dimples on the leg faces so they won't get planed off.) Bevel the top ends of the front legs to match the side rails—trim the waste with a backsaw and plane the ends flush with the side-rail bevels.

Plane the outside corner off the front legs and the two outside corners off the back, as shown at top right. Sand the surfaces flush with the cylinder. With a sharp chisel or knife, fade the rounds neatly into the rails, as shown at bottom right. Don't use sandpaper or a wood file, because inevitably they'll blur the sharpness of the arris that defines the transition.

Now bore the holes for the dowels in the front legs, centered on the dowel-center dimples. Make the holes a fraction deep, so that the dowels won't bottom out and keep the joint from closing. Whether you bore the holes by hand or on the drill press, check that the bit is at right angles to the face of the leg.

Next, bore the holes in the back legs for the round tenons of the back stretcher. Turn the stretcher so its shoulder-to-shoulder length equals the length of the front rail, and size the tenons so they will fit snugly.

Dry-assemble the front rail and stretcher to the glued-up rails and legs, and mark the intersections of the side-rail bevels with the back face of the front rail. Also, hold the chair back on top of the back legs, and

mark its curve on the ends of the legs. Take the chair apart, place the end of the chair seat on the front rail, line up the curve with the marks at each end, and trace the curve on the rail. Bandsaw about ⅛ in. above the line. The top edge of the front rail should be beveled so the seat will lie flat on it. Assemble the chair frame and bevel the rail with a spokeshave to match the angle of the side rails.

Before gluing up the pairs of frames, trim the top of the back legs roughly to fit the back. If you are making only a few chairs, you can estimate the angle at which the back deviates from vertical (the other angle is marked on the ends of the legs) and saw off most of the waste with a handsaw. If you are making a large set of chairs, it would be worth making jigs to cut the correct angle on a tablesaw. (You'll need one jig for the left legs, another for the right.)

After the legs and side rails are glued up, plane the outside corners of the legs flush with the cylinder.

The transition from leg to rail should be smooth, so finish this curve with a knife or chisel after gluing up.

Glue the chair together while it sits on a flat surface, as shown in the photo at top left. Plane the front rail flush with the front faces of the legs, as shown at bottom left. The exact fitting of the back to the legs requires patience—try the back in place and plane off where necessary. When the angles are right, chisel a slight hollow in the bearing surface so the visible joints between back and leg will be tight. Screw through the back into the legs and plug the screw holes with plugs cut from the same wood as the back.

Upholstering the seat—Before fastening the plywood seat to the chair frame, the seat must be padded with foam and covered. You will need about ½ yd. of upholstery fabric for each seat cover, a piece of extra-firm, 1-in. polyurethane foam the same size as the seat, heavy muslin, black cambric, upholstery glue and a staple gun.

First, remove any sharp arrises and corners on the plywood with a spokeshave and sandpaper. Cut the foam to size with a hot-wire cutter or fine saw, using the plywood seat as a pattern. Then lay the foam on the seat and cover it with a piece of muslin large enough to overlap the foam by 6 in. on each side. Glue the muslin to the foam all around the foam's perimeter to within 2 in. from the edges.

When the glue has dried, stretch the muslin over each edge of the foam and the plywood, and staple it to the underside of the seat. The muslin should be taut enough to give a rounded edge, which makes the seat comfortable and helps to keep the seat cover from wearing through.

Cut the seat-cover material 4 in. larger all around than the plywood. Make a 1-in. fold in one of the short sides of the seat cover and staple it to the underside of the plywood, about 3 in. from the edge. Stretch the opposite side taut and staple it to the plywood in the same way. The fabric will now be stretched across the seat in a straight line from side to side.

Turn the long, back edge of the seat cover under, making a neat 45° pleat at the corners, and staple it to the plywood. Do the same with the front edge of the cover, putting enough tension on the fabric to make it follow the shape of the seat. Cut the black cambric the same size as the seat, fold it under ½ in. all around, and staple it to the underside of the seat. Screw the plywood to the frame with No. 8 screws, then sit down and try the chair out.

Glue up the chair on a flat surface. If the diagonals are unequal, wedge out the shortest one. Check that the legs are parallel by measuring top and bottom.

After assembling the chair, plane the front rail flush with the legs.

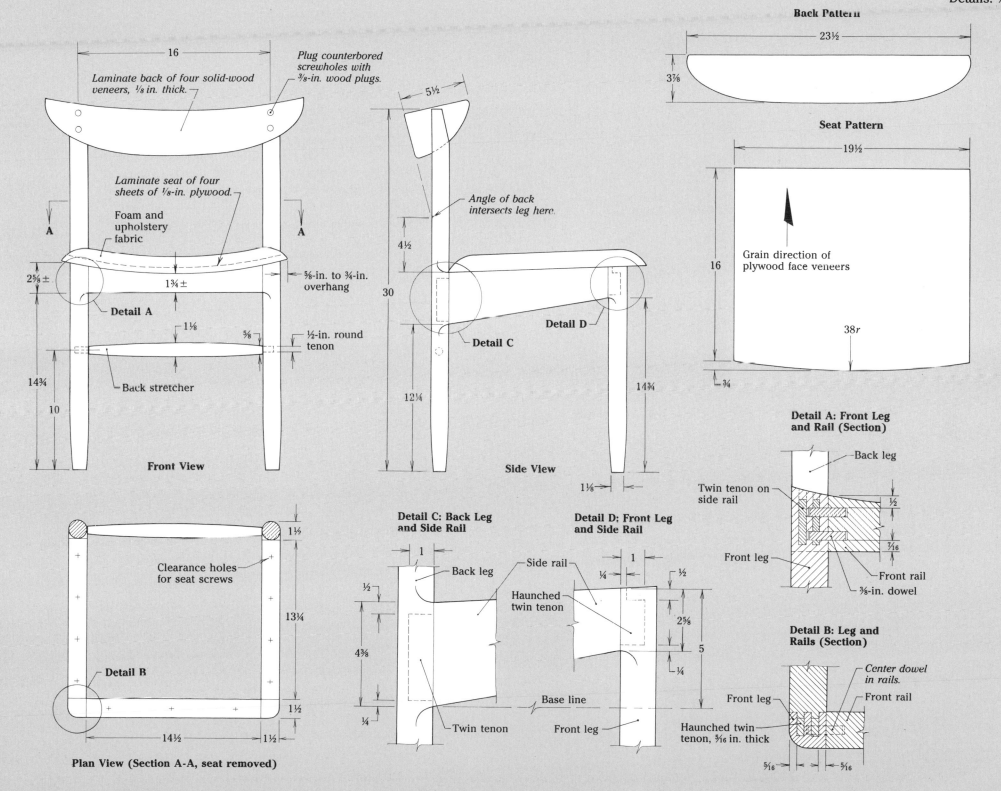

Dining Chair

Scale: ⅛ in. = 1 in.
Details: ¼ in. = 1 in.

Front View

16

Laminate back of four solid-wood veneers, ⅛ in. thick.

Plug counterbored screwholes with ⅜-in. wood plugs.

Laminate seat of four sheets of ⅛-in. plywood.

Foam and upholstery fabric

A   A

⅝-in. to ¾-in. overhang

2⅝ ±   1¾ ±

Detail A

1⅛   ⅝   ½-in. round tenon

Back stretcher

14¾

10

Plan View (Section A-A, seat removed)

1½

Clearance holes for seat screws

13¼

Detail B

1½

14½   1½

Side View

5½

Angle of back intersects leg here.

4½

30

Detail C

Detail D

12¼

14¾

1⅛

Back Pattern

23½

3⅛

Seat Pattern

19½

16

Grain direction of plywood face veneers

38r

¾

Detail C: Back Leg and Side Rail

1

Back leg

Side rail

½

Haunched twin tenon

4⅜

Base line

¼

Twin tenon   Front leg

Detail D: Front Leg and Side Rail

1

¼   ½

2⅝

5

¼

Front leg

Detail A: Front Leg and Rail (Section)

Back leg

Twin tenon on side rail

½

7/16

Front leg

Front rail

⅜-in. dowel

Detail B: Leg and Rails (Section)

Center dowel in rails.

Front leg

Front rail

Haunched twin tenon, 5/16 in. thick

5/16   5/16

Two Stools

Scale: ¼ in. = 1 in.
Details: ½ in. = 1 in.

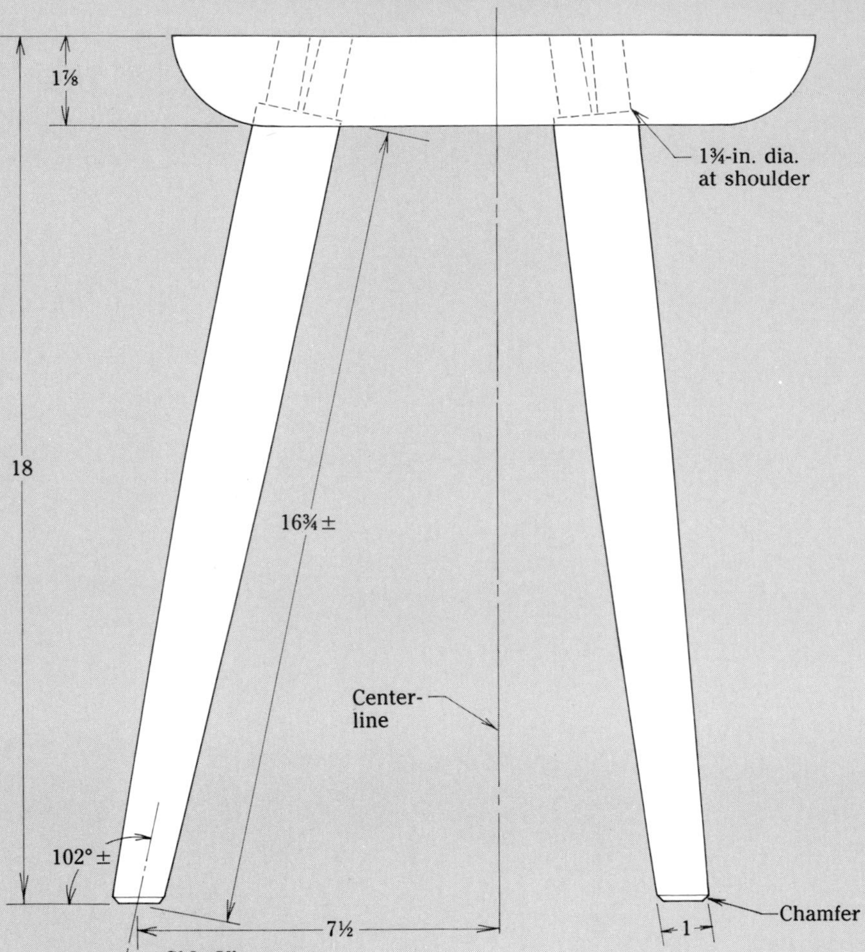

1⅞
1¾-in. dia.
at shoulder
18
16¾ ±
Center-
line
102° ±
7½
1
Chamfer

Side View

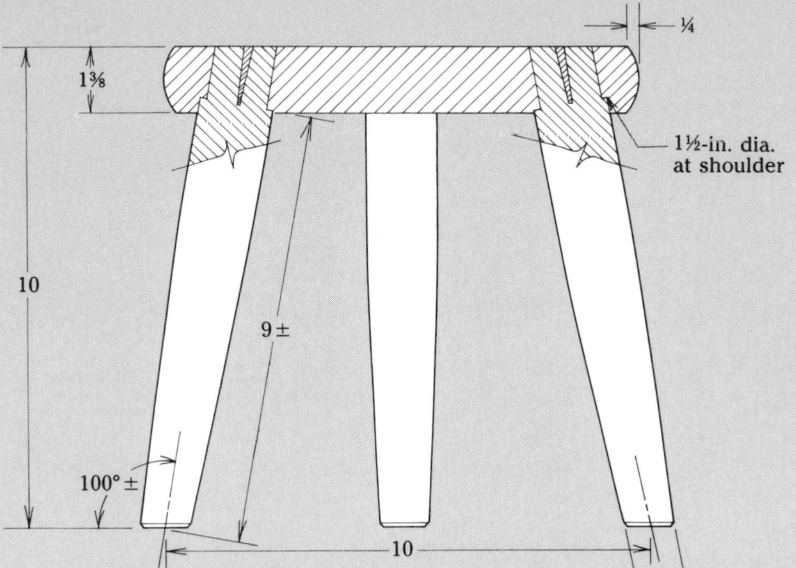

¼
1⅜
1½-in. dia.
at shoulder
10
9 ±
100° ±
10
1

Side View (Partial Section A-A)

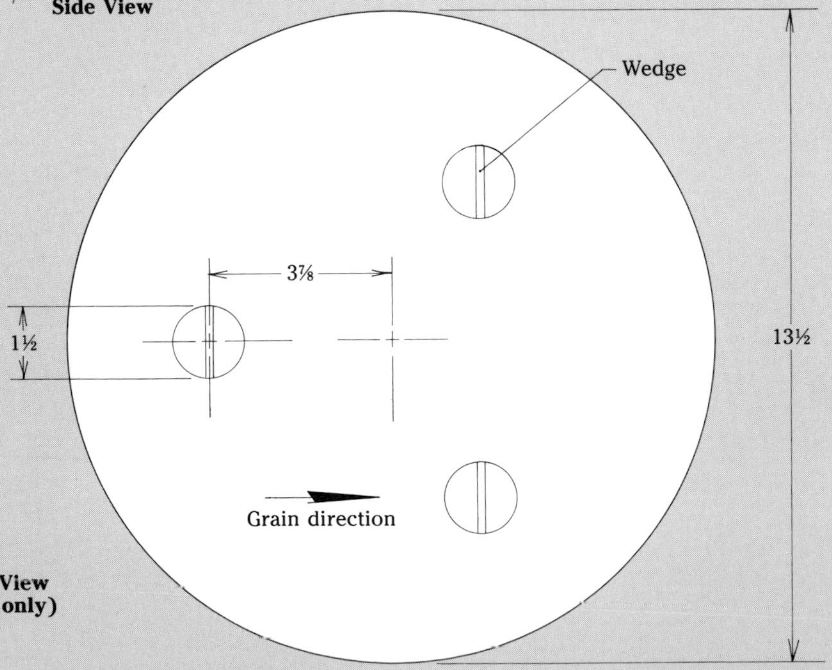

Wedge
3⅞
1½
13½
Grain direction

Plan View
(Top only)

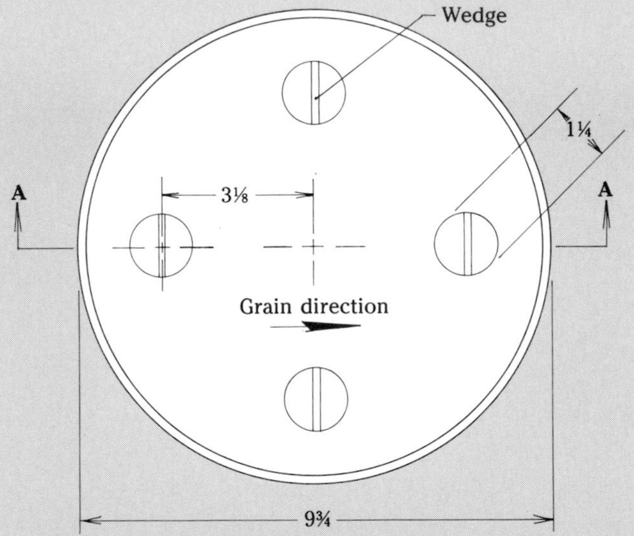

Wedge
1¼
A
3⅛
A
Grain direction
9¾

Plan View (Top only)

Alternate Edge Details

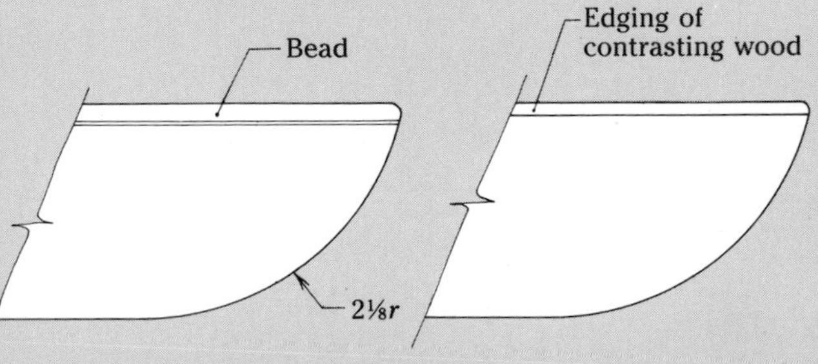

Bead
Edging of
contrasting wood
2⅛r

Two Stools

Stools are handy to have in every room of the house. The mahogany stool shown at right can be used to seat someone at the dinner or kitchen table in a pinch. Three-legged stools are useful on uneven floors, but they are easily knocked over and therefore can be dangerous for young children. A smaller, four-legged version, ideal for children, is also shown in the plan drawings. Stools much higher than 18 in. should have some form of bracing between their legs (pp. 144-147). The legs can be blind-mortised into the seat, as shown in the photo, or through-mortise-and-tenoned, as shown in the plan drawings.

Both stools have turned seats and legs, so you'll need a lathe with a minimum swing of 14 in. (The swing is twice the vertical distance between the headstock center and the lathe bed.) My small Delta-Rockwell lathe has a gap in the bed at the headstock end that allows me to turn work up to 15 in. in diameter and 2 in. thick. The legs should fit on any lathe. The simple turning techniques needed for these stools are described in numerous books on turning (several of which are listed in the bibliography, so I won't repeat them here).

Construction

Any reasonably hard wood that turns well is appropriate for both of these stools, but I don't like to turn oak because it tears easily. You're unlikely to find a 15-in.-wide board for the seat (except, perhaps, in mahogany), so you'll have to join it up. A two-board seat looks best, preferably cut from the same board and joined off center with an inconspicuous glue line.

I'll describe how to make the large stool shown in the plan drawings; the same techniques can be used to make the small stool. Mark a 14-in.-dia. circle on what will be the underside of the seat, and cut it out on the bandsaw. You can screw the underside directly to the lathe faceplate or, if you don't want the screw holes to show, glue the seat to a piece of scrap plywood and screw the faceplate to the plywood. If you sandwich a piece of thick paper between the plywood and seat, the plywood will be easier to remove.

Details become more important as furniture becomes simpler, so the edge profile of the seat should be carefully made. If you don't trust your eye to guide the tool to make a pleasing shape, make a cardboard or Masonite template of the edge profile shown in the

The ebony edging on this mahogany stool bent without breaking, despite the tight curve of the seat. The edging adds a decorative touch to the simple stool.

plan drawings. You can also cut a *V*-groove with a small skew chisel, or add a small edging of contrasting wood around the circumference as shown at left. I cut the rabbet for the edging with a skew after shaping and sanding the seat. Make the edging and glue it in place as described on pp. 94-95. Set the seat aside while you make the legs.

It is essential to turn the legs from straight-grained stock. If the wood fibers are not parallel to the leg's axis, the leg will be inherently weak and liable to break. Blanks for legs used to be split directly from the log, a method that ensures straight grain. I saw out the blanks, however, making them a little over 1¾ in. square, and about ½ in. longer than finished length if I'm using through tenons. Cut the corners off at 45° to make a rough octagon. I center one end of the blank on the headstock drive center, and give the leg a sharp blow with a maul or heavy hammer to set the center. Before fixing the leg to the tailstock, I place a tenon template—a piece of hardwood scrap with a 1½-in. hole in the middle—over the tailstock center. Hanging the template on the tailstock allows you to check the size of the tenon without removing the leg from the lathe.

Rough the leg down to a 1¾-in. cylinder and then turn the round tenon to fit the template exactly. If you're through-tenoning, make the tenon about ½ in. overlong to allow for trimming after assembly. Make blind tenons the finished length.

Shape the legs to a slightly swelling taper. The Greeks discovered that even though the sides of a cylinder are straight, they appear to be concave, so they corrected for this optical illusion by making the middle of their columns swell slightly (this swelling is called entasis). The same principle applies to the legs, and I've indicated the swelling in the plan drawings, though the exact amount is a matter of judgment. Here again, what looks right is right.

Chamfer the bottom of each leg substantially while it is still on the lathe, or it will splinter as it wears down. You can also sand and finish the legs on the lathe. I don't think there is anything wrong with leaving necessary tool marks and neat construction lines in finished work, so I don't attempt to remove the impressions left on the bottom of the leg by the headstock center. Cut slots in the tenons for the wedges as described on pp. 95-96. Stools that are blind-mortise-and-tenoned need no wedges.

Boring the holes for the tenons in the seat at the correct angle takes care. An error of only 1° will throw the leg off by about ⅜ in. at its bottom end. The degree scale on the tilting table of most drill presses is too small for accuracy, so here's the method I use.

Set the drill-press table as close to the correct angle as you can. On a piece of ¾-in. plywood scrap, mark and bore holes for the leg tenons in the same positions they will be on the seat. Put the legs in the plywood and set them on the floor. The center of the bottom ends of the legs should lie on a 15-in.-dia. circle for the large stool and a 10-in.-dia. circle for the small. If they don't, adjust the angle of the drill-press table and try again on the plywood scrap.

When you have the correct angle, mark the position of the holes on the underside of the seat—you can trace through the plywood scrap or measure. Keep the holes well clear of the glue line. Clamp the seat to the drill-press table. For through mortises, place a backing piece under the seat to prevent the top surface from splitting out. Chuck a 1¾-in. bit in the drill press and bore just far enough to make a flat seating for the shoulder of the tenon. Then, without disturbing the top, put the 1½-in. bit used to make the tenon template in the chuck, and bore the mortise. Repeat this procedure for each mortise.

For blind-mortised stools, make sure the ends of the tenons aren't hitting the bottoms of the mortises, keeping the shoulders from seating. Then spread glue on the parts and push them together. Tight mortise-and-tenon joints shouldn't need clamping.

To assemble stools that are through-mortised, insert the legs (without glue) and turn them so the wedge slots are at right angles to the grain of the seat and parallel to each other. Put a pencil line on the seat adjacent to each slot so you can reposition them quickly. Next, mark around the protruding ends of the tenons with a pencil, then remove the legs and saw off the waste. Put glue on the tenons and inside the mortises and insert the tenons. Align the slots with the pencil marks and, with the stool set firmly on a bench, drive in the wedges. I use Titebond for these stools because, though not as strong as a resin glue, it remains slightly elastic and won't give way as the top moves slightly with seasonal changes.

After the glue has set, cut off the wedges and chisel around the tenons before planing them flush with the seat. If you don't chisel the perimeter down first, the unsupported fibers are liable to break off below the surface of the top when planed.

High Chair

This little chair is for children just beyond the food-throwing stage. I don't think younger children are happy at the dining table anyway, and would probably prefer to eat out of a trough on the floor. High chairs with trays have always seemed like appliances rather than furniture to me, so I have never made one. Children like being able to climb in and out of their seats rather than being lifted by a grown-up, so I have splayed the legs for greater stability and provided front and side rungs.

Construction

This high chair is made of cherry, but any good turning wood, such as maple or walnut, will do. Make the seat first—of one piece, if possible, and free from checks, knots or other defects that will weaken the wood. Bandsaw the seat blank to a 13-in. diameter, screw a faceplate to the underside and mount it on the lathe. Turn the edge profile, checking it with a plywood or cardboard template if you don't trust your eye to arrive at a pleasing shape. Dish the top surface of the seat slightly, as shown in the plan drawings, and run the curve out almost to the edge. The perimeter of the top surface should be flat so it will rest without wobbling on the drill-press table while you're boring the holes for the legs and arms.

Turn the legs next. If your tailstock center is small enough, hang a ¾-in. tenon template on it (p. 95) to check the diameter of the tenons. I chamfer the shoulders of all the tenons on this chair so they will not bottom out in the mortise openings. The chamfers also make neat connections between the parts.

The only real difficulty with this piece is boring the round mortises at the correct angles so that the parts fit together. If you were making several chairs at once, it would be worth making jigs, but for a single chair, jigs are hardly worth the trouble. For leg mortises, I set up the drill press by trial and error, using a trial seat made of plywood, as described on p. 140. When assembled in the trial seat and stood on a level floor, the bottom ends of the legs should form the corners of a 16-in. square. If they depart more than a ½ in. from this measurement, adjust the drill-press table and bore the trial seat again.

After boring the mortises in the underside of the seat, insert the legs dry, then position the mortises on the legs for the top two front-to-back stretchers by

measuring up from the floor. At the same time, measure between the legs at this height to establish the shoulder-to-shoulder length of the stretchers. Bore the ⅜-in. mortises while the legs and seat are assembled. I use an electric drill and power-bore bit. Turn the leg slightly to align the bit by eye with the intended position of the stretcher.

Turn these two stretchers, checking the size of the tenons carefully with calipers. Put the stretchers in place, then locate the holes for the two side-to-side stretchers and measure their lengths. Bore the ⅜-in. holes the same way—the drill and bit will fit between the legs. Turn the stretchers and bore holes for the lower front-to-back stretcher. These holes are centered in the length of each side-to-side stretcher and

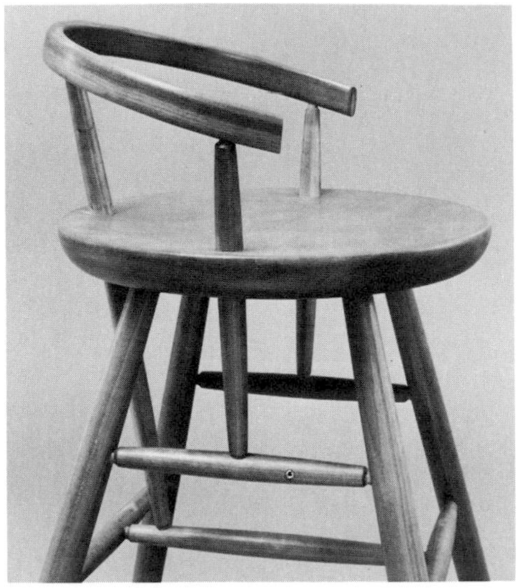

The three back supports pass through the seat without glue and are tenoned into front-to-back stretchers.

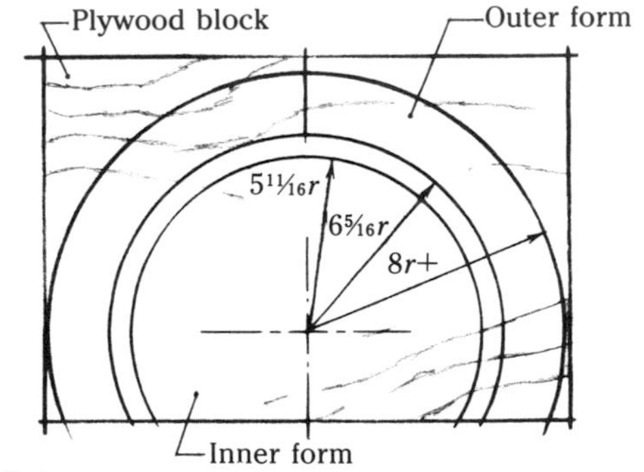

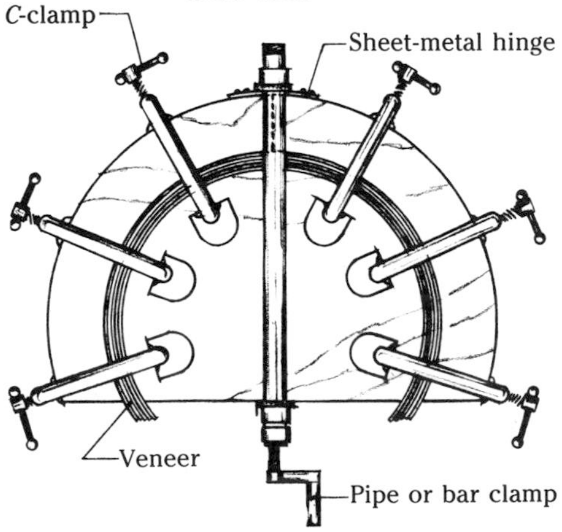

Glue up the back on a simple mold cut from two pieces of ¾-in. plywood glued face to face. Hinge the outer mold with a piece of thin metal. Bore holes in the inner part to take C-clamps.

at a right angle to its long axis. Dry-assemble the chair again (because of the angles, all the pieces must go together at once). Measure the length of the lower stretcher, turn it and fit it in place.

Turn the three back supports next. The portion that fits through the seat isn't tapered, but is a ¾-in.-dia. cylinder, so you can use the ¾-in. tenon template to check this dimension.

The supports for the back run through holes in the seat and are mortised into the front-to-back stretchers, as shown in the photo at left. Lay out the position of these holes in the seat as shown in the plan drawings. To bore the holes, I have someone hold a short piece of dowel under the seat in line with the marks on the underside of the seat and the marks for the mortise on the appropriate stretcher. I line up the drill bit with the dowel so that the hole will be angled correctly. Bore all three holes from the top surface, stopping the bit as soon as its point penetrates the underside of the seat, then disassemble the chair and complete the holes by boring from the underside.

The mortise for the back support in each top front-to-back stretcher is centered in the length of the stretcher and bored at right angles to the long axis. The mortise in the bottom front-to-back stretcher is angled. Bore the mortise by putting a bit with an extension shank through the hole in the seat. If you don't have an extension, set a sliding bevel to the correct angle, disassemble the chair and bore the hole using the bevel as a guide.

The curved back is made of strips of thin veneer laminated in a simple mold. To make the mold, glue two pieces of ¾-in. plywood or particleboard together to make a 1½-in.-thick block. The pieces should be at least 11 in. by 16 in. With a compass, draw part of a 6⁵⁄₁₆-in.-radius circle on the block, as shown in the sketch at left. Then increase the radius of the compass to draw a concentric circle as large as will fit on the block. Bandsaw on these lines and cut the outer, horseshoe-shaped part in half. Hinge this outer part by nailing or screwing a piece of thin sheet metal across the cut so the mold can be opened to accept and release the strips.

Bandsaw ⅝ in. off the inner mold to allow for the thickness of the back. Clean up the bandsaw marks and smooth the curves of both inner and outer parts with rasps, files and sandpaper. Make sure that the mating surfaces remain flat and at right angles to the faces of both parts of the mold.

Bore 1½-in. holes about two thirds of the way through the inner part of the mold to take C-clamps. Leave a bridge of wood at least ½-in. wide between adjacent holes, and chisel a flat on each hole for a better bearing surface. Wax the mating surfaces of the parts thoroughly.

I cut the veneer for the back myself. In order for veneer made of kiln-dried wood to bend to this curvature, it must be straight-grained and no thicker than ⅛ in. I used five ⅛-in. pieces of veneer, which I cut on the tablesaw with a sharp, carbide-tipped blade to ensure a surface suitable for gluing. Cut the veneers about 1⅛ in. wide and 2 in. longer than needed. To check that the veneers won't break, bend each one by hand around the inner mold.

Lay out the molds, clamps and plastic resin glue, and select strips with good faces for the outside veneers. Apply the glue with a brush or short-nap paint roller, and put the whole assembly in the mold. Put a pipe or bar clamp across the center of the mold, and then attach the C-clamps, starting at the center and working to the ends. It's a good plan with a new mold to go through the whole procedure dry. (I mean the veneers, of course, not you.) Glue up on a flat tabletop and keep a short, narrow piece of ½-in.-thick hardwood stock handy so you can drive the veneers down flat on the tabletop as you apply clamping pressure. This ensures that the edges of the veneers are aligned. When the glue is dry, plane the edges of the back flat, then round the arrises with a spokeshave. Trim and round the ends of the back as shown in the plan drawings, or saw them at an angle as shown in the photos. Then finish-sand the faces.

Glue up the chair before boring the round mortises in the back for the supports. As you will have discovered during the dry assembly, the legs, seat and stretchers must all go together at once. Pull the tenons home with padded pipe or bar clamps. Slide the back supports in place and position the bottom edge of the back on the support tenons to mark the mortises. Set two sliding bevels to the angles shown in the plan drawings; use them as guides while boring the mortises for the side-support tenons. Use the same technique for the center-support mortise, then glue the back to the supports and the supports to the stretchers (don't glue them to the seat).

I finished the chair with polyurethane so it could be hosed down at suitable intervals without damaging the finish.

High Chair

Scale: ¼ in. = 1 in.
Detail: ⅛ in. = 1 in.

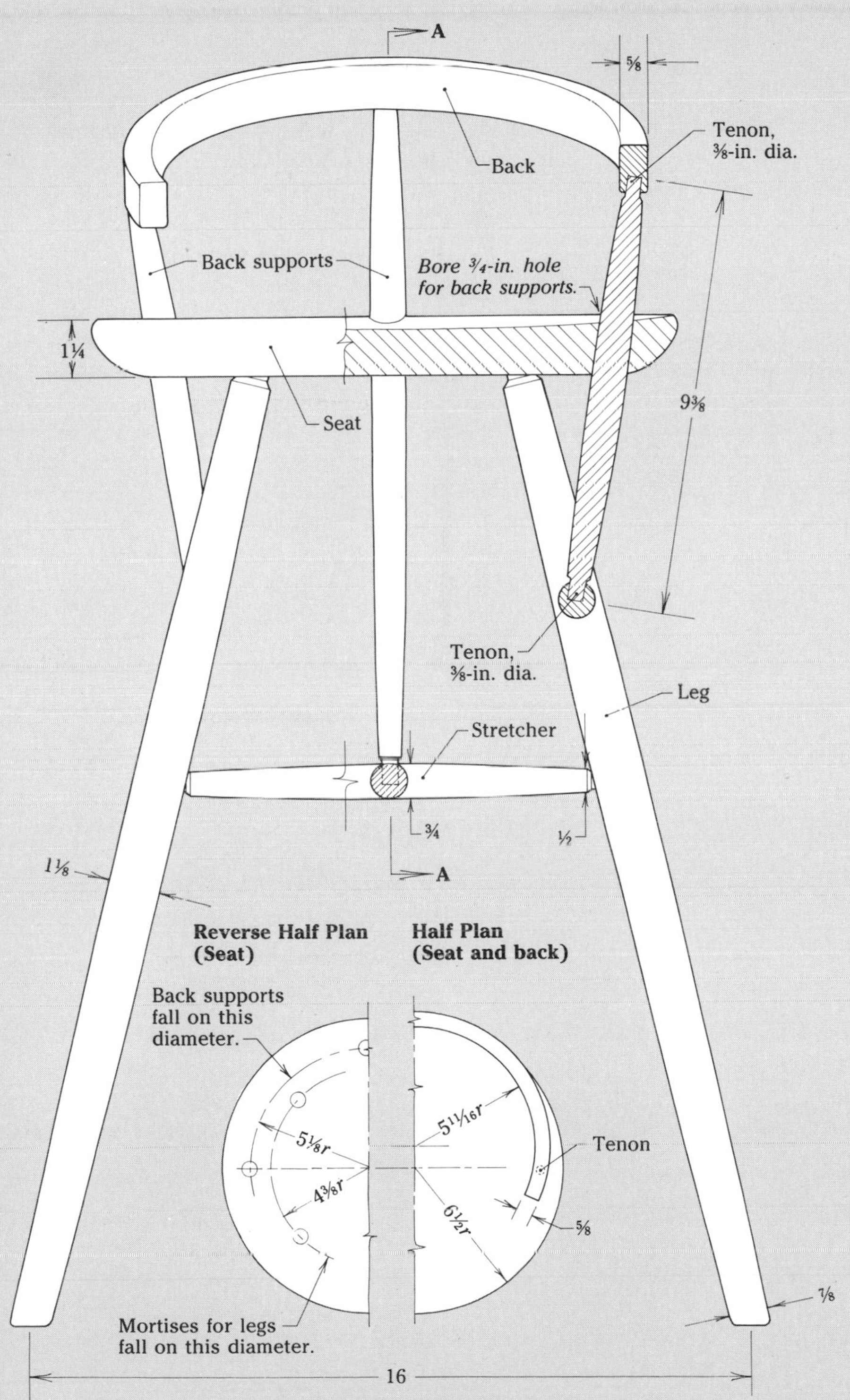

A
⅝
Tenon, ⅜-in. dia.
Back
Back supports
Bore ¾-in. hole for back supports.
1¼
Seat
9⅜
Tenon, ⅜-in. dia.
Leg
Stretcher
¾
½
A
1⅛
Reverse Half Plan (Seat)
Half Plan (Seat and back)
Back supports fall on this diameter.
5⅛r
4⅜r
5¹¹⁄₁₆r
6½r
Tenon
⅝
Mortises for legs fall on this diameter.
⅞
16

Front View (Section B-B)

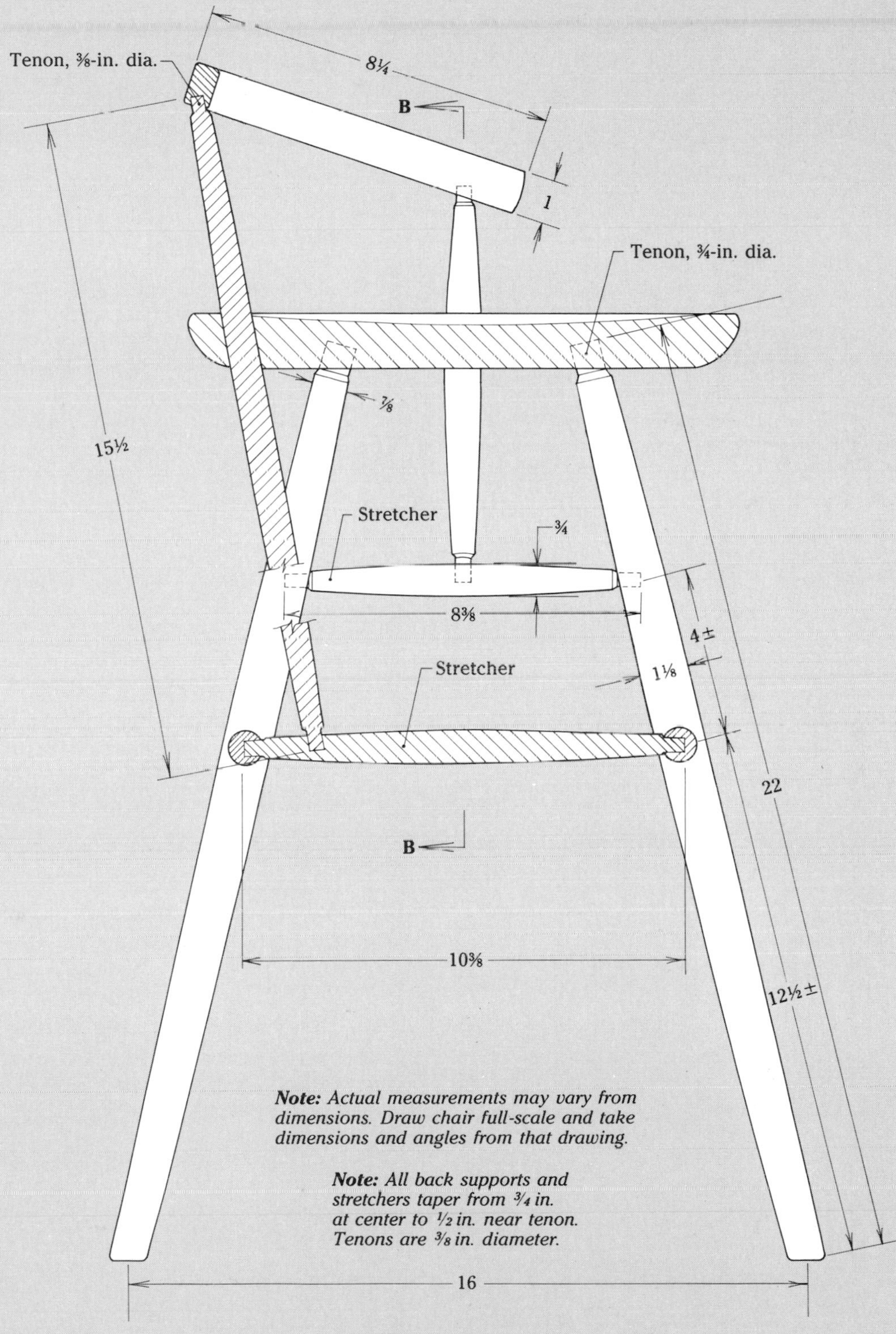

Tenon, ⅜-in. dia.
8¼
B
1
Tenon, ¾-in. dia.
⅞
15½
Stretcher
¾
8⅜
4±
Stretcher
1⅛
22
B
10⅜
12½±
Note: Actual measurements may vary from dimensions. Draw chair full-scale and take dimensions and angles from that drawing.
Note: All back supports and stretchers taper from ¾ in. at center to ½ in. near tenon. Tenons are ⅜ in. diameter.
16

Side View (Section A-A)

Bar Stool

Scale: ¼ in. = 1 in.
Details: ½ in. = 1 in.

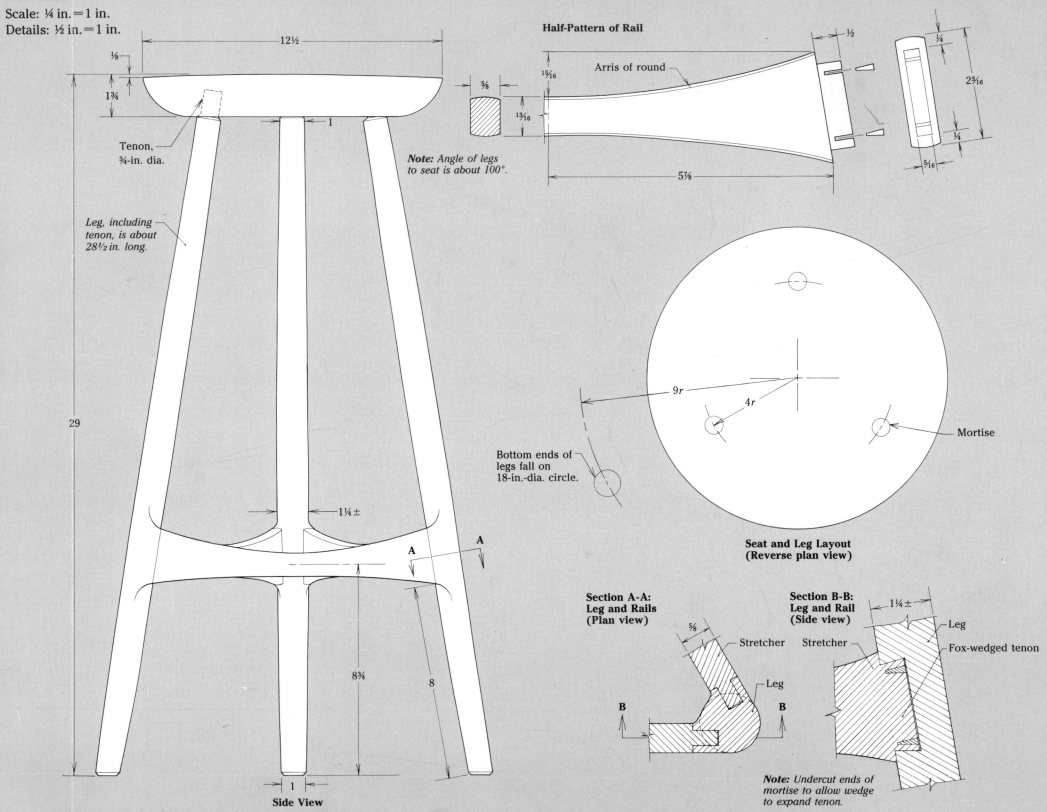

Half-Pattern of Rail

Arris of round

½

15⁄16

5⁄8

13⁄16

5⁷⁄8

¼

2⁵⁄16

¼

5⁄16

Note: Angle of legs to seat is about 100°.

12½

⅛

1¾

Tenon, ¾-in. dia.

1

Leg, including tenon, is about 28½ in. long.

29

1¼ ±

8¾

8

1

Side View

9r

4r

Mortise

Bottom ends of legs fall on 18-in.-dia. circle.

Seat and Leg Layout
(Reverse plan view)

A   A

A

B   B

Section A-A:
Leg and Rails
(Plan view)

5⁄8

Stretcher

Leg

Section B-B:
Leg and Rail
(Side view)

1¼ ±

Stretcher

Leg

Fox-wedged tenon

Note: Undercut ends of mortise to allow wedge to expand tenon.

Bar Stool

I have made a number of these high, three-legged stools to be used at a bar or counter. The first one was inspired by a photo I saw years ago of an ice-fishing stool used in Greenland (bear fur was attached to the bottoms of the legs to prevent slipping). The original design has been through a number of changes, and I like the version shown in the photo at right best. Although the stool appears fragile, its triangulated structure is very strong. The curved stretchers, which are at the right height to be used as footrests, are tenoned into the legs. The weight of the sitter puts this joint in tension, so it must be blind-wedged (the English, with their well-known love of animals, call it fox-wedging) or pinned with small, wooden pegs.

Three-legged stools of this height are not stable enough to be used by young children. If that is a concern, you can make a four-legged version, increasing the splay of the legs slightly.

Construction

Almost any hardwood will do for these stools, as long as it turns well. Pick dry, straight-grained stock for the legs—any cross grain will weaken them. Make the turning blanks for the legs about 30 in. long. Joint two adjacent faces, then saw the other two to make the blanks 1½ in. square in section. Make at least one spare blank, and several shorter, 1½-in.-square pieces of scrap wood for testing machine setups.

The legs are turned except where the stretchers join them, and these joints must be cut before turning. Because the faces of the legs are angled at the joints, it's best to work from a full-scale drawing of a section through the leg, as shown at top right. The sketches at bottom right show the sequence of cuts. Set the blade of a tilting-arbor tablesaw 15° from the vertical for cuts one and two. Cut off two adjacent faces from one of the scrap pieces, and check that the two sawn faces meet at an angle of 120°. Saw all the legs and the remaining scrap pieces with this setting.

The outer face of each stretcher must be tangent to the circle inscribed in the trapezoid and at a right angle to the 120° face of the leg blank. Make the third and fourth cuts with the blade at 90°, running the 120° faces on the saw table, as shown in the sketch. Then measure ³⁄₁₆ in. from the newly cut 90° faces to position the cheeks of the mortise. This leaves a little

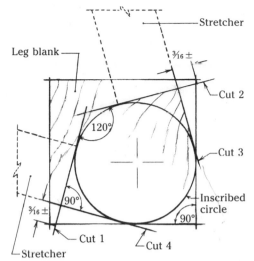

This full-size drawing shows a section through the leg at the joints as the leg develops from the square leg blank. The stretchers must be perpendicular to the 120° faces and tangent to the inscribed circle. If the legs of your stool are slightly different than the size shown here, construct a drawing like this for those dimensions.

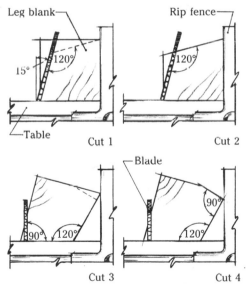

The first two cuts make two adjacent faces of each leg blank form a 120° angle. Make the second two cuts to trim surfaces that are perpendicular to the 120° faces and tangent to the inscribed circle.

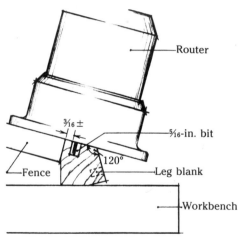

To rout the mortises, fix a fence to the router base, clamp the leg firmly to a workbench and lower the bit carefully into the wood.

wood to trim off to make the stretcher and leg flush after assembly. Measure from the bottom end of each leg to position the ends of the mortise.

I rout the mortises, as shown in the sketch at left. Try out the fence and bit settings on the scrap pieces. Clamp the piece firmly to the workbench and lower the bit carefully onto the leg—this can be tricky because the fence has a rather small surface to bear against. Square the rounded ends of the mortises. (If you are fox-wedging the joints, undercut the mortises just before assembly.)

Make the three stretchers next. They're best laid out using a full-size pattern that includes the tenons and accurately indicates the shoulder lines. I cut the tenons on the tablesaw, using a high rip fence for the cheek cut and a miter gauge set at the correct angle

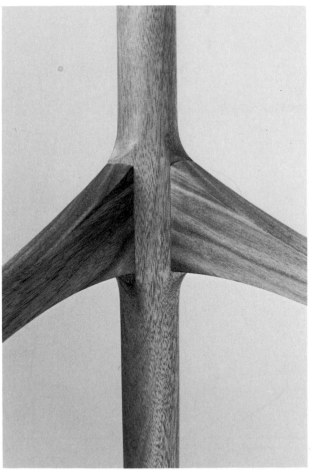

The stool legs are cylinders above and below the stretchers. After turning the legs, the surface between the stretcher joints can be planed to flow into the cylinders.

for the shoulder cuts, with the fence as a stop. Check these settings with scrap wood to make sure that the tenons will fit the mortises snugly. After cutting the tenons, bandsaw the curves, and clean up and round the edges with a spokeshave or router.

To mount the legs on the lathe, you need to find the center of each end. The ends are trapezoids, not squares, so their centers fall on the center of an inscribed circle, as shown in the sketch on p. 145. A cardboard template of the circle or trapezoid, with a hole punched at its center, is helpful.

After you've marked the centers, saw off the one remaining 90° corner tangent to the circle. Turn the legs, mounting the bottom end on the headstock center. It's easy to tear out the fibers of the wood where the round sections change to trapezoidal, so I cut in at these places with a chisel or knife before starting to turn, as shown in the photo on p. 134. The taper is gentle, having a 1-in. diameter at each end to about 1¼ in. just above and below the mortises—make a template for the curve if you don't trust your eye.

After turning, you can use the lathe as a vise while planing off most of the waste on the mortised section. Insert the stretchers, draw lines down their inside faces onto the 120° faces of the leg, and plane to these lines. The photo at left shows how these joints look on the inside of the assembled chair. I also like to do the final sanding by hand while the leg is still mounted on the lathe.

Turn the seat next. It should be made of one wide piece of wood, or at least appear to be. Bandsaw the seat blank round and attach a lathe faceplate to what will be the bottom face of the seat. If you don't want the screw holes to show, glue the blank to a piece of plywood and screw the faceplate to the plywood. Put a piece of newspaper or thin cardboard between the plywood and the blank, so that the glue joint will be easy to break. Turn the edge profile, judging the curve by eye or with a template.

Before turning the top surface of the seat convex, you must bore the holes for the legs. Mark the faceplate and the seat bottom so you can screw them back together later in the same position. The holes must be bored at the correct angle, or the legs and stretchers will not fit without forcing. The only foolproof way to ensure accuracy is to try out the drill-press settings on a trial seat made of ¾-in. plywood scrap (p. 140). Lay out the holes on a 4-in.-radius circle, as shown in the plan drawings, set the drill- press table as close to 80° as you can and bore the holes. Insert the legs and see if the centers of their bottom ends lie ¼ in. to either side of an 18-in.-dia. circle drawn on the floor. If they don't, adjust the angle of the drill-press table and try again. For a final check, assemble the legs, stretchers and plywood trial seat. (The shoulders of the stretchers may need slight adjustment later.) You'll discover that because of the angles, all the pieces have to go together at once — this is good practice for final assembly.

After boring the holes, replace the faceplate and turn the top surface of the seat slightly convex. The convex surface is a little easier on the sitter's thighs than a flat surface, and it looks better. I sand the curved edge profile on the lathe, then clamp the faceplate in a bench vise while sanding the seat's top surface parallel with the grain.

Dry-assemble the legs, stretchers and seat again. Because the legs are angled, the shoulders of the stretchers will gap slightly. (This problem also occurs on the angled posts of the cradle, pp. 24-27.) Mark where wood needs to be removed from the shoulders, trim with a chisel and reassemble the stool. Repeat this procedure until the shoulders fit tightly.

If you are fox-wedging the joints, cut the slots in the tenons, make the wedges and taper the mortises before gluing up. A fox-wedged joint works rather like a dovetail—the wedges force the tenon apart so that it can't be pulled out of the tapered mortise. The wedges are driven in by the bottom of the mortise as the tenon is pushed home during assembly. Therefore, a fox-wedged joint must be cut very accurately. If the wedges are too long or too thick, the joint won't close; if they are too thin, the joint will be loose.

I cut the slots for the wedges on the tablesaw, about ¼ in. from the edges of the tenon, and just shy of the shoulders, as shown in the plan drawings. The wedges should be about 1/16 in. shorter than the depth of the slot, and should fit halfway into the slot without forcing. The difference between the thickest end of the wedges and the width of the slots should equal the amount that each end of the mortise is tapered. The actual sizes needn't be those shown in the plan drawings, but this relationship must hold. For short tenons like these, I wouldn't make the wedges more than twice the width of the slot—any wider and you risk splitting the stretcher. I make the wedges first, then taper the mortises accordingly. It's a good idea to make and assemble a fox-wedged joint in scrap wood, then cut it in half to see if you've gauged the mortise tapers and sizes of the wedges correctly.

Because all six joints must go together at once, this is a difficult piece to glue up. I recommend dry-assembling again to check how best to assemble and determine the positions of the clamps. Do not insert the wedges when dry-assembling—you won't get the joints apart. The ideal way to pull the stretcher-to-leg joints together when gluing up is with a band clamp. If you are fox-wedging, you'll need to force the wedges into their slots with additional pressure from a bar or pipe clamp placed on top of the band. Remove the bar clamp as soon as the joint is closed up. As you tighten the band clamp, pull the seat tight onto the legs with three suitably padded pipe clamps hooked on the seat and ends of the legs.

When the glue has set, plane or scrape the outside faces of the stretchers and legs flush. Then take a sharp chisel or knife and continue the curve of the stretcher until it fades into the leg, as shown in the photo below.

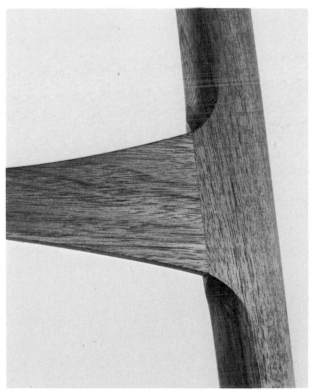

The transition from the leg to the stretcher should be smooth. After assembly, trim the legs and stretchers with a chisel or knife to make the transition curve continuous.

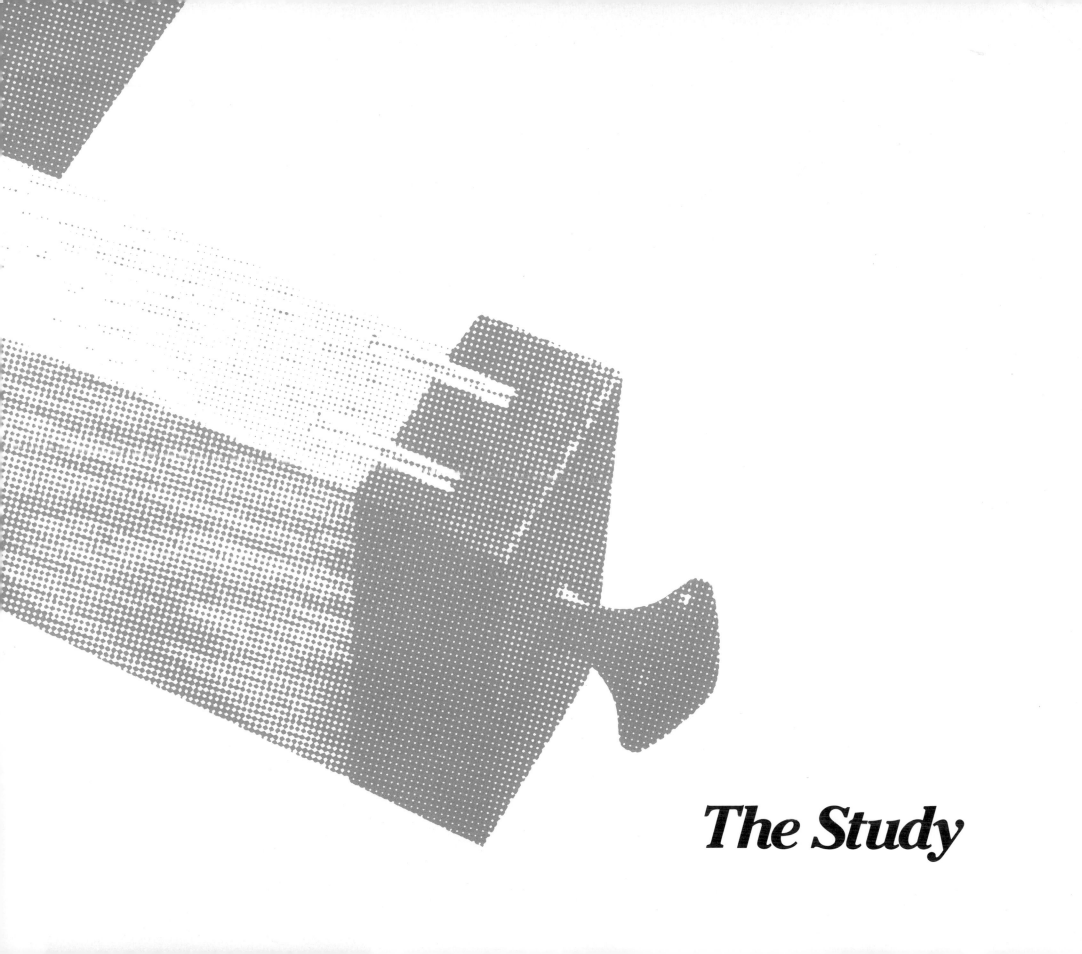

The Study

Desks 8

About Desks

After spending twenty years in a woodworking shop, lifting, carrying and mostly on the move, I have found the long hours I have spent at a desk writing this book extremely tiresome. This experience has increased my awareness of the importance of a well-designed desk, a comfortable chair and good lighting for desk work.

The desk must be the proper size, shape and height, and its drawers must suit their contents and the writer's convenience. Some people, particularly male business executives, bolster their egos with excessively large desks. There is no point, however, in having a work surface that you can't comfortably reach across. Desktops longer than 5½ ft. to 6 ft. and wider than 30 in. tend to collect piles of books and papers that would be better kept in a bookcase or file drawer, or on an adjacent table.

No height is perfect for all desks. The usual height, 28½ in., is slightly lower than that of a dining table. Try out existing desks, or mock up different desktop heights to find the one best for you. Typewriters require a surface about 2 in. to 3 in. lower than desk height. If you do a lot of typing, though, it's best to have a separate typing table adjacent to the desk.

The arrangement of the drawers is a matter of personal preference and common sense. Small drawers for frequently needed items should be placed top right or top left, where they will be most accessible. Drawers for things less frequently needed, such as files, should be placed lower. Right-handed people like a file drawer to be on their right; left-handed people prefer the reverse. Drawers under the center of the desktop must be shallow, so that they won't interfere with the writer's knees. To make drawers more useful, you can add vertical dividers, or a shallow sliding tray on runners attached to the drawer sides for small items. You should be able to open a drawer easily without getting up from the desk; for this reason, I prefer knobs to conventional brass handles because you can grasp them from any direction.

Good natural or artificial light at a desk is essential. Right-handed people usually prefer the light to come from their left so that they are not writing in the shadow cast by their own hand. For typing, the light source should be above and slightly behind the typist and positioned to avoid shadows.

A desk chair should have a comfortably shaped seat, not more than 10 in. lower than the writing surface. The chair should also have a firm back. The dining chair (pp. 131-137) is well suited to a desk, though I put a cushion on it because it's a little lower than comfortable writing height for me.

Writing Table

I have always thought of this piece as a lady's writing table, perhaps because the first one was commissioned by a woman writer. She liked to keep reference books and dictionaries within easy reach along the back, hence the table is 28 in. deep and has a raised edging to keep things from falling off. The table is unobtrusive and will fit comfortably in the corner of the study or living room.

The writing table in the photo is made of mahogany and has two small drawers to store paper and pens. I prefer mahogany for this table over all other woods. It has a wonderful color, enhanced by age, and its grain tends to be uniform. One mahogany version of this table that I especially liked had rosewood knobs and edging. A leather or felt writing pad will protect the top from being marred by ball-point pens.

Construction

The table's construction is straightforward and conventional. The legs and rails of the base are mortise-and-tenoned, and the top is held in place with metal tabletop fasteners or wooden buttons to allow for movement. The drawers, whose fronts are cut out of the wide front rail, are hung on runners screwed to the front and back rails.

Make the base first. Square up the stock for the rails and legs, and cut the mortises and tenons before tapering the legs. The outside faces of the legs and rails are flush, so you can lay out the joint with one setting of a mortise gauge. I double-tenon the rails; too much wood would have to be removed to make one long tenon, and this would weaken the leg. For added insurance against a weak joint, offset the tenons slightly toward the inside face of the rail, as shown in the plan drawings, to leave thick outer cheeks for the mortises.

I cut the mortises with a hollow chisel attachment on a drill press (p. 134), and then cut the tenons on the tablesaw using a high, wooden auxiliary rip fence. Groove the inside faces of the rails for tabletop fasteners or wooden buttons before assembly. All four faces of each leg are tapered, beginning below the line of the rails. You can taper the leg with a hand plane as described on pp. 5-6.

I like to cut the drawer fronts out of the front rail so the grain pattern is continuous. (If you are left-handed, you may want to put the large drawer on the left.)

The drawer fronts are too small to cut out on the tablesaw, because the saw kerf would be too wide, but you can cut them out with a coping saw. Accurately knife-mark the outline of each drawer on the outside face of the rail. Bore a $\frac{1}{16}$-in. hole in all four corners of each drawer front, placed so the knife marks are tangent to the holes. Knife-mark the other face, joining the holes. Remove the pin from one end of a medium coping-saw blade (about sixteen teeth per inch) and thread the blade through a hole. Replace the pin, attach the saw frame and cut out the drawer front, leaving the knife mark just visible on the rail.

To clean up the openings in the rail, clamp the rail firmly to a bench, face up, with a piece of hardwood scrap beneath, then chisel to the knife marks. Make sure that you keep the chisel at a right angle to the face of the rail. Lay out the curve on the front rail with a beam compass or by springing a thin wooden batten, bandsaw the waste and clean up the curve with a spokeshave to the rounded section shown in the plan drawings.

Glue up the ends of the base first, applying clamping pressure only over the tenons. The legs are parallel if the measurement from the outside face of one leg to the inside face of the other is the same at the top and bottom. I position the clamps to spread the legs about $\frac{1}{4}$ in. wider at the bottom than the top to counteract the perspective distortion that makes parallel legs seem to be toeing in. (The closer the observer is to the legs, the more apparent this effect is.)

When the glue has dried on the ends, add the two longer rails. Clamp each end of the front rail by placing one pad of a *C*-clamp inside the drawer opening, the other pad on the leg. Pulling the joints together with a pipe or bar clamp stretched from leg to leg might split the rail at the drawer opening.

Clean up the edges of the drawer fronts with a hand plane and the ends with a disc sander. Fit each front to its opening so there is a gap of about $\frac{3}{32}$ in. all around the front. The drawers are lap-dovetailed at the front and through-dovetailed at the back, and the $\frac{1}{2}$-in.-thick sides are grooved for the runners on the drawer hangers. The drawers and drawer hangers are made and installed as described for the bed with drawers (pp. 15-16). This method of attaching hangers to the rails is the quickest and most accurate way I have found to ensure that the drawer fronts are centered in their openings. It's easier to attach stops to the hangers behind the drawers than to try to position the runners to act as stops. When the hangers and stops are screwed in place, insert the drawers, and plane or scrape the drawer fronts and the rail perfectly flush. The drawer pulls are easy to turn on the lathe. Because the drawers are light, there is no need for through-wedged tenons on the pulls—round stub tenons, shown in the plan drawings, will do.

You'll have to glue up this wide top. Match the pieces for color and grain pattern, joint the edges and glue them up as described in Appendix 2. The edging shown in the plan drawings, which keeps things from falling off the back of the table, is optional. The grain of the short pieces of edging on the ends must run vertically to allow for seasonal movement.

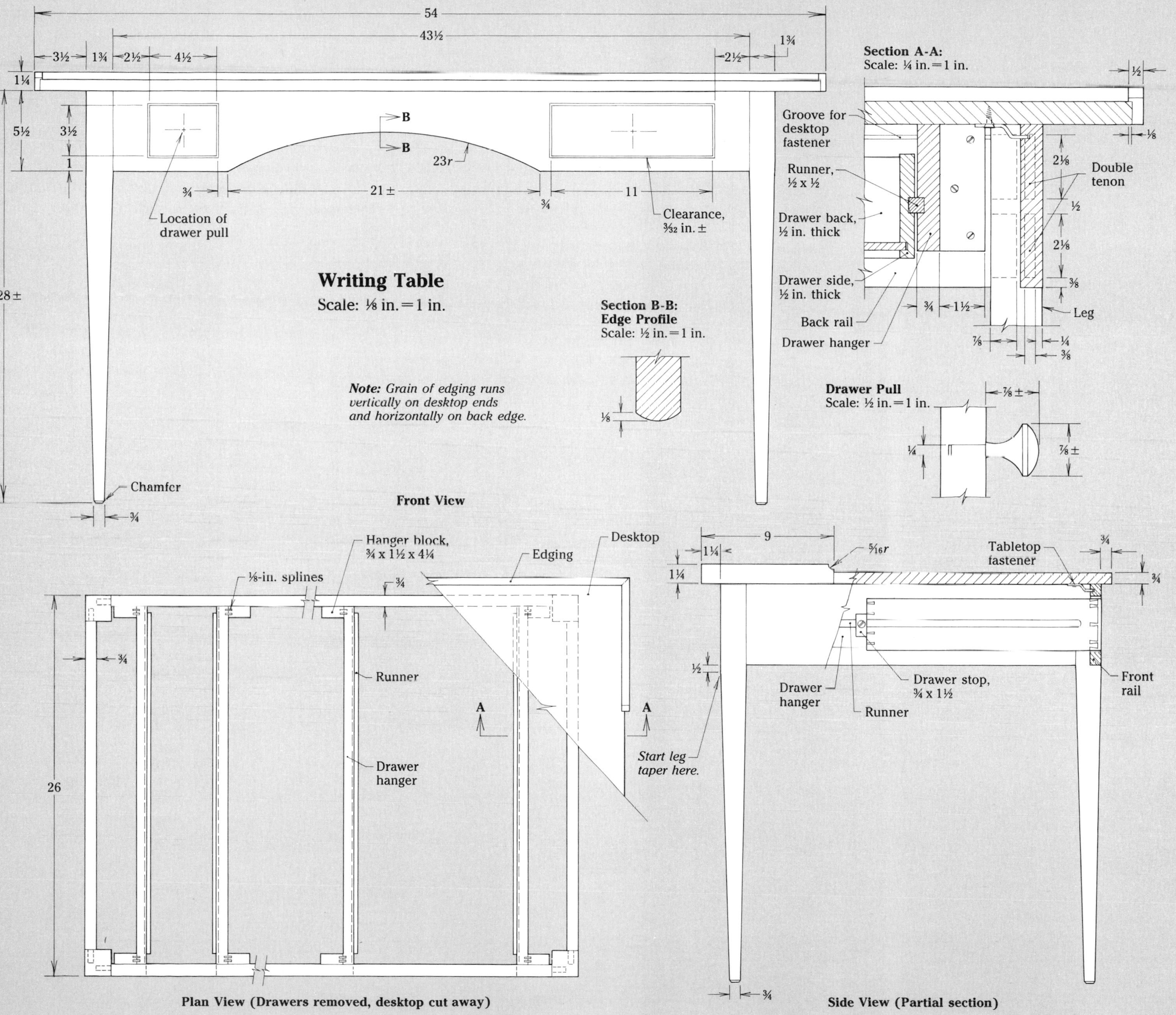
Writing Table
Scale: ⅛ in. = 1 in.
Front View
54
43½
3½
1¾
2½
4½
2½
1¾
1¼
5½
3½
1
B
B
23r
¾
21 ±
¾
11
Location of drawer pull
Clearance, 3⁄32 in. ±
28 ±
Chamfer
¾
Note: Grain of edging runs vertically on desktop ends and horizontally on back edge.
Section A-A:
Scale: ¼ in. = 1 in.
½
⅛
Groove for desktop fastener
Runner, ½ x ½
Drawer back, ½ in. thick
Drawer side, ½ in. thick
Back rail
Drawer hanger
Double tenon
2⅛
½
2⅛
⅜
Leg
¾
1½
⅞
¼
⅜
Section B-B:
Edge Profile
Scale: ½ in. = 1 in.
⅛
Drawer Pull
Scale: ½ in. = 1 in.
⅞ ±
⅞ ±
¼
Plan View (Drawers removed, desktop cut away)
Hanger block, ¾ x 1½ x 4¼
Edging
Desktop
⅛-in. splines
¾
¾
Runner
Drawer hanger
26
A
A
Start leg taper here.
Side View (Partial section)
9
1¼
5⁄16r
1¼
Tabletop fastener
¾
¾
½
Drawer hanger
Runner
Drawer stop, ¾ x 1½
Front rail
¾

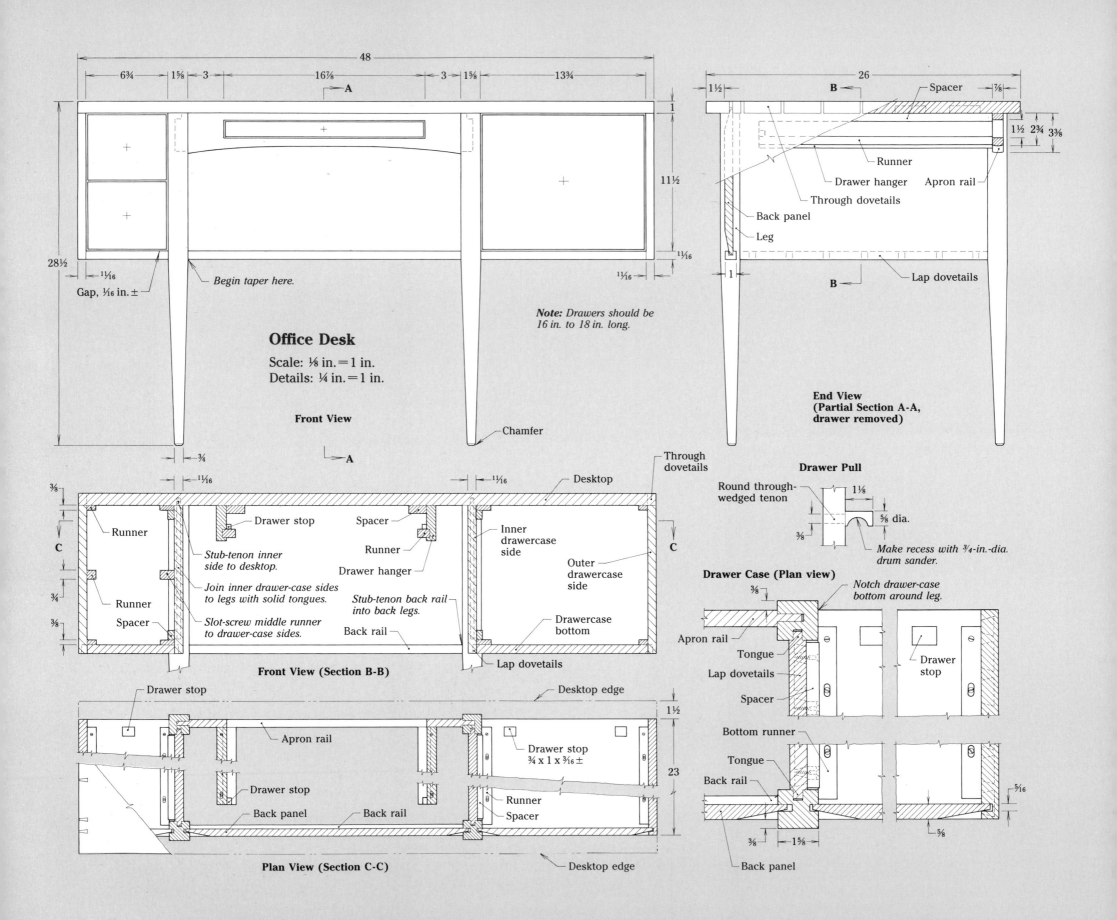

Office Desk

Scale: ⅛ in. = 1 in.
Details: ¼ in. = 1 in.

Front View

48

6¾ · 1⅝ · 3 · 16⅞ · 3 · 1⅝ · 13¾

A

1

11½

1¹⁄₁₆

28½

1¹⁄₁₆

Begin taper here.

Gap, ¹⁄₁₆ in. ±

1¹⁄₁₆

¾

A

Chamfer

End View
(Partial Section A-A,
drawer removed)

26

1½

B

Spacer

⅞

1½ 2¾ 3⅜

Runner

Drawer hanger   Apron rail

Through dovetails

Back panel

Leg

B

Lap dovetails

Note: Drawers should be
16 in. to 18 in. long.

Front View (Section B-B)

1¹⁄₁₆

1¹⁄₁₆

Through dovetails

Desktop

⅜

Runner

C

Drawer stop   Spacer

Runner

Drawer hanger

Stub-tenon inner
side to desktop.

Join inner drawer-case sides
to legs with solid tongues.

Slot-screw middle runner
to drawer-case sides.

Stub-tenon back rail
into back legs.

Back rail

Inner
drawercase
side

Outer
drawercase
side

Drawercase
bottom

Lap dovetails

Runner

Spacer

¾

⅜

C

Drawer Pull

Round through-
wedged tenon

1⅛

⅜

⅝ dia.

Make recess with ¾-in.-dia.
drum sander.

Drawer Case (Plan view)

⅜

Notch drawer-case
bottom around leg.

Apron rail

Tongue

Lap dovetails

Spacer

Drawer
stop

Bottom runner

Tongue

Back rail

Back panel

⅜   1⅝

5⁄16

⅝

Plan View (Section C-C)

Drawer stop

Apron rail

Drawer stop

Back panel   Back rail

Desktop edge

1½

Drawer stop
¾ x 1 x ³⁄₁₆ ±

Runner

Spacer

23

Desktop edge

Office Desk

The desk in the photo was designed to fit in the rather small office of a local doctor. I don't recommend this design for people who like to perch on a desk because this kind of mistreatment could tip it over. The file drawer on the right takes letter-size Pendaflex files; the other drawers are for smaller items. You may want to put a sliding tray for small items in the top left-hand drawer.

For anyone fond of dovetailing, this desk is an ideal project, because there are twenty-two sets to cut: six sets for the carcase and four for each drawer. The construction is somewhat unusual, but very strong. The desktop and two drawer cases are assembled as a single *U*-shaped carcase, and then the front legs and apron rail and back legs and back panels are slid into place. The bottom of each drawer case is lap-dovetailed to the two sides of the case. The outer side of each case is through-dovetailed to the top, and the inner side is stub-tenoned into the underside of the top and fixed by tongues to the legs, as shown in the drawing on p. 156.

Construction

It is best to use a wood with moderate to low seasonal movement (see Appendix 1). Although the desk can swell and shrink across its width without conflict, the $1\frac{1}{16}$-in.-thick sides and bottoms of the drawer cases will respond more rapidly to changing humidity levels than the 1-in.-thick desktop. The drawer sides, particularly for the deep file drawer, should also be made of stable wood.

Join up the pieces for the top and the drawer cases. It's important that these pieces be flat, so select boards that are thick enough to plane out any warp or wind. I use $1\frac{1}{4}$-in. or $1\frac{1}{2}$-in.-thick rough-sawn stock for the top and 1-in.-thick rough-sawn stock for the rest. The outer sides and bottoms of the drawer cases are the same width, but the inner sides are narrower because they fit between the legs. When you cut the pieces to final dimension, make sure that they are square, otherwise the drawers will jam or rattle in the assembled carcase.

The carcase joinery is conventional, except for the inner sides, which have joints on both ends and both edges. To avoid confusion and errors later, lay out all the carcase joints and mark the mating pieces before cutting any of them. Mark the notches for the legs on

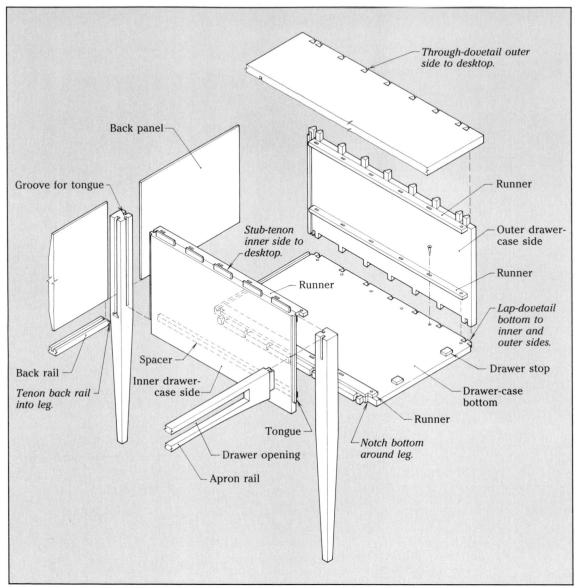

Through-dovetail outer side to desktop.

Back panel

Groove for tongue

Stub-tenon inner side to desktop.

Runner

Runner

Outer drawer-case side

Runner

Lap-dovetail bottom to inner and outer sides.

Back rail

Tenon back rail into leg.

Spacer

Inner drawer-case side

Drawer stop

Drawer-case bottom

Runner

Tongue

Notch bottom around leg.

Drawer opening

Apron rail

The inner sides of the drawer cases are joined to the desktop, case bottoms and legs with lap dovetails, stub tenons and tongues, as shown here. Add the drawer runners and spacers after assembly.

two corners of the bottom of each drawer case, and position the inner side accordingly when marking its lap dovetails. (Though you could through-dovetail the bottoms and sides, I think that this would distract the eye.)

I cut the tenons and the tongues on the inner sides with the tablesaw, using a high wooden fence screwed to the rip fence for extra stability, as when tenoning a rail. The tenons are ¾ in. long and the tongues ⅜ in. long; both are ⅜ in. thick. Saw the waste between the tenons and chisel to the shoulders.

Cutting the tails on the tablesaw on a piece as wide and heavy as the desktop is very awkward, so I prefer to cut them by hand. (See pp. 30-31 for tips on dovetailing wide pieces.) The drawer-case bottoms are more manageable—the tails can be cut on both of them at once by clamping the bottoms together and pushing them over the angled tablesaw blade with the miter gauge, as shown in the sketch on p. 44.

After completing the dovetail joints, lay out the mortises on the underside of the top. Dry-assemble the two drawer cases—just start the tails in the sockets, don't drive them home. Make sure that the sides are at right angles to the desktop and the drawer-case bottom, then knife-mark the positions of the mortises from the tenons. Clear the waste in the mortises with a brace and bit or electric drill, and chisel to the lines. The tenons should fit snugly.

Next, cut out five legs (one is a spare). Make the legs 1⅝ in. square, and cut the joints in them before tapering the bottom half of the leg. Groove the legs for the tongues on the inner sides. These grooves are stopped just above where the bottom of the drawer cases meet the legs, and they extend through the top end of the leg so that the leg can be slid into place during assembly. I rout these grooves because it's easier to make a stopped groove with a router than a tablesaw. They must not fit the projecting tenons too snugly or they may jam when glue is applied and the legs are slid into place.

The legs are connected by an apron rail at the front and a narrow rail at the back, which also supports the middle panel. Dry-assemble the carcase again, slide the legs into position and measure between them to find the shoulder-to-shoulder dimension of the rails. Lay out and cut the mortise-and-tenon joints that join the rails to the legs. Both rails are set back ⅜ in. from the front faces of the legs, so they will fall in the same plane as the edges of the drawer cases. Mark the joints with pencil or crayon for easy reference at assembly. (Don't be tempted to simplify the construction by omitting the back rail and middle panel. The rail is a strut, and a structural necessity. Without it, the desk would droop at its ends.)

Cut the 5/16-in.-wide grooves for the back panels next. Position the grooves so the faces of the panels will be in the same plane as the edges of the drawer cases, as shown in the plan drawings. It is essential that these grooves line up with each other. Set up a tablesaw or router to groove the sides and bottoms of the drawer cases and the back rail. Then dry-assemble the carcase and legs, and mark the position of the grooves in the desktop and legs from the grooves you just cut. Make the grooves in the legs for the wide middle panel deeper than for the two end panels, because the middle panel will move more.

Glue up the 5/8-in.-thick back panels, cut them to size and bevel them to fit the grooves. The grain of all the panels should run vertically. The grain of the middle panel, therefore, will run parallel to its shortest dimension, not longest as is usually done to minimize seasonal movement. It would have been visually confusing to have the grain run vertically on the end panels and horizontally in the middle. Once again, what looks right usually is right.

Lay out the curve on the bottom edge of the front apron rail by springing a thin batten. Then bandsaw the curve and give the edge a slight round with a spokeshave. I cut the front for the small center drawer out of the rail with a coping saw, as described on pp. 151-152. (The drawer and drawer hanger will be made after assembling the carcase.)

I dry-assemble the entire desk to make sure that everything fits properly before gluing. If you are confident of your accuracy, you needn't push the dovetail joints home—they can be difficult to pull apart. It's convenient to finish the panels and legs before final assembly (I use an oil finish), and to wax the inside faces of the drawer cases. Squeezed-out glue won't adhere to the finished and waxed surfaces, which makes clean-up easier, but be sure the surfaces to be joined are bare wood.

The desk is best assembled in three stages: first the carcase, then the two front legs and front rail, and finally the back legs, rail and panels. Use a plastic resin glue, such as Weldwood, that will allow ample assembly time. Place the desktop upside down on sawhorses or a low bench, push the drawer-case sides in

The back panels are beveled to fit in grooves in the carcase, legs and back rail. The back rail is tenoned into the legs and acts as a strut, making the desk rigid.

place, then add the lap-dovetailed bottoms. Make clamping blocks to bear on the dovetails and pull them home with pipe or bar clamps as described on pp. 31-32. You may need to use clamps and a stiff, slightly crowned bearer at top and bottom to pull the dovetails and tenons of the inner sides home (place the bearer on top of the dovetail-clamping blocks). Measure the diagonals of the drawer cases to check that the openings are square. Plane the tails and pins flush after the glue has cured.

Glue the front legs and rail together. Pull the joints together with C-clamps that bear on the ends of the drawer opening and the legs—a pipe or bar clamp across the rail might split it. When the glue has cured, spread glue in the grooves in the legs and on the tongues, and push the assembled legs and rail into place. Next, slide the two small back panels into the carcase. Then slide the back legs, rail and middle

These desk drawers require a lot of dovetails. You can clamp pairs of sides together and cut the tails on the tablesaw. Use locking tails on the drawer sides for even stronger drawers. Finish just the tails and end grain of the front to highlight the joints, and wax the sides for easy running.

panel as a unit onto the tongues of the inner sides. If the tongues fit tightly, it might be wise to put glue in the grooves only; the glue may swell the tongues, making them jam, rather than slide, in the grooves. When assembly is complete, add pipe or bar clamps across the top and under the drawer-case bottoms to pull the legs tight onto the tongues.

Make the drawers next. The drawer sides are lap-dovetailed to the front and through-dovetailed to the back—this requires a lot of dovetailing, as shown at left. The drawers in the cases slide between runners slot-screwed to the carcase sides, top and bottoms. The drawer sides bear against the outer carcase sides, but spacers are needed to pack the faces of the inner sides out about ⅟₃₂ in. beyond the faces of the legs. You can position the runners for the top drawer on the left-hand side using strips of scrap wood, as shown in the sketch on p. 43.

Make the shallow center drawer next. Trim the drawer front to fit the opening, leaving about ⅟₁₆-in. clearance all around, then add sides, back and bottom. (Unlike the other drawer fronts, which have lips at top and bottom, this front is flush with the edges of the sides.) The drawer is supported by two runners, each housed in a groove in a hanger that is slot-screwed to the underside of the desktop. (You can substitute slotted washers for slots cut in the hanger, as shown on p. 71.) Make the hangers and runners of a stable wood, such as maple. Position each hanger so its inside face is flush with the end of the drawer opening and the runner is about ⅟₁₆ in. above the lower edge of the opening. Slot-screw a spacer above the drawer sides, as shown in the plan drawings—this keeps the drawer from tipping down as it's pulled out.

To stop the drawers, I glue blocks to the drawer-case bottoms and the underside of the desktop. The blocks on the case bottoms must be thin enough to fit beneath the drawer bottoms. Position the stops to strike the back face of the drawer front and rub-glue them in place. Trim them with a chisel so the drawers will sit about ⅟₁₆ in. back from the front edge of the drawer cases. Because of its weight, the large drawer needs two stops at top and bottom. Stops for the center drawer can be placed behind the drawer and glued to the runners.

You can turn pulls for the desk, like those shown in the plan drawings, or use metal pulls. I don't find loose-bail pulls convenient for desks, so I don't use them unless I'm asked to.

Folding Desk

I first made this desk to fit in the hallway of a rather small house in Weston, Vermont. The desktop had to fold to give easy passage when the desk was not in use, rather than just to conceal the pigeonholes. Over the years, I made eight or nine more folding desks, each a little different. The one shown in the photos is the final version, and I would make no more changes in this particular design.

Construction

This is a difficult piece of furniture to make because it involves some fairly complex joinery. I urge anyone who is not familiar with a technique to try it out first on scrap wood and avoid the frustration and expense of spoiling good material. For example, if you haven't attempted a haunched mortise-and-tenon joint before, keep making them in scrap until you can make one with confidence. It's also a good plan, when making a number of identical parts, such as legs, to make one or two extra. Then, if you make a wrong cut in one piece, you don't have to go back and repeat each step to replace it. The extra piece, if not needed, can be kept as a pattern for future projects.

I've made this desk in teak, mahogany, cherry, walnut and padauk, but not in any blond woods such as oak or ash. I prefer to use walnut or mahogany, perhaps because the desk is akin to those made in the late eighteenth and early nineteenth centuries when those two woods were in vogue. This is not to say that a furniture maker is bound by traditions and historical precedents, but I think that he or she should be aware of them.

The desk consists of three assemblies—a carcase, a base and a pigeonhole unit—each of which is made separately. The carcase, which houses the fixed desktop, four drawers and the two slides that support the folding top, is the most complex of the three, and should be made first.

The carcase—The carcase top and sides are solid pieces, but its bottom is a mortise-and-tenoned frame, constructed with loose tenons to allow the top and sides to move with seasonal changes in humidity. (The isometric drawing on p. 164 shows an exploded view of the desk construction.)

Select the stock for the top and sides, and for the front and back rails of the bottom. Plane it ¾ in. thick.

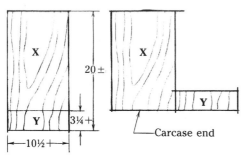

Glue up each carcase side from one board, 10½ in. to 11 in. wide, to ensure uniform color and grain pattern.

(You can make the rails of an inexpensive wood and lip them with the wood you're using for the desk.) If possible, use a single board for the 10½-in.-wide top. Unless you can cut the *L*-shaped sides from 18-in.-wide boards, join them as shown in the sketch at left, so that the color and grain will be uniform. Plane the top end of the short piece flat before assembly—it's impossible after. When you trim the pieces to final dimension, make sure the ends are square to the edges, or the assembled carcase won't be square.

Lay out and cut the through dovetails that join the top and sides, and the lap dovetails that join the bottom rails and sides. (See pp. 30-31 for tips on laying out and cutting carcase dovetails.) Mark the curve on the front edge of the carcase top by springing a thin batten, then bandsaw to the line and clean up the curve with a spokeshave.

A solid back panel is housed in a ¼-in.-wide groove just inside the back edge of the carcase. I rout the groove, taking care to stop it just short of the ends of the carcase top and the ends of the bottom rail so that it won't show on the outside of the carcase. Because the grain of the panel runs parallel to the length of the carcase, the grooves in the carcase top and bottom rail should be at least ⅜ in. deep to allow the panel to expand and contract across its width. (See Appendix 1 to calculate the probable movement of the wood you are using.) The grooves in the sides needn't be so deep, because there is almost no shrinkage along the panel's length.

Join up the back panel and plane it to finished thickness. Trim it to length and width (allow for movement), and then bevel the ends and edges to fit the groove. I rough-cut the bevel on the tablesaw, then I do the final fitting with a hand plane.

The front and back rails of the carcase bottom are joined by five short rails, which support the dividers for the drawers and desktop slides. These short rails are tenoned into each long rail, but are glued only to the front rail. The tenons slide in the back-rail mortises to accommodate seasonal changes in the carcase. Plane the short rails ¾ in. thick, cut them to width, then lay out the mortises in the long rails. Make the mortises about half as deep as the long rails are wide. Mark the depth of a pair of mortises on the faces of the two long rails, tap the rails into the carcase sides and measure between the marks. Cut the short rails about ⅜ in. less than this dimension to allow room for movement, then cut the tenons on the

tablesaw, using a high wooden fence screwed to the rip fence to support the rails. Dry-assemble the bottom and sides to check that the short rails fit—the shoulders of the back tenons should be about ⅜ in. from the back rail.

Next, cut the ¾-in.-wide by ⅜-in.-deep dadoes in the carcase sides for the fixed desktop. Position the dadoes so the desktop will rest on the wide part of each side. Stop the dadoes in the groove for the back panel, or they will show from the back. I cut the dadoes on the tablesaw with a dado head, clamping a stop block to the rip fence to stop the cut. In order to run the wide end of each side against the fence, you'll have to move the fence to the other side of the blade for one cut.

Before assembling the carcase, sand the surfaces that will show on the inside. If you finish these surfaces now, remember to keep the finish off the joints. Assemble the bottom frame first. Glue the front mortises and tenons only, but put the back rail in place so you can pull the joints tight and check that the frame is square. Leave a gap of about 1/16 in. or less between the outer edge of each end rail and the shoulders of the dovetails.

When the glue has cured on the bottom frame, glue up the carcase. Push the top onto the sides, slide the back panel in place and add the bottom frame. Make sure to keep glue out of the panel grooves. Pull the dovetails home with pipe or bar clamps and clamping blocks (pp. 31-32), and measure the diagonals to check that the carcase is square. When the glue has cured, flush off the dovetails with a sharp plane.

The base—It's convenient to make the base next, so that you have something on which to set the carcase. The base, a simple structure of four tapered legs connected by rails, is similar to the base used for the drop-leaf table (pp. 102-105). For strength and appearance, select straight-grained wood for the legs. Plane and saw the rails and legs to dimension, but cut the joints before cutting the curve on the rails and tapering the legs. Because the rails are flush with the outside faces of the legs, you can lay out the mortises and the tenons with one setting of a mortise gauge. The haunched mortise-and-tenon joint provides a little extra gluing surface and lessens the chance of the mortise cracking through the end of the leg. The base has no additional bracing, such as a stretcher, so these joints must fit snugly.

Lay out the tapers as described on pp. 5-6, beginning them ¼ in. below where the bottom edges of the rails meet the legs. You can rough-cut the taper on the bandsaw and finish with a hand plane. Tapering legs this thin on the jointer can be dangerous. I like to plane the faces of the legs slightly convex in their length because the flat surfaces will appear to be concave due to the distortions of perspective.

The shallow curve on the bottom edge of each rail echoes the curves of the carcase and desktop, and helps keep the desk from looking too severe. The curves are best laid out by springing a thin batten. Bandsaw to the line, then clean up the curve and round the edge with a spokeshave. Before assembly, cut a groove for tabletop fasteners or wooden buttons (p. 98) on the inside face of each rail.

Glue up the ends of the base first. I adjust the clamping pressure to toe the legs out slightly. This helps to overcome another perspective distortion that makes two parallel legs, when seen from above, appear to converge. Measure from the outside face of one leg to the inside face of the other, top and bottom. The bottom measure should be about ¼ in. greater than the top. When the glue has cured on the ends, add the two long rails. Clamp them so the legs toe out slightly, too.

Plane the faces of the rails and legs flush after the glue has cured, then screw the base to the carcase. Make sure to stand the desk on a flat surface while fitting the desktop, drawers and pigeonhole unit.

Desktop, drawers and slides—Select the stock for the desktop. The fixed top is held in place by the carcase sides, so the wood can be chosen for figure and color alone. The folding top isn't restrained by any structure, so it should be made of quartersawn or rift-sawn wood (growth rings perpendicular to the faces), preferably one wide piece. The folding top will be cut to size and hinged later.

Glue up the fixed top, if necessary, and thickness-plane it to slide into the ¾-in. groove in the carcase sides. Notch the top so that its back edge butts against the carcase back, and the edge of the notch butts against the sides. I make most of the long, cross-grain cut for the notch on the tablesaw, then I finish the notch with a handsaw and chisel.

The exposed ends of the fixed top overhang the carcase sides by ¼ in., and the front edge overhangs the sides by ½ in. Each exposed end is fastened to the

carcase by a single, long wood screw running vertically through the carcase side, as shown in the plan drawings. Bore the clearance holes for these screws now, but don't fasten the top yet—it must be removed to fit the slides for the folding top, the drawer dividers and the drawers.

The drawers have false fronts and the slides have facings. Cut the fronts and facings from one long piece of wood so that the grain pattern will be continuous across the front of the desk. Select this piece, cut it at least 1 in. over finished length and then plane it ¾ in. thick. Cut it approximately 1/16 in. over the finished width of 2½ in. and set it aside. You'll cut off the individual false fronts and facings later.

The slides for the folding top should be maple or oak, 1 in. thick, 2½ in. wide and 15⅞ in. long. (This length allows for the ¾-in.-thick facing and clearance at the back. If the slides were too close to the back panel, shrinkage of the carcase would cause them to project.) The five dividers that separate the drawers and slides from each other can be made of the same wood as the slides. Plane the dividers ½ in. thick, rip them to width using the same saw setting as for the slides, and cut them 13¾ in. long. (If the dividers extend further than the shoulders of the back tenons on the short rails, they might hinder the rails from moving.) Make sure that the slides and dividers are all dead flat.

The facings are attached to the slides with two ⅛-in.-thick plywood splines, as shown in the photo at top right. Each facing is flush with the face of the slide that runs against the carcase side, and it protrudes ¼ in. beyond the slide's other face. The overhang strikes the drawer divider, which acts as a stop. It's safer to cut the grooves for the splines on the tablesaw before cutting the facings off the long strip. Use the rip fence as a stop, and cut the grooves in the ends of the slides, using the same fence setting, by running them vertically over the saw. Glue the facings in place and plane them flush with the two edges and the outside face of each slide.

The false drawer fronts are screwed to through-dovetailed drawers, as shown in the photo at bottom right. I use ⅜-in. maple for the drawer sides, and ⅝-in. maple for the drawer front and back. Make the drawer sides 15¼ in. long and wide enough to be an easy sliding fit between the carcase bottom and the fixed desktop. To find the width of the drawers, set the slides in place against the ends of the carcase and measure the

Join the facings to the slides with ⅛-in. plywood splines. The overhang on the facing strikes an adjacent divider to stop the slide.

The through-dovetailed drawers are screwed to false fronts. This mahogany false front has a rosewood pull.

Hinge the fixed top to the folding top with folding-table hinges notched into the top surfaces of both pieces.

distance between them. Subtract 2½ in. from this measurement for the five ½-in.-thick dividers, and divide the remainder by four. Make all the drawers this wide (don't worry if they are fractionally larger). When gluing up, measure the diagonals to make sure the drawers are square. Plane the tails and pins flush when the glue has dried.

Next, put both slides, all four drawers and as many of the dividers as will fit, into the carcase. Plane a little off each divider until all the dividers and drawers fit between the carcase sides without being forced into place.

The dividers must be positioned and screwed to the short rails of the bottom one at a time. Put a slide and a divider at one end of the carcase. Push the divider tight against the slide facing, and position the facing flush with the front edge of the front rail. Clamp the divider to the rail, front and back, bore clearance holes up through the rail and screw the divider in place. Repeat this procedure with the slide and divider at the other end of the carcase.

Before positioning the remaining dividers, cut a narrow piece of scrap the same thickness as the false fronts and clamp it flush with the edge of the front carcase rail—this positions the dividers to act as drawer stops. Put a drawer against the fixed dividers at each end and place dividers against the exposed sides of the drawers. Push the ends of the dividers against the scrap, then clamp and screw them to the short rails. Put the two center drawers in place and the last divider between them, and repeat the procedure. When all the dividers are screwed in place, plane the sides of the drawers and slides if necessary until they slide smoothly in the openings.

Cut the false fronts to overlap each drawer side a fraction more than ¼ in. and screw them to the drawers from the inside. Try the drawers in the openings, and plane the edges of the fronts so they clear the carcase by about ¹⁄₁₆ in. The ends of the fronts can fit closely together because there will be virtually no movement along the grain. I think the fronts look best set back about ¹⁄₁₆ in. from the edge of the carcase. To do this, lay the desk on its back and place ¹⁄₁₆-in.-thick strips of wood on the ends of the dividers, then insert the drawers. Plane and scrape the fronts flush with the carcase edge, and remove the strips of wood. The drawers will all be set back a uniform distance.

The drawer pulls should be made of wood that contrasts with the color of the carcase without being too

extreme. A walnut or cherry desk with rosewood pulls looks good, but a maple desk with ebony pulls would contrast too greatly—your attention would be drawn to the pulls, not the overall appearance of the desk. You can turn the pulls shown in the plan drawings, but if no lathe is available, you can carve them, or simply use small, brass pulls.

The next step is to cut the folding desktop to size. The curve on the outer edge of the folding top is identical to the curve on the carcase top, and can be laid out and cut in the same manner. Notch the front corners to fit around the carcase sides when the top is folded. Before hinging the fixed and folding tops, I round the edges that take the hinges, as shown in the photo at top left. Do this with a hand plane, making sure to keep the arrises perfectly straight.

Hinge the two tops with a folding-table hinge, as shown at left. (See Appendix 5 for sources of supply.) The hinges must be set flush with both tops, and I strongly recommend trial-fitting a hinge to pieces of scrap before cutting into the desktops. Place the mating edges of the fixed top and folding top together on a flat surface and knife-cut around the hinge outline into both surfaces, then neatly chisel out the waste. Rectangular folding-table hinges are easier to fit than ones with semicircular ends, but I think that the semicircular ones are more elegant.

Pegs fixed to the outer short rails of the carcase bottom keep the slides from being pulled out of the carcase. The ¼-in.-dia. pegs run in a stopped groove in the bottom edge of each slide. The length of the groove and the position of the peg determine how far the slide can be pulled out of the carcase. The slide should extend to within about 1 in. of the edge of the folding top. Fix the pegs to the rails, and rout a ⁵⁄₁₆-in. groove in the bottom edge of each slide. Put the slides into the carcase, slide the desktop in place and fix it with the two screws. Gluing the top is unnecessary and messy. You may need to take a shaving off the edges of the slides so they run easily, but don't plane off too much or the folding top will droop.

Pigeonhole unit—The pigeonhole unit is a rectangular, through-dovetailed box made of ½-in.-thick wood. The box contains ¼-in.-thick vertical and horizontal dividers housed in dadoes. Make the box ¹⁄₃₂ in. longer than the inside dimension of the carcase so that you can plane the ends to fit the carcase opening tightly. The curved front edges of the top and bottom of the box run parallel to the curve of the carcase top, and can be laid out, cut and cleaned up in the same way. Cut a small recess in the bottom large enough to permit grasping the folded desktop, as shown in the photo at top right.

Rout the ¼-in. by ¼-in. dadoes for the vertical dividers in the top and bottom—for each dado, I run the router against a fence clamped to the piece. Rout from the back edges, and stop the dadoes about ⅜ in. from the front edges. Practice routing the dadoes on scrap; if crooked or misplaced, they are difficult to repair. Glue up the box, making sure that it is square.

Thickness-plane the stock for all the dividers ¼ in. thick—make them a snug sliding fit in the dadoes. Then rout dadoes ¼ in. wide by ⅛ in. deep in all six long vertical dividers and two of the horizontal ones in order to house the other dividers. The widths of the dividers vary with their positions, as shown in the plan drawings. All the dividers are flush with the back edge of the box. The long vertical dividers are set back ¼ in. from the front edge of the top and bottom of the box. The horizontal dividers and the short vertical dividers are flush with the edges of the long vertical dividers. After cutting the dividers to correct width and length, notch their front corners to cover the stopped dadoes. The cutout in the edge of each short vertical divider looks nice and makes it easier to grasp papers in the pigeonholes.

Slide the dividers into the box from the back, gluing only the long vertical dividers. I dovetail the three small drawers, as shown in the plan drawings, but you can substitute simple rabbet joints, glued and nailed with panel pins. You can turn pulls for these drawers, or make pulls of ¼-in.-dia. brass rod epoxied into a hole in each drawer front.

Fit the pigeonhole unit into the carcase. You can taper the ends slightly to make it easier to slide the unit in, but make sure the front edges are tight to the carcase sides, as shown in the photo at bottom right. Bore the holes for the four ¼-in.-dia. brass or ⅜-in.-dia. wood pins that support the unit. After finishing the pigeonhole unit, insert it into the carcase and tap the pins into the holes.

I think an oil finish is best for this desk. There is no need to oil surfaces that won't be seen, but wherever wood is sliding on wood, I use a good-quality paste wax, which makes for a smooth action and reduced wear. The insides of the drawers are best waxed, too. It makes them easier to keep clean.

Cut a small recess in the bottom of the pigeonhole unit so you can open the folding top.

The pigeonhole unit is supported by brass or wood pins in the carcase sides. Fit the unit so its front edges are tight to the carcase. Tap the pins in horizontally.

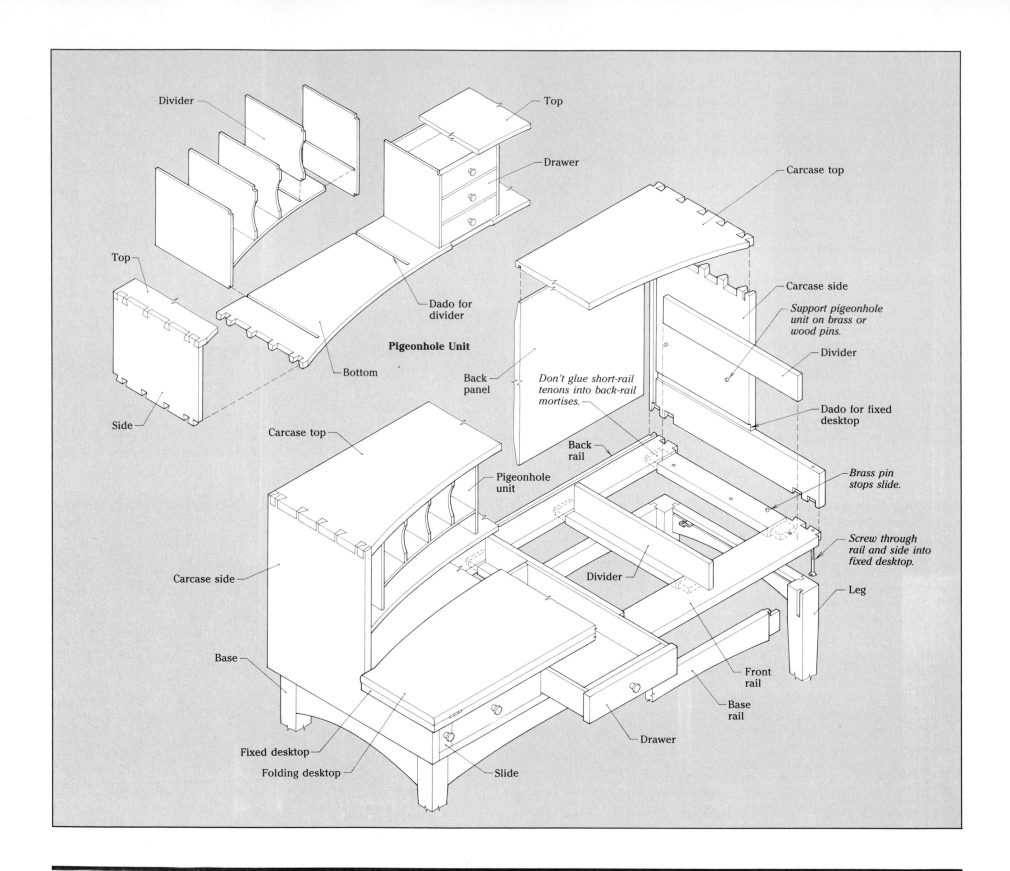

Divider

Top

Drawer

Carcase top

Carcase side

Support pigeonhole unit on brass or wood pins.

Divider

Dado for divider

Pigeonhole Unit

Top

Don't glue short-rail tenons into back-rail mortises.

Dado for fixed desktop

Side

Bottom

Back panel

Back rail

Brass pin stops slide.

Carcase top

Pigeonhole unit

Screw through rail and side into fixed desktop.

Carcase side

Divider

Leg

Base

Front rail

Base rail

Fixed desktop

Folding desktop

Slide

Drawer

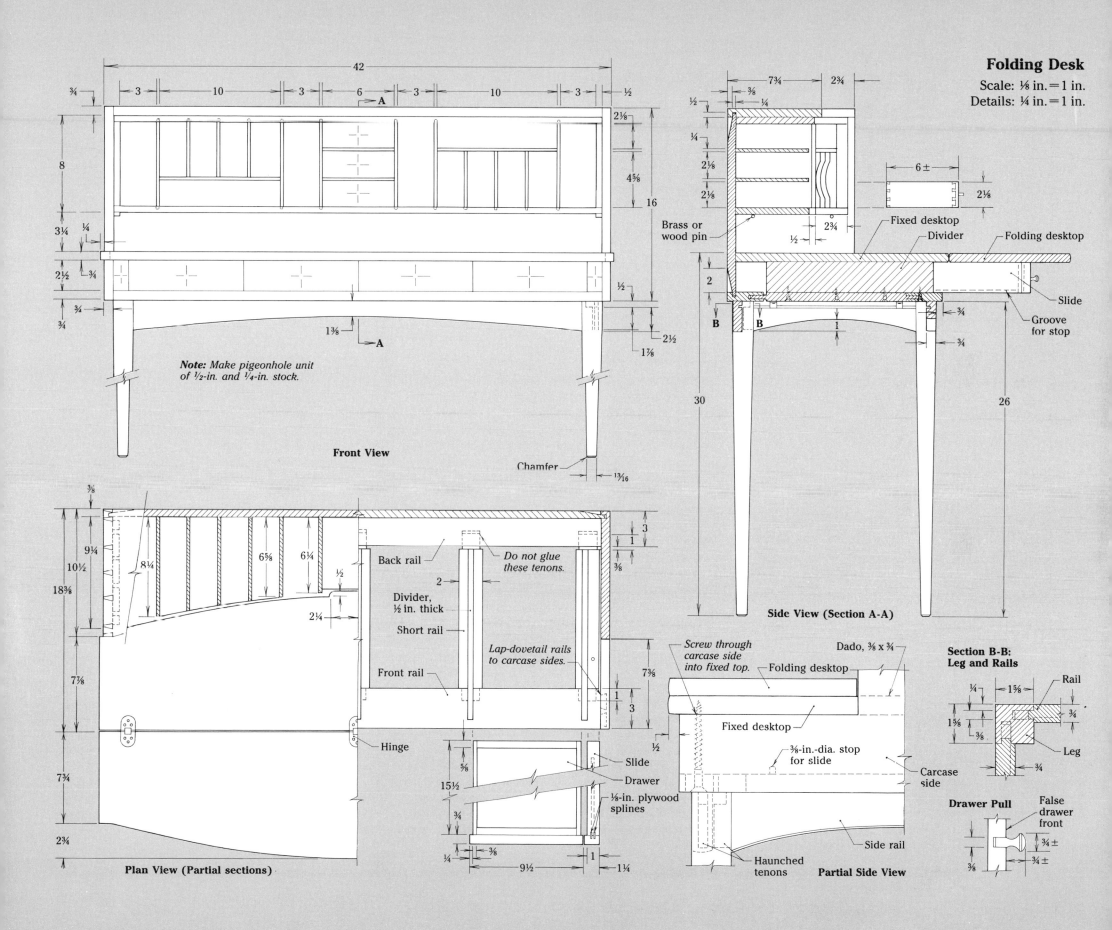

Folding Desk
Scale: ⅛ in. = 1 in.
Details: ¼ in. = 1 in.

Front View

Note: Make pigeonhole unit of ½-in. and ¼-in. stock.

Chamfer

Brass or wood pin

Fixed desktop
Divider
Folding desktop
Slide
Groove for stop

Side View (Section A-A)

Plan View (Partial sections)

Back rail
Do not glue these tenons.
Divider, ½ in. thick
Short rail
Lap-dovetail rails to carcase sides.
Front rail
Hinge

Slide
Drawer
⅛-in. plywood splines

Screw through carcase side into fixed top.
Dado, ⅜ x ¾
Folding desktop
Fixed desktop
⅜-in.-dia. stop for slide
Carcase side
Side rail
Haunched tenons
Partial Side View

Section B-B: Leg and Rails
Rail
Leg

Drawer Pull
False drawer front

Accessories

Library Steps

Several years ago, some people from St. Louis stopped by the shop and asked if I would make them some library steps. I had never been asked to make any before, so had no immediate image of what they should look like. The only similar things I knew of were the steps the Shakers made to reach their high storage drawers and the marvelous three-tread spiral steps made by the Pennsylvania woodworker Wharton Esherick.

The requirements of the clients were straightforward. The steps had to be 27 in. high, which suggested three treads, with a 9-in. rise from tread to tread. They also had to be easily moved, sturdy and handsome. After looking at various woods, the clients and I decided on cherry for its strength and the beauty of its grain. It also seemed an appropriate wood for a library. We considered adding a post as a handhold for people standing on the top tread, but finally left it off because the piece had to travel across the country in the trunk of a car.

I had a very able student at the time who was itching to try his hand at a complex piece of joinery, so he and I worked on the design together. This piece was then made mostly by him. (I later made several more steps without changing the original design.) After deciding on the number of treads and basic shape of the piece, we drew various full-size profiles for the curved sides. I usually work out designs full-size and always keep a roll of brown paper and a crayon nearby for the purpose—I've never been able to make the mental transfer from a scale drawing to the actual piece.

Once the student and I had a side profile that we both liked and that satisfied the requirements, we needed to determine the slope and distance between the sides. We traced the profile onto two pieces of cardboard, cut them out and set the cardboard sides up in the shop, positioning them at different slopes and at various distances apart until they looked right.

What looks right can't be prescribed, but must be found by trial and error and close observation. Try an extreme position that is obviously wrong and then an extreme in the other direction. Gradually, by trying less extreme positions, thereby narrowing the range of possibility, you find what looks right. It's much better to go through this process with two people—one person moves the pieces and the other watches what happens and suggests new positions. For the library steps, the only two variables were the slope of the pieces and their distance apart. Other projects may have one variable or many variables that will need to be juggled until they look right.

Years after making these steps, I still find them pleasing to the eye. I like the contrast between the rear curve and the straight front edge, and also the way in which all the structural elements are securely locked together. Its sturdiness is obvious even to people who are not woodworkers.

Construction

First, make accurate, full-size drawings of the side view and half front view. You can scale up by ruling ¼-in. squares on the plan drawings and transferring the lines in each of these squares to a corresponding 1-in. square ruled on a large sheet of paper. Or you can make the full-size drawing by measuring, using a thin batten to draw the curves. The batten will make smooth curves, though not exactly the same as those in the plan drawings.

The treads can be made of single boards, but the sides will need to be glued up of at least two boards. Ideally, the grain of each side should be parallel to the axis of each leg, but the end-grain-to-side-grain joint this would require is impractical and unattractive. I joined the boards for each side so that the grain of the two pieces met at an acute angle, as shown in the photo. This created a pleasing pattern, and because the grain of the back leg is perpendicular to the floor, the leg is stronger than if the boards had been joined so that their grain patterns were parallel to each other and to the front edge of the side. If possible, when joining up the sides, select boards whose grain has a sweep consistent with the curve of the back edge of the sides.

Plane the treads to thickness and cut them to width and a little over finished length, taking the measurements from the full-size drawings. Make sure that the ends of the treads are square with the edges. Cut out the full-size side view and use it as a pattern. If you're making more than one set of steps, you may want to make a Masonite pattern, which can be used over and over. Bandsaw the sides, then clean up the curves with a spokeshave.

The dovetails for these steps are harder to make than ordinary ones because the top tread and the sides don't meet at a right angle. (Anyone wishing to complicate this piece further could try angling in the treads toward the back.) Before laying out the tails and pins, bevel the top ends of the sides and the ends of the top tread. The angle at which these pieces meet when seen from the front is the bevel angle; it's the same for both ends of all three pieces. I set a sliding bevel to the bevel angle as drawn on the full-scale front view, then bevel the ends of the treads on the tablesaw and those of the sides with a hand plane.

Next, set a marking gauge to slightly more than the thickness of the sides and top tread. Gauge a line on one face and two edges of each piece, as shown in the

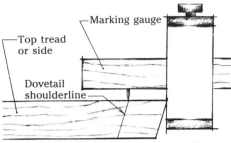

To lay out the dovetail shoulders on the ends of the top tread and sides, gauge a line on one face and both edges. Reset the gauge to make the other line, or mark it with a knife.

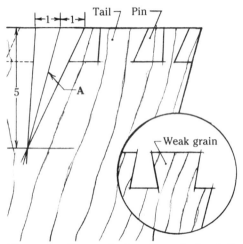

The centerlines of the skewed dovetails should be parallel to the grain direction of the sides. To establish the slope of the dovetails, draw line A parallel to the grain direction. Then measure 1 in. from either side of the line and 5 in. from the end and connect these points. (Change these dimensions to make the dovetail angles more or less acute.) The insert shows the weakness of a standard dovetail when used on the sloping grain of the stair sides.

sketch at top left. The line on the remaining face can be made by resetting the marking gauge or by knife-marking along a straightedge connecting the two lines on the edges.

The plan drawings show the dovetail layout. The tails are narrow near the edges to lock the joint and are wider toward the center of the joint. The tails must also be skewed—their centerlines must be parallel with the grain direction of the side. Ordinary dovetails on these pieces would have some short grain and would be liable to split. To lay out skewed dovetails, first set a sliding bevel parallel to the direction of the grain on the side and draw line A, as shown at bottom left. For a dovetail slope of 1 to 5, mark a point on the line 5 in. from the end of the side. Measure along the end 1 in. on either side of the line and connect those points with the first point. These two lines establish the angles of the two sides of each dovetail, sloped in accordance with the grain. Determine the spacing of the tails, and mark them on the outside face of each side, using a sliding-bevel setting for each slope.

Don't be tempted to cut the tails in the top tread—the compound angles would make assembly more difficult. When making the steps, I was extra sensitive about ease of assembly because I had recently cut joints for a small cabinet that interlocked in such a way it could not be put together.

Saw the tails, taking care not to cut beyond the gauge lines on either face. Clear the waste with a coping saw and chisel to the gauge lines in the usual way. Scribe the pins from the tails with a sharp knife and cut the pins.

The two lower treads are housed in shallow dadoes in the sides, and fixed by wedged through tenons. Knife-mark the dadoes parallel to the top tread, and stop them at the back edge of each tread. Before cutting the dadoes, lay out and cut the mortises for the through tenons, taking the positions from the full-scale drawing. Notice that the edges of the tenons are parallel to the front edge of the steps. Clear the waste from the mortises by boring from both sides and chisel carefully to the lines.

The dadoes should be about 3/16 in. deep. The walls of the dadoes must be cut at the bevel angle on the ends of the sides and top tread, and the bottoms must be parallel to the faces of the sides. Setting up a table-saw to make these angled cuts would be more trouble than it's worth, so I bore out the waste on the drill

press by making a series of shallow holes with a Forstner bit. Then I chisel to the knife marks by hand. For chiseling, you can bevel the edge of a piece of scrap to the correct angle and then clamp it along the knife mark. By resting the blade of the chisel on the beveled edge while paring to the line, you can make sure that the walls are accurate. Clean up the bottoms of the dadoes with the chisel, working bevel down.

Next, cut the tenons on the treads. Lay them out according to the positions of the mortises, and check the shoulder-to-shoulder length with the full-scale drawing. (You could assemble the sides and top tread and measure these lengths, but it's not good practice to drive dovetails home more than once.) Trim the treads slightly over the shoulder-to-shoulder length plus the length of the tenons on both ends. Leave the ends of the treads square to the faces, and scribe the shoulder line of the tenons around each end. The shoulders must be beveled to the same angle as the dovetails, so it's easiest to knife-mark the lines on the edges using a sliding bevel, then square lines across the faces connecting the beveled lines.

Make the cheek cuts and the slots for the wedges on the tablesaw, running the tread against a high wooden fence. Using the miter gauge, cut to within about 1/32 in. of the shoulder lines to clear the waste from the tenon cheeks. Trim to the lines with a chisel resting against scrap beveled to the correct angles. Cut away the waste between the tenons and then make these surfaces flush with the shoulders to complete the tenons.

Round the edges of the treads, as shown in the plan drawings, then sand the pieces. You might want to cut some kind of handhold in the top tread to make the steps easier to move around. The angles aren't great enough to cause the clamps and bearers to slip when gluing up. Leave the clamps on just long enough to pull the joints home and drive in the wedges.

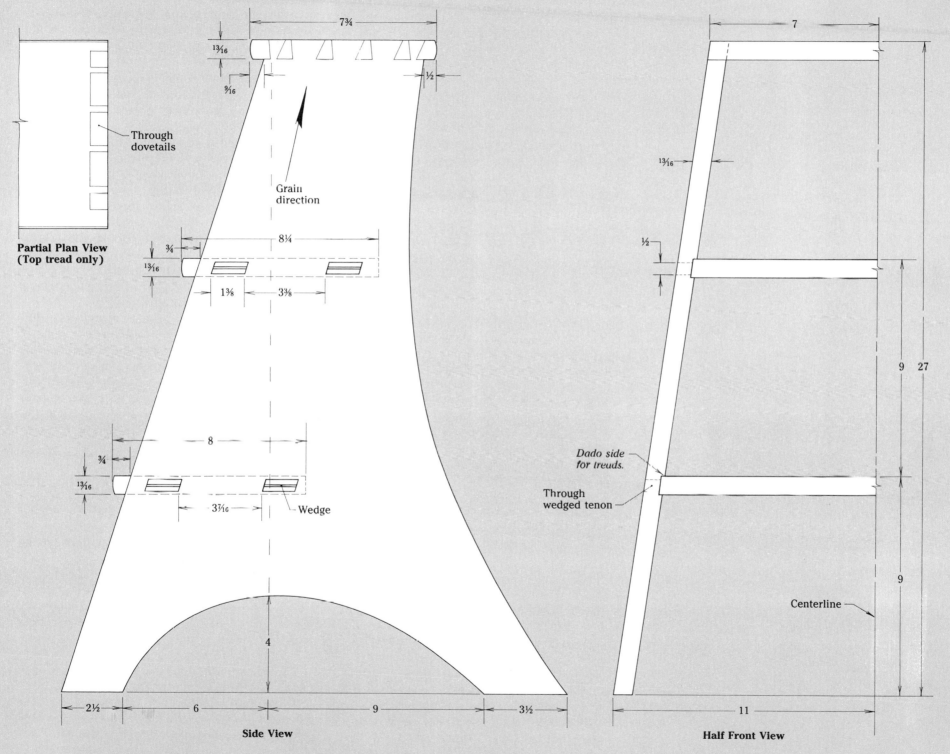

Library Steps

Scale: ¼ in. = 1 in.

7¾

13⁄16

9⁄16

½

Through
dovetails

Grain
direction

**Partial Plan View
(Top tread only)**

8¼

¾

13⁄16

1⅜   3⅜

7

13⁄16

½

8

¾

13⁄16

3⅛6   Wedge

Dado side
for treads.

Through
wedged tenon

9   27

4

2½   6   9   3½

Centerline

9

11

Side View

Half Front View

Two Bookcases

Both of the bookcases in this section can be altered to suit your particular needs. The exact dimensions will depend on the wall space available and on the size and number of books to be shelved. Before changing the dimensions too drastically, however, you should consider the arrangement of the books and the load limit of the shelves. A groaning table is symbolic of lavish hospitality, but no one wants a groaning bookshelf.

Placing large, heavy books on the bottom shelves and lighter ones above is the most stable arrangement for freestanding bookcases, because it weights the bottom, keeping the center of gravity low. Hardcover books that are 8 in. or 9 in. high weigh about 13 lb. per lineal foot of shelving, paperbacks weigh about 7½ lb. per foot. Magazines average 26 lb. per foot of shelving, and reference works, such as dictionaries, can weigh as much as 34 lb. per foot. (Each volume of the compact edition of the Oxford English Dictionary weighs 8¼ lb. and is only 3 in. wide.)

A ¾-in.-thick oak shelf, resting on supports at each end, will carry the heaviest books up to a span of about 27 in. without sagging. For an average collection of books, a 36-in. span is the maximum for a ¾-in. hardwood shelf. The maximum span increases with the thickness of the shelf—support a board at both ends and experiment if you are worried about the weight of your books on a given length and thickness of shelving.

Hanging bookcase—I designed the bookcase shown in the photo at left to hang adjacent to a desk in a study. It had to be strong because the books were all weighty reference works. The wedged-tenon construction is also rigid enough to support plants, clocks or anything else needing a place off the floor. The center shelf is adjustable, and the case can be knocked down for transportation or storage by removing the loose wedges. The bookcase could easily be made taller, but if you make the shelves longer than 30 in., and they are loaded with heavy books, you may have to increase their thickness to prevent sagging. You can bevel the front edge of a thick shelf to make the bookcase appear less bulky.

If you can't find boards wide enough for the sides and shelves, make sure the glue lines of edge-joined boards don't pass through a mortise or tenon. Plane the boards flat and ⅞ in. thick. Remember to cut the top and bottom shelves long enough for the through tenons. The curves on the sides can be laid out with a thin batten using the measurements given in the plan drawings. Bandsaw the curves to the line and clean up their edges with a spokeshave and sandpaper.

Knife-mark the mortises for the through tenons on both faces of each bookcase side. Bore out the waste and chisel carefully to the marks. Lay out and cut the tenons on the top and bottom shelves. Because they won't be glued, there is no need to make the tenons a snug fit—they should just slip easily into the mortises. I clear the waste between the tenons with a coping saw and chisel to the marking-gauge line. Make the ¼-in.-thick loose wedges, then lay out and cut the mortises for them as described on p. 98. I like to chamfer the ends of the tenons with a chisel.

The movable center shelf shown on the opposite page is supported on ¼-in. brass pins that fit into holes bored into the sides. You can make wooden pins and shelf standards, as shown in the photo below. The method for making the shelf standards, which are housed in shallow grooves in the sides, is

The top and bottom shelves of the hanging bookcase are through-tenoned into the sides and fixed with loose wedges.

These adjustable shelves are supported by wooden shelf standards housed in shallow grooves in the bookcase sides. The shelves are notched around the shelf standards, and the wooden pegs are housed in short grooves in the bottom of each shelf.

on p. 124. The bookcase can be hung in exactly the same manner as the headboard with night tables (p. 21)—fasten one angled strip to the underside of the top shelf and the other to the wall.

Freestanding bookcase—The little bookcase shown at left is a straightforward design that can be made in any reasonably strong hardwood. The top is dove-tailed to the sides and the bottom shelf is through-tenoned-and-wedged to the sides to help stiffen the case. For extra stiffness, you could rabbet the back edges of the sides, top and bottom shelves and set a back in the rabbet.

When cutting the mortises and through tenons, make them a close fit because they will show. The wedges must be parallel to the width of the shelves (at right angles to the grain of the sides) to avoid splitting the sides. If you plan to use the bottom shelf for exceptionally heavy books or records, house it in a shallow dado in each side to take some of the load off the through tenons. The layout of the dovetails and through mortises is shown in the plan drawings.

The shape of the cutout that forms the feet on the bottom of each side is best traced from a half-pattern that can be laid out by springing a thin batten. The adjustable shelves are supported by wood pins and shelf standard, as shown in the photo on p. 171.

The bookcase can also be made with an overhanging top, as shown in the plan drawings. (This design might be more suitable for a room furnished with antiques.) Each side is joined to the top by three bare-face tenons housed in blind mortises. The sides are long and a bit awkward to handle when cutting the tenons on the tablesaw, so I use the high fence described on p. 5. The mortise-and-tenon joint isn't as sturdy as a dovetail, so I recommend through-tenoning all shelves to stiffen the case, as shown in the plan drawings, or you can add a plywood back.

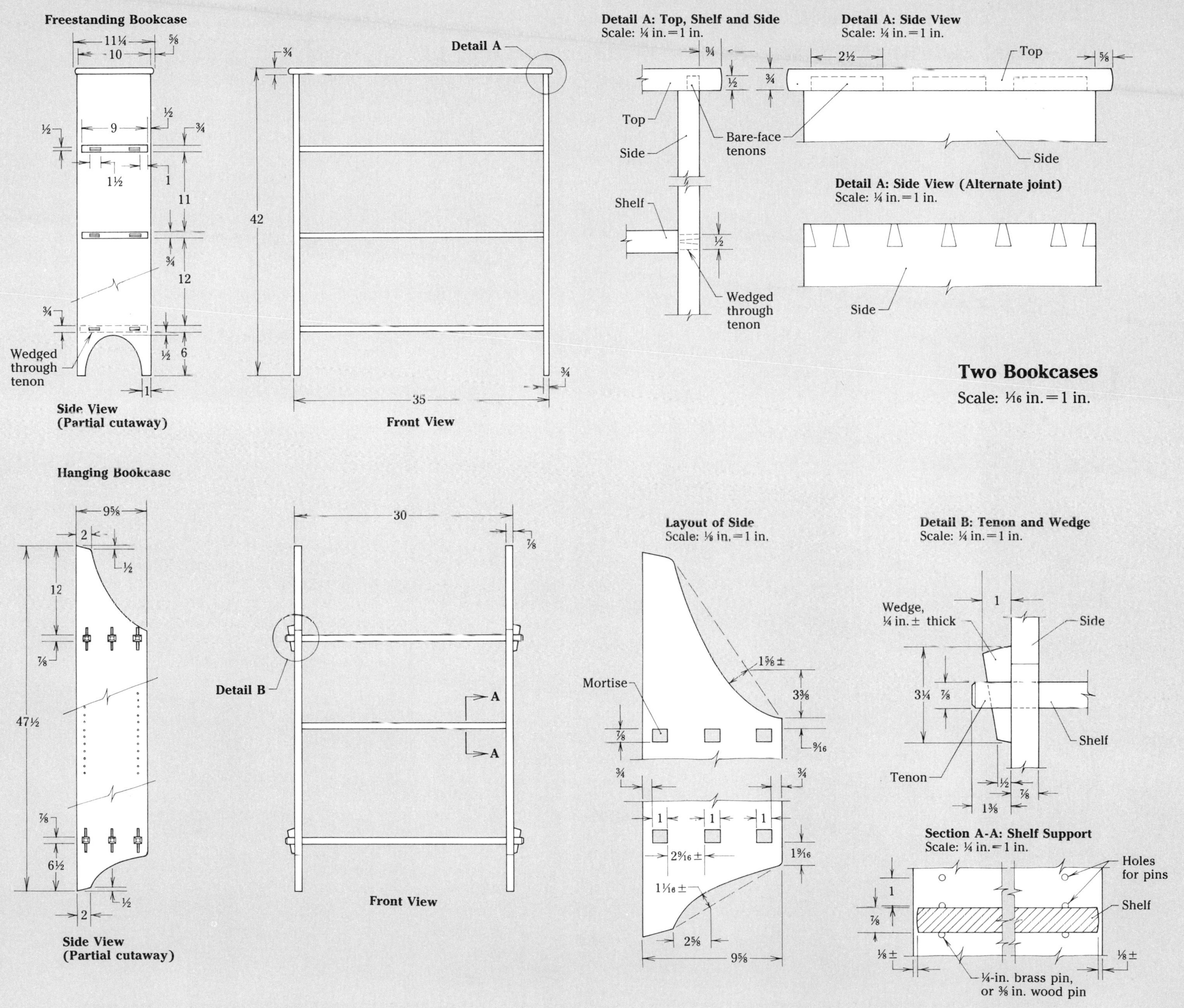

Freestanding Bookcase

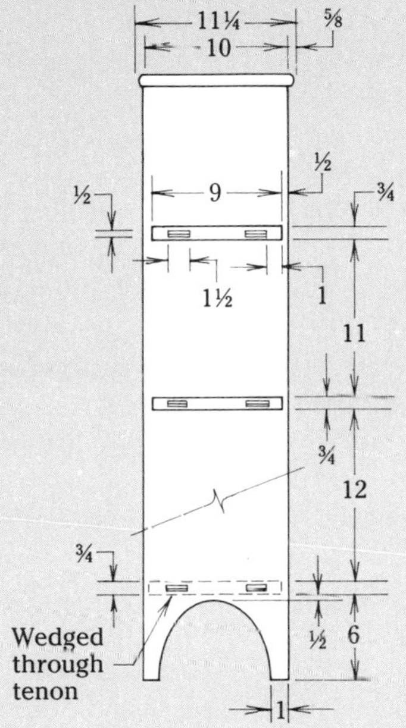
11¼
10
⅝
9
½
½
¾
1½
1
11
¾
12
¾
Wedged through tenon
½
6
1

Side View (Partial cutaway)

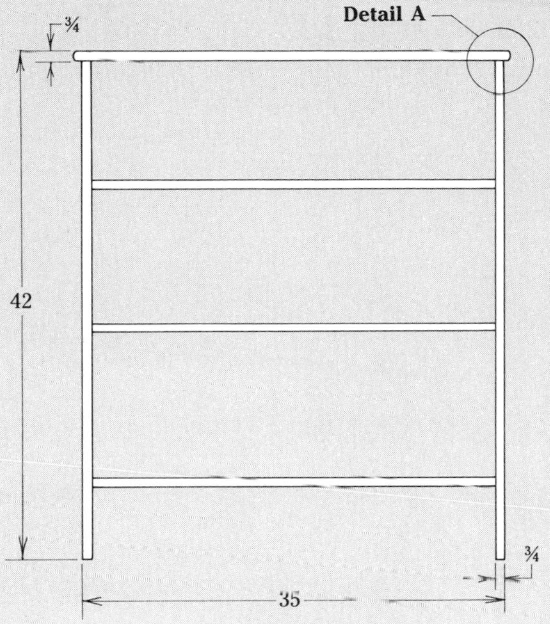
Detail A
¾
42
35
¾

Front View

Detail A: Top, Shelf and Side
Scale: ¼ in. = 1 in.

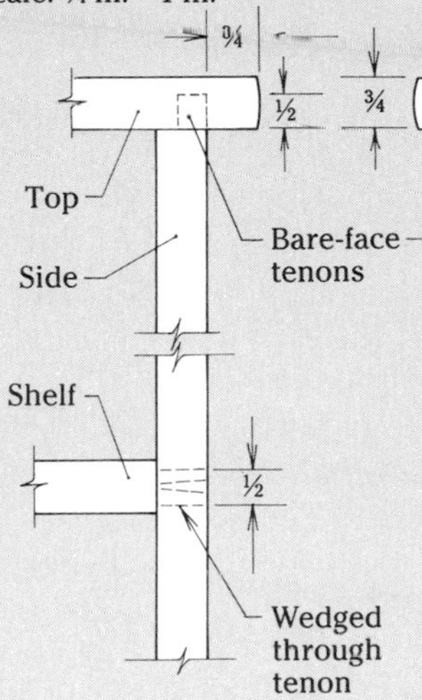
¾
½
¾
Top
Side
Bare-face tenons
Shelf
½
Wedged through tenon

Detail A: Side View
Scale: ¼ in. = 1 in.

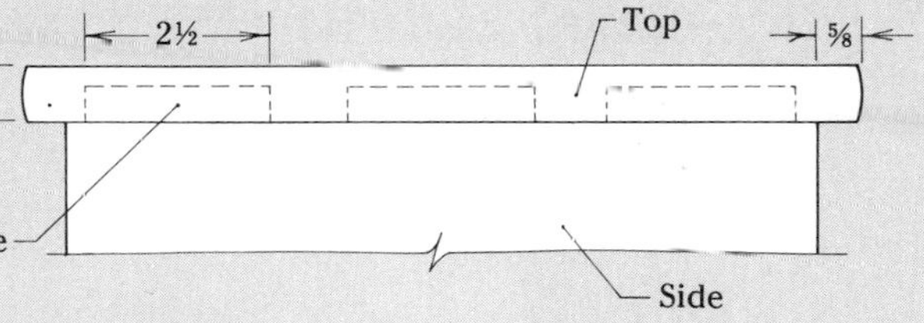
2½
Top
⅝
Side

Detail A: Side View (Alternate joint)
Scale: ¼ in. = 1 in.

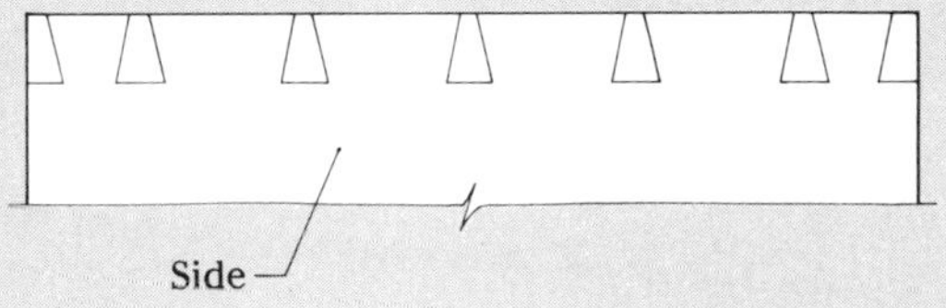
Side

Two Bookcases

Scale: 1/16 in. = 1 in.

Hanging Bookcase

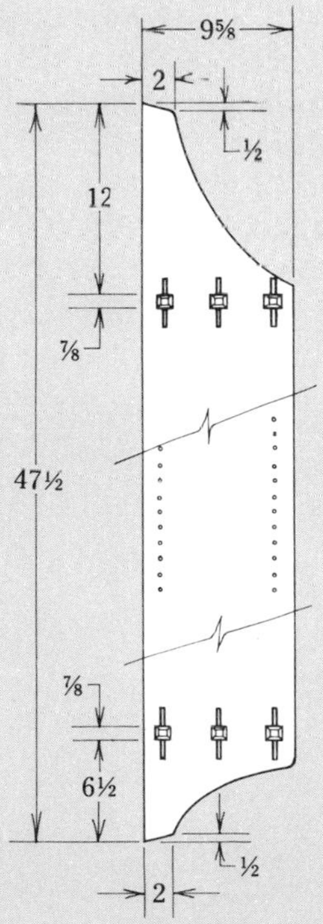
9⅝
2
½
12
⅞
47½
⅞
6½
½
2

Side View (Partial cutaway)

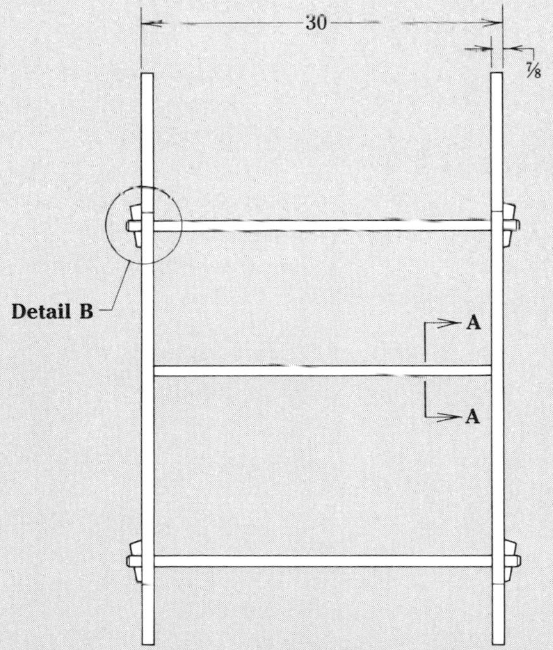
30
⅞
Detail B
A
A

Front View

Layout of Side
Scale: ⅛ in. = 1 in.

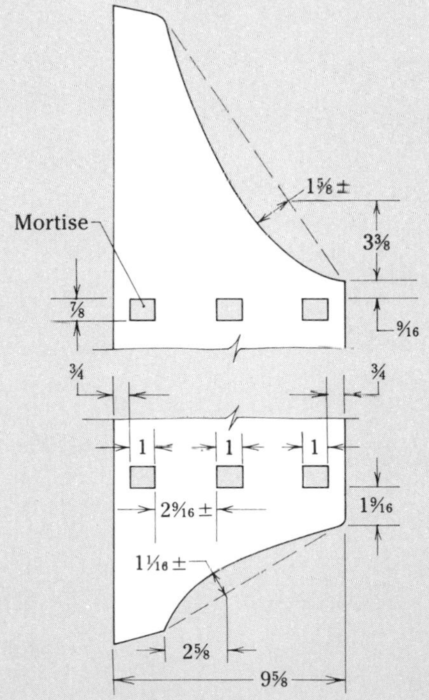
1⅝ ±
3⅜
Mortise
⅞
9/16
¾
¾
1
1
1
1 9/16
2 9/16 ±
1 1/16 ±
2⅝
9⅝

Detail B: Tenon and Wedge
Scale: ¼ in. = 1 in.

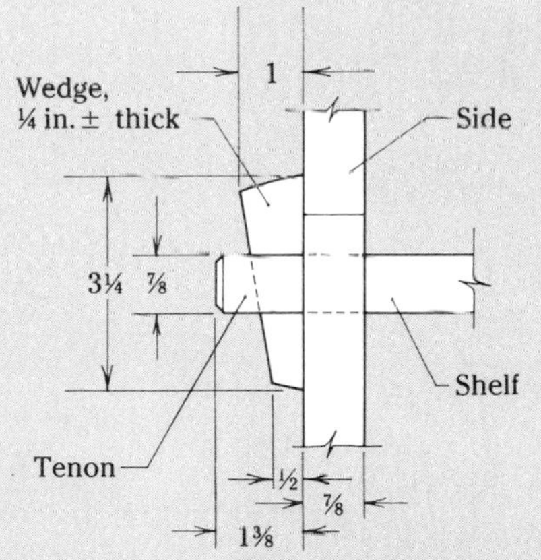
1
Wedge, ¼ in. ± thick
Side
3¼
⅞
Shelf
Tenon
½
⅞
1⅜

Section A-A: Shelf Support
Scale: ¼ in. = 1 in.

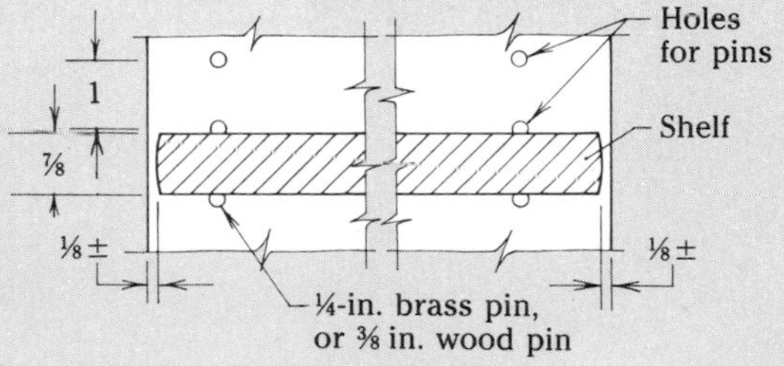
Holes for pins
1
Shelf
⅞
⅛ ±
⅛ ±
¼-in. brass pin, or ⅜ in. wood pin

Armchair

Scale: ⅛ in. = 1 in.
Details: ½ in. = 1 in.

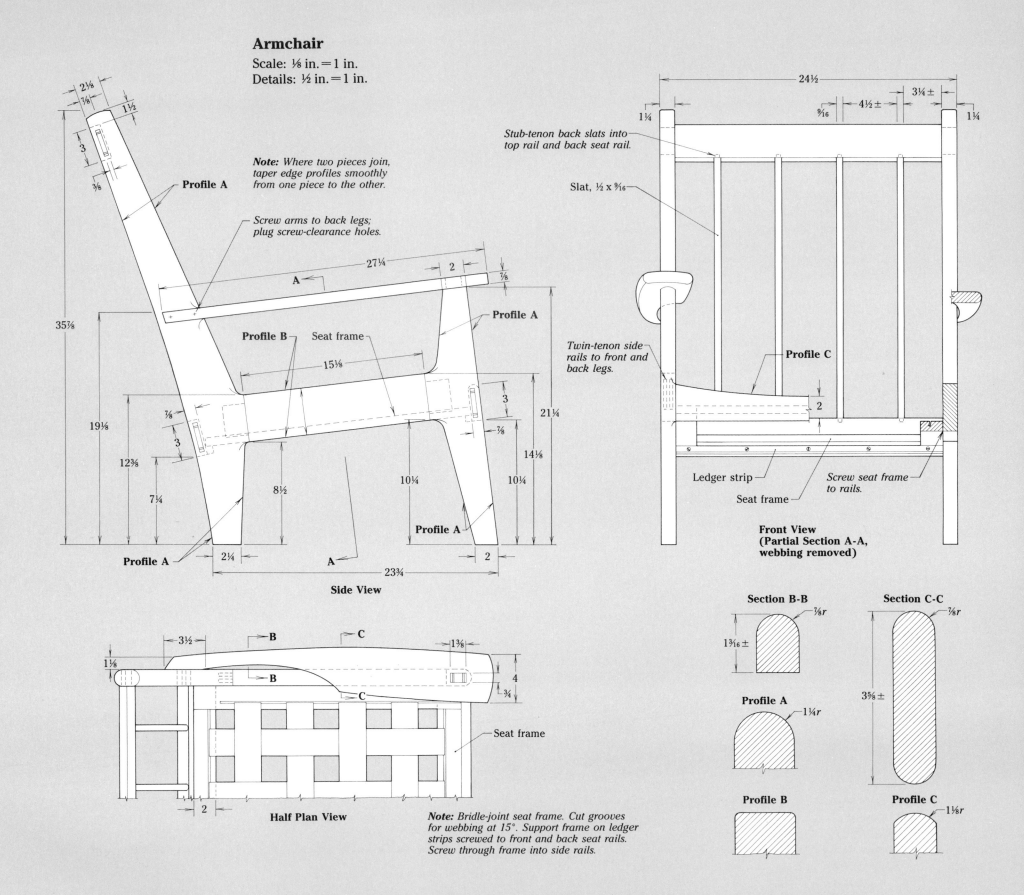

Note: *Where two pieces join, taper edge profiles smoothly from one piece to the other.*

Screw arms to back legs; plug screw-clearance holes.

Profile A

Profile A

Profile B   Seat frame

Profile A

Profile A

2¼

A

23¾

Side View

2⅛
⅞
1½
3
⅜
35⅞
19⅛
12⅜
7¼
8½
10¼
10¼
14⅛
21¼
3
⅞
3
⅞
27¼
2
⅞
15⅛

Stub-tenon back slats into top rail and back seat rail.

Slat, ½ x 9⁄16

Twin-tenon side rails to front and back legs.

Profile C

Ledger strip

Screw seat frame to rails.

Seat frame

**Front View
(Partial Section A-A,
webbing removed)**

24½
1¼
9⁄16
4½ ±
3¼ ±
1¼
2

Half Plan View

3½
1⅜
1⅛
4
¾
2
B
B
C
C

Seat frame

Note: *Bridle-joint seat frame. Cut grooves for webbing at 15°. Support frame on ledger strips screwed to front and back seat rails. Screw through frame into side rails.*

Section B-B   ⅞r
1³⁄16 ±

Profile A   1¼r

Profile B

Section C-C   ⅞r
3⅝ ±

Profile C   1⅛r

Armchair

Winston Churchill's saying "We shape our buildings—and then our buildings shape us" is equally true of furniture. Certain styles elicit certain kinds of behavior. This is not just a matter of association, usage or historical precedent, but of the actual physical relationship between the form of the furniture and the shape of the human body.

Around 1900, Charles Rennie Mackintosh designed a number of side chairs, characterized by straight, very tall backs in latticelike patterns. The effect was theatrical and exaggerated, dramatizing the sitter, while telling him plainly to sit up straight and to try to look dignified. They were not chairs to slouch in.

The familiar bean-bag chairs, popular in the 1960s, provide a complete contrast to the formality of the Mackintosh designs. These malleable chairs tell the sitter, "Be yourself, be comfortable. I don't really have any shape of my own so I can accommodate myself to any posture or position you like."

All chairs fall somewhere between these extremes. The dining chair on p. 131 is comfortable, but not a chair in which you'd curl up with a good book, like the easy chair on p. 78. The walnut armchair at right is a formal chair, quite different in character from either the dining chair or easy chair. It creates a different kind of presence in the room and needs a different kind of space, such as a quiet, orderly study, in which it makes a very comfortable reading chair. This chair, or the version with rockers, shown on p. 177, would also be appropriate for the living room.

Construction

The armchair consists of two end frames joined by two seat rails, a seat frame and a top rail. The seat cushion is supported by Pirelli webbing stretched in the seat frame. The back cushion rests against four narrow slats that are mortised into the back seat rail and the top rail. This chair involves quite a bit of hand-shaping, so if you haven't worked much with spokeshaves or drawknives, I suggest you make one of the chair's end frames in softwood to get the hang of those tools.

Make the end frames first. It's best to make a full-size pattern of ⅛-in. plywood or Masonite for each of the two legs and the rail that joins them. The rail is rectangular, so its pattern can be laid out by measuring. To make patterns for the legs, superimpose ⅛-in.

squares on the side view in the plan drawings and then reproduce the lines in these small squares in corresponding 1-in. squares ruled on the plywood or Masonite. A pantograph (a copying instrument with arms that form a parallelogram) would also work.

Mark the positions of the through mortises on the leg patterns, but don't include the tenons on the rail. Make the pattern accurate and the curves smooth, and you'll have less waste to remove later when shaping and trimming. Assemble the end-frame patterns on a flat surface and check to be sure they conform to the drawing.

Select the wood for the frames and plane it 1¼ in. thick. For the back legs, try to find pieces with grain that follows the curve of the legs, which will make a better-looking and stronger chair. Mark out the legs

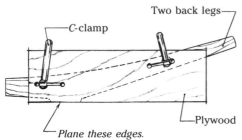

To plane the shoulders of the twin mortises in the legs, clamp a pair of legs between two pieces of plywood, and joint or plane the whole assembly. By repositioning the clamp and turning the assembly over, you can use this jig to hold the legs while mortising.

and rails for each frame using the patterns; add 2 in. to each end of the rails for the tenons. Cut the pieces on the bandsaw and arrange the pieces for each frame so the best color and grain will face out. Then letter or number each joint clearly with a crayon. (The bandsawn edges will be cleaned up later.)

I mark the through mortises for the top rail and seat rails from the leg patterns. First, bore $\frac{1}{16}$-in. holes at each corner of the mortises on the pattern. Then position the pattern on a leg and mark the leg through the holes with a brad awl. At the same time, put two or three registration marks on the edges of the pattern and square lines across the edges of the leg at those marks. Turn the leg over, align the pattern's registration marks with those on the leg, and mark the corners of the mortise on the other face. (If you have a drill press, you could just bore holes through the leg from the first face to position the mortise on the other face.) Connect the holes with knife marks to outline the mortises, bore from both faces to clear the waste, and chisel to the lines.

The side rails are twin-tenoned to the front and back legs, which makes the end frames very strong. The shoulders of the mortises on each leg must be flat and square to the faces of the leg, or the chair will be twisted. To trim the mortise shoulders, I clamp the two back legs together, face to face, between two pieces of plywood, about 36 in. by 5 in., as shown in the sketch at left. Align the through mortises of the legs (you might insert a small plug through them) and align the straight edges of the plywood with the shoulders of the twin mortises. Then run the whole assembly over the jointer, taking a light cut. You can do the same with the front legs.

Knife-mark the limits of the mortises on each pair of legs while the pieces are still clamped up, to ensure proper alignment. When you scribe the cheeks with a mortise gauge, you can mark the tenons on the rails with the same settings. (Remember to run the mortise gauge against the outside faces of the legs and rails for both mortises, so they will be aligned.) If you are making one chair, it's quickest to cut the mortises by hand. For more than one chair, it is worth setting up a mortising machine or mortising attachment on a drill press.

I cut the twin tenons on the tablesaw, using a high wooden fence, as described on p. 134. The arm and front leg are joined by a through-mortise-and-tenon joint, so cut the tenon on the ends of the front legs

now, before assembling the end frames. (The arms are screwed to the back legs.)

I glue up the end frames next, because they are more easily held in a vise while shaping the edges. (Clamp them up dry first to make sure the joints are tight and that the frames are flat.) After the glue has dried, plane the faces of the pieces flush, then mark the rounds on the edges with a crayon. It is all too easy to round over a section that is supposed to be left square—especially when working with parts that are not identical but are mirror images of each other. Wrongly cut, such places are impossible to repair.

The rounds are indicated in the plan drawings. The round on the inside edge of each leg tapers into the square edges of the rail. Start these tapers with a sharp chisel and complete the shaping with a spokeshave, drawknife or Surform. (A rasp leaves deep scratches.) The round also tapers on the inside edge where the arm meets the back leg. Mark the position of the arm from your full-size drawing, then spokeshave the round close to the marks—leave the final tapering until the chair is assembled. On the outside edges of the legs, the rounds taper into the seat rails and top rail. Mark these rail positions, spokeshave near the marks, and finish after assembly.

Tapering the round where one piece meets another isn't mere fussiness, but a simple, effective way to emphasize the junction. Where the arm crosses the back leg, for example, the taper makes it clear that the arm is intended to be joined at this point and not $\frac{1}{2}$ in. up or down.

Next, make the two seat rails and the top rail, and cut their tenons to fit the through mortises in the legs. The tenons should project no more than $\frac{1}{16}$ in. Remember the saw kerfs for the wedges. The edges of all the rails should be left square, except the top edge of the front seat rail, which is curved in its length and has a rounded top edge so it doesn't cut into the sitter's thighs. Lay out the curve with a thin batten, bandsaw to the line, then clean up the edge and round it with a spokshave.

The back cushion is supported by four narrow slats that are mortised into the top rail and back seat rail. Lay out and cut the mortises at right angles to the faces of the rails. The shoulders of the tenons will need to be trimmed because the edges of the two rails are at a slight angle to one another. Cut the shoulders a bit long, then trim them to fit with a chisel.

Dry-assemble the chair to make sure that everything fits, then glue it up. Drive the pairs of wedges in each tenon by alternating light blows of a hammer, otherwise the end of the tenon will be forced off center in the mortise. I glue the chair up while it sits on the tablesaw, or some other dead-flat surface, to ensure that it goes together without twisting.

Make a full-size pattern for the arms so they will be identical in shape. You could rip a 2-in.-thick board in half to make the arms, and the grain patterns on each piece would be mirror images. Mark the mortise for the front-leg tenon on both faces of each arm, bore out the waste and chisel cleanly to the lines. Trim the tenons, if necessary, to make a snug fit. Shape the edges of the arms, as shown in the plan drawings, with a spokeshave, then bore the holes for the screws that attach the arms to the back legs. Counterbore the holes first, so the screws can be hidden by ⅜-in.-dia. wood plugs, then bore the screw-clearance holes. Add the arms to the chair and glue and wedge the through tenons; just screw (no glue) to the back legs.

Now finish the tapers on the assembled chair. Cut the tapers in cleanly with a sharp chisel or knife to make a fair, clean line that fades away into the round. Even a finely set spokeshave will have left small flats on the rounds, and these must be removed with sandpaper. This is one task where the hand is surer than the eye—you will *feel* irregularities before you see them. At the same time, feel all the arrises, and if any are uncomfortably sharp, break them with sandpaper. I prefer an oil finish for this chair.

The seat cushion is supported on Pirelli webbing (p. 86) that has been stretched on a bridle-jointed frame. The metal ends of the webbing fit into angled grooves in the frame. Make the frame to fit the assembled chair, so that it will be even with the bottom edges of the end-frame rails. Support the frame on small ledger strips that have been screwed and glued to the front and back seat rails, and then screw through the side rails of the frame into the end frames. Mark the position of the webbing straps before boring the clearance holes for the No. 10 screws in the side rails of the frame, so that the screws don't interfere with the straps. Before screwing the frame in place, you'll need to bevel the back edge to conform to the slope of the back rail.

The seat and back cushions are both 22 in. square, made of 4-in.-thick foam rubber, wrapped in Dacron batting and covered with slipcovers. You can make the cushions as described on pp. 81-82.

The armchair can be made into a rocker without altering the basic design. Examine existing rockers to determine the length and curve of those for your chair.

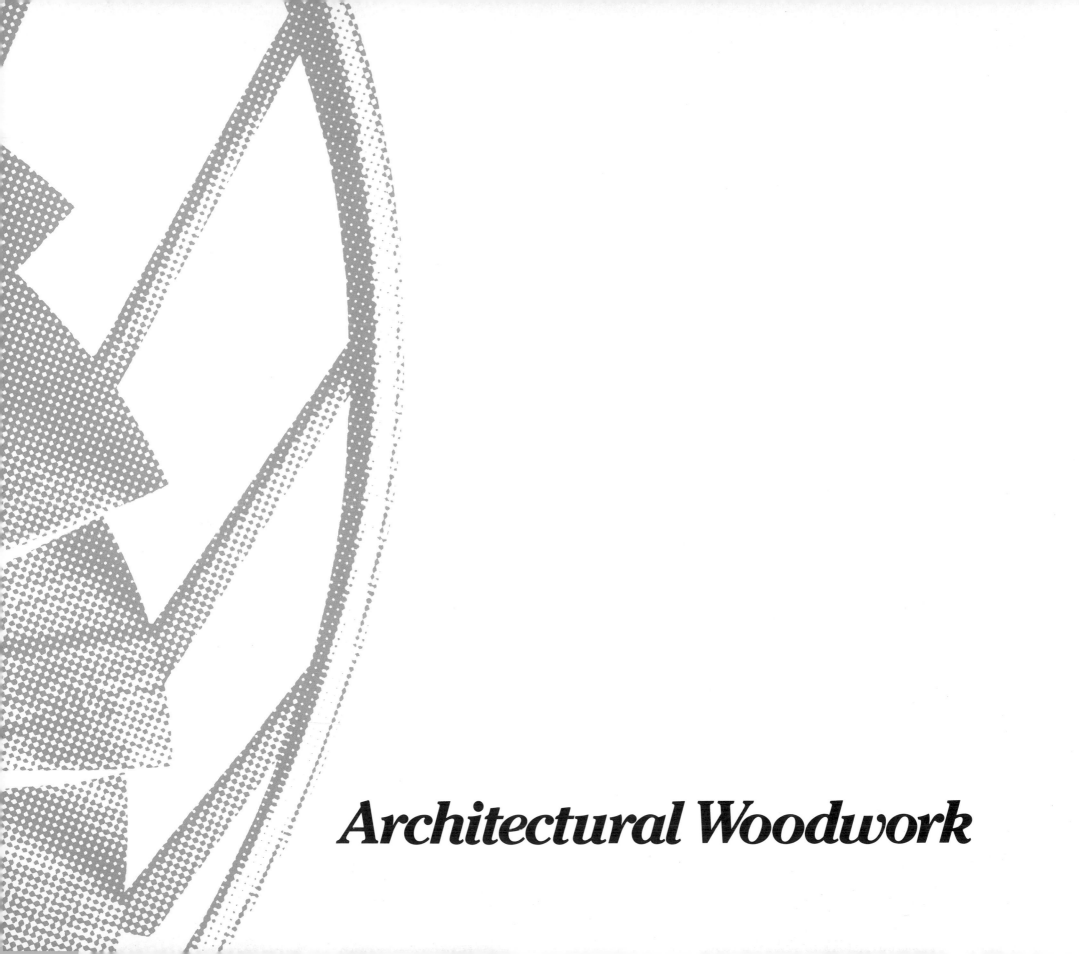

Architectural Woodwork

Doors and Staircase 10

Lightweight Door

The lightweight door shown in the photo acts mostly as a visual screen and has little effect on noise penetration. I designed it for a client who lives alone, for whom I have made a number of kitchen cabinet doors of similar style. The house is old, and every door opening is a different size. The slatted construction makes it easy to vary the width of the doors while keeping the style consistent throughout the house. The door is only ⅞ in. thick, too thin for standard door handles and latches, so I made wooden ones that mount on the surface of the door.

Construction

This door is practically identical to the doors for the serving table (p. 123). Like those doors, it has a bridle-jointed frame and loose slats held in place by tongues. The main difference, apart from size, is the wide, middle rail that stiffens this door and provides a surface for mounting the handle and latch.

The center rail is joined to the stiles by ¼-in. plywood splines, the slats are held in place by ¼-in. splines cut from the same wood as the slats. The center rail is glued in place, but the slats must be free to move with changes in humidity. (For a lightweight door like this, I don't feel it's necessary to mortise-and-tenon the center rail to the stiles.)

Almost any wood is suitable for this door, but avoid woods that will move a lot with changes in humidity—swelling in the slats might push the frames apart.

(See Appendix 1 for shrinkage values of common woods.) You will also want to consider matching or contrasting the door with the furniture, the trim or the floors in the room.

I make the door of 1¼-in.-thick rough-sawn boards. If possible, cut all the rails and stiles oversized and allow the wood to adjust to the workshop humidity for at least a week or two. Then plane each piece ⅞ in. thick, taking an equal amount off both faces. Plane the slats to the same thickness. Lay out and cut the bridle joints on the top and bottom rails and stiles, as described on p. 36. Cut the mortises in the rails and the tenons on the stiles. (It's helpful to test the tablesaw setups on scrap before cutting into either). Push the frame together, clamp it lightly and measure the distance between the inside faces of the stiles. Cut the center rail to this length, insert it between the stiles at the correct height, and cut the slats to fit the openings. Their ends can fit snugly against the rails, but you should allow some room for expansion across the width of the door. Arrange them as you please, then make a large, *V*-shaped crayon mark across the face of each set of slats so you can reposition the slats quickly in the same order. Before you disassemble the frame, chamfer the arrises around the openings with a ball-bearing router bit. Mark the position of the center rail, take the door apart and chamfer the ends and edges of both sides of the slats using the same router setup.

I cut the grooves for the splines using a dado head on the tablesaw. Make them ½ in. deep and a snug, but not tight, fit for the ¼-in. plywood. The top and bottom rails and the stiles are grooved on their inside edges only, the center rail is grooved on both edges, and each slat is grooved on both edges and both ends. Because all the pieces are the same thickness, only one saw setup is needed. Stop the grooves in the edges of the stiles, so that they won't show as gaps on the ends of the door.

Cut the plywood splines next, about ⅞ in. wide. For the solid-wood splines, I plane a board ⅞ in. thick, then rip a few more splines than I need off the edges on the tablesaw. Before assembly, sand and finish the solid-wood splines—if the slats shrink, you'll be able to see them.

To assemble the door, first glue and clamp the center rail to the stiles. Align it with the marks and make sure that the pieces meet at right angles. Next, slide the slats into place, complete with splines, but no glue. Last, add the top and bottom rails, pulling the shoulders of the bridle joints tight with bar or pipe clamps placed vertically and horizontally. Clamp across the faces of the bridle joints with C-clamps, using wooden blocks to distribute the pressure and protect the wood. Remove the bar clamps when all the C-clamps are in place.

When the glue has cured, plane the edges and faces lightly to remove any unevenness, then sand and finish the door. Because this door isn't exposed to the weather, most any finish will do, but oil or wax finishes can become grimy in a household with children.

Hang the door before installing the handle and latch. If you set the hinges in the edge of the door in the conventional way, use solid, drawn-brass butt hinges, not hinges stamped from brass sheet. I prefer to mount wide brass butts on the face of the stile and the casing, as shown in the photo at right. Or you can face-mount brass or wrought-iron H-hinges, as shown in the plan drawings. (See Appendix 5 for sources of supply.) Most H-hinges don't have loose pins, so they're a little harder to install than butt hinges. Regardless of the hinge you use, keep the gap between the door and the casing uniform, and as narrow as the shrinkage value of the wood will allow. Plane a 5° bevel on the handle stile so the stile won't hit the casing.

Handle and latch—If the door is to be used for a closet, a single handle and a magnetic catch at top

Two Doors

Scale: 1⁄16 in. = 1 in.
Details: ¼ in. = 1 in.

Exterior Door

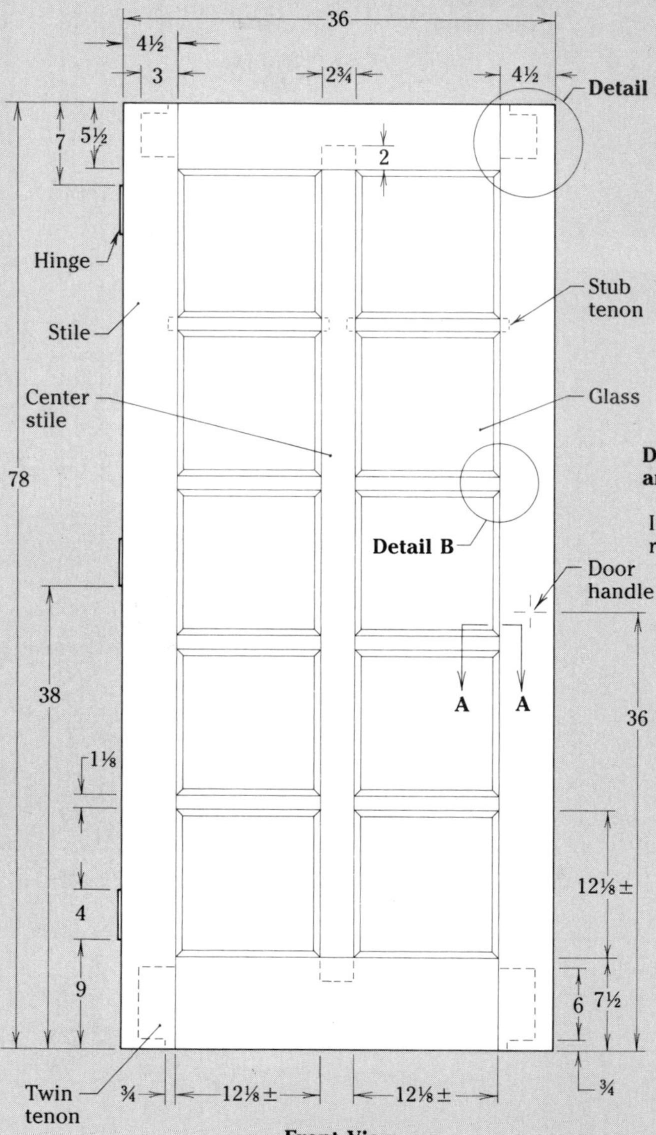
36
4½
3
2¾
4½
Detail A
7
5½
2
Hinge
Stile
Stub tenon
Center stile
Glass
78
Detail B
Door handle
38
A
A
36
1⅛
4
12⅛ ±
9
6
7½
Twin tenon
¾
12⅛ ±
12⅛ ±
¾

Front View

Detail A: Top Rail and Fillets (End view, stile removed)

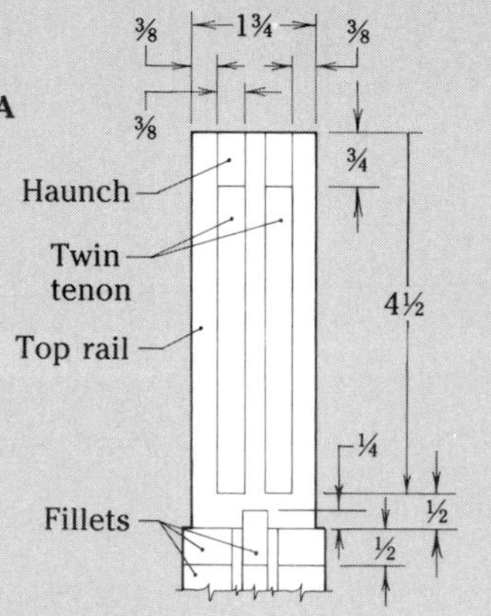
⅜
1¾
⅜
⅜
Haunch
¾
Twin tenon
4½
Top rail
¼
½
Fillets
½

Detail B: Intermediate Rail and Fillets (End view, stile removed)

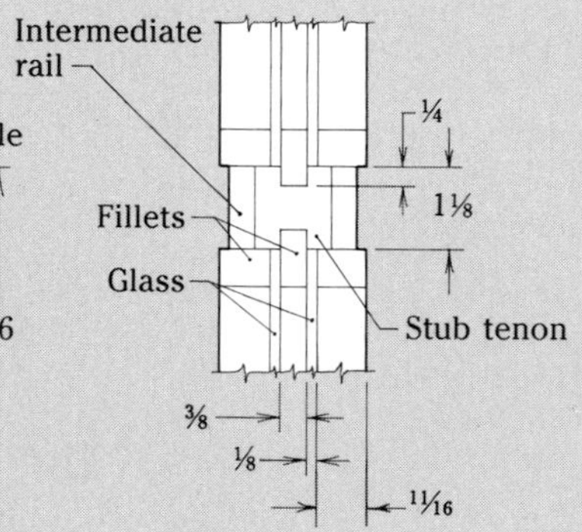
Intermediate rail
¼
1⅛
Fillets
Glass
Stub tenon
⅜
⅛
11⁄16

Note: *To substitute wood panels for glass, set the panels into the grooves in rails and stiles.*

Interior Door

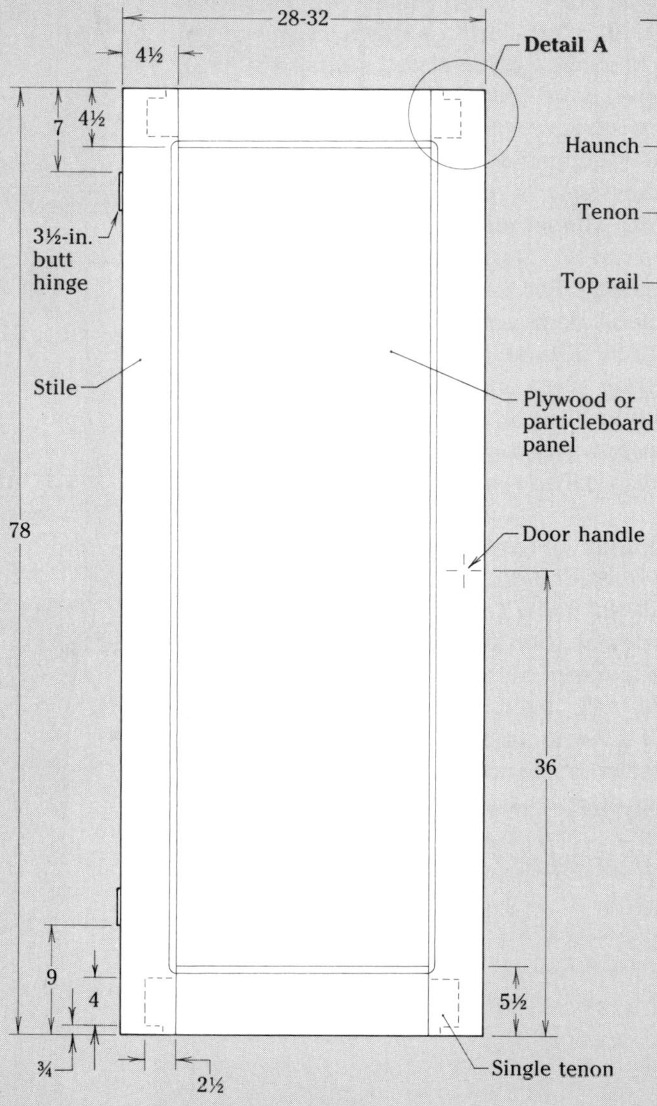
28-32
4½
Detail A
7
4½
3½-in. butt hinge
Stile
Plywood or particleboard panel
78
Door handle
36
9
4
5½
¾
2½
Single tenon

Front View

Detail A: Top Rail and Panel (End view, stile removed)

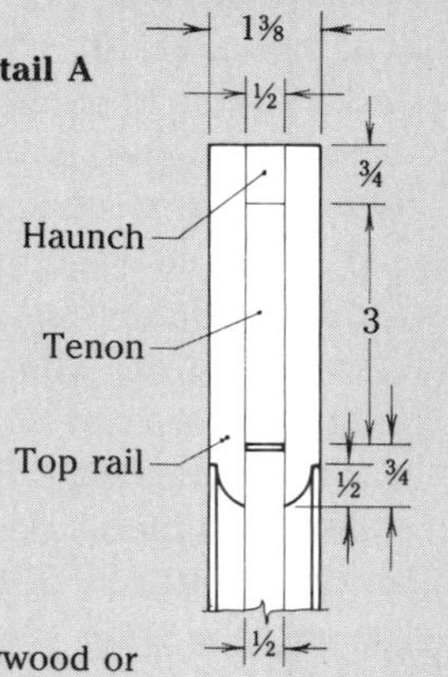
1⅜
½
¾
Haunch
3
Tenon
Top rail
½
¾
½

Note: *Glue panel in groove.*

Section A-A: Intermediate Rail and Stile

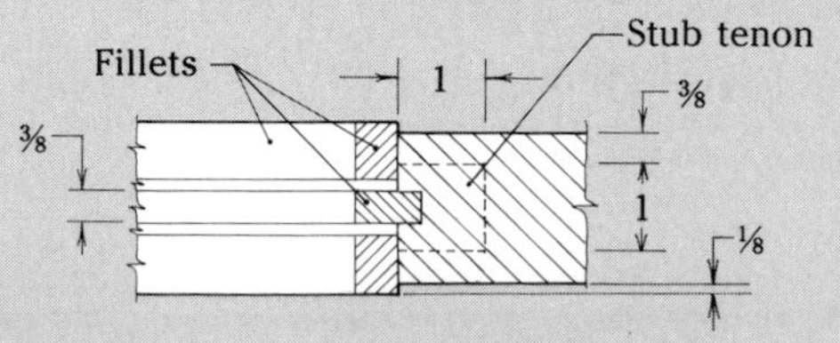
Fillets
1
Stub tenon
⅜
⅜
1
⅛

Two Doors

I have always believed that the things most used around the house should also be the handsomest. Well-fitted, solid doors with good hardware are a satisfaction to make and a pleasure to use. If made badly, however, they are a constant source of aggravation: When it rains, they stick and have to be kicked open or slammed shut; when it's dry, they rattle and let in the cold. Practically all doors are now mass-produced. Many have only a ⅛-in. plywood skin and a cardboard interior, and you hesitate to rap too hard on them. A good door is not difficult to make, but it must be designed and made to suit its particular use.

Doors are hung for many different purposes, and if I may misquote Robert Frost, "Before I built a door, I'd want to know what I was shutting out or keeping in." A door can keep the cold out and the heat in, or the reverse. It can be only a visual or sound barrier, or a barrier to water, fire or intruders, like an iron-clad city gate that is defended by archers, portcullis and boiling oil against the assaults of enemies.

The closest I came to defending a door was in 1941. England was more seriously threatened by invasion than at any time since Napoleon. Our house had a good, solid front door, but even so, I remember that every night for several months we reinforced it with a heavy piece of timber. My mother also made a point of removing the distributor cap from her car, thus denying the Germans the use of her Morris Minor. I am sure it never occurred to us children that the invaders might use the kitchen door, or bring their own transportation.

Because they are fixed along only one edge, doors tend to sag under their own weight. I once wandered into the Victoria and Albert Museum in London and came across an Egyptian temple door 5000 years old. Made of edge-joined vertical planks, 2½ in. thick, it had only two horizontal stiffeners. I could not understand how such a massive door had been prevented from sagging. Looking closely, however, I saw the answer, faintly visible under the paint. The edge of each plank had been notched like the teeth of a sawblade, and the notches fit perfectly into those of the neighboring planks. The edges couldn't slip, so the door couldn't sag.

The two doors shown in the plan drawings prevent sagging in different ways. The frame-and-panel exterior door, shown in the photo at right, relies almost en-

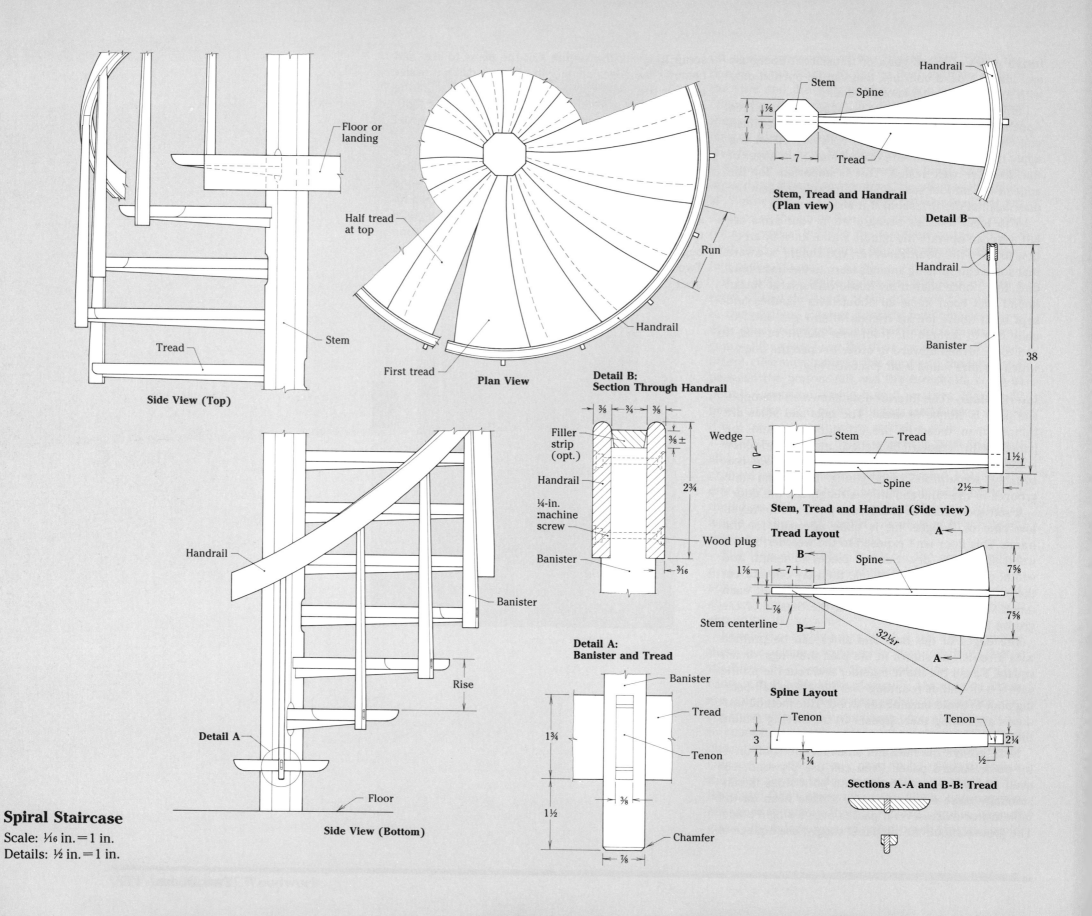

Side View (Top)

Floor or landing

Half tread at top

Tread

Stem

Plan View

First tread

Handrail

Run

Stem, Tread and Handrail
(Plan view)

Stem

Spine

Handrail

7/8

7

7

Tread

Detail B

Handrail

Banister

38

1½

2½

Stem, Tread and Handrail (Side view)

Wedge

Stem

Tread

Spine

**Detail B:
Section Through Handrail**

3/8   3/4   3/8

Filler strip (opt.)

3/8 ±

Handrail

2¾

¼-in. machine screw

Wood plug

Banister

3/16

Tread Layout

A

B

Spine

7 +

1⅞

7/8

Stem centerline

B

32½r

7⅝

7⅝

A

Spine Layout

Tenon

Tenon

3

¼

½

2¼

Sections A-A and B-B: Tread

Side View (Bottom)

Handrail

Banister

Rise

Detail A

Floor

**Detail A:
Banister and Tread**

Banister

Tread

Tenon

1¾

3/8

1½

Chamfer

7/8

Spiral Staircase

Scale: 1/16 in. = 1 in.
Details: ½ in. = 1 in.

Spiral Staircase

The red oak spiral staircase shown in the photos at right was erected in a Vermont barn and is 1½ stories high. It was built and fitted together in the shop, then knocked down and reassembled in the barn. It took myself and two apprentices eight days to make, and another fifteen hours to install. Much of that time was spent fussing with the joints in the handrail, so I devised a simpler method, which is shown in the plan drawings. These drawings show a portion of a spiral staircase, rather than the whole 14-ft. staircase we built for the barn. Because no two houses (or barns) are exactly alike, you will have to adapt the design and construction for the staircase that you want to build. If you are building a spiral staircase for an existing house, you will be more restricted in determining its position and design than if you were designing the house and staircase at the same time. In both instances, however, the same basic decisions must still be made.

Design

A few definitions are needed before proceeding further. The staircase consists of a stem into which are through-mortise-and-tenoned the steps, which are called treads. (In this discussion, the top floor or landing, but not the bottom floor, is considered a tread.) A handrail is bolted to banisters, which are mortised to the ends of the treads.

The distance between the top surface of one tread and the top surface of the next is called the rise. The width of each tread, measured from the front edge of one tread to a point directly below the front edge of the next, is called the run. The ratio of run to rise tells you the angle at which a person going up the staircase is climbing—a 1-to-1 ratio is a 45° incline, a 1¾-to-1 ratio is about 30°.

Here's how I determine the dimensions necessary to build a spiral staircase. First, measure the vertical distance between the top surfaces of the two floors. This measurement, which is the height of the staircase, must be accurate to within ⅛ in., or the rest of the calculations will be thrown off. Let us use as an example a height of 104 in.

Next, decide on the number of turns (or fractions of a turn) that you want the staircase to make, and which way it will turn, clockwise or counterclockwise. Both decisions may be dictated by the geometry of

the house. If possible, I use sixteen treads (including the top floor), and have them turn through a full circle. This allows me to mortise each tread into a facet of a sixteen-sided stem, which makes layout easier. Divide the staircase height by the number of treads to determine the rise: 104 in. ÷ 16 = 6½ in. This rise is acceptable, requiring a person to take neither too large nor too small a step up from tread to tread.

Suppose, on the other hand, that a staircase turning through three quarters of a circle (270°) would fit into the space better. This would contain only twelve treads (three quarters of sixteen), and the rise would be 104 in. ÷ 12 = 8½ in. This rise is still acceptable, but near the upper limit of comfort recommended by stair safety rules.

Let us take another example to illustrate a different point. The height of this staircase must be 80 in., and you want it to make one complete turn of sixteen treads. The rise, therefore, will be 80 in. ÷ 16 = 5 in. This is a pretty short step to take, but not completely impossible. There is a problem, however. As you step onto the first tread, you may strike your head on the underside of the last one, because there will be only 72 in. of clearance (given treads 3 in. thick). A 6-ft. headroom, while a luxury on a boat, is too short for stairs in a house. A solution would be to use fewer treads to make less than a complete turn.

You must also consider the ratio of the run of the treads to the rise. Suppose the height of the staircase must be 12 ft., and you want to gain this height in one complete turn of sixteen treads. The rise will be 9 in., which is just at the recommended limit. Let's also assume that the staircase can be no more than 5 ft. in diameter. Because the treads radiate from the stem, they are tapered, and the widest portion of each one is on the circumference of this circle. The maximum run of each tread, therefore, will be just under 12 in., which is the circumference of the circle divided by the number of treads.

Climbing this staircase, you will be walking a little over 2 ft. away from the post, because of the space occupied by the handrail. The run of the treads where you will be walking will be about 10 in. The ratio of run to rise will be almost 1 to 1, and you'll be climbing what amounts to a 45° incline. This is a dangerous angle, because if you slip, you're likely to keep falling and end up on the floor in a heap.

This staircase should probably have more treads and turn through more than a complete circle to in-

crease the run-to-rise ratio and decrease the angle of the climb. With twenty treads turning through 450° (1¼ turns), the rise would be about 7¼ in. If there were no problems in positioning the first and last treads in relation to the existing structure, the diameter and the run could stay the same. The run-to-rise ratio would now be about 1⅓ to 1, or an incline between 35° and 40°, which is just acceptable.

I have climbed some terrifyingly steep, winding stairs, sometimes without handrails, built within the walls of English castles. Their narrowness and dangerousness were advantages when they were built. Only one person at a time could ascend the stairs, so they were easily defended. Falling down a stone spiral staircase in full armor must have taken the starch out of even the hardiest knight, as well as discouraged his supporters.

To summarize, here are some rules of thumb for designing spiral stairs. Don't attempt to have the stairs turn a full circle if the floor-to-ceiling height is less than 7 ft. The rise should be between 6 in. and 7 in., but not less than 5 in. or more than 9 in. The run-to-rise ratio should be about 1¾ to 1, which will give an incline of about 30° to 35°. Avoid inclines of more than 40° and less than 25°. Make the outside diameter of the stairs at least 5 ft.—decreasing the diameter decreases the run and makes the stairs cramped as well. (For more information on stair specifications, see the bibliography.)

When you have made the calculations for your stairs, consult an architect or engineer to help you determine what alterations to the structure of the house will be needed. The barn staircase, for example, weighs 1500 lb.—more with people on it—and a post had to be placed directly under the stem to support the load. The upper end of the stem must be solidly braced. I had an iron strap made for this purpose; it slipped over the stem and was lag-bolted to a beam. (Check to make sure that you aren't violating the local building codes—the building inspector is also a source of useful information.)

Construction

When you are ready to start construction, check your measurement of the distance between the surfaces of the two floors, and double-check your calculations—it's not easy to correct errors after the staircase has been made. Draw a full-scale plan view and a full-scale elevation that includes at least three treads.

Also make a full-scale pattern for one tread and for one banister. I'll describe how my apprentices and I made the spiral staircase for the barn; you can alter the procedure to suit your staircase.

The stem—We made the stem first. It was 7 in. square and extended beyond the top tread to form a newel post for the handrail on the landing. We toyed with the idea of hauling an oak tree out of the woods (with a team of horses, of course), hewing it with a broadax and then using an adze to shape it, as though it were a mast for a schooner. It was a romantic notion, which the owner vetoed without hesitation.

We then decided to glue up 16-ft. lengths of 8/4 oak, the thickest stock available in that length. The oak was specially ordered (at extra expense), but when it arrived it was too twisted to be used in continuous lengths. Our solution was to cut the boards into two or three lengths, depending on how badly they were warped, plane and joint them flat and end-glue them back together with Titebond. Then we skimmed the faces of the five reconstituted boards in the planer and face-glued them to make the stem, staggering the end-grain joints by at least 1 ft.

If you use this method, you'll need long pipe clamps or pinch dogs to draw the end-grain joints together while the glue sets. To my surprise, these simple end-grain joints were strong enough to be picked up and machine-planed before face-gluing, but you should handle the pieces carefully. Scarf joints are a much stronger and less risky alternative to end-gluing. The length of each scarf bevel should be at least eight times as long as the thickness of the pieces.

The photo at right shows how we face-glued and clamped the stem together. Sight across the top edges of the sawhorses to check that they all lie along the same plane. Gluing up such a large assembly takes time, so we used a plastic resin glue and a short-nap paint roller to spread the glue evenly. Don't be tempted to end-glue and face-glue at the same time—it would be practically impossible to get good joints, and any gaps would be very unsightly.

The stem does not have to be made of oak nor does it have to be laminated. Solid Douglas fir, for example, would do very well. The wood for a solid stem should be dry and it should be reasonably stable, otherwise it might shrink away from the shoulders or ends of the tread tenons. I would also avoid using elm and beech, which tend to warp as they dry.

Face-gluing the pieces for the stem requires at least one assistant, several sturdy sawhorses and a lot of pipe or bar clamps. Align the edges of the pieces by pushing them tight against the clamps.

The center spine on each tread is mortised into a banister and the stem. The spine also stiffens the tread.

Cut facets for treads that are tenoned into the stem on an arris. A facet directly opposite the one shown here is a bearing surface for the tenon shoulders.

After the stem has been glued up (or cut roughly to size if it's solid), joint one edge square to a face and feed the stem through a thickness planer. Take an equal amount off all four surfaces until the stem is 7 in. square. Lacking a large-enough jointer or a thickness planer, you can square up the stem with an electric hand plane, or a hand plane powered only by your arms. Make sure the faces are square to one another, and sight over winding sticks to check that the faces aren't twisted along their length. (Winding sticks are two identical pieces of wood, 2 in. or 3 in. wide and 1 ft. to 3 ft. long, each one with parallel edges. Set one on edge at each end of a face and sight over one winding stick to the other. Both edges should be parallel; if not, the face is twisted.)

Next, make the stem octagonal. We cut the corners off on the tablesaw. This required a very large shop—the saw needed 16 ft. of clearance on either end—and the efforts of three people to steady the stem as it was cut. (If working alone, I would use an electric hand plane.) Whatever method you use, it is important that the stem be a true octagon, and that each face be straight and untwisted—if not, the positioning of the treads will be thrown off (see the plan drawings on p. 9 for a layout of an octagon in a square). Make a template to check the angles and width of three adjacent faces at the same time.

Next, mark the position of the top surface of each tread, measuring from the bottom of the stem. There were sixteen treads on our staircase, but instead of making a sixteen-sided stem, we cut eight additional facets into the arrises of the octagon at appropriate heights. The first tread falls on a face of the octagon, the second on an arris, the third on an adjacent face, and so on. Place the treads accurately; even a ¼-in. variation in the distance between pairs of treads can cause people to trip.

The sixteenth tread on our staircase was at the level of the second floor. It was mortised into the stem, like the other treads, but was only half as wide as the others, and was edge-joined to the floor at the site. This requires extremely accurate measurements and placement of the treads, but the results look good.

Extend the tread marks around the stem to the opposite face or arris, so that you can lay out and cut the other end of the through mortise. Cut the facets in the arrises (two opposite ones for each mortise), making them about ½ in. wider than the thickness of the tread spines, as shown in the photo at bottom left.

An apprentice cut the facets on our stem with his sheath knife, but a sharp chisel and spokeshave would do the job. Make sure the facets are flat and extend equally into each adjacent face of the octagon.

Mark the mortises on the faces and facets. You can do this by measurement, or by making a pattern that will key off the arrises. The top end of each mortise falls on the line you've drawn to indicate the top surface of the tread. Make sure that the mortises are centered on the octagonal faces and the facets.

We cut the mortises in from both sides using a mortising attachment on a drill press and a ¾-in. hollow chisel, then chiseled to the lines. We set up supports for the stem on each side of the drill-press table; it was easier to move the drill press than the stem for each new mortise. For the mortises centered on the facets, we made a cradle to hold the stem on the drill-press table so that the stem wouldn't rock on the arris. The mortises could be cut by hand by boring out the waste first and chiseling to the lines.

Regardless of how you cut the mortises, take the time to lay out and cut them accurately. If the mortises aren't positioned correctly and aren't perpendicular to the axis of the stem, the tread spacing will be irregular, making it dangerous to climb the stairs. If the mortises aren't cleanly cut, the staircase won't look as crisp as it should.

The treads—Each tread is made up of three pieces: a spine and two tread halves, doweled and glued together. Tenons on the spine attach the tread to the stem and banister, as shown in the top photo on the opposite page. All the treads are identical, so full-size templates will speed the work and help ensure accuracy. The shape of the treads is important; seen together, they give a sense of motion, as if the staircase were a great, wooden turbine pivoting on an axle.

Make the banisters for the handrails next. Trace them from the pattern, then bandsaw the shape and joint or plane the edges. The small shoulders on the top end of each banister position the handrail. Cut them on the tablesaw, running the inside (not the tapered) edge against the rip fence for both cuts. Set a stop so that the cut comes to within about ¹⁄₁₆ in. of the finished shoulder line. You will chisel the correct angles when assembling the handrail. Lay out the curves for the treads as shown in the sketch at right, or scale the curves up from the plan drawings using squared paper.

Thickness-plane the spines to fit snugly in the mortises, then bandsaw the taper and round the edge. Cut the shoulder on the stem tenon, leaving the tenon long enough to protrude slightly from the stem when assembled. Cut the tenon for the handrail banister, as shown in the plan drawings. I cut the wedge slots in all the tenons on the tablesaw, with the blade raised to maximum height and a stop clamped to the rip fence to prevent cutting into the shoulders.

The wood for the tread halves should be free of checks and other defects. Plane the pieces flat and 1¾ in. thick, and joint one edge flat and square to the faces. I cut each tread half just a little long so I can chisel the end flush with the shoulder of the stem tenon after assembly. Lay out and bandsaw the curved edges, but leave the final shaping until after the treads are glued up. Clean up the end-grain surfaces on a disc sander.

Bore the dowel holes in the treads, then use dowel centers to position the corresponding holes in the spines. Glue the treads together using a strong glue, such as Aerolite 306 or an epoxy. When the glue has cured, shape the curved edges using a spokeshave, and then chisel the narrow ends flush with the shoulders of the stem tenons.

Mortise the bottom end of each banister to fit the tenon on the tread. (Unless you can dry-assemble the staircase in your shop, you'll have to make the handrail after installing the staircase.)

Assembly and installation—You would need a large truck and plenty of help to deliver an assembled staircase, so it is best to assemble it on site. With an architect, engineer or building inspector, you will have determined the best way to support the stem and attach it to the upper floor or ceiling joists. If the staircase has a tread half that is even with the top floor, install that tread and fit it to the floor before fixing the stem. I like to put a few thin shims under the stem so the whole assembly can be lowered slightly if necessary to align the tread and floor. The photo at right shows how the tread on the barn staircase aligned with the framework of the landing. The bottom end of the stem is positioned by a hardwood collar, which is made in two halves, shaped to fit the stem, and screwed to the floor. The collar will also hide any shims under the stem.

You will probably need to fit each tread tenon to its mortise in the stem before gluing the treads in place.

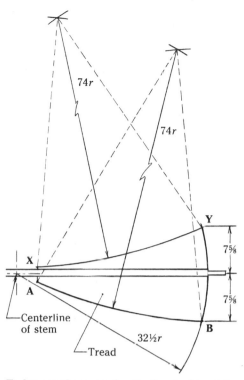

To lay out the curve for the front edge of the tread, set a beam compass to 74 in. and strike two arcs, centered on points A and B. The intersection of these arcs gives the center for the curve. Lay out the back-edge curve in the same way; use X and Y as centers.

The top tread can butt against the top floor or landing. Make sure the surface of the tread aligns exactly with the floor.

A heavy scrap-wood bearer and two pipe clamps will pull the tread into position while gluing, as shown in the photo below. Use a framing square to check that the tread is exactly at right angles to the stem, then drive in the wedges. Alternate hammer blows so you drive the wedges in equally, then remove the clamps. When the glue has cured, saw off the wedges and most of each protruding tenon, and chisel it flush with the surface of the octagon face or facet.

The handrail—The handrail not only prevents people from falling off the staircase, but spreads the weight of someone climbing the stairs to adjacent treads. For these reasons, the handrail must not be omitted, nor should its construction be substantially changed. In the plan drawings, the handrail is placed at the proper height for adults, but if young children are likely to be climbing around, you must add an extra handrail closer to the treads. (Check your town's building code, too, as many have strict requirements for handrails and banisters.) Though sound design can minimize dangers, spiral staircases are inherently less safe than conventional ones. You may be a trained acrobat, but there is no telling what person—old, young, sober or otherwise—may one day climb your staircase.

It is best to make and assemble the handrail on site. I learned this the hard way: The barn's staircase handrail was made of steam-bent sections, ¾ in. thick and 8 ft. long. We used the partially assembled staircase as a form, steam-bent sections of the handrail in the shop, then joined them on site. This turned out to be a time-consuming and quite maddening job. The owner subsequently decided that he did not like the gap between the two sides of the handrail, so we went

A bearer and two pipe or bar clamps will pull the treads tight to the stem. Check with a framing square to make sure the tread is perpendicular to the stem. Remove the clamps after driving the wedges.

back once more and cut helical pieces of oak to fill the gap, which also took a long time and was equally as exasperating.

I have modified the handrail here, making the pieces thinner to eliminate steam-bending and to simplify assembly; these alterations are shown in the plan drawings. Glue the banisters in place and wedge them, checking that they are at right angles to the treads. Then measure the length of the helix at the position of the handrail along the top ends of the banisters (our handrail was over 20 ft.). Add 1 ft. to this measurement and make two continuous pieces of oak of this length, 3 in. wide and ⅜ in. thick, joined by as many scarf joints as necessary. Use air-dried wood if possible, because it bends more readily than kiln-dried wood. Cut the pieces to width, plane them to thickness, then cut the scarfs and glue them together. Make the scarf bevels at least 3 in. long. When the glue has cured, plane the edges and faces flush by hand, or run the entire strip through a thickness planer. If the rails are too stiff to bend to the radius easily, plane them thinner until they will bend.

Clamp the handrails in position on the banisters to mark the correct angles of the banister shoulders. You can mark the shoulders using dividers, or mark them by eye if the saw cuts are almost correct. Then remove the rails and chisel to the marks. (If the shoulders are close to accurate, you can trim them while bolting or nailing the rails in place.)

The rails are fastened on either side of the banisters with ¼-in. or ⁵⁄₁₆-in. machine screws, counterbored and plugged, as shown in the plan drawings. An attractive and simple alternative would be copper nails and roves—a rivet-like fastening system used in lapstrake boat building (see Appendix 5 for sources of supply). You could also clamp and glue the handrail to the posts using epoxy or another high-strength glue, but wood screws will split the banisters. Start at the bottom of the staircase, leaving a few inches that can be trimmed off perpendicular to the floor after installation. Clamp the rails to two or three banisters in a row—you may have to adjust the shoulders slightly with a chisel. Then bore the holes and install the machine screws or copper nails. Fix the rails to the rest of the banisters in the same way.

There is no structural need for the filler strip between the rails, so it can be omitted. If you want to add one, use straight-grained wood for ease of bending. Make up a test strip, 4 ft. or 5 ft. long and ⅜ in.

thick, and try it in the rail. If it's too stiff, plane it thinner until it makes the curve without being forced. Saw a slight taper on the strips, as shown in the plan drawings, so that the widest face is a hair wider than the distance between the rails. Pushing the strip into place will make tight joints. Scarf-joint enough strips to make the length, then glue the long strip between the rails.

Finishing—Treads get a lot of wear and should be finished as carefully as a hardwood floor. You can use a penetrating oil finish (there are types especially formulated for floors) or a hard coating such as polyurethane. Beware of creating a slick, dangerous surface. The decks of boats are often dusted with a fine, quartz sand to roughen the surface, and this treatment would be appropriate here. Sprinkle it on very lightly when the finish is still wet. I would definitely use varnish or polyurethane on the handrail, but the rest of the staircase could be oiled or coated with a good paste wax. If you're in doubt about finishes, check with a local paint store or professional painter.

An interesting variation of this staircase intrigues me, and someday I would like to make it. By increasing the length of each successive tread, the spiral becomes a volute. For example, an increase of ⅝ in. would make the diameter at the top of the spiral 10 in. greater than at the bottom. Ascending an expanding volute is a very different experience from walking up a spiral staircase. The idea has symbolic overtones that take us beyond the confines of this book, and thus, this is an appropriate place to stop.

Appendices

Appendix 1　Wood Selection and Movement

Wood Selection

Choosing an appropriate wood for a particular design may seem difficult, but it isn't as subjective as it appears to be. Leaving aside questions of cost and availability, there are certain criteria that always apply.

Most obviously, the wood should have the right mechanical properties for its particular function—which may mean using more than one species in the same piece of furniture. Years ago, for example, chairs were commonly made out of three different woods: pine, which could be easily carved, for the seat; maple, an ideal turning wood, for the legs and rungs; and oak, which bent well, for the back.

You should also consider the suitability of the wood to the tools and construction techniques you plan to use. For example, oak can be a miserable material in which to hand-cut dovetails, because its coarse grain can be difficult to cut cleanly. Teak, which dulls edge tools rapidly, should be avoided for pieces that will require a lot of machining, unless you have carbide cutters. The tendency of wood to move with changes in humidity will also affect the choice of wood. Climates with great fluctuations in humidity demand a stable wood, such as mahogany, or an ingenious design and construction to neutralize the inevitable shrinkage and expansion.

Stability, ease of working, durability, strength, hardness and resistance to decay—even when all these criteria have been satisfied, there are still considerable possibilities for wood choices. Why is it that certain designs look better in one wood than another? Part of the answer lies in the color and texture of the wood. All woods have grain patterns, which range from the almost invisible, as in holly and ebony, to the inescapable, as in red oak. If you use an aggressively grained wood to make a piece characterized by simplicity and careful proportions, like the desk on p. 159, the result may be striking and dramatic, but not anything a sensible person would want to live with. I think that the smaller the surfaces and the finer the detailing of a piece, the more restrained the color and figure of the wood should be. But, like any rule, this one can be disregarded by the inspired with triumphant results.

If you wish to combine different kinds of wood in the same piece, it is important that the woods enhance each other, and that all be subordinated to the overall design. A colleague of mine once made a small oval vanity table, the surface of which was veneered with alternating strips of ash and ebony. The result, though superbly executed, was a visual nightmare. A large table in ash with a thin edging or inlay of ebony or rosewood, however, could be both striking and tasteful. If, on the other hand, the contrast between the two materials is too subtle, there will be an irritating doubt as to whether more than one wood has been used, and you will get what a teacher of mine called "the monotony of faint variation."

A similar consideration when choosing wood is how it will look with the hardware on the piece. I find certain combinations more pleasing than others: polished brass with walnut or mahogany, wrought iron with oak, stainless steel with rosewood.

We often think of furniture in a particular setting and want to select the wood for a new piece to match existing furniture and trim. Although this is a valid consideration, occasionally the dominant wood in the room will not be appropriate for the design of the new piece. When this happens, I think the appropriate wood, not the matching wood, is the best choice. It isn't having identical woods and finishes that make two pieces of furniture good neighbors, but shared qualities of scale, simplicity and proportion.

Wood Movement

All wood, no matter how old or how thoroughly dried, expands and contracts with changes in humidity. You must account for this movement in the design and the construction of a piece of furniture (and anything else made of wood) or suffer jammed or rattling drawers and doors and split tabletops and carcase sides.

A lot of the trouble caused by seasonal movement is a result of bad design. I have learned the hard way not to disregard the effects of wood movement. Customers who cannot retrieve their tennis shorts in the spring because their bureau drawers have swollen shut are not easily mollified. Even with good design and sound construction, a knowledge of wood movement is required on the part of the maker. You must resist the temptation to fit parts such as doors, drawers and framed solid-wood panels to close tolerances in the controlled climate of the workshop. Fit them instead to allow for the conditions to which they will be exposed. If you're making furniture for the fairly constant climates of coastal California or the Southwest, you can probably ignore seasonal changes in wood. If you're making furniture for the changeable climate of New England or for an unknown destination, make sure that solid wood has been allowed sufficient room to move, or use veneered construction.

Most of the movement problems for the furniture in this book concern fitting drawers in a carcase and loose panels in frames. The amount of clearance to allow for any part depends on its width (movement is greatest across the grain), the species of wood used, the way the boards are sawn from the log, and the range of humidity to which the furniture will be subjected.

The table on the opposite page lists the shrinkage values of common North American woods and some imported woods. The numbers indicate the percentage that a piece of wood will shrink

Hardwoods	Tangential	Radial
Alder, red	7.3	4.4
Ash, black	7.8	5.0
Ash, white	7.8	4.9
Aspen, quaking	6.7	3.5
Basswood, American	9.3	6.6
Beech, American	11.9	5.5
Birch, paper	8.6	6.3
Birch, yellow	9.2	7.2
Buckeye, yellow	8.1	3.6
Butternut	6.4	3.4
Catalpa	4.9	2.5
Cherry, black	7.1	3.7
Chestnut	6.7	3.4
Chinkapin, golden	7.4	4.6
Cottonwood, eastern	9.2	3.9
Dogwood, flowering	11.8	7.4
Elm, American	9.5	4.2
Elm, rock	8.1	4.8
Hackberry	8.9	4.8
Hickory, pecan	8.9	4.9
Hickory, shagbark	10.5	7.0
Holly, American	9.9	4.8
Honeylocust	6.6	4.2
Hophornbeam, eastern	10.0	8.5
Hornbeam, American	11.4	5.7
Locust, black	7.2	4.6
Madrone, Pacific	12.4	5.6
Magnolia, southern	6.6	5.4
Maple, red	8.2	4.0
Maple, sugar	9.9	4.8
Oak, black	11.1	4.4
Oak, live	9.5	6.6
Oak, northern red	8.6	4.0
Oak, overcup	12.7	5.3
Oak, red	8.9	4.2
Oak, southern red	11.3	4.7
Oak, white	10.5	5.6
Persimmon	11.2	7.9
Sassafras	6.2	4.0
Sweetgum	10.2	5.3
Sycamore, American	8.4	5.0
Tupelo, black	8.7	5.1
Walnut, black	7.8	5.5
Willow, black	8.7	3.3
Yellow poplar	8.2	4.6

Softwoods	Tangential	Radial
Baldcypress	6.2	3.8
Cedar, Alaska	6.0	2.8
Cedar, eastern red	4.7	3.1
Cedar, incense	5.2	3.3
Cedar, northern white	4.9	2.2
Cedar, western red	5.0	2.4
Douglas fir (coastal)	7.8	5.0
Doulgas fir (inland)	7.6	4.1
Fir, balsam	6.9	2.9
Fir, white	7.1	3.2
Hemlock, eastern	6.8	3.0
Hemlock, western	7.9	4.3
Larch, western	9.1	4.5
Pine, eastern white	6.1	2.1
Pine, loblolly	7.4	4.8
Pine, lodgepole	6.7	4.3
Pine, longleaf	7.5	5.1
Pine, pitch	7.1	4.0
Pine, ponderosa	6.2	3.9
Pine, red	7.2	3.8
Pine, shortleaf	7.7	4.6
Pine, slash	7.6	5.4
Pine, sugar	5.6	2.9
Pine, western white	7.4	4.1
Redwood, old growth	4.4	2.6
Redwood, young growth	4.9	2.2
Spruce, Engelmann	7.1	3.8
Spruce, red	7.8	3.8
Spruce, Sitka	7.5	4.3
Tamarack	7.4	3.7
Yew, Pacific	5.4	4.0

Imported Woods	Tangential	Radial
Apitong	10.9	5.2
Avodire	6.5	3.7
Balsa	7.6	3.0
Banak	8.8	4.6
Cativo	5.3	2.3
Greenheart	9.0	8.2
Khaya	5.8	4.1
Lauan	8.0	3.8
Limba	5.4	4.4
Mahogany	5.1	3.7
Obeche	5.3	3.1
Parana pine	7.9	4.0
Primavera	5.2	3.1
Ramin	8.7	3.9
Spanish cedar	6.3	4.1
Teak	4.0	2.2
Walnut, European	6.4	4.3

This table shows the approximate percentage that tangentially and radially sawn woods will shrink from green to oven-dry.

when it is taken from green (freshly cut) wood to oven-dried (all moisture is baked out). A piece of tangentially sawn red oak, 10 in. wide when green, will be .89 in. narrower when oven-dried.

The table also shows that wood of the same species will shrink across the grain less when sawn at right angles to the growth rings (called radially sawn, quartersawn or rift-sawn), than when sawn at a tangent to the growth rings (tangentially sawn, flat-sawn or slash-sawn). Flat-sawn boards are the staple of most lumberyards. At the mill, these boards are sliced off one after another, without turning the log on the carriage, and the growth rings of most will be more or less parallel to the board's faces. The growth rings of a few of the boards near the center of the log will be radially sawn. A skilled sawyer can increase the number of radially sawn boards by rotating the log, but this takes longer and is considerably more trouble. If you ask your lumber dealer for radially sawn boards, you are likely to be disappointed. However, if the dealer will let you sort through the pile, you will probably find some. Examine the growth rings on the ends of the boards, selecting boards whose growth rings are between 45° and 90° to the faces.

The final factor to consider is the moisture content of the wood. A tree contains a great deal of water—the interior of its cells and the cell walls are full of it. When a tree is cut and converted to lumber, the water inside the cells, called free water, drains away relatively quickly. The water in the cell walls, called bound water, leaves more slowly. The cell walls will lose water until their moisture content is in equilibrium with the surroundings. At equilibrium, the amount of water in the wood as a percentage of the weight of the wood is called the equilibrium moisture content (EMC). This gain and loss of water by the cell walls cause the movement in wood that a woodworker is concerned with.

The EMC of any wood varies according to the relative humidity, as shown for white spruce in the chart at right. At 0% relative humidity, the EMC is also 0%—the wood is bone-dry (this is the oven-dried condition mentioned above). At 100% relative humidity, the EMC is about 30%—the cell walls have absorbed water amounting to 30% of the weight of the wood. (EMC at 100% relative humidity is called the fiber saturation point.) Though each wood species varies, the EMC for most will fall within the outside lines on the chart.

A look at the table suggests that it is best to make drawer sides from a wood with low shrinkage, preferably radially sawn. Given the variations in relative humidity where you live, you can figure out from the chart what the moisture content should be for the wood you use. In Vermont, I prefer to use wood with an EMC of about 12% to 14%, which corresponds to a relative humidity of 65% to 75%. The only reliable way to ensure that the wood is at the moisture content that you want is to control the workshop humidity and keep the wood in

the shop long enough for it to reach equilibrium. For kiln-dried or air-dried rough-sawn wood, you should allow one to three months for boards 1 in. thick and at least six months for boards 2 in. thick. The amount of time the wood takes to reach equilibrium can be shortened considerably by cutting the pieces roughly to size first.

There is a relatively simple formula for determining the amount of movement that will occur in a drawer side, panel or any other piece of wood over a given change in the relative humidity. You need to know the initial width of the piece (W), the shrinkage value for the species of wood (S), the change in EMC for the range of relative humidity (M), and the fiber saturation point (fsp), which can be averaged at 28% to cover most species. The formula is:

$$\text{Dimensional change} = \text{WSM} \div \text{fsp}$$

Let's use the bottom drawer from the tall bureau (pp. 43-45) as an example, and figure the movement for a flat-sawn red oak drawer side that must fit into a carcase opening 8½ in. high. Assume that the bureau will be used in a climate where the seasonal changes of relative humidity vary from a low of 60% to a high of 90%. The initial width (W) is 8.5 in. From the chart, we see that over this range the EMC will go from about 11% to about 20%, so M is about 9% (0.09).

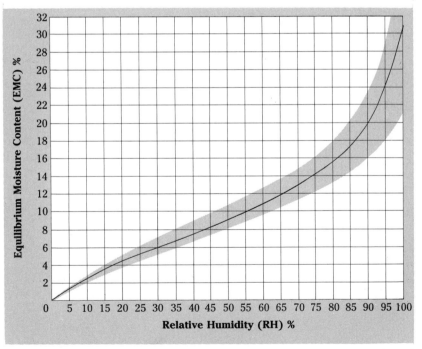

This chart shows the equilibrium relationship between the amount of bound water in white spruce and the amount of water in the air in which the spruce is kept. Spruce is typical of most woods, which will fall within the area indicated by the shading on the chart.

The shrinkage value (S), taken from the table, is 8.9% (0.089). Plugging these figures into the formula gives:

Dimensional change = (8.5 in.)(0.089)(0.09) ÷ 0.28 = 0.24 in.

The drawer side will become about ¼ in. wider as the relative humidity moves from 60% to 90%. If your shop is at 60% relative humidity when you fit the drawers, and the bureau is going to be subjected to stretches of 90% relative humidity in the home, you'd better fit the drawers very loosely, or use a more stable wood—a flat-sawn mahogany drawer side would move only a bit over ⅛ in.:

(8.5 in.)(0.09)(0.51) ÷ 0.28 = 0.139 in.

Radially sawn mahogany would be even better, moving only about ³⁄₃₂ in. You may decide to alter the construction of the piece and use a side-hung drawer, for example.

If the drawer side is in the middle of its moisture range when fitted, say 15% EMC at about 75% relative humidity for the drawers above, you'd need to plane the red oak side at least ⅛ in. narrower than its opening so it won't jam when the humidity reaches 90%.

The same formula can be used to figure other similar clearances, such as for a drawer front in an opening, a panel in a frame, a tabletop buttoned to a base. The movement in a wide panel can be quite surprising. The paneled chest (pp. 34-37) requires panels about 15 in. wide. Flat-sawn red oak panels in a climate varying between 30% and 90% relative humidity would expand and contract nearly ¾ in. If the chest was made when the wood was at the bottom of this range, about 6% EMC, you would have to make the grooves at least ⅜ in. deep to accommodate the potential swelling. It is good practice to pin the ends of panels in the center of the grooves so that the two edges will move equally in the grooves.

Sudden humidity changes can be very destructive to furniture. People often think the damage is caused by heat, but it is not; it is caused by the wood's rapid drying out upon exposure to dry air. (Moisture absorption isn't as damaging because it takes longer.) The outer fibers respond first to an increase in the surrounding level of humidity, the interior of the wood responds more slowly. This creates a temporary imbalance within the wood, which can cause cracks and broken glue lines. When the change in humidity is gradual, the wood has time to adjust slowly with much less interior stress. Turning the heat on after a wet autumn can be hard on furniture—especially with a hot-air heating system and no humidity control. Room humidifiers can be a good buy for those who value their furniture.

The table and chart are adapted from *Understanding Wood: A craftsman's guide to wood technology* by R. Bruce Hoadley (see the bibliography). Hoadley's book covers wood movement in great detail and includes charts of the average moisture content of interior woodwork in the United States in January and July.

Appendix 2   Joining Boards

Edge-Joining

A tabletop, carcase side or panel might look best made from a single, wide board, but such boards are rare, and if found, they require a large planer or a hand plane and a fair amount of time and energy. Edge-joining several boards to make a wide board is an important part of the furniture maker's trade, requiring judgement in selecting the boards and skill in making the joints.

When edge-joining boards, you must first decide whether you want to emphasize that a tabletop, for example, is made of separate boards joined together or whether you wish the top to have the appearance of a single, wide board. There is no right or wrong here, just a difference in approach. I decide according to the design and scale of the piece, and according to the boards that are available.

There are several ways to draw attention to the joined-up quality of a tabletop. You can select and arrange the boards for maximum contrast of color and grain. Alternating the heartwood and sapwood of cherry, to use an extreme example, gives a dramatic, striped effect. The rosewood and teak table (pp. 62-63) is a subtler version of this treatment. Another method is to V-groove the edges of adjacent boards. These V-grooved boards can be edge-glued or splined and screwed to frames without edge-gluing, as for the slat-top table (pp. 59-61) and the record cabinet (pp. 72-74). You could also sandwich a thin, contrasting strip between adjacent boards, inlay dovetail-shaped keys of a different wood across the joints, as shown below, or offset adjacent boards so that the surface is stepped, rather like the hull of a lapstrake boat.

It is possible to select, arrange and join individual boards so carefully that the joints themselves are almost invisible. I take great pains to achieve this effect with the fixed top and leaves of a drop-leaf table (pp. 102-105) or the top of an oval table (pp. 114-119). If you are fortunate enough to have boards cut in sequence from the same log, this matching is not difficult. If you don't have boards cut

To accent the joint between two boards, you can inlay a dovetail key of a contrasting wood, centered on the joint.

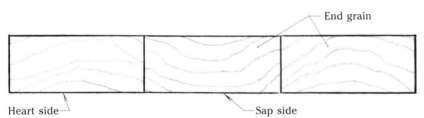

End grain

Heart side — — Sap side

When edge-gluing, alternate the heart side and the sap side of adjacent boards to keep the top from cupping excessively.

in sequence, it helps to be able to choose from a stock of wood large enough to yield boards that are consistent with each other in grain and color. Choosing from a limited stock may force you to use boards that are unsuitable because they are twisted, have the wrong grain pattern or color, or have imperfections such as knots, splits or wormholes. When selecting boards, plane off a patch here and there on the surface of each one to check the grain and color, particularly if the boards have any surface discoloration. I am not suggesting that wood used in furniture should always be free from natural irregularities, but such boards should be used by choice and not out of necessity.

The joined-up tabletop or panel that is most difficult to arrange is one that appears to be randomly selected (the two words contradict each other). It takes a great deal of care to place boards or strips so they make no discernable pattern.

Radially sawn boards (quartersawn or rift-sawn) are less likely to twist or cup than tangentially sawn boards (flat-sawn). If you use flat-sawn boards, try to alternate the heart side and the sap side of adjacent boards to reduce the likelihood of the glued-up boards curling. Arrange them so that the semicircular pattern of rings on the end of one board opens up and that of its neighbor opens down and so on, as shown in the sketch above. (The rings open toward the heart side.) This alternation is far less important for joining radially sawn boards.

I won't describe the techniques of edge-joining boards in detail, but I will offer some comments. Whenever possible, plane the faces of boards to be edge-joined flat. It is difficult to join boards that are twisted or cupped, because the angle of the edge to the face of a twisted or cupped board isn't uniform. Also, twist can't be remedied by clamping when gluing up. A bowed board, however, can usually be straightened when clamping if both of its edges are joined to a straight board, or if it is paired with a board bowed in the opposite direction. A badly twisted board, which would require the removal of too much wood to plane it flat, can often be saved. Saw the board down the middle lengthwise, plane each half flat and edge-join the halves back together.

If you machine-joint the edges, make sure the jointer knives are sharp and the infeed and outfeed tables are accurately set. The fence should be as near perpendicular to the tables as possible. Any slight divergence from 90° can be compensated for by placing the opposing faces of adjacent boards against the fence when planing, so that the divergence will cancel, not accumulate. The slower you feed the edge over the knives, the smoother the cut will be.

If you hand-plane the edges and haven't mastered the skill yet, just keep practicing. Remember that the goal for each board is to plane the edge at a right angle to the faces and dead straight or just slightly hollow in its length—not convex. I often machine-joint the edges, then do the final fitting with a long hand plane.

To check the fit of the edges, I clamp one board, edge up, in the vise, then set its neighbor in place on the edge. The edges should sit fair, without any rocking. If they rock, it means one or both edges are twisted and need to have a little planed off. Check each pair of boards in turn, or if there are only three or four, stack them up all at once. Lay a straightedge or framing square across all the faces to make sure they are in the same plane.

I like to dowel the edges of the boards with ⅜-in. by 2-in. hardwood dowels placed about 8 in. to 12 in. apart. The dowels keep the edges aligned while gluing, but contribute little to the strength of the joint. Alignment of the dowel holes is essential, and a self-centering doweling jig is a good investment. You could align the edges with splines, but unless the grooves are stopped near the ends of the boards, they will show.

I always glue the boards up vertically, because the glue runs down the edges if the boards are lying flat, and the joints can be starved. Clamp the bottom board in a vise or stand it on sawhorses, and stack the rest on top—the dowels keep them from falling off. As you add boards, spread glue evenly on both mating edges—don't just run a bead down the center of one edge. A quick way to close up the joints before putting on clamps is to stand the whole assembly on edge on the bench, pick up one end and slam it down hard, then do the same with the other end. It makes an awful racket, but is far quicker than winding up the clamps one by one.

Pipe clamps or bar clamps will work equally well for almost all applications. Bar clamps are more rigid, but unwieldy when they are more than 6 ft. long. Pipe clamps can be threaded at each end and coupled together to any length required. Place a clamp over every dowel, alternating from side to side of the assembly to keep it from cupping, and put a clamp at each end with its pipe or bar in the same plane as the boards. Press the bars or pipes flush with the faces of the boards to keep the assembly flat. If the boards are not to be replaned, slip waxed paper or plastic under them to keep the clamps from staining the wood.

Apply only enough clamping pressure to pull the joints tight. There should be plenty of glue squeezing out of the joints, but too much pressure can squeeze out too much glue and starve the joint. Wipe off surplus glue and leave the clamped-up boards in the vise for the glue to cure, or stand them up, supporting the clamps against a wall. When the glue has cured, feed the assembled boards through a thickness planer or plane and scrape off any squeezed-out, hardened glue.

End-Joining

It is perfectly feasible to join up 1½-ft. or 2-ft.-long pieces like bricks in a wall to make boards of any length and width. These composite boards can then be dovetailed, hinged or whatever, just like other boards. You may want to use this technique for appearance, for economy (short boards are often substantially cheaper than longer stock of the same quality and species), or because the boards you have are too twisted or crooked to be used in a continuous length.

To make long, wide pieces of short boards, I glue the boards end to end, then edge to edge. First, joint one face of all the short pieces, then thickness-plane them to a uniform thickness, leaving at least ¹⁄₁₆ in. to be planed off later. Check the faces as they come out of the planer for tear-out. Mark an arrow on each face to indicate the direction the piece should be fed into the thickness planer to minimize tear-out. The widths need not be uniform, but there should be enough boards of each width to extend the full length of the piece when placed end to end. Joint one edge of each board, then sort the boards into groups according to width and rip each board in a group to the same width. Saw each end square using a planer blade or carbide blade for a smooth cut.

Now lay all the pieces out on the floor or bench and arrange them as you want, keeping all the arrows pointing in the same direction. (Remember that boards of different widths can't be placed end to end, only edge to edge.) Stagger the end-grain joints of adjacent boards by at least two or three times the width of the widest boards. Number each joint and letter each strip.

Now glue up the boards in each strip end to end with Titebond or an equivalent glue. Lay the boards on a flat surface, align their edges and pull the ends together with one long clamp, applying only moderate pressure. Check that the boards stay flat. When the glue has cured, treat each glued-up strip as a single board—just don't drop them. Thickness-plane the strips to clean the faces up, joint the edges and place a few dowels to help align the joints and keep them from sliding. Glue them up in the numbered order. When the glue has cured, plane the assembly to its finished thickness. A composite board such as this looks best with a continuous strip glued along each of its edges. These strips could be a different wood, to emphasize and delineate the composite board more clearly.

Appendix 3 Estimating Materials

To figure the amount of lumber that you need for a project, make a complete bill of materials. I follow the format given below, which shows the bill for the base of the folding desk (pp. 159-165). List each part and its finished dimension—include joints, such as tenons, and round off to a convenient number. Next, calculate the number of square inches per part, divide that figure by 144 to find the area in square feet, then multiply by the number of those parts to get the square-foot total. Solid lumber is sold by the board foot (1 sq. ft., 1 in. thick = 1 bd. ft.), rather than by the square foot, so multiply the square-foot total by the thickness to get the board-foot total.

List all the parts for the project on the billing, grouping parts by the thickness of the wood. Remember that you can lose quite a bit of thickness when planing long boards flat. A tabletop, ⅞ in. thick and 6 ft. long, for example, may require rough lumber 1¼ in. thick rather than 1 in. thick.

Rough lumber is sold in ¼-in. increments of thickness—a board 1 in. thick is called 4/4 stock, one 1½ in. thick is 6/4 stock and so on. The width of the boards is measured when the board is green, so when you buy 12-in.-wide stock, you will actually get boards that average about 11¼ in. wide. To account for this discrepancy, I increase the board-foot total by 10%. Lumber is graded according to quality, and I allow at least 20% waste for the top hardwood grade, firsts and seconds (FAS). Lower grades are cheaper, but more wasteful. The amount of lumber needed is therefore about 30% greater than the amount on the bill of materials—it will take about 3¾ bd. ft. of 8/4 stock to make the legs, for example.

You can buy lumber retail, or if you buy enough, wholesale. When you buy retail, you can sometimes pick out the boards you want, but this is more expensive than buying wholesale. If you choose an exotic wood that you won't use again, buying retail makes more sense.

When buying wholesale, you can't specify the exact widths and lengths of the boards, nor, generally speaking, can you pick them out. Consequently, you have to order more wood than you will need for a particular job if you want to match boards for color and grain. If you can build up a stock of lumber over the years, you will have more choice for each piece of furniture that you make.

4/4 stock, walnut	Size (in.)	Area (sq. in.)	Area (sq. ft.)	No. parts	Total (sq. ft.)	Total (bd. ft.)
long rails	2½ x 40	100	.69	2	1.38	1.38
short rails	2½ x 18	45	.31	2	.62	.62
8/4 stock, walnut						
legs	26 x 2	52	.36	4	1.44	2.88

Appendix 4   Glues and Finishes

I use only two kinds of wood glue for furniture making, each of which has advantages and drawbacks. I use Titebond, a creme-colored, aliphatic resin glue, for general-purpose edge-gluing, for simple joints that will not be heavily stressed, and for small laminations. Titebond sets up in one or two hours, thus freeing up clamps and speeding the work. However, it has an assembly time of five minutes or less, and it cannot be easily sanded off after it has cured. Like Elmer's Glue-All, a white, polyvinyl acetate glue, Titebond deteriorates in ultraviolet light. It can also creep under stress and therefore shouldn't be used for heavy, bent laminations.

For gluing complicated joints that require long assembly time, such as dovetailed carcases, I usually use Weldwood Plastic Resin Glue. Weldwood has an assembly time of ten to twenty minutes, and takes at least six hours at 70°F to cure. It is easy to clean up squeezed-out glue with water before the glue sets, and when dry, Weldwood won't gum up sandpaper. Unlike Titebond, it is practically waterproof and won't deteriorate in the sun.

Finishing Wood

A neighbor of mine, who liked to make his own furniture, never started with stock less than 2 in. thick. He didn't like the raw newness of machine-planed pine, so he would hitch the boards up behind his jeep and tow them up and down his gravel driveway. Patina is too delicate a word to describe the effect—the wood looked glaciated. After this preparation, he would make his table or dresser, adding hardware from the local blacksmith. The results were monumental and exactly right for his large, rambling house. He was a forceful man, and this was reflected faithfully in his furniture.

Most of us prefer a smoother surface than this, and we want it to be sealed against dirt and stains. There are many different ways to finish wood, and your choice will reflect your own needs, as well as your attitude toward wood and furniture. There is no right or wrong finish, so I'll just point out some of the possibilities in order to help you make an informed choice. As an old carpenter friend used to say when asked his opinion on a matter of detail, "It's all according to what you want."

Between the wood-finishing extremes of bare wood and polyurethane, there is a vast array of sealers, lacquers, varnishes and oils, both natural and synthetic. To pick a finish, you must first decide whether you are willing to allow the minor accidents of everyday living—spills, dents, burns and scratches—to be written into your furniture, or whether you want to try to keep them out.

Polyurethane and other clear, hard film finishes that seal the wood like a plastic coating (paints, varnishes and lacquers) will certainly protect the wood. But, like plastic, these finishes don't age with charm. Film finishes prevent the furniture from acquiring that mature richness of tone conferred only by time. A well-used piece of furniture, like a fine old face, inevitably has its history written into it. Film finishes are unequaled for wood on countertops in kitchens and bathrooms and in other places where it will be exposed to water. For other applications, however, I only use them when asked, and always with reluctance.

When I put my hand on a table, I don't want to feel the finish—however fine—I want to feel the wood. All film finishes prevent this. My sister has a sturdy kitchen table, made of hard pine, that has never had any finish on it at all. After a hundred years of scrubbing with soap and water, the wood has bleached to a very pale and beautiful yellow. The softer parts of the grain have worn away, and the table looks well used, without being shabby.

If you like the quality and feel of wood, but don't like it enough to want to scrub your table every day for a hundred years, you'll probably want to finish with an oil or penetrating sealer. In the past, many different kinds of animal and vegetable oils were used to seal furniture against dirt and moisture. In Nova Scotia, cod liver oil, mixed with lampblack and thinned with kerosene, is still used to preserve wooden roofs. On a warm day you can smell these roofs for a couple of miles downwind, which probably explains why the finish has never been popular for furniture.

Today there is a wide range of oils and penetrating sealers for furniture on the market. These finishes don't coat the surface of the wood. They soak into the wood fibers and saturate them so that any spilled liquids will remain on the surface. Most oils and sealers change their chemical composition when exposed to the air. This polymerization (the formation of long molecular chains) is irreversible, so alcohol or other solvents have little effect on them.

Boiled linseed oil, which has been used for centuries, is a durable finish that is easy to apply and maintain. It isn't toxic, doesn't have a strong smell, and it won't yellow or deteriorate in sunlight. When it hardens, it is tough, elastic and inert. I always thin the first application with turpentine (half turpentine, half oil), so that it soaks deep into the wood fibers. Warming this mixture—not over an open flame—also helps penetration. The excess oil from each application must be thoroughly wiped off before it gets tacky. The next coats are unthinned oil. Putting three or four coats of linseed oil on a piece of furniture is a tedious process because you have to wait at least twelve hours between applications for the oil to dry. Also, you accumulate a collection of oily rags, which, like incendiary bombs, can ignite and burn fiercely hours later.

Because of the problems with linseed oil, I switched to Watco oil, a penetrating, synthetic sealer with most of the good qualities of linseed oil, but none of its drawbacks. As with linseed oil, it is important that the first coat penetrate the surface of the wood. Watco is thin enough that it needn't be diluted or heated. The number of applications needed depends on the porosity of the wood and the way it is cut—the steeper the angle of the wood fibers to the surfaces, the more oil the fibers will absorb. Three applications is the minimum for medium-density woods like walnut. Teak needs less and oak more. When the wood will absorb no more oil, the fibers are saturated, and it is pointless to continue adding oil. Too much oil builds up an unsightly yellow coating that can only be removed by scraping.

Use lint-free rags, such as old cotton sheeting, not paper towels, for wiping excess oil off the surface after each application. Beads of oil will appear like perspiration on the freshly wiped surface. The beads will continue to appear for some time and you must wipe them off as many times as necessary, otherwise they will eventually harden and make a rough surface.

For the final application of oil, I usually wet-sand the surface with 600-grit wet/dry paper, using the oil as lubricant. Always sand with the grain. Steel wool (0000, the finest grade) serves the same purpose as sandpaper, but beware of leaving any metal fibers. If metal fibers come into contact with water, they will cause iron stains, which are difficult to remove, particularly on light-colored woods, and especially on oak.

A gentle wet-sanding is the best way to maintain an oil finish, and this should be done whenever the surface has lost its sheen. A coating of wax over an oil finish will keep the furniture shining and make dusting easier—if that is one of your preoccupations. You can probably tell from my tone that I do little dusting.

Appendix 5 Sources of Supply

These suppliers carry many materials useful to woodworkers, in addition to the items mentioned—ask for catalogs when ordering.

Brass *H*-hinges: Ball and Ball, 463 W. Lincoln Hwy., Exton, PA 19341

Brass stays for chest lid: Woodcraft, 41 Atlantic Ave., P.O. Box 4000, Woburn, MA 01888

Chest lifts: Period Furniture Hardware Co., Inc., 123 Charles St., Boston, MA 02114

Copper nails and roves: The Wooden Boat Shop, 1007 N.E. Boat St., Seattle, WA 98105

Deks Olje varnish: The Flood Company, Hudson, OH 44236

Extending-table slides: Craftsmen Wood Service Co., 1735 W. Cortland Court, Addison, IL 60101

Fasteners in a variety of nonferrous metals: Majestic Fasteners, Inc., P.O. Box 193, Morris Plains, NJ 07950

Folding-table hinge: Woodcraft, 41 Atlantic Ave., P.O. Box 4000, Woburn, MA 01888

Gauged slate: Vermont Structural Slate Co., P.O. Box 98, Fair Haven, VT 05743

Hinge for rule joints: Woodcraft, 41 Atlantic Ave., P.O. Box 4000, Woburn, MA 01888

Iron *H*-hinges: Horton Brasses, Nooks Hill Rd., P.O. Box 95, Cromwell, CT 06416

Masonry sealer: Gawet Marble Co., Rte. 4 West, Center Rutland, VT 05736

Metal tabletop fasteners: Paxton/Patterson, 5719 W. 65th St., Chicago, IL 60638

Paper-fiber seating (a substitute for rush): The Woodworkers' Store, 21801 Industrial Blvd., Rogers, MN 55374

Pirelli webbing: General Rubber, 131 Portland St., Boston, MA 02114

Recessed brass handle: The Renovators Supply, Renovator's Old Mill, Millers Falls, MA 01359

Rush seating: H.H. Perkins & Co., P.O. Box AC, Amity Station, Woodbridge, CT 06525

Soss hinges: Constantine, 2050 Eastchester Rd., Bronx, NY 10461

Texweb (a substitute for Pirelli webbing): The Woodworkers' Store, 21801 Industrial Blvd., Rogers, MN 55374

Bibliography

Francis, D.K. Ching. **Building Construction Illustrated.** New York: Van Nostrand Reinhold Co., 1975.

Building specifications, including staircases. Less comprehensive, but much more comprehensible than Architectural Graphic Standards, *cited below.*

Frid, Tage. **Tage Frid Teaches Woodworking—Joinery: Tools and Techniques.** Newtown, Conn.: The Taunton Press, 1979. **Tage Frid Teaches Woodworking—Shaping, Veneering, Finishing.** Newtown, Conn.: The Taunton Press, 1981.

These two books cover all the standard techniques of furniture making.

Hoadley, R. Bruce. **Understanding Wood: A craftsman's guide to wood technology.** Newtown, Conn.: The Taunton Press, 1980.

The best account I've found of the properties and behavior of wood.

Joyce, Ernest. **The Encyclopedia of Furniture Making.** New York: Drake Publishers, 1970.

Although somewhat outdated, this book is a classic and still immensely useful.

Miller, Bruce W., and Widess, Jim. **The Caner's Handbook.** New York: Van Nostrand Reinhold, 1983..

Includes information on cane, rush, wicker and other seating materials.

Pain, F. **Practical Wood Turning.** New York: Sterling Publishing Co., 1979.

An informative, if idiosyncratic, book by a professional turner.

Ramsey, Charles G., and Sleeper, Harold R. **Architectural Graphic Standards.** Seventh edition. New York: John Wiley & Sons, 1982.

Specifications for staircases and just about everything else in a building.

Stokes, Gordon. **Modern Wood Turning.** New York: Drake Publishers, 1973.

A concise introduction to wood turning that more than covers the techniques necessary for the turning projects in this book.

U.S. Forest Products Laboratory. **Wood handbook: Wood as an engineering material.** Washington, D.C.: U.S. Government Printing Office, 1974.

A detailed and authoritative analysis of the mechanical and physical properties of wood.

Index

We wish to thank the following photographers for their contributions:

Alan Gill
Brian Gulick
Richard Starr

We also wish to thank the following organizations and individuals for permission to reprint their photographs:

Page 5
Reproduced by courtesy of the trustees of the British Museum
      Egyptian headrest
Victoria and Albert Museum, Crown Copyright
      The Greate Bed of Ware
      Aumbrey

Page 29
Reproduced by courtesy of the Dean and Chapter of Westminster, London
      Coffer
National Monuments Record, Crown Copyright
      Dug-out chest
      Chip-carved chest
      Linen-fold chest
      Nailed chest

Page 91
Victoria and Albert Museum, Crown Copyright
      Carved table
      Draw-top table
Reproduced by permission of Viscount De L'Isle, V.C., K.G., Penshurst Place, Kent, England
      Trestle table

Page 129
Reproduced by courtesy of the Dean and Chapter of Westminster, London
      Coronation chair
Photography by Egyptian Expedition, The Metropolitan Museum of Art
      Tutankamen's throne
Victoria and Albert Museum, Crown Copyright
      Linen-fold chair

Page 167
Bruce Beeken
      Library steps

Editor: Laura Cehanowicz Tringali
Assistant Editor: Roger Holmes
Copy Editor: Deborah Cannarella
Indexer: Harriet Hodges

Design Director: Roger Barnes
Associate Art Director: Lee Hochgraf Hov
Assistant Art Director: C. Heather Brine
Staff Artist: Kathryn Olsen
Illustrators: Brian Gulick, thumbnail sketches; Roy Lewando,
inks; Jean D. McPherson, plans and isometrics
Illustration Assistants: Jean Zalkind Anderheggen, Barbara Hamill,
Karen Pease

Manager of Production Services: Gary Mancini
Production Manager: Mary Galpin
Typesetter: Nancy-Lou Knapp
Darkroom: Annette Hilty, Deborah Mason, Jay Smith
Production Assistants: Dorothy Dreher, Barbara Wills

Typeface: Cheltenham 9½ point
Paper: Warren Patina, 70 lb., Neutral pH
Printer: Connecticut Printers, Bloomfield, Connecticut
Binder: A. Horowitz & Sons, Fairfield, New Jersey